Guide to
Network Defense and Countermeasures,
Second Edition

by
Randy Weaver

THOMSON
COURSE TECHNOLOGY

Australia • Canada • Mexico • Singapore • Spain • United Kingdom • United States

THOMSON
™
COURSE TECHNOLOGY

Guide to Network Defense and Countermeasures, Second Edition
is published by Thomson Course Technology

Managing Editor:
William Pitkin III

Product Manager:
Sarah Santoro

Product Marketing Manager:
Gayathri Baskaran

Production Editor:
Danielle Slade

Senior Manufacturing Coordinator:
Justin Palmeiro

Copyeditor:
Lori Cavanaugh

Technical Editor:
Sydney Shewchuk

Quality Assurance Coordinator:
Christian Kunciw

Proofreader:
Marc Masse

Editorial Assistant:
Allison Murphy

Cover Design:
Abby Scholz

Indexer:
Sharon Hildenberg

Compositor:
GEX Publishing Services

Developmental Editor:
Lisa M. Lord

ISBN-13: 978-1-4188-3679-5
ISBN-10: 1-4188-3679-6

TABLE OF
Contents

CHAPTER FIVE
Virtual Private Network (VPN) Concepts   **161**

CHAPTER SIX
VPN Implementation   **203**

Introduction

This book is an introduction to one of the most important and urgent concepts in protecting computers and networks: intrusion detection. In a narrow sense, intrusion detection is the capability of hardware and software to alert users to suspicious connection attempts that could represent attackers trying to gain unauthorized access to a computer and/or its resources. This specific function is covered extensively throughout several chapters of this book, along with other key security topics. However, in a wider sense, the practice of intrusion detection encompasses virtually all aspects of network security, and these activities—such as risk analysis, security policies, damage assessment, intrusion response, anticipating future attacks, and prosecuting intruders—are also examined.

This book was written with two goals. The first goal is to give students a solid foundation in advanced network security fundamentals. Although emphasis is placed on intrusion detection, the book also covers essential practices, such as developing a security policy and carrying out that policy by performing Network Address Translation (NAT) and packet filtering and by installing proxy servers, firewalls, and virtual private networks (VPNs). The second goal is to prepare students to take the Network Defense and Countermeasures exam, which is the second exam for the Security Certified Network Professional (SCNP) certification.

Intended Audience

Guide to Network Defense and Countermeasures, Second Edition is intended for students and professionals who need hands-on introductory experience with installing firewalls and intrusion detection systems (IDSs). This book assumes that students are familiar with the Internet and fundamental networking concepts, such as TCP/IP, gateways, routers, and Ethernet. It also assumes that students have fulfilled the prerequisites for exam SC0-402, which include IP troubleshooting; subnetting, subnet masking, IP datagram structure, routing, Web security, and common attack techniques.

Overview

Chapter 1 should be a review for students. It covers IP addressing, subnetting, routing, IP packet structure, and different types of network attacks that a perimeter security configuration should defend against. Chapters 2 and 3 cover risk analysis and the development of a well-defined security policy. Chapter 4 explains network traffic signatures, an essential concept to understand before planning intrusion detection and firewall configurations. Chapters 5 and 6 address using VPNs for secure remote access, and Chapters 7 and 8 explain the use of IDSs. Chapters 9 to 11 explore firewalls and include installation guidelines for Check Point NG and Microsoft ISA Server 2000. Students also learn about Linux's built-in command-line tool for packet filtering, Iptables. Chapter 12 discusses ongoing security management, including auditing, maintaining and monitoring systems, and managing security events. Most chapters incorporate encryption, authentication, and other security concepts that contribute to intrusion detection and countermeasures.

How To Use This Book

This book should be studied in sequence. The first chapter offers a solid refresher on network security and establishes the basis for the running case project (discussed later in "The Running Case Project"). Each chapter builds on the previous one and expands the basic knowledge students already have from prerequisite courses. Additionally, the sequence of chapters has been arranged to conform more closely to accepted information security best practices.

About the Organization of Topics

You might have noticed that the risk analysis and security policy chapters have been placed at the front of the book, unlike most security books. The reason for this is simple: Best practices state that your security policy dictates what security measures are needed to support organizational security goals. Your policy is the basis for security, so it follows that security policies should be learned first. To formulate an accurate and comprehensive security policy, you must first do the following:

(1)   Identify, evaluate, and prioritize assets to be protected.

(2)   Assess vulnerabilities and threats to assets, and evaluate the potential impact if threats become a reality.

(3)   Determine how to manage risks.

(4)   Create a security policy based on your risk assessment and the organization's needs and security stance.

This process can be more detailed, but these steps are the basic procedure for developing an initial security policy. Keep in mind, too, that a security policy is never truly completed. Risk analysis and policy review should be conducted regularly, especially in response to security incidents or changes. Your security policy must be updated to address your network's current needs.

After a security policy is in place, you can begin securing the network. At this stage, you begin evaluating hardware and software approaches to securing resources, such as VPNs for remote access, IDSs to monitor for unauthorized access, and firewalls to filter traffic.

The Running Case Project

The running case project is designed so that students can benefit from immediate practical application of newly learned skills and concepts. At the end of Chapter 1, students are asked to design a basic network for a fictitious company, LedGrafix. LedGrafix is a small video game design company that has recently released a new game that's a huge success. This explosive success means the company will be expanding rapidly and needs a new location. You have been hired to design and secure its new home. Throughout the book, you'll be working on a full-scale network design and security project.

The project attempts to mirror a real-life setting as closely as possible. In Chapter 1, you use your existing security knowledge and network design skills to draft an initial diagram for the new site and develop a full hardware and software inventory. Using this initial design, in subsequent chapters you conduct a risk analysis, draft a security policy, research equipment, plan a VPN deployment, and modify your security policy at each step to reflect the changes in your plan. You also design your IDS and firewall and update your security policy with the new VPN, IDS and firewall policies.

Although this project sounds time consuming, doing this same job in a real-world setting would be much more time intensive. At times it might seem that you don't have all the information you need to complete the project, but as in real life, answers aren't always definitive. You need to make judgment calls based on your own expertise, and choose the best solution you can when there doesn't seem to be a right answer. Real networks and businesses seldom have clear answers or needs.

The case project has three primary goals:

- To teach students how to find and use resources such as information security Web sites, newsgroups, mailing lists, and so forth

- To teach students how to apply concepts to solving problems and how to document their work effectively

- To guide students in carrying out an information security project in a logical and structured manner so that outcomes are more predictable and manageable

Throughout the project, your instructor can guide you with information, templates, or other materials the author has provided and will let you know his or her expectations for the final deliverable, a complete security policy and procedures manual for the LedGrafix network.

Chapter Descriptions

Here is a summary of the topics covered in each chapter of this book:

Chapter 1, "Network Defense Fundamentals," is intended as a review of previously learned concepts. Basic TCP/IP networking concepts that play a role in thwarting intrusions and attacks are covered, including IP addressing, subnetting, IP packet structure, DNS, and routing and access control. It also examines the goals of a network security program, which balances the need for connectivity and access with the need to maintain privacy and integrity. Chapter 1 also explores common security threats and vulnerabilities that intrusion detection systems (IDSs) and other security devices need to address and offers an overview of the basic tools for blocking those threats, including packet filters, antivirus software, log files and analysis software, and IDSs.

Chapter 2, "Security Policy Design: Risk Analysis," explains a key factor in security design: a comprehensive risk analysis. Often neglected, risk analysis provides key information needed to determine what security methods are best suited to the resources to be protected. An initial security policy is based largely on a comprehensive risk analysis and risk assessment.

Chapter 3, "Security Policy Implementation," examines the development of a security policy that tells organization members what resources must be protected, how to protect critical resources, and how to respond if an intrusion occurs.

Chapter 4, "Network Traffic Signatures," delves into the approaches IDS hardware and software use to detect unauthorized access attempts and block them. In particular, you examine different types of intrusion detection signatures. You learn how to capture packets, compare normal traffic signatures to suspicious ones, and develop filters based on traffic signatures.

Chapter 5, "Virtual Private Network (VPN) Concepts," discusses the basic concepts of VPNs, including the three core activities a VPN performs: encapsulation, encryption, and authentication. You also learn about tunneling protocols, IP Security (IPSec), and Internet Key Exchange (IKE), and then explore some advantages and disadvantages of VPNs.

Chapter 6, "Virtual Private Network (VPN) Implementation," explains how business needs figure into the equation of designing and deploying VPN connectivity. You learn about client security and see how to configure VPNs, how to use different topologies to secure a network, and how VPNs and firewalls work together. Finally, you learn how a VPN policy should be incorporated into your overall security policy.

Chapter 7, "Intrusion Detection System Concepts," introduces fundamental IDS concepts, including the components that make up an IDS and the basic step-by-step process of intrusion detection. Different options for setting up an IDS are covered, such as network-based, host-based, and hybrid IDS implementations. Finally, you examine some widely used IDS packages, ranging from freeware software to expensive hardware systems that use multiple network sensors to detect suspicious traffic.

Chapter 8, "Intrusion Detection: Incident Response," explains how to develop and refine IDS filtering rules. The primary task of the IDS is to detect suspicious activity, but it's still up to the response team to determine whether the activity is a problem or a false alarm and take steps to respond to the incident. You learn options for assembling a response team and see how to deal with false alarms. You also learn some guidelines for preparing evidence for prosecution.

Chapter 9, "Choosing and Designing Firewalls," explains the functions of a firewall and describes how perimeter networks are designed. This chapter provides an overview of basic types of firewalls and their primary functions so that you can choose the right one to meet your needs. You also learn about the firewall rule base, the heart of a firewall's operation, and the basic firewall security function—packet filtering.

Chapter 10, "Firewall Topology," discusses how proxy servers work to shield hosts on an internal network and explains how to select and configure a bastion host. You also learn about other common security functions that firewalls perform, including NAT, authentication, and encryption.

Chapter 11, "Strengthening and Managing Firewalls," discusses how to maintain and edit a rule base, manage log files, and improve firewall performance. This chapter also offers guidelines on installing Check Point NG and Microsoft ISA Server 2000 and using Linux's built-in packet-filtering tool, Iptables.

Chapter 12 "Strengthening Defense Through Ongoing Management," discusses the management of security measures so that they continue operating efficiently and continue detecting and protecting against attacks. You learn about real-time event monitoring and developing an IDS to keep pace with a growing network. This chapter also covers the importance of conducting regular security audits, enhancing a defense in depth strategy, and keeping your knowledge base up to date.

Appendix A, "SC0-402 Objectives," maps the objectives in the Security Certified Professional (SCP) SC0-402 Network Defense and Countermeasures exam to this book's corresponding chapter and section. If you need to brush up on a specific topic to prepare for the exam, you can use this appendix as a handy reference.

Appendix B, "Security Resources," lists several security-related organizations, groups, and information sources. If you're looking for up-to-the-minute news about virus attacks or security problems, turn to the resources listed in this appendix as a good starting point, but remember to develop your own security resources, too.

Features

To help you fully understand networking security concepts, this book includes many features designed to enhance your learning experience:

- **Chapter Objectives.** Each chapter begins with a detailed list of the concepts to be mastered in that chapter. This list gives you a quick reference to the chapter's contents and serves as a useful study aid.

- **Figures and Tables.** Numerous diagrams of networking configurations help you visualize common perimeter defense setups. In addition, tables provide details and comparisons in an organized, easy-to-grasp manner. Some tables include specific examples of packet-filtering rules you can use to build a firewall rule base. Because most labs use Microsoft operating systems, Microsoft products are used for most of the screen shots and Hands-on Projects in this book; however, some Linux coverage is included as well.

- **In-Chapter Activities.** Each chapter has short projects integrated into the main text. The purpose of these short activities is to provide immediate reinforcement of a newly learned skill or concept and give students an opportunity to apply knowledge and skills as a way to maintain interest and motivation.

- **Chapter Summaries.** Each chapter's material is followed by a summary of the concepts introduced in that chapter. These summaries are a helpful way to review the ideas covered in each chapter.

- **Key Terms.** Following the Chapter Summary, a list of all terms introduced in the chapter with boldfaced text are gathered together in the Key Terms list, with full definitions for each term. This list encourages a more thorough understanding of the chapter's key concepts and is a useful reference.

- **Review Questions.** The end-of-chapter assessment begins with a set of review questions that reinforce the main concepts in each chapter. These questions help you evaluate and apply the material you have learned.

- **Hands-On Projects**. Although understanding the theory behind networking technology is important, practice in real-world applications of this theory is essential. Each chapter includes projects aimed at giving students experience in planning and development tasks or hands-on configuration tasks.

- **Case Projects.** Each chapter closes with the corresponding segment of this book's running case project (described previously in "The Running Case Project"), which gives you a chance to draw on your common sense as well as skills and knowledge you have learned. Some chapters contain additional scenario-based Case Projects on intrusion detection and security-related situations to help you sharpen your decision-making and troubleshooting skills, which are essential in network security systems administration.

Lab Setup

The lab setup for this book is straightforward, requiring each student to have access to a computer capable of supporting Windows XP Professional with Service Pack 2 and Fedora Core 3 in a dual-boot configuration. Students also need access to the Internet for projects and research.

Text and Graphic Conventions

Where appropriate, additional information and exercises have been added to this book to help you better understand the topic at hand. Icons throughout the text alert you to additional materials. The following icons are used in this book:

NOTE

The Note icon draws your attention to additional helpful material related to the subject being covered.

TIP

Tips based on the author's experience offer extra information about how to attack a problem or what to do in real-world situations.

CAUTION

The Caution icon warns you about potential mistakes or problems and explains how to avoid them.

HANDS-ON PROJECTS

Each hands-on activity or project in this book is preceded by the Hands-On icon and a description of the exercise that follows.

CASE PROJECTS

These icons mark Case Projects, which are scenario-based assignments. In these case examples, you're asked to apply independently what you have learned.

INSTRUCTOR'S MATERIALS

The following supplemental materials are available when this book is used in a classroom setting. All supplements available with this book are provided to instructors on a single CD. You can also retrieve these supplemental materials from the Thomson Course Technology Web site, *www.course.com*, by going to the page for this book, under "Download Instructor Files & Teaching Tools."

Electronic Instructor's Manual. The Instructor's Manual that accompanies this book includes additional instructional material to assist in class preparation, including suggestions for classroom activities, discussion topics, and additional case projects.

Solutions. Solutions to all end-of-chapter material are included with answers to Review Questions and, when applicable, Hands-on Activities, Hands-on Projects, and Case Projects.

ExamView. This book is accompanied by ExamView, a powerful testing software package that instructors can use to create and administer printed, computer (LAN-based), and Internet exams. ExamView includes hundreds of questions that correspond to the topics covered in this book, enabling students to generate detailed study guides that include page references for further review. The computer-based and Internet testing components allow students to take exams at their computers and have them graded automatically to save instructors time.

PowerPoint Presentations. This book comes with Microsoft PowerPoint slides for each chapter. These slides are meant to be used as a teaching aid for classroom presentation, to be made available to students on the network for chapter review, or to be printed for classroom distribution. Instructors are also at liberty to add their own slides for other topics introduced to the class.

Figure Files. All figures in the book are reproduced on the Instructor's Resources CD. Similar to the PowerPoint presentations, they are included as a teaching aid for classroom presentation, to make available to students for review, or to be printed for classroom distribution.

COPING WITH CHANGE ON THE WEB

Sooner or later, all the specific Web-based resources mentioned in this book will become out of date or be replaced by newer information. In some cases, the URLs listed here might lead you to their replacements; in other cases, the URLs will lead nowhere, leaving you with the dreaded 404 error message, "File not found."

When that happens, don't give up! There's always a way to find what you want on the Web, if you're willing to invest some time and energy. Most Web sites offer a search engine, and if you can get to the main site, you can use this tool to help you find what you need. You can also use general search tools, such as *www.google.com, www.hotbot.com,* or *www.lycos.com,* to find related information. In addition, although standards organizations offer the most specific information about their standards, many third-party sources of information, training, and assistance are also available. The bottom line is that if you can't find something where the book says it's located, start looking around. It's an excellent way to improve your research skills.

Visit Our World Wide Web Site

Additional materials designed especially for you might be available for your course on the World Wide Web. Go to *www.course.com* periodically and search for this book title for more details.

ACKNOWLEDGMENTS

I would like to thank Thomson Course Technology for the opportunity to write this book on a topic of such value and importance. Thanks also go to the editorial and production staff, including Sarah Santoro, Product Manager; Danielle Slade, Production Editor; and the testers in the Manuscript Quality Assurance Department: Christian Kunciw, John Freitas, and Danielle Shaw. Thanks also to Lisa Lord, Development Editor, for her guidance, her words of encouragement, and her periodic reminders that kept me on track. Sydney Shewchuk, the Technical Editor, went above and beyond the call of duty to provide suggestions based on his experience and knowledge. I would also like to thank the following reviewers, who guided me with helpful feedback on each chapter:

Michael Anderson, ECPI College of Technology, Newport News
Robert Bruen, Springfield Technical Community College
Dr. Philip Craiger, University of Central Florida
Mark Krawcyzk, Greenville Technical College
David Pope, Ozarks Technical Community College

Special thanks goes to my best friend, wife, and co-writer, Dawn, whose skills and insight made this project possible. Also, thanks to my family for their patience and support and to Ann Marie for starting this journey.

1

NETWORK DEFENSE FUNDAMENTALS

After reading this chapter and completing the exercises, you will be able to:

♦ Explain the fundamentals of TCP/IP networking

♦ Describe the threats to network security

♦ Explain the goals of network security

♦ Describe a layered approach to network defense

♦ Explain how network security defenses affect your organization

This chapter introduces you to the fundamental network security concepts you need to know. Some material might be a review for you, but it will serve to get you warmed up. To secure a network, understanding the TCP/IP protocol suite is vital. You review IP addressing briefly, and then move on to examining the "guts" of packets and seeing how attackers can use them to breach your network defenses. You also see how your knowledge of protocols can be used to block harmful communications.

Next, you learn about different kinds of intruders and threats to network security, such as malicious code and natural disasters. Attackers have many motivations for hacking into networks, and your job is to figure out what they're doing (before they do it, if possible) and to prevent them from carrying out their plans.

When you're warmed up, you'll dive in to the goals of network security. You learn about the challenges of ensuring privacy, confidentiality, integrity, and availability for your network resources. Your organization's security policy (covered in Chapters 2 and 3) is the first step toward defining specific security goals.

After reviewing the basics, you'll dig in to the real meat of network defense technologies. You discover how layering technologies can ensure better protection than any single technology used alone. The method of layering defenses is called defense in depth (DiD). Although you'll probably encounter some concepts that seem overwhelming, don't worry about that now. Ancient Techno-ese secrets will be shared, and you will soon know all.

TCP/IP NETWORKING REVIEW

Transmission Control Protocol/Internet Protocol (TCP/IP) is actually a suite of many protocols that allow information to be transmitted from point to point on a network. This section gives you a refresher on networking basics, such as IP addressing, packet structures, and header information. You also review how to determine a local computer's IP address.

The Open Systems Interconnect (OSI) Model

You're probably familiar with the Open Systems Interconnection (OSI) model of network communications, which divides communications into seven separate layers. TCP/IP has its own stack of protocols that roughly correspond to these layers. The two models are shown in Figure 1–1.

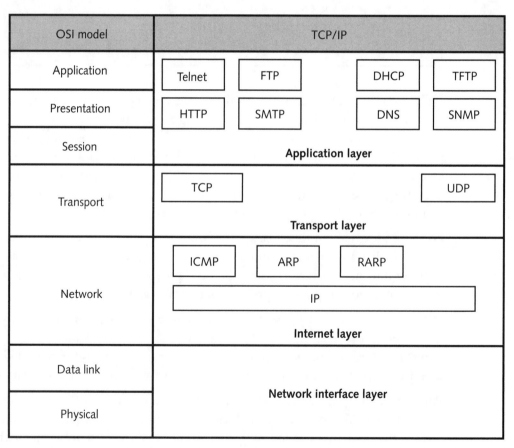

Figure 1-1   The OSI model and the TCP/IP stack

You should be familiar with most of these protocols and their functions. If you need a quick refresher on the TCP/IP stack, the OSI model, and the major protocols operating at different layers, simply run an Internet search on "TCP/IP and the OSI Model." Dozens of helpful sites are available for every level of knowledge, such as *www.tcpipguide.com/free/index.htm*.

IP Addressing

One way attackers can gain access to your network is by determining the IP addresses of computers. After they have an address, they can attempt to take over the computer and use it to launch attacks on other computers in the network or access resources on the network. Therefore, one of the fundamental requirements of network security is to understand IP addresses and other network addresses so that you can conceal or change them to deter attackers.

IP addresses currently in use on the Internet conform to **Internet Protocol version 4 (IPv4)**, which calls for addresses with 32 bits or 4 bytes of data. Each of the 4 bytes (which is also called an octet) in an IP address has a value between 0 and 255, and each octet is separated by dots, as in 192.168.10.1. An IP address consists of two main parts:

- The **network address**, the part of the address shared among computers in a network
- The **host address**, which is unique to a computer in its subnet

These two parts are combined with a third value, the **subnet mask**, which tells another computer which part of the IP address is the network address and which part is the host address.

IP addresses are valuable commodities. If attackers can find a computer's IP address, they can run a port scan to look for open ports that can be exploited. If you can hide IP addresses, you can prevent certain attacks. To hide the addresses of computers on your network, you can use **Network Address Translation (NAT)** to translate your private network's nonroutable internal addresses into the address of the NAT server's external interface connected to the Internet, thereby hiding the internal addresses.

Security is not the only reason for using NAT. The Internet has grown at a rate not expected by those who created the IPv4 32-bit addressing scheme. Today, IP addresses are in short supply, so **Internet Protocol version 6 (IPv6)** is under development. By sharing one or more of the NAT server's IP addresses with internal hosts, NAT has allowed more time to work out the details of IPv6. You can also use a **proxy server** to effectively conceal IP addresses of internal machines (see Figure 1-2).

NOTE   Technology standards are explained in documents called Requests for Comments (RFCs). You can look up RFCs at *www.rfc-editor.org*. IPv6, specified in RFC 2460, has several improvements over IPv4. IPv6 is autoconfiguring and incorporates Internet Protocol Security (IPSec, explained in Chapter 5) for authentication and encryption. IPv6 addresses are 128 bits, increasing the number of possible addresses from about 4 billion to 3.4 times 1038. That's 34 with 37 zeros. How would you like that number for a bank balance?

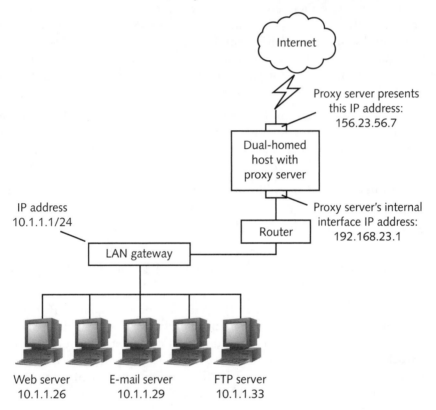

Figure 1-2   Proxy servers concealing IP addresses on the internal network

In IPv4, addresses are separated into address categories called "classes." An IP address class is determined by the number of its networks compared to the number of its hosts. For example, a Class A address uses 8 bits for the network portion of the address and 24 bits for the host portion. The classes have been divided as shown in Table 1-1. Remember that private network addresses can never be used on the public Internet.

Table 1-1 IP address classes

Class	First Octet Decimal Range	Default Subnet Mask	Reserved Private Address Range	Purpose
Class A	1–127	255.0.0.0	10.0.0.1 to 10.255.255.254 (127.0.0.1 reserved for TCP/IP local interface testing)	Large corporations and governments
Class B	128–191	255.255.0.0	172.16.0.1 to 172.16.255.254	Medium networks
Class C	192–223	255.255.255.0	192.168.0.1 to 192.168.255.254	Small networks
Class D	224–239	N/A	N/A	Multicasting
Class E	240–254	N/A	N/A	Experimentation

TIP

You can find a number of IP address calculators on the Web; an excellent one is at *www.subnetmask.info/*. For more on IP addresses and subnets, refer to *Guide to TCP/IP*, Second Edition, by Ed Tittel and Laura Chappell (Thomson Course Technology, 2004, ISBN 0-619-21242-X).

ACTIVITY

Activity 1-1: Determining Your Computer's IP Address

Time Required: 10 minutes

Objective: Determine the IP address of your computer.

Description: Every computer connected to the Internet is assigned an IP address. Often the address is dynamically generated and changes from session to session. With some DSL connections and many T-1 or other connections, a static IP address is used. ISDN connections also use a static IP address; however, for dial-up users, the Internet service provider (ISP) assigns an address dynamically at the time of the connection. In this activity, you use the Ipconfig command to determine your computer's IP address.

1. Power on your computer, if necessary.

2. Click **Start**, point to **All Programs**, point to **Accessories**, and then click **Command Prompt** to open a command prompt window. (You can also click **Start**, **Run**, type **cmd**, and click **OK**.)

3. At the command prompt, type **ipconfig /all**. (Be sure to leave a single blank space between "ipconfig" and the forward slash.)

4. Press **Enter**. The screen displays your IP address as well as other information. Your IP address is four numbers separated by periods. In some cases, you might have several addresses. The IP address assigned to your Ethernet adapter is the external address.

5. Write down your IP address, subnet mask, and default gateway address on the following lines. In addition, write down the address assigned to your Ethernet adapter, if applicable.

_____

_____

_____

_____

6. Type **exit** and press **Enter** to close the command prompt window. Leave your system running for the next activity.

For a complete listing of Ipconfig commands, type ipconfig /? at the command prompt.

Exploring IP Packet Structure

TCP/IP is packet-based; it gives computers a fairly simple framework for transmitting information in small packages called packets. Unfortunately, TCP/IP packets give attackers another way to gain entry into a network. They can intercept packets and falsify the information in them or manipulate the packets in a way that makes it impossible for receiving servers to respond, which then disables those servers and opens the network to attack.

IP Datagrams

TCP/IP is transmitted along networks as discrete chunks called packets or **datagrams**. Each complete message is usually separated into multiple datagrams. In addition, each datagram contains information about the source and destination IP addresses, a variety of control settings, and the actual data exchanged by the client and host.

Each IP datagram is divided into different sections. The primary subdivisions are the header and the data, described in the following sections. Besides the header and data sections, some packets have an additional segmented section at the end called a **footer** (or sometimes "trailer") containing data that indicates it's the end of the packet. An error-checking algorithm, called a **Cyclic Redundancy Check (CRC)**, might also be added.

IP Header Structure

The **data** in an IP packet is the part that end users see, but the **header** is the part that computers use to communicate, and it plays an important role in terms of network security and intrusion detection. An IP header (similar to a TCP header, described in "TCP Headers" later in this chapter) contains a number of components. Figure 1-3 shows a common way of depicting the information in an IP header, which is divided into different sections of 32-bit layers.

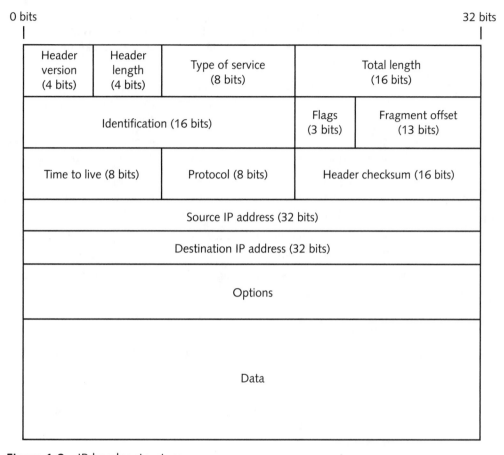

Figure 1-3 IP header structure

It's helpful to divide the IP header sections into components because they have varying degrees of value for configuring packet filters. Each section has varying importance to attackers, too, so it's vital to know what each one does to protect against different types of attacks. These are the components in the IP header structure:

- *Header version*—This component identifies the IP version used to generate the packet.

- *Header length*—This component describes the length of the header in 32-bit words and is a 4-bit value. The default value is 20.

- *Type of service*—This component expresses the quality of service in the transmission of the packet through the network. Four options are available: minimize delay, maximize throughput, maximize reliability, and minimize cost. Most IP network setups don't enable an application to set this value.

- *Total length*—This 16-bit field specifies the packet's total length to a maximum of 65,535 bytes.

- *Identification*—This 16-bit value helps divide the data stream into packets of information. The receiving computer (possibly a firewall) uses each packet's identification number to reassemble the packets that make up the data stream in the correct order.

- *Flags*—This 3-bit value indicates whether the packet is a fragment—one packet within a sequence of packets that make up an entire communication—and whether it's the last fragment or more are to follow.

- *Fragment offset*—If the data received is a fragment, this value indicates where it belongs in the sequence of fragments so that a packet can be reassembled.

- *Time to live (TTL)*—This 8-bit value identifies the maximum time the packet can remain in the system before it's dropped. Each router or device the packet passes through reduces the TTL by a value of one.

- *Protocol*—This component identifies the type of transport packet being carried (for example, 1 = ICMP, 2 = IGMP, 6 = TCP, and 17 = UDP).

- *Header checksum*—This component is the sum of the 16-bit values in the packet header expressed as a single value.

- *Source IP address*—This component is the address of the computer or device that sent the IP packet.

- *Destination IP address*—This component is the address of the computer or device receiving the IP packet.

- *Options*—This component can include items such as a security field and several source routing fields that the packet sender uses to supply routing information. Gateways can then use this routing information to send the packet to its destination.

Programs that capture packets as they pass through a network interface give you another way to view packet header information. Most network operating systems (OSs) have some type of built-in or add-on program to monitor network activity, such as Windows Network Monitor. Many security administrators, however, prefer third-party applications for their versatility and extra features. One such program called Ethereal tracks packets and supplies detailed information on them (see Figure 1-4).

IP Data

Firewalls, covered in Chapters 9 through 11, and virtual private networks (VPNs, covered in Chapters 5 and 6) can protect data in a packet in a number of ways. Firewalls inspect inbound and outbound traffic and compare it to a set of rules to decide whether the packet can pass. VPNs use the public Internet to send and receive, but they create a secure private tunnel for the transmission. A proxy server is another method of securing data. Proxies receive a packet from a host on the internal local area network (LAN) that they're protecting and completely rebuild the packet from scratch before sending it to its destination. The receiving computer then thinks the packet has come from the proxy server rather than the originating host.

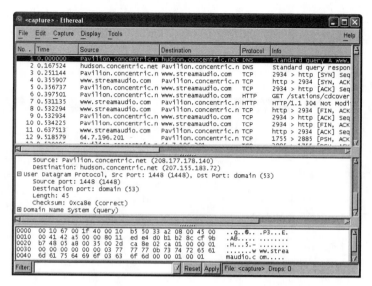

Figure 1-4   TCP/IP header information displayed by Ethereal

IP Fragmentation

Fragmentation of IP packets was originally developed as a means of allowing large packets to pass through routers that couldn't handle them because of frame-size limitations. Routers were then able to divide packets into multiple fragments and send them along the network, where receiving routers reassembled them in the correct order and passed them along to their destination.

Fragmentation creates a number of security problems, however. Because the TCP or User Datagram Protocol (UDP) port number is supplied only at the beginning of a packet, it appears only in fragment number 0. Fragments numbered 1 or higher are passed through the filter without being scrutinized because they don't contain any port information. An attacker simply has to modify the IP header to make all fragment numbers of a packet start at 1 or higher. All fragments then go through the filter and can access internal resources.

To be safe, you should configure the firewall/packet filter to drop all fragmented packets, especially because fragmentation is seldom used now because of improvements in routers. You could also have the firewall reassemble fragmented packets and allow only complete packets to pass through.

ICMP Messages

Internet Control Message Protocol (ICMP) is a protocol designed to assist TCP/IP networks with troubleshooting communication problems. When used correctly, ICMP produces messages that tell a host whether another host can be reached through a ping signal.

A firewall or packet filter must be able to determine, based on a packet's message type, whether an ICMP packet should be allowed to pass. Table 1-2 lists some common ICMP type codes.

Table 1-2   ICMP type codes

ICMP Type	Name	Possible Cause
0	Echo Reply	Normal response to a ping
3	Destination Unreachable	Host is listed on the network but cannot be contacted
4	Source Quench	Router receiving too much traffic
5	Redirect	Faster route located
6	Destination Network Unknown	Network cannot be found
7	Destination Host Unknown	Host cannot be found on the network
8	Echo Request	Normal ping request
11	Time Exceeded	Too many hops to a destination
12	Parameter Problem	There is a problem with the IP header and the packet cannot be processed

TIP

You'll find a complete list of ICMP message types at *www.iana.org/ assignments/icmp-parameters*.

TCP Headers

TCP/IP packets don't contain just IP header information. They also contain TCP headers (shown in Figure 1-5) that provide hosts with a different set of flags—and give attackers a different set of components they can misuse in an attempt to attack networks.

From a security standpoint, the Flags section (labeled as "Offset reserved" in Figure 1-5) of a TCP header is important because it's the one you can filter for when you create packet-filtering rules. For example, the TCP header portion of a TCP packet that has an **acknowledgement (ACK) flag** set to 1 rather than 0 indicates that the destination computer has received the packets that were sent previously. RFC 793 includes specifications for these six control flags in a TCP header:

- URG (urgent)
- ACK (acknowledgment)
- PSH (push function, which forces TCP to forward and deliver data)
- RST (reset the connection)
- SYN (synchronize sequence numbers)
- FIN (finished—no more data from the sender)

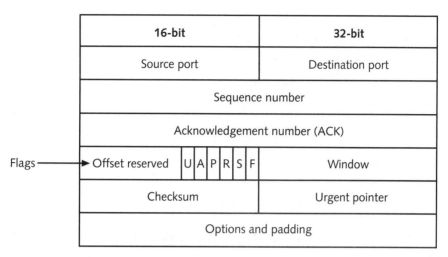

16-bit	32-bit
Source port	Destination port
Sequence number	
Acknowledgement number (ACK)	
Offset reserved U A P R S F	Window
Checksum	Urgent pointer
Options and padding	

Flags ⟶

Figure 1-5   A TCP header

UDP Headers

UDP provides a datagram transport service for IP, but this protocol is considered unreliable because it's **connectionless**. In other words, a UDP packet doesn't depend on an actual connection being established from host to client. This makes it easier for an attacker to send a malformed or dangerous UDP packet to a client.

UDP is used for broadcasting messages or for protocols that don't require the same level of service as TCP. For example, Simple Network Management Protocol (SNMP) and Trivial File Transfer Protocol (TFTP) are normally used on LANs, where packet loss is less of a problem. Attackers can scan for open UDP services to exploit by sending empty UDP datagrams to a suspected open port. If the port is closed, the system sends back an ICMP "Destination Unreachable" message (type 3).

UDP packets have their own headers, as shown in Figure 1-6, in addition to the data part of the packet.

UDP is described in detail in RFC 768.

TIP

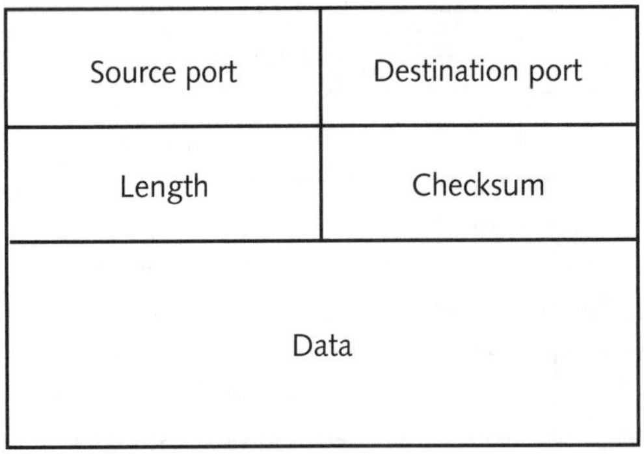

Source port	Destination port
Length	Checksum
Data	

Figure 1-6 A UDP packet header and data

Activity 1-2: Downloading and Installing a Network Traffic Analyzer

Time Required: 45 minutes

Objective: Monitor and analyze network traffic.

Description: To get a better idea of what TCP/IP packet headers look like, using a network traffic analyzer to capture packets as they enter or leave your network can be helpful. In this activity, you download and use Ethereal to observe packets. You also need to download and install a packet capture utility called WinPcap for running Ethereal.

To do this activity, you must stop any firewall programs you're running currently.

1. Start your Web browser, enter the URL for the WinPcap Web site (**http://winpcap. org**), and then press **Enter**.

2. Click **Downloads** on the left side of the page.

3. Start to download WinPcap by clicking the **WinPcap auto-installer (driver +DLLs)** link for the latest version of the software.

4. When the File Download dialog box opens, click **Run**. If you see a security warning about an unknown publisher, click **Run** again. The file is downloaded to a temporary directory on your computer, and the WinPcap setup utility opens automatically.

5. Click **Next** in the first setup window.

6. Click the **I Agree** button. In the Completing the WinPcap 3.1 Setup Wizard window, click **Finish**. Restart your computer to complete the installation.

7. Start your Web browser, enter the URL for the Ethereal Web site (**http://www.ethereal.com**), and then press **Enter**.

8. Click **Download** to go to the Ethereal: Download page.

9. Under Official Releases, click the **Main Site** link next to Windows.

10. Scroll down the Ethereal for Windows page and click the latest **ethereal-setup-[*version number*].exe** file.

11. When the File Download dialog box opens, click **Run**. If you see a security warning about an unknown publisher, click **Run** again. Then click **Next** to continue the setup.

12. In the Ethereal Setup: License Agreement window, click **I Agree**.

13. In the Choose Components window, accept all defaults, and then click **Next**.

14. If the Select Additional Tasks window is displayed, accept all defaults and click **Next**.

15. In the Choose Install Location dialog box, select the directory where you want to install the software, and click **Next**.

16. If necessary, in the Install WinPcap? window, click to clear the **Install WinPcap 3.1 beta 4** check box to keep your current version of WinPcap, and then click **Install**. The Installing dialog box opens, displaying a series of messages about the installation progress. When you see the message "Installation Complete," click **Next** and then click **Finish**.

17. Click **Start**, point to **All Programs**, point to **Ethereal**, and click **Ethereal**. The Ethereal Network Analyzer window opens.

18. Click **Capture**, **Options** from the Ethereal menu. If you see a warning, click **OK**, and then click **Capture**, **Options** from the Ethereal menu again.

19. Click the **Interface** list arrow, and select your network interface device in the drop-down list. Click the **Start** button at the bottom of the Options dialog box. The Ethereal: Capture dialog box opens with a series of 0% readings, reporting that no data has been captured yet.

20. Click **Start**, point to **All Programs**, point to **Accessories**, and click **Command Prompt** to open a command prompt window.

21. At the command prompt, type **ping *IPaddress*** (substituting the IP address you found in Activity 1-1 for *IPaddress*).

22. Click **Stop** at the bottom of the Ethereal: Capture dialog box. A wealth of information about the packets that have passed through your network gateway should appear in the main Ethereal window. The first line should contain information about your ping request. Write down what protocol is listed, and explain what the abbreviations mean. (*Hint:* Look at the middle section of the Ethereal window, where detailed information about the packet is displayed.)

_____

_____

23. Type **exit** and press **Enter** to close the command prompt window.

24. Click **File**, **Quit** from the Ethereal menu, and then click **Continue without saving** to close the Ethereal window and return to the Windows desktop. Leave your system running for the next activity.

Domain Name Service (DNS)

Domain Name Service (DNS) is a general-purpose service used mainly on the Internet. DNS servers translate host names to IP addresses used to identify the host computer. To connect to Web sites, users need a DNS server that can translate the **fully qualified domain names (FQDNs)** they enter, such as *www.course.com*, to the corresponding IP addresses so that the appropriate computers can connect to one another.

In terms of network security, DNS is important because it gives network administrators another tool for blocking unwanted communication. With firewalls, Web browsers, and proxy servers, administrators can enter DNS names to block Web sites containing content that's considered offensive or unsuitable. In addition, networks that use DNS servers need to enable traffic through the DNS servers when packet filtering is set up.

DNS can be exploited in many ways. Attackers often attempt buffer overflow, zone transfer, or cache poisoning attacks. In a DNS buffer overflow attack, an overly long DNS name is sent to the server. When the server is unable to process or interpret the DNS name, it can't process other requests. A DNS cache poisoning attack exploits the fact that every DNS packet contains a "Question" section and an "Answer" section. An older, more vulnerable server has stored answers that are sent in response to requests to connect to DNS addresses. Attackers can break into the cache to discover the DNS addresses of computers on the network. Most (but not all) DNS servers, however, have since been patched to eliminate this vulnerability.

DNS zone files contain a list of every DNS-configured host on a network as well as their IP address. Microsoft DNS-enabled networks also list all services running on DNS-configured hosts. When an attacker attempts to penetrate the network, the DNS zone file can provide a list of exploitable targets on the internal network. When configuring DNS servers connected to the Internet, you should disable zone transfers to all hosts except those internal to the network. Internal hosts must be able to transfer zone information to update their records.

Encryption

Packet filters, firewalls, and proxy servers provide protection for packets of information that pass through a gateway at the perimeter of a network or subnet. However, corruption can also occur between the sending gateway and the gateway of the destination network. To protect a packet's contents from being intercepted, firewalls and other security components often encrypt the contents of packets leaving the network and are prepared to decrypt incoming packets. Encryption is the process of concealing information to render it unreadable to all but the intended recipients. Encryption turns ordinary (plaintext) information into encoded ciphertext.

Much of the encryption on the Internet makes use of digital certificates—electronic documents containing an encrypted series of numerals and characters called a digital signature, which authenticates the identity of the person sending the certificate. Certificates make use of keys, which are long blocks of encoded text generated by algorithms. The sending host uses a key to encrypt data before transmission, and the receiving host uses the key to decrypt data back into readable form. The encryption key can be any length, but most current encryption methods use key lengths from 40 to 256 bits. Longer keys are more secure but at the cost of performance.

An organization that wants to encrypt data often needs to set up Public Key Infrastructure (PKI), which is needed to make digital certificates and public and private key distribution possible for users. The PKI framework is the foundation of some popular and highly trusted security schemes, including Pretty Good Privacy (PGP) and Secure Sockets Layer (SSL).

NOTE

Digital signatures and PKI are important concepts to understand and are crucial to security on the internet. Fore more information on these topics, run an Internet search, or consult the relevant RFCs. (Try *www.rfc-editor.org.rfcxx00.html* for the current Internet standards.)

ACTIVITY

Activity 1-3: Examining a Digital Certificate

Time Required: 20 minutes

Objective: Examine a default digital certificate on a Windows XP computer.

Description: A digital certificate, an electronic document that encrypts communication between networked computers, can be difficult to conceptualize. However, your Windows XP computer already has a number of digital certificates that have been issued by organizations called certification authorities (CAs). You can view these certificates to get a better idea of the information they contain. In this activity, you open the Microsoft Management Console, add the Certificates snap-in, and then view the components of a certificate.

1. Click **Start**, **Run**, type **mmc**, and then click **OK**. The Microsoft Management Console window (labeled Console1) opens.

2. Click **File**, **Add/Remove Snap-in** from the menu.

3. In the Add/Remove Snap-in dialog box, click **Add**. In the Add Standalone Snap-in dialog box, click **Certificates**, and then click **Add**.

4. In the Certificates snap-in dialog box, verify that My user account is selected, and then click **Finish**.

5. In the Add Standalone Snap-in dialog box, click **Close**. Click **OK** to close Add/ Remove Snap-in and return to Console1.

6. Click to expand **Certificates – Current User** and **Trusted Root Certification Authorities**.

7. Under Trusted Root Certification Authorities, click **Certificates**, and scroll down the list of certificates in the pane on the right. Double-click the first certificate labeled **VeriSign Trust Network**.

8. In the Certificate dialog box (which lists the certificate's components), click **Details**.

9. Click **Public key** to see the public key associated with the digital signature. Click **Enhanced key usage (property)** to see the ways in which the digital certificate can be used. Click **OK** to close the Certificate dialog box.

10. Click **File**, **Exit** to close the MMC window. When prompted to save the settings, click **No**. Leave your system running for the next activity.

OVERVIEW OF THREATS TO NETWORK SECURITY

A variety of attackers might attempt network intrusions, causing loss of data, loss of privacy, and other consequences. The threat is one that concerns a growing number of corporate managers. More businesses are actively addressing this problem, but many others have not taken steps to secure their systems from attack.

This section gives you a general overview of who might want to attack your systems and other threats you might encounter. The first step in defeating the enemy is to know the enemy! Next, you learn about major security concerns on the Internet and see how network security and defensive technologies are used to combat threats. Finally, you learn about access controls and auditing and see how defense measures affect your network and organization.

Types of Attackers

When planning network security measures, knowing the types of attackers (discussed in the following sections) likely to attempt breaking in to your network is important. This knowledge can help you anticipate and set up detection systems, firewalls, and other defenses to block them as effectively as possible. Before getting into the types of attackers, an overview of motivations for attempting to break into systems can be helpful:

- *Status*—Some attackers attempt to take over computer systems just for the thrill of it. They like to keep count of how many systems they have access to as a sort of notch on their belt.

- *Revenge*—Disgruntled current or former employees might want to retaliate against an organization for policies or actions they consider wrong. They can sometimes gain entry through an undocumented account (back door) on the system.

- *Financial gain*—Other attackers have financial profit as their goal. Obviously, attackers who break into a network can gain access to financial accounts. They can steal individual or corporate credit card numbers and make unauthorized purchases. Just as often, attackers defraud people out of money with scams carried out via e-mail or other means.

- *Industrial espionage*—Proprietary information is often valuable enough that it can be sold to competing companies or other parties who want to upgrade their technological capabilities in some way.

Crackers

A **cracker** is anyone who attempts to gain access to unauthorized resources on a network, usually by finding a way to circumvent passwords, firewalls, or other protective measures. They seek to break into computers for different reasons:

- "Old school" hackers consider themselves seekers of knowledge; they operate on the theory that knowledge is power, regardless of how they come by that knowledge. They are not out to destroy or harm; they want to discover how things work and open any sources of knowledge they can find. They believe the Internet was intended to be an open environment and anything online can and should be available to anyone.

- Other less "ethical" crackers pursue destructive aims, such as the proliferation of viruses and e-mail bombs, much like vandals and graffiti artists.

- Some bored young people who are highly adept with computers try to gain control of as many systems as possible for the thrill of it. They enjoy disrupting systems and keeping them from working, and they tend to boast about their exploits online.

TIP

A good overview of crackers' motivations is available at The Learning Channel's Web site, *http://tlc.discovery.com/convergence/hackers/articles/psych.html*.

Disgruntled Employees

Who would try to access customer information, financial files, job records, or other sensitive information from *inside* an organization? Disgruntled employees. These employees are usually unhappy over perceived injustices and want to exact revenge by stealing information. Often they give confidential information to new employers. When an employee is terminated, security measures should be taken immediately to ensure that the employee can no longer access the company network.

Sometimes the most serious vulnerabilities facing a company are those inside the firewall, not outside it. For example, in November 2002, the FBI broke up the largest identity theft ring in U.S. history. A help desk worker at a computer software company allegedly agreed to give passwords and access codes for consumer credit reports to another person, who was then able to make unauthorized purchases using the stolen information (the credit card numbers and other personal information of more than 30,000 people).

The 2004 CSI/FBI Computer Crime and Security Survey is available at *www.gocsi.com*. Click the Download Survey PDF link on the right, and follow the instructions to download the survey. You need to register, but registration is free.

Criminals and Industrial Spies

No matter how ethical "old school" hackers consider themselves to be, many other crackers are out to steal anything they can get their hands on. They might be interested in selling information to the top bidder or using it to influence potential victims. Many companies would certainly be interested in getting the plans for a new product from their competitors.

Script Kiddies and Packet Monkeys

The term **script kiddie** is often used to describe young, immature computer programmers who spread viruses and other malicious scripts and use techniques to exploit weaknesses in computer systems. They lack the experience to create viruses or Trojan programs on their own, but they can usually find these programs online and spread them for their own aims. The assumption among supposedly more sophisticated crackers is that script kiddies seek only to break in to as many computers as possible to gain attention and notoriety.

Another type of mischievous attacker is a **packet monkey**, who's primarily interested in blocking Web site activities through a distributed denial of service (DDoS) attack. In a DDoS attack, the attacker hijacks many computers and uses them to flood the target with so many false requests that the server can't process them all, and normal traffic is blocked. Packet monkeys might also want to deface Web sites by leaving messages that their friends can read.

Packet monkeys, script kiddies, and their exploits are explained in the Jargon File, an online version of the Hacker's Dictionary that you can research at *www.eps.mcgill.ca/jargon/jargon.html*.

Terrorists

Until September 11, 2001, most people didn't consider a terrorist attack on an information infrastructure a likely threat. Since that awful day, however, the threat posed by terrorists has been taken more seriously. A terrorist group might want to attack computer systems for several reasons: making a political statement or accomplishing a political goal, such as the release of a jailed comrade; causing damage to critical systems; or disrupting the target's financial stability. Attacking the World Trade Center certainly accomplished the latter goal, given the nature and location of the structures. Terrorists might also want to simply cause fear.

It might be hard to understand why a terrorist attack on computers would be considered a serious threat, until you think about how many critical systems are controlled by computers. Consider the chaos a successful attack on a computer system controlling a nuclear power plant's reactors would cause. The overall psychological effect would be just as detrimental as the damage to the infrastructure and even the loss of life.

Malicious Code

In 2001, the Code Red worm infected millions of computers, costing around $2.4 billion in cleanup, lost productivity, and so on. (For more information, see the story "Code Blue Worm Strikes in China, May Migrate" at *www.newsfactor.com/perl/story/13405.html*.) This self-propagating malicious code (**malware**) exploited systems using Internet Information Services (IIS, Windows Web server software) that were susceptible to a buffer overflow vulnerability in the Indexing Service. When the worm appeared, Microsoft had already released a patch. The vulnerability was well known, and instructions were freely available explaining how to exploit it, yet many administrators hadn't taken steps to protect their systems.

Information security has come a long way since the Code Red worm, but there will always be a new vulnerability right around the corner, and security professionals must stay one step ahead of attackers. The following sections review types of malware you might encounter.

Viruses, Worms, and Trojan Programs

Although most users think of any type of virus, worm, or Trojan program as a virus, they are completely different types of attacks. A **virus** is computer code that copies itself from one place to another surreptitiously and performs actions that range from benign to harmful. Viruses are spread by several methods: running executable code, sharing disks or memory sticks, opening e-mail attachments, or viewing Web pages that use malicious ActiveX objects.

A **worm** creates files that copy themselves repeatedly and consume disk space. Worms don't require user intervention to be launched; they are self-propagating. Some worms can install **back doors**—a way of gaining unauthorized access to a computer or other resource, such as an unused port or terminal service, that makes it possible for attackers to access and gain control over a computer. Others can destroy data on a hard disk. At this writing, for instance, one antivirus software company reports the top virus threat to be another Mydoom variant called W32.Mydoom.BU@mm (see the Symantec Security Response Web site at *http:// securityresponse.symantec.com/avcenter/venc/data/w32.mydoom.bu@mm.html*). Just like a cold or flu virus, computer viruses and worms can mutate or be altered to defeat antivirus software.

A **Trojan program** is also a harmful computer program but one that appears to be something useful—a deception much like the Trojan horse described in Greek legends. The difference between a virus and a Trojan program is in how the malicious code is used. Viruses replicate themselves and can potentially cause damage when they run on a user's computer. Trojan programs can also create a back door. In addition, the often hidden or obscure nature of a back door makes the attacker's activities difficult to detect.

Viruses, worms, and Trojan programs are a major security threat. They can damage files, enable attackers to control computers, and cause applications to stop functioning correctly. In creating a network defense perimeter, you need to consider guarding against them. Firewalls and intrusion detection systems don't block malicious code on their own, however; you need to install antivirus software or proxy servers that can be configured to filter them out and delete them before they cause harm.

Macro Viruses

A macro is a type of script that automates repetitive tasks in Microsoft Word or similar applications. When you run a macro, a series of actions are carried out automatically. Macros are a useful way to make performing some tasks more efficient. Unfortunately, **macro viruses** perform the same functions, but they tend to be harmful. For example, in March 1999, the Melissa macro virus caused Microsoft to shut down incoming e-mail. Melissa spread rapidly and arrived as an attachment with the subject line "Important message from [name of someone]." The body text read, "Here is that document you asked for . . . don't show anyone else." If the recipient opened the attachment, the macro virus infected the computer and carried out a series of commands. Melissa was a fast-spreading virus, infecting more than 100,000 computers in the first few days. Macro viruses remain a threat today, but the good news is that the user must perform some action for the virus to be activated; therefore, educating users not to open these attachments is essential.

Other Threats to Network Security

It isn't possible to prepare for every possible risk to your systems. At best, you can maintain a secure environment for today's threat and have a comprehensive plan for integrating safeguards against tomorrow's threat into your defenses. The next threat might be infection by a new virus or the exploit of a recently discovered vulnerability, or it might be an earthquake that destroys your facility. There are many threats you can't mitigate entirely, such as a natural disaster. Although you might have prepared for natural disasters by maintaining an alternate site complete with all necessary equipment, the fact remains that your primary site's network and equipment suffered total or near total loss.

Social Engineering: The People Factor

Another common way in which attackers gain access to an organization's resources is one that can't be defended against with hardware or software. The vulnerability, in this case, is gullible employees who are fooled by attackers into giving out passwords or other access codes. Attacks that involve personnel who don't observe accepted security practices (or who willfully abuse them) can best be addressed with a strong and enforced security policy. Chapters 2 and 3 cover security policies in depth.

Common Attacks and Defenses

Table 1-3 describes some of the common attacks you need to guard against and the defensive strategies you can use to defeat them. These concepts are discussed in more depth throughout the remainder of the book.

Table 1-3   Attacks and defenses

Attack	Description	Defense
Denial of service (DoS) attack	The traffic into and out of a network is blocked when servers are flooded with malformed packets (bits of digital information) that have false IP addresses or other data inserted into them or contain other fake communications.	Keep your server OS up to date; log instances of frequent connection attempts against one service.
SYN flood	A network is overloaded with packets that have the SYN flag set.	Keep your firewall and OS up to date so that these attacks are blocked by means of software patches and updates, and review your log files of access attempts to see whether intrusion attempts have been made.
Virus	Network computers are infected by viruses.	Install antivirus software and keep virus definitions up to date.
Trojan program	An attacker delivers a malicious Trojan program through a "back door."	Install antivirus software and keep virus definitions up to date.
Social engineering	An employee is misled into giving out passwords or other sensitive information.	Educate employees about your security policy, which is a set of goals and procedures for making an organization's network secure.
Malicious port scanning	An attacker looks for open ports to infiltrate a network.	Install and configure a firewall, which is hardware and/or software designed to filter out unwanted network traffic and protect authorized traffic.
Internet Control Message Protocol (ICMP) message abuse	A network is flooded with a stream of ICMP echo requests to a target computer.	Set up packet filtering.

Table 1-3   Attacks and defenses (continued)

Attack	Description	Defense
Finding vulnerable hosts on the internal network to attack	An attacker who gains access to one computer on a network can get IP addresses, host names, and passwords, which are then used to find other hosts to attack.	Use proxy servers.
Man-in-the-middle	An attacker operates between two computers in a network and impersonates one computer to intercept communications.	Use VPN encryption.
New files being placed on the system	A virus or other program causes new files to proliferate on infected computers, using up system resources.	Install system-auditing software, such as Tripwire.
Remote Procedure Calls (RPC) attacks	The operating systems crash because they are unable to handle arbitrary data sent to an RPC port.	Set up an IDS.

Internet Security Concerns

As you probably know from your study of basic networking concepts and TCP/IP, a port number combined with a computer's IP address constitutes a network connection called a **socket**. Software commonly used by attackers attempts to identify sockets that respond to connection requests. The sockets that respond can be targeted to see whether they have been left open or have security vulnerabilities that can be exploited. **Hypertext Transport Protocol (HTTP)** Web services use port 80. HTTP is among the most commonly exploited services.

The following sections briefly cover some aspects of using the Internet that you need to be aware of from a security standpoint. These sections cover e-mail vulnerabilities such as viruses, scripts that enter the network through e-mail or downloaded files, and broadband connections that enable computers to connect to the Internet with IP addresses that never change and can easily be attacked.

E-Mail and Communications

For a home user who regularly surfs the Web, uses e-mail, and engages in instant messaging, a firewall's primary job is to keep viruses from infecting files and to prevent Trojan programs from entering the system through hidden back door openings. Personal firewall programs, such as Norton Internet Security, come with an antivirus program that alerts users when an e-mail attachment or a file containing a known virus is found.

Scripting

A widespread network intrusion that's increasing in frequency and severity is the use of scripts—executable code attached to e-mail messages or downloaded files that infiltrates a system. It can be difficult for a firewall or intrusion detection system (IDS) to block all such files; specialty firewalls and other programs should be integrated with existing security systems to keep scripts from infecting a network.

A specialty e-mail firewall can monitor and control certain types of content that pass into and out of a network. These firewalls can be configured to filter out pornographic content, junk e-mail, and malicious code. MailMarshal by NWTECH (*www.nwtechusa.com/ mailmarshal.html*), for instance, unpacks and scans the content of each e-mail message before it reaches the recipient. E-mail filtering programs, however, introduce privacy issues that need to be balanced against an organization's need for protection—a trade-off that applies to almost all aspects of network security, not just e-mail messages.

Always-on Connectivity

The proliferation of affordable high-speed connections, such as cable modems and DSL lines, brings up special security concerns for network administrators. Computers using always-on connections are easier to locate and attack because their IP addresses remain the same as long as they're connected to the Internet—which might be days at a time if computers are left on overnight or over a weekend. Some users pay extra for static IP addresses that never change and that enable them to run Web servers or other services. Static IP addresses, however, make it easier for attackers to locate a computer and scan it for open ports.

Another problem happens when remote users (employees who are on the road, contractors who work at home, or business partners) want to connect to your organization's internal network. With the popularity of the Internet, more home computers started using modems. These connections were usually made through temporary dial-up connections that used protocols such as Point-to-Point Protocol (PPP). Now it's increasingly likely that remote users connect to a network through an always-on DSL or cable modem connection, which means they might be connected to your network for hours at a time.

Always-on connections effectively extend the boundaries of your corporate network, and you should secure them as you would any part of your network perimeter. At the very least, your network security policy should specify that remote users have their computers equipped with firewall and antivirus protection software. After all, if attackers can break in to a remote user's computer while that user is connected to your network through a VPN or other connection, your network becomes vulnerable as well.

ACTIVITY

Activity 1-4: Identifying Open Ports

Time Required: 15 minutes

Objective: Use the Netstat command to look for open ports on your computer.

Description: A computer you're securing, particularly one that's hosting firewall or IDS software, should have a minimal set of resources and open ports on it. How do you determine which ports are open on your computer? You can do so with the Netstat utility, which is built in to both UNIX and Windows systems. The following steps apply to a Windows XP computer, but you can also run the Netstat –a command on a UNIX system to get the same information.

1. Click **Start**, point to **All Programs**, point to **Accessories**, and click **Command Prompt**.

2. At the command prompt, type **netstat –a** (leave a blank space between "netstat" and the hyphen). Press **Enter**.

3. Netstat presents information in columns. The first column, Proto, indicates the protocol being used. The last column, State, tells you whether a connection has been established (ESTABLISHED) or the computer is listening for connections (LISTENING). How many TCP ports did you find that were reported in the State column as LISTENING? How many UDP ports? Write your findings here:

   _____

   _____

4. Type **exit** and press **Enter** to close the command prompt window.

GOALS OF NETWORK SECURITY

So far, you have reviewed basic TCP/IP knowledge and an overview of the threats networks face. In the following sections, you learn what's needed to begin building secure systems. You need to enable business partners, mobile workers, and contractors to connect securely to the main network, and you need a way to authenticate authorized users reliably. You must also have a clear picture of the overriding goals of a network security effort, including privacy and data integrity.

Providing Secure Connectivity

In the early days of the Internet, network security primarily emphasized blocking attackers and other unauthorized users from accessing the corporate network. Now secure connectivity with trusted users and networks is the priority. When people go online to conduct business, they often engage in the following activities that could make them vulnerable:

- Placing orders for merchandise online, revealing both personal and financial information during payment
- Paying bills by transferring funds online
- Accessing account information
- Looking up personnel records
- Creating authentication information, such as user names and passwords

The growth of the Internet and e-commerce isn't likely to slow down, so methods to secure these transactions must be set up and maintained. Several methods can be combined in a layered security scheme, as you see later in "Using Network Defense Technologies in Layers."

Secure Remote Access

One of the biggest security challenges facing organizations that communicate via the Internet is the need to provide secure remote access for contractors and employees who are traveling. A VPN, with its combination of encryption and authentication, is an ideal and cost-effective solution (see Figure 1-7). (VPNs are explained in more detail in Chapters 5 and 6.)

Ensuring Privacy

Corporations, hospitals, and other organizations with databases full of personal and financial information need to maintain privacy not only to protect their customers but also to maintain the integrity and credibility of their own companies. In addition, legislation exists that protects private information and mandates severe penalties for failure to adequately protect private information. Examples of these laws include Sarbanes-Oxley, Health Insurance Portability and Accountability Act (HIPAA), and the Gramm-Leach-Bliley Act. You probably won't need to know much about these laws for the SCNP certification exam, but if you work in an industry affected by these or other laws governing privacy protection, you definitely want to keep up on the legalities.

One of the most important and effective ways to maintain the privacy of information on an organization's network is to educate all employees about security dangers and to explain security policies. Employees are the ones most likely to detect security breaches *and* to cause security breaches accidentally through their own behaviors. They can also monitor activities of their fellow employees and stay aware of suspicious activity that could indicate a security problem.

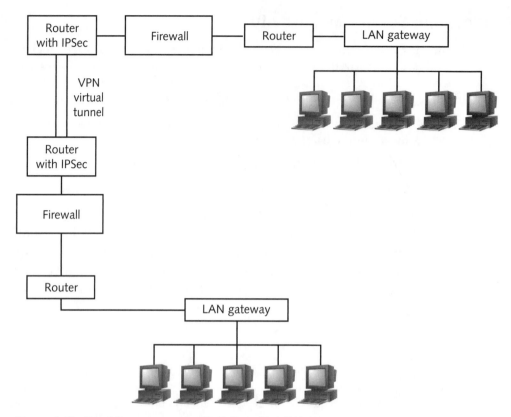

Figure 1-7   Providing secure connectivity with VPNs

Providing Nonrepudiation

Nonrepudiation is an important aspect of establishing trusted communication between organizations that do business across a network rather than face-to-face. Encryption protects the integrity, confidentiality, and authenticity of digital information. Encryption can also provide **nonrepudiation**, which is the capability to prevent one participant in an electronic transaction from denying that it performed an action. Nonrepudiation simply means ensuring that the sender can't deny sending a message and the receiver can't deny receiving it.

Confidentiality, Integrity, and Availability: The CIA Triad

Security professionals are familiar with the term "CIA triad" (not to be confused with our friends in Langley, Virginia) to refer to the goals of ensuring confidentiality, integrity, and availability—the tenets of information security. **Confidentiality** refers to preventing intentional or unintentional disclosure of communications between a sender and recipient. **Integrity** ensures the accuracy and consistency of information during all processing (storage, transmission, and so forth). **Availability** is making sure those who are authorized to access resources can do so in a reliable and timely manner. The CIA triad is often represented as a triangle, as shown in Figure 1-8.

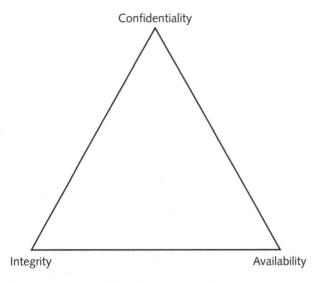

Figure 1-8   The CIA triad

USING NETWORK DEFENSE TECHNOLOGIES IN LAYERS

No single security component or method by itself can be expected to ensure complete protection for a network—or even an individual host computer. Instead, you need to assemble a group of methods that work in a coordinated fashion to provide protection against a variety of threats.

The components and approaches described throughout the rest of this book should be arranged to provide layers of network defense. This layering approach to network security is often called **defense in depth (DiD)**. The National Security Agency (NSA) originally designed DiD as a best practices strategy for achieving information assurance. In general, the layers are as follows (each layer in discussed in the following sections):

- Physical security
- Authentication and password security
- Operating system security
- Antivirus protection
- Packet filtering
- Firewalls
- Demilitarized zone (DMZ)
- Intrusion detection system (IDS)
- Virtual private network (VPN)
- Auditing and log files
- Routers and access control

For more information on DiD, visit *www.nsa.gov/snac/support/ defenseindepth.pdf*.

TIP

Physical Security

The term **physical security** refers to measures taken to physically protect a computer or other network device from theft, fire, or environmental disaster. Along with installing computer locks that attach the device to a piece of furniture in your office, critical servers should be in a room protected by a lock and/or burglar alarm. It's been said many times but is worth repeating: "If the bad guys can touch it, they own it." This statement means it takes only seconds for a computer to be compromised. Within minutes, an attacker can defeat most common locks and steal anything from a password file to the whole server.

In addition, uninterruptible power supply (UPS) devices help maintain a steady level of electrical power, thus avoiding possible damage from voltage spikes—sudden and dramatic increases in power that can damage hardware.

Use an engraving tool to mark serial numbers, phone numbers, or other identifiers on portable devices, such as laptops, that can be lost or stolen easily. Specialized locks are available for PCs and laptops; many have alarms that go off if someone tries to take the device. You can also store portable computers in locked cabinets, such as the ones sold by Datamation Systems (*http://pc-security.com*).

TIP

Authentication and Password Security

After you have physically secured your computers, you can begin to protect them from the inside as well. One simple but effective strategy is **password security**—having your employees select good passwords, keep them secure, and change them as needed. Using multiple passwords, including screen-saver passwords and passwords for protecting critical applications, is also a good idea to guard against unauthorized employees gaining control of unattended computers.

Authentication uses one of three methods: something the user knows, something the user possesses, and something the user is. In the field of network computing, authentication is performed in one of several ways. Basic authentication makes use of *something the user knows*, such as a user name/password pair. In challenge/response authentication, the authenticating device generates a random code or number (the challenge) and sends it to the user who wants to be authenticated. The user resubmits the number or code and adds his or her secret PIN or password (the response) or uses *something the user possesses*, such as a smart card swiped through a card reader.

In large organizations, a centralized server typically handles authentication. The use of *something the user is*—biometrics (retinal scans, voiceprints, fingerprints, and so on)—is also growing in popularity because of increasing concerns over terrorist attacks and other criminal activities.

TIP You can provide an extra layer of protection for a laptop by setting the Basic Input Output System (BIOS)—a password that keeps intruders from starting a computer. However, this protection can be circumvented easily if the computer is booted from a floppy disk.

Operating System Security

Another way to secure computers and their data from the inside is by installing OS patches that have been issued to address security flaws. It's your responsibility to keep up with patches, hot fixes, and service packs and install them when they become available. In addition, stopping any unneeded services and disabling Guest accounts help make an OS more secure.

Antivirus Protection

Virus scanning refers to the process of examining files or e-mail messages for file names, file extensions such as .exe (for executable code) or .zip (for zipped files), or other indications that viruses are present. Many viruses have suspicious file extensions, but some seem innocuous. Antivirus software uses several methods to look for malware, including comparisons to the software's current signature files, which contain a pattern of known viruses. Signature files are the primary reason for keeping your antivirus software updated; antivirus software vendors frequently create updates and make them available for customers to download. When antivirus software recognizes the presence of viruses, it deletes them from the file system or places them in a storage area called a "quarantine" where they can't replicate themselves or do harm to other files.

Firewalls and IDSs, by themselves, aren't equipped to scan for viruses and eliminate them. However, many enterprise-level firewalls come with integrated antivirus protection. Antivirus software is a must-have for every computer in a network; if your firewall doesn't provide antivirus software, you need to install it on the computer that hosts the firewall and on all network computers.

Packet Filtering

Packet filters block or allow the transmission of packets of information based on port, IP address, protocol, or other criteria. Like firewalls and IDSs, they come in many varieties. Some are hardware devices, such as routers placed at a network gateway. Others are software programs that can be installed on a gateway or a computer. Here are a few examples:

- *Routers*—These devices are probably the most common packet filters. Routers process packets according to an access control list (ACL) the administrator defines.

- *Operating systems*—Some systems, such as Windows and Linux, have built-in utilities for packet filtering on the TCP/IP stack of the server software. Linux has a kernel-level packet filter called Ipchains; Windows has a feature called TCP/IP Filtering. Ipchains are covered in detail in Chapter 11, which also covers Iptables, the replacement for Ipchains in Linux kernel versions 2.4 and later.

- *Software firewalls*—Most enterprise-level programs, such as Check Point NG, perform packet filtering; Check Point's product specializes in stateful filtering. Personal firewalls, such as ZoneAlarm and Sygate Personal Firewall, have a less sophisticated version called stateless packet filtering.

Whatever type is used, the packet-filtering device evaluates information in the header and compares it to the established rules. If the information corresponds to one of the "allow" rules, the packet is allowed to pass; if the information matches one of the "deny" rules, the packet is dropped.

Firewalls

The foundation for installing a firewall is your organization's overall security policy. After you have a solid security policy as your guide, you can design security configurations to support your organization's goals. Specifically, you can create a packet-filtering rule base for your firewall that reflects your overall approach to network security. (Don't worry if this information seems a bit overwhelming now; you learn all about security policies in Chapters 2 and 3 and firewalls in more detail in Chapters 9 to 11.) The following sections describe two ways in which a firewall can control the amount of protection a network receives: permissive versus restrictive policies.

Permissive Versus Restrictive Policies

A firewall, following the direction given in a security policy, typically adopts one of these general approaches to security (see Figure 1-9):

- *Permissive*—Calls for a firewall and associated security components to allow all traffic through the network gateway by default, and then block services on a case-by-case basis.

- *Restrictive*—Calls for a firewall and associated network security components to deny all traffic by default. The first rule denies all traffic on any service and using any port. To allow a specific type of traffic, a new rule must be placed ahead of the "deny all" rule.

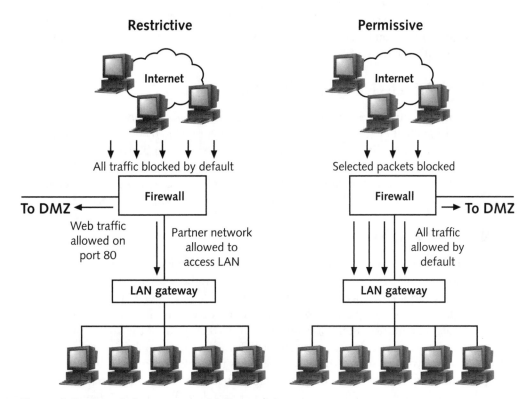

Figure 1-9   Permissive versus restrictive policies

A firewall should enforce the overall policy established by the network administrator. Enforcement is handled primarily through setting up packet-filtering rules, and a rule base contains a set of these rules. The order of rules in the rule base is important to how the firewall processes traffic.

Demilitarized Zone (DMZ)

A subnet called a **demilitarized zone (DMZ)**, which is a network that sits outside the internal network but is connected to the firewall, makes services publicly available yet protects the internal LAN. A DMZ might also contain a DNS server, which resolves domain names to IP addresses. The subnet attached to the firewall and contained in the DMZ is sometimes called a "service network" or "perimeter network."

Intrusion Detection System (IDS)

Firewalls and proxy servers ideally block intruders or malicious code from entering a network. However, an IDS used with these tools offers an additional layer of protection for a network. An IDS works by recognizing the signs of a possible attack and sending a notification to an administrator that an attack is underway. The signs of possible attacks are commonly called **signatures**—combinations of IP address, port number, and the frequency of access attempts. You learn the details of IDS concepts and implementation in Chapters 7 and 8.

Virtual Private Networks (VPNs)

When companies need to share files or exchange confidential financial information, traditionally they turn to expensive leased lines provided by telecommunications companies. Although these lines create a point-to-point connection between company networks and, therefore, ensure a high level of security, the monthly costs are excessively high for many budget-conscious companies. A growing number of organizations are turning to VPNs to provide a low-cost and secure connection that uses the public Internet.

Network Auditing and Log Files

Auditing is the process of recording which computers are accessing a network and what resources are being accessed and then recording the information in a log file. IT managers often overlook detailed and periodic review of log files generated by firewalls and IDSs. By reviewing and maintaining log files, you can detect suspicious patterns of activity, such as regular and unsuccessful connection attempts that occur at the same time each day. You can identify—or at least gather enough information to begin to identify—those who have attacked your network. You can set up rules to block attacks and keep your network defense systems up to date by examining attack attempts that have penetrated firewalls and other protective devices. Effective management of log files is an essential activity that goes hand-in-hand with any perimeter security configuration.

Log File Analysis

Compiling, reviewing, and analyzing log files are among the most tedious and time-consuming tasks associated with network security. Network administrators read and analyze log files to see who is accessing their networks from the Internet. All connection attempts that were rejected should be recorded in the hope of identifying possible intruders or pinpointing vulnerable points in the system.

When you first install intrusion detection or firewall hardware or software on your network, you'll probably be asked to prepare reports stating how the network is being used and what kinds of filtering activities the device is performing. It's a good idea to sort logs by time of day and per hour. (Sorting log files produces more organized material that's easier to review than the log files produced by the server, firewall, or other device.)

Be sure to check logs to learn when the peak traffic times are on your network, and try to identify the services that consume the largest part of your available bandwidth. If your firewall or IDS can display log file entries graphically (as shown in Figure 1-10), showing these graphs to management is always a good idea because they illustrate trends with more impact than lists of raw data.

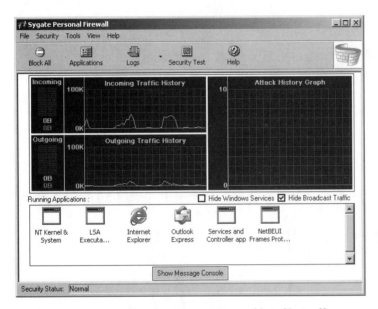

Figure 1-10   A graphical representation of log file traffic

Configuring Log Files

Typically, the log files compiled by firewalls or IDSs give you different options. You can view active data (data compiled by the firewall as traffic moves through the gateway in real time) or data that the device has recently recorded. You can also view the information in these ways:

- *System events*—These events usually track the operations of the firewall or IDS, making a log entry whenever it starts or shuts down.

- *Security events*—These events are records of any alerts the firewall or IDS has issued.

- *Traffic*—This is a record of the traffic that passes through the firewall.

- *Packets*—Some programs enable you to view information about packets that pass through them.

With more elaborate programs, you can customize what you see in log files and search for specific items or events.

GUI Log Viewers

You can always view log files with a text editor, but if you have ever used this method, you know how tedious it can be. A graphical tool organizes logged information into easy-to-read columns and lets you sort them by date, IP address, or other criteria. One GUI product is Sygate Personal Firewall's log viewer, shown in Figure 1-11.

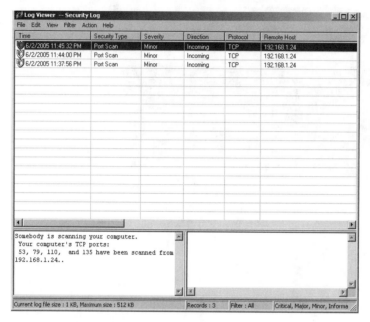

Figure 1-11   Sygate Personal Firewall's log viewer

Routing and Access Control Methods

Routing and access control are important network concepts because routers at the perimeter of a network are critical to the movement of all network traffic, regardless of whether the traffic is legitimate or harmful. Because of routers' positions on the perimeter of networks, they can be equipped with their own firewall software so that they can perform packet filtering and other functions.

To set up a defense, you need to know what kinds of attacks to expect and what services and computers might present openings that could be exploited. As a security professional, it's your job to ensure that no unauthorized access occurs. You must find points of access that would allow attackers to gain access to your network. An attacker might attempt to access open points of entry, such as:

- *Vulnerable services*—The attacker might be able to exploit known vulnerabilities in a server program.

- *E-mail gateways*—The attacker might be able to attach a virus payload to an e-mail message. If a recipient clicks the attachment to open it, the program runs and the virus installs itself on the user's system.

- *Porous borders*—Computers on the network might be listening (that is, waiting for connections) on a virtual channel called a port that's not being used. If an attacker discovers a port that the computer has left open and that isn't being used, this open port can give the attacker access to that computer's contents.

Users must have access to the resources necessary to do their jobs, but unauthorized people must not be able to gain access to exploit those resources. Access control is a vital facet of network security and encompasses everything from complex permission configurations on domain controllers to a locked door. There are three main methods of access control you should be familiar with:

- *Mandatory Access Control (MAC)*—This method defines an uncompromising manner of how information can be accessed. With the MAC method, all access capabilities are defined in advance. System administrators establish what information users can and cannot share.

- *Discretionary Access Control (DAC)*—With this method, network users are given more flexibility in accessing information. This method allows users to share information with other users; however, the risk of unauthorized disclosure is higher than with the MAC method.

- *Role Based Access Control (RBAC)*—This method establishes organizational roles to control access to information. The RBAC method limits access by job function or job responsibility. An employee could have one or more roles that allow access to specific information.

THE IMPACT OF DEFENSE

Although the cost of securing systems—and the data they contain—might seem high, in terms of **return on investment (ROI)**, the cost of a security breach can be much higher. As mentioned, several laws exist to protect privacy, and those laws can carry severe monetary penalties. When added to the direct and indirect costs of a security breach, implementing a sound security scheme can seem inexpensive by comparison.

A key factor in successfully securing systems is the support you gain from upper management. Before security efforts ever start, executives and managers have to be sold on the idea. This serves several key purposes:

- First, the project is going to cost money, and you need to have funding for the project approved beforehand.

- Second, the project will require IT staff time, and managers, supervisors, and employees from all departments must participate to paint a clear picture of priorities and carry out the security plan.

- Next, the process of actually implementing security systems might require downtime for the network, which translates into lost productivity and inconvenience to everyone.

- Last, and most important for the long-term success of security efforts, executives and management need to fully support the project from start to finish. If they don't, development, testing, implementation, and maintenance are nearly impossible to complete. The necessary resources and enforcement won't be available. Besides, if management doesn't seem to care and doesn't support the new order, why would anyone else?

In addition, remember that it isn't enough to simply plan and implement security systems. Probably the most challenging facet of information security is keeping up-to-date on new threats and other developments in the industry. Security systems must be maintained continuously and updated to provide protection against new threats.

This chapter has given you a rundown of network security fundamentals. You should already be familiar with most of the material. If you find you aren't familiar with a concept discussed here, you might want to pick up a copy of *Guide to Networking Essentials, Fourth Edition*, by Greg Tomsho, Ed Tittel, and David Johnson (Thomson Course Technology, 2004, ISBN 0-619-21532-1). Most network professionals keep a library of reference materials, so there's no shame in needing a quick refresher. After all, the security field is constantly changing, and many employers consider the ability to adapt and learn new concepts a prized "soft skill." Besides, who can remember the exact details of a TCP/IP packet if the information isn't used daily?

CHAPTER SUMMARY

- Some basic knowledge of TCP/IP networking is important not only to configure the equipment that helps form a defensive configuration but also to be aware of vulnerabilities related to IP addresses. Proxy servers or Network Address Translation can be used to shield the IP addresses of internal hosts from external users.

- The IP and TCP (or UDP) header sections of IP packets contain a variety of settings that attackers can exploit. These settings include header information, such as the source or destination IP address.

- Attackers can misuse ICMP messages to intercept traffic and direct it to a server they control or to flood a server with so many requests that it can no longer handle other traffic.

- Domain Name Service (DNS) is a general-purpose service that translates fully qualified domain names, such as *www.course.com*, into IP addresses. Computers use IP addresses to locate other computers. Attackers can exploit DNS, but administrators also use it to block unwanted traffic.

- Encryption protects data as it passes from one network to another, and authentication limits access to authorized users.

1

- Network intruders might simply be motivated by a desire to see what kind of data is available on a network and to gain control of computers. Revenge by disgruntled current or former employees might be the primary motivation, however. Some attackers break in to accounts and networks for financial gain. Others want to steal proprietary information for their own use or for resale to other parties.

- Because the Internet is playing an increasingly important role in the movement of business-related traffic from one corporate network to another, an understanding of network security concerns pertaining to online communication is essential. E-mail is one of the most important services to secure because of the possibility of malicious scripts being delivered in e-mail attachments. In addition, always-on connections present new security risks that need to be addressed with firewall and VPN solutions.

- Goals for a network security program originate with an analysis of the risks you face and an assessment of the resources you want to protect. One of the most important goals of any network security effort should be to maintain the privacy of customer and employee information. Other goals include preserving data integrity, authenticating approved users of network resources, and enabling remote users to connect securely to the internal network.

- An effective network security strategy involves many layers of defense working together to prevent many different kinds of threats.

- Auditing is the process of recording which computers access a network and what resources are being accessed, and then recording the information in a log file. Firewall, packet filtering, and IDS logs should be reviewed regularly as a way to detect vulnerable points that should be closed.

- Routing and access control are important network concepts because the routers at the perimeter of a network are critical to the movement of all traffic into and out of the network.

- Defense affects the entire organization. Before beginning a security project, a company's upper management must agree and fully support the project. IT staff need input from managers, supervisors, and employees from all departments to create an effective policy and carry out security measures.

KEY TERMS

acknowledgement (ACK) flag — A TCP header field that contains the value of the next sequence number the sender is expecting to receive. After a connection is established (TCP three-way handshake), the ACK flag is significant and this value is always sent.

availability — Making sure those who are authorized to access resources can do so in a reliable and timely manner.

authentication — The process of determining the identity of an authorized user through matching a user name and password, a fingerprint or retinal scan, a smart card and PIN, and so on.

back doors — A way of gaining unauthorized access to a computer or other resource, usually through an opening in a program that's supposed to be known only to the program's author.

confidentiality — The goal of preventing intentional or unintentional disclosure of communication between a sender and recipient.

connectionless — A feature of the UDP protocol, which does not depend on a connection actually being established between a host and client for a UDP packet to be sent from host to client.

cracker — A person who attempts to gain access to unauthorized resources on a network, usually by finding a way to circumvent passwords, firewalls, or other protective measures.

Cyclic Redundancy Check (CRC) — An error-checking algorithm sometimes added to the end of a TCP/IP packet.

data — The part of a packet that contains the actual data being sent from client to server.

datagrams — Discrete chunks of packets, each of which contains source and destination addresses, control settings, and data.

defense in depth (DiD) — A layering approach to security that protects a network at many different levels by using a variety of strategies and methods.

demilitarized zone (DMZ) — A subnetwork of publicly accessible Web, e-mail, and other servers that's outside the LAN but still protected by the firewall.

footer — Another section added to a TCP/IP packet that tells a computer it's the end of the packet.

fully qualified domain name (FQDN) — The complete DNS name of a computer, including the computer name, domain name, and domain name extension, such as *www. course.com*.

header — The part of a packet that contains source and destination information and general information about the packet.

host address — The part of an IP address that's unique to a computer in its subnet.

Hypertext Transport Protocol (HTTP) — A protocol used by Web services that communicates via TCP/IP port 80.

integrity — The goal of ensuring the accuracy and consistency of information during all processing (storage, transmission, and so forth).

Internet Control Message Protocol (ICMP) — A protocol that reports network communication errors to support IP communications. The Ping command is a common troubleshooting utility based on ICMP.

Internet Protocol version 4 (IPv4) — The IP addressing system currently in widespread use on the Internet, in which addresses are created with 32 bits (4 bytes) of data.

Internet Protocol version 6 (IPv6) — A new version of IP that's gaining support among software and hardware manufacturers and that will eventually replace IPv4; this version calls for 128-bit IP addresses.

macro viruses — A type of malware that performs the same functions as a macro but tends to be harmful.

malware — Software, such as viruses, worms and Trojans, designed to purposely cause harm, allow theft, or otherwise compromise a computer system.

network address — The part of an IP address that a computer has in common with other computers in its subnet.

Network Address Translation (NAT) — NAT translates internal network address into external interface address, which hides the internal LAN addressing scheme and decreases the need for Internet-usable addresses.

nonrepudiation — Ensuring that the sender can't deny sending a message and the receiver can't deny receiving it.

packet filters — Devices or software that block or allow the transmission of packets of information based on port, IP address, protocol, or other criteria.

packet monkey — An attacker who's primarily interested in blocking the activities of a Web site through a distributed denial-of-service attack.

password security — Selecting good passwords, keeping them secure, and changing them as needed contributes to password security. Using multiple passwords, including screen-saver passwords and passwords for protecting critical applications, also helps guard against unauthorized access.

physical security — A term that refers to measures taken to physically protect a computer or other network device from theft, fire, or environmental disaster.

proxy server — A program that provides Web browsing, e-mail, and other services for network users to conceal their identity from those outside the network.

return on investment (ROI) — The total value gained after a solution has been deployed. A positive return on investment is desirable because it means the solution has solved more problems than it creates.

script kiddies — Attackers (often young people) who spread viruses and other malicious scripts and use techniques to exploit weaknesses in computer systems.

signatures — Combinations of flags, IP addresses, and other characteristics indicating an attack that are detected by a firewall or IDS.

socket — A network connection that uses a TCP/IP port number combined with a computer's IP address.

subnet mask — A value that tells another computer which part of a computer's IP address is its network address and which part is the host address.

Transmission Control Protocol/Internet Protocol (TCP/IP) — This suite of protocols allows information to be transmitted from point to point on a network.

Trojan programs — A type of program that appears to be harmless but that actually introduces viruses or causes damage to a computer or system.

virus — Computer code that copies itself from one place to another surreptitiously and performs actions that range from benign to harmful.

worm — A type of malware that creates files that copy themselves repeatedly and consume disk space. Worms don't require user intervention to be launched; they are self-propagating.

REVIEW QUESTIONS

1. What advantages does IPv6 have over IPv4? (Choose all that apply.)

    a. IPv6 uses DHCP for its configuration settings.

    b. IPv6 uses a 128-bit address space.

    c. IPv4 cannot support IPSec.

    d. IPv6 incorporates IPSec.

2. Which of the following is a method of hiding internal host IP addresses? (Choose all that apply.)

    a. Network Address Translation (NAT)

    b. configuring a firewall to insert a fake source IP address into outgoing messages

    c. proxy servers

    d. setting up software firewalls on all internal hosts, thus hiding them

3. A Class C address has a first octet decimal range of _____ to _____ .

    a. 172, 191

    b. 191, 224

    c. 192, 239

    d. 192, 223

4. Class D addresses are reserved for experimentation. True or False?

5. The reserved Class A address 127.0.0.1 is used for which of the following?

    a. broadcasting to all hosts on a subnet

    b. testing the TCP/IP local interface

    c. experimentation

    d. your firewall's internal interface address

6. What are the primary subdivisions of an IP datagram? (Choose all that apply.)

    a. data

    b. flags

    c. body

    d. header

7. Fragmentation of IP packets causes several security problems. How should you configure the firewall or packet filter to prevent harm from fragmented packets? (Choose all that apply.)

    a. Reassemble the packets and allow only completed packets to pass.

    b. Forward fragments to the destination address for reassembly.

    c. Drop all fragmented packets.

    d. Request authentication from the source.

8. Most network intrusions originate from what location?

   a. inside the company

   b. script kiddies

   c. back doors

   d. industrial spies

9. Why is UDP considered unreliable?

   a. The header does not contain a checksum.

   b. The data is transmitted in clear text.

   c. It is connectionless.

   d. Routers typically drop a large number of UDP packets.

10. A DNS server translates _____ to _____ .

    a. encrypted IP addresses, clear text

    b. IP addresses, MAC addresses

    c. FQDNs, IP addresses

    d. static addresses, DHCP

11. How can DNS help network administrators?

    a. Filtering devices (routers, firewalls, and so on) can use DNS names to block certain traffic, such as offensive Web site content.

    b. DNS can automatically configure client protocol settings.

    c. DNS can forward or drop requests based on the source address and protocol used.

    d. DNS can translate all protocols to TCP/IP, enabling cross communication between different types of networks.

12. DNS is vulnerable to what types of attacks? (Choose all that apply.)

    a. zone transfer attacks

    b. cache poisoning attacks

    c. targeted SYN flood attacks

    d. buffer overflow attacks

13. What kind of network communication requires a third-party program rather than a firewall or an IDS to scan for viruses or harmful executables?

    a. e-mail message content

    b. e-mail message headers

    c. Web pages

    d. all of the above

14. What are some of the reasons for network attacks? (Choose all that apply.)
    a. social engineering
    b. revenge
    c. financial gain
    d. status

15. A port number combined with a computer's IP address constitutes a network connection called a(n)_____ .
    a. always-on connection
    b. executable connection
    c. socket
    d. VPN tunnel

16. Why is fragmentation considered a security risk?
    a. Fragments numbered 0 contain port information.
    b. Fragments numbered 1 or higher are passed through filters.
    c. Fragmented packets can't be assembled.
    d. Fragmentation is frequently used.

17. The ability to prevent one participant in an electronic transaction from denying that it performed an action is called _____ .
    a. plausible deniability
    b. integrity
    c. nonrepudiation
    d. undeniability

18. Firewall enforcement of policies is handled primarily through setting up packet-filtering rules, a set of which is contained in the _____ .
    a. routing table
    b. rule base
    c. access control list
    d. packet filter

19. Servers with outside access to the public should never be located where?
    a. on their own subnet
    b. on a DMZ
    c. on the internal LAN
    d. on the network perimeter

20. The signs of possible attacks detected by an IDS are commonly called signatures. What information do signatures contain? (Choose all that apply.)

   a. port number

   b. open ports

   c. time of access attempts

   d. IP address

HANDS-ON PROJECTS

Hands-On Project 1-1: Assessing Your Network Interface

Time Required: 10 minutes

Objective: Examine active connections to computers with the Netstat utility.

Description: As you saw in Activity 1-4, the Netstat utility can provide a wealth of information. In this project, you use it to learn more about the active connections to your computer.

1. Click **Start**, point to **All Programs**, point to **Accessories**, and then click **Command Prompt** to open a command prompt window.

2. Type **netstat** and press **Enter** to view the computer's current active connections.

3. Type **netstat -a** and press **Enter** to view the currently established connections and the ports on which your computer is listening for new connections.

4. Type **netstat -p TCP** and press **Enter** to view information about TCP connections.

5. Type **netstat -p UDP** and press **Enter** to view information about UDP connections.

6. Type **netstat -n** and press **Enter** to view the IP address of the remote computer connected to your computer. This information can be useful in tracking an attacker connected to your network.

7. To get a summary of Netstat's switches, type **netstat /?** and press **Enter**.

8. Type **exit** and press **Enter** to close the command prompt window. Leave your system running for the next project.

Hands-On Project 1-2: Determining Network Connectivity with Linux

Time Required: 15 minutes

Objective: Use a Linux terminal window to observe the output from the Ifconfig command.

Description: In this project, you view network connectivity in Fedora or Red Hat Enterprise Linux, which is already configured with the X Window GNOME interface. You need to log in with the root account or an account that has superuser (root) permissions. (*Note:* The steps are similar for other Linux versions and some UNIX versions.)

1. Right-click the GNOME desktop, and then click **Open Terminal**.

2. At the command line, type **ifconfig**, and then press **Enter**.

3. Notice the left side of the display. If you see an entry for "eth0," that means the system is configured to access an Ethernet network, such as through a network interface card. If you see an entry for "ppp," that means the system is configured for access to the Internet, such as through a dial-up modem. The "lo" connection is a local loopback connection used for diagnostic testing of the network connection.

For detailed information on the Linux ifconfig command, type man ifconfig in a terminal window. Press the spacebar to scroll through the pages. Press q to return to the terminal.

TIP

4. Type **exit**, and then press **Enter** to close the terminal window.

Case Projects

CASE PROJECTS

Case Project 1-1: Defining and Designing a Network

The overview of this book's running case project is in the front matter. Please review this information carefully to guide you in completing each chapter's project as you work through the remaining chapters.

You have been hired as a consultant to design a network for LedGrafix, a video and PC game design company. LedGrafix's newest game has become a hot seller, and the company anticipates rapid growth. It's moving into a new facility and will be installing a new network. Because competition is fierce in the game industry, LedGrafix wants the network fully secured, documented, and maintained while providing high availability, scalability, and performance.

1

Based on your current network technology and information security knowledge, for this project you design a network to meet the specified requirements and create a network diagram detailing your design. After you have created the diagram, you create a hardware and software inventory for the network. In addition to designing the network, you must also provide full documentation. The network should meet the following requirements:

❏ One location in Phoenix, AZ

❏ Capable of supporting 62 users in these departments: Accounting and Payroll, 4; Research and Development, 12; Sales and Marketing, 10; Order Processing, Shipping, and Receiving, 14; secretarial and office management staff, 4; upper management (including the president, vice president, and general manager), 10; Customer Relations and Support, 6; Technology Support, 2.

❏ Full T-1 Internet connection

1. Design a network that meets the preceding requirements.

2. Examine the facility diagram your instructor provides. Using whatever drawing application you have available (MS Paint will work, if you have no other options), create a diagram of your network, showing the physical layout of the system.

3. Create a hardware and software inventory. Your instructor has blank forms you can use, or you can create or find your own. Your inventory should include at least the following:

❏ Operating systems

❏ Server operating systems

❏ Office applications

❏ Antivirus software

❏ Computers, servers, and peripherals

❏ Network connectivity equipment, such as hubs, switches, or routers

❏ Specialized imaging or multimedia devices or software

❏ Developer tools (you can make up tool names, if necessary)

❏ Other applications you think are necessary

4. After you have finished the diagram and inventory, turn them in to your instructor. Strive for a professional look in your work, and don't forget to proofread your work carefully before submitting it.

2

SECURITY POLICY DESIGN: RISK ANALYSIS

After reading this chapter and completing the exercises, you will be able to:

♦ Explain the fundamental concepts of risk analysis

♦ Describe different approaches to risk analysis

♦ Explain the process of risk analysis

♦ Describe techniques to minimize risk

Computer crime is becoming more sophisticated. As one vulnerability is patched, another threat crops up to take its place. Those charged with securing systems and the data stored on them must be vigilant. They must also have the support of management and develop a plan to deal with security for their organization. This plan is called a security policy.

One of the first steps toward an effective security policy is risk analysis. This chapter, along with Chapter 3, explains the processes in creating and carrying out a security policy. First, you learn the fundamentals of risk analysis, and then you explore different methods of performing risk analysis. Next, you need to decide how to deal with or manage those identified risks. Risk analysis is not a one-time deal that, when it's complete, can be trusted to remain accurate. Threats are ever changing, so risk analysis must be conducted regularly to reassess the environment and determine whether changes to policies and procedures are needed.

FUNDAMENTAL CONCEPTS OF RISK ANALYSIS

The consensus among security professionals is that there is no zero-risk situation—in other words, there is no situation in which security is perfect. Your first task, when undertaking the formulation of a security policy, is to assess the risk faced by your employees, your network, and your databases of customer, job-related, and personnel information. Your ultimate goal is not to reduce the risks to zero, but to devise ways to manage risks in a reasonable fashion. This process, called **risk analysis**, determines the threats that face the organization, precisely what resources are at risk, and what priority should be given each asset. It's the first step in formulating a **security policy**, a statement that spells out exactly what defenses should be configured to block unauthorized access, how the organization will respond to attacks, and how employees should safely handle the organization's resources to discourage loss of data or damage to files.

Because threats are changing constantly along with technology, the process of determining risks and developing a security policy to manage those risks is an ongoing process, as shown in Figure 2-1, rather than a one-time operation.

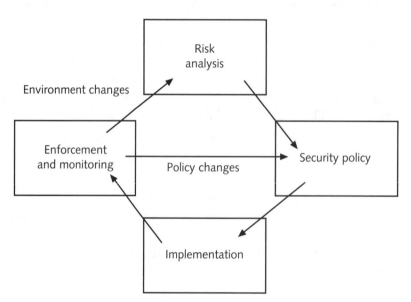

Figure 2-1 The process of risk analysis

Of course, you're likely to encounter skepticism when you begin working at an organization that hires you to manage its IT and security needs. Many companies overlook security policies and risk assessments in the process of developing network defenses and countermeasures. When you ask whether a security policy is in place, don't be surprised to hear remarks such as "*What* security policy?" or "We started working on one three years ago but it never got anywhere." In the rush to cope with everyday business processes and amid the normal turnover of employees, security policies can easily be placed on the "back burner" and overlooked. One of your first tasks, then, might be selling managers and employees alike on the need to develop a risk analysis and security policy cycle for your organization.

The following sections lay the groundwork for a clear understanding of risk analysis, the first step in developing a network security policy. You'll learn about the fundamental concepts that underlie risk analysis, different approaches to conducting a risk analysis, principles to keep in mind to make risk analysis an ongoing process rather than an isolated occurrence, and ways to analyze the economic effect of threats should they become realities.

TIP If you're looking for statistics to back up your risk analysis and security policy drafts, visit the CERT Coordination Center *(www.cert.org)*, which maintains current information on new threats and statistics of virus attacks and other security incidents.

Risk Analysis Factors

Risk is defined as the possibility of damage or loss. Risk analysis, then, is the study of the likelihood of damage or loss is in a particular situation or environment. In terms of a network of computers connected to the wider Internet, risk analysis should encompass the computer hardware and software in an organization plus its data warehouses—the store-houses of valuable customer, job-related, and personnel information that a company needs to safeguard.

People who conduct risk analysis for a living break the field into a group of related fundamental factors. The following sections describe these six factors that go into creating a risk analysis:

- Assets
- Threats
- Probabilities
- Vulnerabilities
- Consequences
- Safeguards

Assets

Assets in an organization play a central role in risk analysis—after all, they are the hardware, software, and informational resources you need to protect by developing and implementing a comprehensive security policy. You're likely to encounter four different types of assets:

- *Physical assets*—Equipment and buildings in the organization
- *Data assets*—Databases, personnel records, customer or client information, and other data the organization stores

- *Application software assets*—Server programs, security programs, and other applications used on a day-to-day basis to communicate and carry out the organization's typical activities

- *Personnel assets*—People who work in the organization as well as customers, business partners, contractors, and freelance employees who contribute to the organization

Some assets are tangible objects that you can actually touch or work with, such as computers. Other assets are intangible; they include a company's reputation and the level of trust it inspires in its customers. In addition, you might consider other assets essential business concepts, such as confidentiality, integrity of information, and availability of resources. The most valuable information, such as a database with contents that need to be confidential and accurate, is what you should focus on first. Data, even though it isn't something you can touch, might be the most important asset to continuing business operations. It's also the most difficult to evaluate. In fact, listing every single asset you have can be difficult. You might be able to analyze only the most important ones in detail.

Threats

Threats are events and conditions that haven't occurred but could potentially occur, and their presence increases risk. Some dangers are universal, such as weather-related disasters. Others are more specific to your own system, such as a server storing a customer database, with the obvious danger being the threat of an attacker gaining access to the system. Other examples of circumstance-specific threats include the following:

- *Power supply*—The power supply in your area might be unreliable, making your company subject to brownouts, blackouts, and sudden surges called voltage spikes.

- *Crime rate*—If you work in a high-crime area, or if other offices in your area have been broken into, your risk is increased.

- *Facility-related*—If your building has old wiring prone to fluctuations or has insufficient fire suppression, the risk of water or fire damage increases.

- *Industry*—Your organization operates in a highly competitive industry or in one that requires high security. A security breach could result in litigation or major loss of revenue or even closure of the business.

The seriousness of a threat depends on the probability that it will occur. This, in turn, depends on conditions such as geographic location, the organization's physical location, existing security defenses (such as locks and alarm systems), and how carefully your employees manage passwords and other sensitive information.

Probabilities

Geographic or physical location, habitual, and other factors affect the **probability** that a threat will actually occur. A geographic factor might include a regional proclivity to earthquakes. The physical location might influence threat probability because of an electrical problem with the building housing your systems. Habitual factors could be a result of poor security awareness in your organization. If your employees have developed a habit of using other employee's accounts or keeping passwords written down near their computers, the probability of a security breach increases. Each set of factors that increase or decrease threat probabilities are specific to a given situation. These factors are a large part of what risk assessment seeks to uncover. Risk analysis evaluates each factor and rates its potential impact or exposure.

Your **exposure** is increased if you have one or more factors that increase threat probabilities. For example, if you live in a part of the country with frequent severe storms or floods, the threat of weather-related damage increases. If you have a group of disgruntled employees who have just been fired and who work with sensitive information, the probability of losing some of that information increases unless you take steps to protect it before they leave the premises. If your office has an alarm system wired to a security service, the probability of a burglary is reduced.

Make a list of the biggest threats to your computer network, and rank them in order of probability. The Australian Standard AS 4360 Risk Management, developed by Standards Australia (*www.riskmanagement.com.au*) uses seven steps to describe probability: Negligible, Very Low, Low, Medium, High, Very High, and Extreme. It can be helpful to rank the threats facing your own organization using the form in Table 2-1.

Table 2-1   Sample threat probabilities

Threat	Probability
Earthquake	Medium
Fire	Low
Flood	High
Attack from the Internet	Very High
Virus infection	Very High
Employees giving out information	Low

The Australian Standard is a generic guide for risk management. It can be applied to any industry or sector and customized to fit different businesses' needs. It offers a framework for organization-wide risk assessment, analysis, and management. The big downside to the Australian Standard is that you must purchase it from Standards Australia, and the price isn't cheap. If an organization can afford it, the standard is worth the price; however, plenty of free resources for risk analysis are available.

NOTE   For risk management guidelines specific to computer networking and IT, the Risk Management Guide for Information Technology Systems from the National Institute of Standards and Technology (NIST) outlines the risk assessment and management process step by step. NIST is a great resource for information, and best of all, the guide is free. You can find NIST's Risk Management Guide at *http://csrc.nist.gov/publications/nistpubs/800-30/sp800-30.pdf*.

Vulnerabilities

Vulnerabilities are situations or conditions that increase the probability of a threat, which in turn increases risk. Examples include connecting computers to the Internet, putting computers out in the open where anyone can use them, installing Web servers outside the corporate network in the vulnerable demilitarized zone (DMZ), and so on.

You can easily come up with examples of vulnerable situations that can affect networked hardware and software. Some of the most common flaws involve OS software (particularly different versions of Windows, although Linux needs to be secured as well and has fallen victim to attacks such as the Lion worm). They also involve application software (most notoriously, Internet Information Services, Internet Explorer, and Outlook Express). Even the freeware Web server Apache has fallen victim to security compromises as a result of software flaws. Although some systems have more security flaws than others, remember that every system can and will have flaws. Opening a network to remote users whose desktop computers are unprotected by antivirus or firewall software can expose it to intrusions and virus infections. Poorly configured firewalls or packet filters, unprotected passwords, log files that aren't reviewed closely or regularly, new intrusion threats affecting wireless networks, and the complexity of modern computer networks mean that any number of components can give an attacker an opening. If you remember that your system always has at least one more vulnerability than what you have found, you'll be a successful information security professional.

By identifying any vulnerability associated with a client's network, you can determine which type of attack the network is susceptible to. Security professionals have many resources for finding information on current vulnerabilities or possible network attacks. One site that should be bookmarked in any security professional's Web browser is the Common Vulnerabilities and Exploits (CVE) list (*www.cve.mitre.org*) sponsored by US-CERT (*www.us-cert. gov*). The primary mission of the CVE is to standardize naming of vulnerabilities and exploits, but its database is essentially a dictionary of security threats. The list is free to download and can be searched easily. As of this writing, the CVE contained 10,423 entries.

 Other helpful sites and security resources are listed in Appendix B.

TIP

Consequences

Substantial consequences can result from a virus that forces you to take your Web site offline for a week or a fire that destroys all your computer equipment. You can extend the earlier identification of threats to include ratings that evaluate the consequences of those threats, as shown in Table 2-2.

Table 2-2 Probability and consequences of threats

Threat	Probability	Consequences
Earthquake	Medium	Significant
Fire	Low	Significant
Flood	High	Minor
Attack from the Internet	Very High	Serious
Virus infection	Very High	Serious
Employees giving out information	Low	Significant

In Table 2-2, the probability of threats has been extended to a rating of the significance of their impact. Ranking these items can be difficult because the severity often depends on the specific virus or your particular physical location. A flood doesn't have as much impact on computers stationed on the 50th floor of an office tower as it does on the ground floor, for instance (although a flood can be devastating to any electrical equipment in the office).

Besides the consequences of getting a system back online after an attack, there's a cost impact as well as other effects that can be more difficult to anticipate. They include insurance claims, police reports, shipping or delivery charges, and the time and effort to obtain and reinstall software or hardware. A return on investment (ROI) calculator, such as the one offered by Cisco Systems Cisco Security Agent, can help you calculate these losses, which can amount to far more than the actual price of hardware (see Figure 2-2).

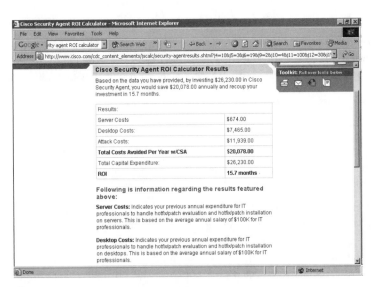

Figure 2-2 Cisco Security Agent ROI calculator

As you can see in Figure 2-2, an investment in Cisco Security Agent software of $26,230.00 would be recovered in 15.7 months, based on the calculated dollar savings of avoiding attacks, downtime, and recovery time.

ACTIVITY

Activity 2-1: Calculating ROI

Time Required: 15 minutes

Objective: Learn how to find and use online resources, such as a ROI calculator, to evaluate different products and help justify equipment investments.

Description: Part of risk analysis is estimating the value of lost data and the computers that store your data as well as the indirect costs of lost productivity and recovery. Cisco Security Agent (CSA) is a powerful enterprise security solution that uses behavior-based assessment to detect suspicious traffic and prevent malicious behavior. CSA can perform firewall and intrusion detection system (IDS) functions as well as operating system assurance and audit log consolidation. The ROI calculator is intended to help customers justify the purchase of CSA. In this activity, you determine the length of time needed to recoup the purchase costs of CSA. You can enter random values or values your instructor specifies.

1. Start your Web browser. Enter the address for the CSA ROI calculator (**http://www.cisco.com/en/US/products/sw/secursw/ps5057/prod_brochure09186a00801e1249.html**), and press **Enter**.

2. When the calculator is displayed, enter values to answer each question or use values your instructor supplies. (*Tip*: For Question 19, enter the number of agents you need to secure all your servers and desktops. Based on the preceding values, enter or select appropriate values from the drop-down lists.)

3. After you've finished entering values, click **Submit** at the bottom of the page.

4. How long would it take you to recover the investment cost of CSA? Did you expect the total costs avoided per year (basically, the cost of attacks, downtime, disasters, and so on that your organization incurs each year) to be higher or lower than the value shown?

   _____

   _____

   _____

5. If time permits, go back and enter different values to better understand how each cost affects your results. After reading the results, close your browser.

The actual cost of an incident is usually much higher than the cost of replacing equipment and restoring data (if it can be restored). When you go to management to justify investing in security, estimating the cost of the investment and benefit to the company (commonly called a **cost-benefit analysis**) is vital. The most critical numbers you want management to understand are the ones for the actual cost per year the company is paying because of security incidents. The benefit is the amount per year saved by preventing incidents.

Safeguards

Safeguards are measures you can take to reduce threats, such as installing firewalls and IDSs, locking doors, and using passwords and encryption. These measures interact with one another to help manage risk. There are a few decisions to make when deciding how to manage risk. First, you must identify and classify risks. Next, you determine priorities of threatened assets. The next step is to determine whether to accept the risk, transfer the risk, or mitigate the risk.

An asset has an associated amount of risk. Threats and vulnerabilities increase the risk; countermeasures work to reduce risk. **Residual risk** is what's left over after countermeasures and defenses are implemented; risk never actually equals zero. Figure 2-3 illustrates this process.

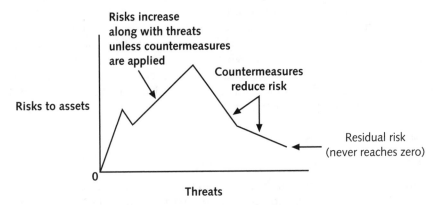

Figure 2-3   Countermeasures reduce, but never completely eliminate, risk

ACTIVITY

Activity 2-2: Conducting Asset Identification, Threat Analysis, and Safeguards in Your Environment

Time Required: 45 minutes

Objective: Learn to apply risk assessment concepts by performing a brief analytical exercise.

Description: One of the first steps in risk analysis is identifying the assets to be protected. In this activity, you perform asset identification and a threat analysis of your environment. Your instructor will set the boundaries of the environment. Your task is to conduct a thorough and objective assessment of the assets in your classroom. After you have determined the assets and threats, you prioritize the assets and propose ideas for safeguards. This activity can be done individually or in groups.

1. First, make a chart with four columns, and label the columns **Asset**, **Threats**, **Probabilities**, and **Safeguards**. Be sure to leave enough room for your notes.

2. Starting at the classroom door, begin writing down assets. Write a short description of each asset in the Asset column, such as "student computer."

3. After you have listed all the assets in your classroom, you assess the threats. Starting with the first asset listed, write down threats that could damage or destroy the asset. Examples of threats are a leaky roof, exposed wires, food or drink that could spill, and so forth. Be sure to look in all directions, including the ceiling. (*Hint:* Be sure to note drop ceilings or false floors because they represent a potential point of access for intruders.)

4. Now that you have assessed the threats, you examine the probabilities of a threat occurring. Use the information in Table 2-2 as a guide. For example, if you listed a leaky roof as a threat and live in an area with frequent rainfall, the probability of that threat occurring and causing damage is high. If you live in an arid desert climate, that probability is not as high.

5. Now that you have performed asset identification and threat assessment (perhaps not as thoroughly as the chapter describes, but the depth of coverage in this project is appropriate to the location), you can begin to determine safeguards that can reduce threats. Beginning with your first asset, look for ways to manage risks to that asset. For a leaky roof directly above an expensive computer, the cost of repairing the roof might be warranted, but simply moving the computer would reduce the risk and be more cost-effective. On the other hand, if the power supply to your server room is prone to fluctuations that could damage delicate electronics, the investment in uninterruptible power supplies (UPSs) and/or a generator could be lower than the cost to replace damaged equipment. Remember that the priority level determines what investment in security is needed.

6. Write down your recommended safeguards.

7. If time permits, share your findings with the class. Discuss the results and justify your assessments and recommendations. Were the results similar? Discuss the similarities and differences in findings.

APPROACHES TO RISK ANALYSIS

After you have made a list of the assets you need to protect, the threats to those assets, the probability that they will occur, the consequences if they occur, and the safeguards you can take to protect them, you have the building blocks you need to prepare a risk analysis.

You can use different types of risk analysis to create a security policy to evaluate how well the policy is performing so that you can update and improve it. The following sections describe the two approaches you're most likely to use.

Survivable Network Analysis

Survivable Network Analysis (SNA) is a security process developed by the CERT Coordination Center security group (*www.cert.org*). SNA starts with the assumption that a computer system or network will be attacked. It leads you through a four-step process designed to ensure the **survivability** (the capability to continue functioning during attacks, system faults, accidents, or disasters) of a network if an attack actually occurs.

Survivability focuses on a network's essential services and assets and critical capabilities. Survivability also depends on four key properties of a network:

- *Resistance*—The capability of a system to repel attacks

- *Recognition*—The capability to detect attacks when they occur and to evaluate the extent of damage and compromise

- *Recovery*—The capability to maintain essential services during an attack and to restore all services following an attack

- *Adaptation and evolution*—The capability to improve system survivability based on knowledge gained from attacks

The study of a network's survivability builds on other concepts related to risk analysis, including **fault tolerance** (the capability of an object or a system to continue operations despite a failure, such as a system shutdown), safety procedures, security systems, and ongoing testing. Most software products aren't designed with survivability in mind. That's why survivability studies can be valuable. Instead, software is often designed to work for a certain number of users or a certain amount of information, until it's replaced by new and improved versions of the same or other software.

The steps in SNA are as follows:

- *System definition*—First, you create an overview of the system's organizational requirements. You analyze system architecture while taking into account its hardware components, software installations, databases, servers, and other computers that store your information.

- *Essential capability definition*—You identify a system's essential services and assets that are critical to fulfilling your organization's missions and goals.

- *Compromisable capability definition*—You design scenarios in which intrusions to the system occur, and then trace the intrusion through your system architecture to identify what can be accessed and what sorts of damage can occur.

- *Survivability analysis*—You identify potential points of fault in the system—integral components that can be compromised. You then make recommendations for correcting the points of fault and suggest specific ways to improve the system's resistance to intrusions and its capability to recover from attacks, accidents, and other disasters.

The emphasis is on an ongoing process rather than a series of steps ending in a report of a configuration regarded as secure and permanent. You might start with better password management, then upgrade the system to encrypt critical data, and then install software that filters out potentially harmful e-mail messages so that the system's capability to survive trouble improves continually.

Threat and Risk Assessment

Threat and Risk Assessment (TRA) approaches risk analysis from the standpoint of threats and risks to an organization's assets and the consequences of those threats and risks if they occur. Like SNA, TRA has four steps:

- *Asset definition*—You identify software, hardware, and information you need to defend.

- *Threat assessment*—You identify the kinds of threats that place the asset at risk. These threats include vandalism, fire, natural disasters such as floods, and attacks from the Internet. Threat assessment also includes an evaluation of the probability and consequences of each threat.

- *Risk assessment*—You evaluate each asset for any existing safeguards, the severity of threats and risks to assets, and the consequences of the threat or risk actually taking place. The combination of these factors creates an assessment of the actual risk to each asset.

- *Recommendations*—Based on the risks and current safeguards, you make recommendations to reduce the risk. These recommendations should then be made part of a security policy.

TRA is carried out in different ways by security agencies all over the world. One of the clearest and most systematic statements of how to perform TRA is by the Information Security Group of the Australian Government's Defense Signals Directorate. The document "Australian Communications – Electronic Security Instruction 33 (ACSI 33)" describes a variety of ratings systems. Instead of assigning numeric values to risks and threat levels, these systems use terms such as "high," "low," and "medium." Often, these systems are enough to assess risk and are easier to use than statistical tools. For instance, Table 2-3 shows ratings you can assign to describe the probability that threats will occur.

Table 2-3   Threat ratings system

Rating	What It Means
Negligible	Unlikely to occur
Very Low	Likely to occur only two or three times every five years
Low	Likely to occur within a year or less
Medium	Likely to occur every six months or less
High	Likely to occur after a month or less
Very High	Likely to occur multiple times per month or less
Extreme	Likely to occur multiple times each day

ACSI 33 is available online at *www.dsd.gov.au/_lib/pdf_doc/acsi33/acsi33_u_0904.pdf*. If you want to research other governments' approaches to TRA, you'll find a set of links to TRA guidelines in Canada and other countries at *www.infosyssec.net/infosyssec/threat1.htm*.

After you have rated the severity of the threat or risk, you need to evaluate the consequences if it actually occurs. Here, too, a set of standard descriptors has been developed and published in ACSI 33. They are shown in Table 2-4.

Table 2-4   Describing consequences

Description	Consequences
Catastrophic	Threatens the continuation of the program as well as causing major problems for customers
Major	Threatens the continuation of basic functions of the program or project and requires senior-level management intervention
Moderate	Does not threaten the program; however, the program could be subject to significant review and modification of operating procedures
Minor	Could threaten the program's efficiency or effectiveness but can be dealt with internally
Insignificant	Can be dealt with by normal operations

After you have evaluated the threats to assets and described the consequences, you can combine the two ratings (the level of threat and consequences of the threat occurring) to come up with an analysis of the risk to each asset, as described in the following section.

RISK ANALYSIS: AN ONGOING PROCESS

Risk analysis is not a one-time activity used solely to create a security policy. Rather, risk analysis evolves to take into account an organization's changing size and activities, the progression to larger and more complex computer systems, and new threats from both inside and outside the corporate network.

The initial risk analysis is used to formulate a security policy; the security policy is then enforced and security is monitored. New threats and intrusion attempts create the need for a reassessment of the risk the organization faces.

Risk Analysis: General Activities to Follow

Whatever method you use, risk analysis is not a single activity but a group of related activities that typically follow this sequence:

- *Holding initial team sessions*—First, hold meetings to get groups of workers together in one place; hold individual interviews or hand out questionnaires to collect pertinent information. It's especially important to talk to all managers in the organization to set the objectives and scope for the risk analysis, to schedule how long the project should take, and to define the important people you need to interview.

- *Conducting asset valuation*—After you get an overview of the scope of the risk analysis, you need to identify the assets you need to protect and determine their value. This activity can be subjective or speculative. If it's subjective, you're assessing the impact of losing assets that might not be tangible, and you should use your best judgment or solicit opinions from other qualified staff. If it's speculative, you're estimating whether information might fall into the hands of unauthorized people, and if it does, what the company's cost would be to recover the information. Personal interviews with managers can help you determine a realistic assessment.

- *Evaluating vulnerability*—You investigate the levels of threat and vulnerability in relation to the value of the organization's assets. Ask IT staff to evaluate what they consider the threat of virus attacks or other intrusions on a scale of one to five, for instance.

- *Calculating risk*—After you have the asset value and an idea of the vulnerabilities threatening those assets, you can calculate risk. Usually, a numeric value is assigned. For instance, 1 is given to a low-level baseline security need and 7 to a very high security priority.

NOTE

Remember that the first step in risk management and designing and implementing a security policy is gaining the backing of upper management (board of directors, CEO, CIO, and so on). This high-level support makes your efforts much easier. The cooperation you get from colleagues, other departments, and employees will be more forthcoming if they know you're acting with full support and authority from the highest levels. "Selling" a security policy to managers isn't a bad thing, nor is it a difficult task if you know what they care about: the bottom line, profits. If you consider how security affects profitability, selling the point isn't hard. Just remember that you need to be able to back up the numbers you give them, and don't exaggerate potential costs of a security incident.

Analyzing Economic Impacts

An important part of conducting a risk analysis is preparing estimates of the financial impact of losses. If you're familiar with statistics, you can use a number of different models for estimating impacts. You can also use a software program to help you prepare reports that substantiate your estimates and to produce charts and graphs to support your figures. A program called Project Risk Analysis by Katmar Software gives you a structure for listing hardware and software assets in your organization (see Figure 2-4). You have an opportunity to work with this program in Activity 2-3.

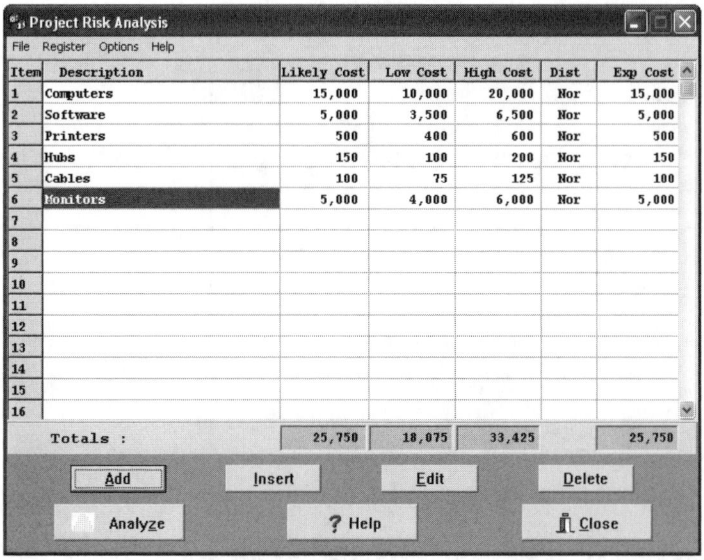
Project Risk Analysis
File Register Options Help
Item Description Likely Cost Low Cost High Cost Dist Exp Cost
1 Computers 15,000 10,000 20,000 Nor 15,000
2 Software 5,000 3,500 6,500 Nor 5,000
3 Printers 500 400 600 Nor 500
4 Hubs 150 100 200 Nor 150
5 Cables 100 75 125 Nor 100
6 Monitors 5,000 4,000 6,000 Nor 5,000
7
8
9
10
11
12
13
14
15
16
Totals : 25,750 18,075 33,425 25,750
Add
Insert
Edit
Delete
Analyze
? Help
Close

Figure 2-4 Project Risk Analysis offers a structure for making cost estimates

With this program, you can make cost estimates by using a variety of statistical models. For those who are unfamiliar with statistics, the simplest model uses the following:

- *Likely cost*—The most realistic estimate of the money you'll have to spend to replace the item
- *Low cost*—The lowest dollar amount for replacing the item
- *High cost*—The highest dollar amount for replacing the item

When you create a record of an asset in Project Risk Analysis and estimate its replacement cost, you enter these terms using the Normal distribution setting, as shown in Figure 2-5.

One desirable feature of a risk analysis program, such as Project Risk Analysis, is being able to analyze cost estimates and present them in a report format (see Figure 2-6). In addition, these programs can quickly calculate the mean cost of replacing hardware, software, or other items.

Project Risk Analysis performs calculations by using a statistical formula called a **Monte Carlo simulation**—an analytical method meant to simulate a real-life system by randomly generating values for variables. The graphical charts and reports these programs create provide valuable documentation you can use in preparing a risk analysis; these visuals have a lot of impact when presented to managers.

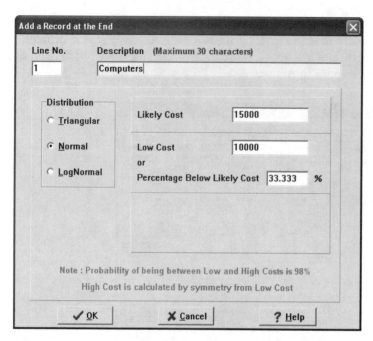

Figure 2-5   Entering values for likely cost and low cost to estimate replacement cost

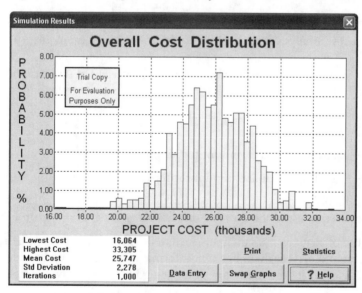

Figure 2-6   Graphical reports in risk analysis software

You'll find more information about Monte Carlo simulations at *www. decisioneering.com/monte-carlo-simulation.html*.

TIP

ACTIVITY

Activity 2-3: Calculating Replacement Costs

Time Required: 15 minutes

2

Objective: Use a risk analysis tool to calculate replacement costs for equipment.

Description: Risk analysis can be subjective when it's done by intuition, hunches, or "gut feelings." A software tool can help bring some consistency and objectivity to the process. In this activity, you download a trial version of a risk analysis tool for Windows called Project Risk Analysis (PRA) by Katmar Software. You then enter the characteristics of network resources in your own school's lab and calculate the contingency funds needed to replace your lab equipment if a disaster strikes. For this activity, you need a computer running Windows XP and a file-archiving utility, such as WinZip. Enter values for computer equipment in your lab as well as an estimate of the data on them. If you aren't in your computer lab or don't know about all the equipment in it, assume you're in a lab with 10 PCs, two printers, one network hub, and one removable disk drive. Each PC has a replacement value of $1,500, is equipped with approximately $1,000 worth of software, and stores data valued at $500.

1. Start your Web browser. Enter the URL for the Project Risk Analysis and Contingency Analysis page (**http://www.katmarsoftware.com/pra.htm**), and then press **Enter**.

2. Read the description of the program, and then click the **Download Now!** link.

3. When you're prompted to open or save the Projrisk.zip file, click **Save** and save it to a directory on your file system.

4. When the file download is finished, click **Close** in the Download Complete dialog box. Close your Web browser. Then double-click the file to open it with WinZip. Extract the files to the same directory where you placed the .zip file you downloaded.

5. Double-click the **ProjRisk_Setup.exe** file and follow the steps in the setup program to install it on your computer.

6. Click **Start**, point to **All Programs**, point to **Risk Analysis**, and click **ProjRisk** to start the program. The first time you run the program, you see a Thank You for Installing PRA window, which states the terms under which the program can be run. (It runs 30 times as an evaluation.) Click **OK**, and then click **OK** again when you see a second shareware reminder.

7. Click **Add** to open the Add a Record at the End dialog box. In the Description text box, type **Computers**.

8. In the Distribution section, click the **Normal** option button.

9. In the Likely Cost text box, type **15000**. (*Note*: Don't use commas in these number entries.)

10. In the Low Cost text box, type **10000**.

11. Click **OK** to return to the main Project Risk Analysis window, where your estimate is entered in the first row.

12. Repeat Steps 7 through 11 for **Software** (likely cost 5000, low cost 3500), **Printers** (likely cost 500, low cost 400), **Hubs** (likely cost 150, low cost 100), **Cables** (likely cost 100, low cost 75), and **Monitors** (likely cost 5000, low cost 4000). (*Note*: Remember to click **Normal** for Step 8 each time.)

13. In the main Project Risk Analysis window, click the **Analyze** button to see the Overall Cost Distribution graph. What are the Lowest Cost, Highest Cost, and Mean Cost figures displayed in this window? Record the answers here:

_____

_____

_____

14. Click the **Statistics** button. What is the mean cost listed in the Simulation Statistics Report dialog box? Record the answer here:

_____

15. Close the Simulation Statistics Report dialog box and the Project Risk Analysis window to return to the Windows desktop. If necessary, click **Yes** in the message box warning you that the data has not been saved. Leave your system running for the next activity.

DECIDING HOW TO MINIMIZE RISK

After you have come up with an analysis of the level of risk to hardware and software assets in your network, you can come up with recommendations of safeguards for minimizing the risk. **Risk management**, in fact, is the term that describes the process of identifying, choosing, and setting up countermeasures justified by the risks you identify. The countermeasures you describe are the statements that go into your security policy. In the following sections, you learn about important points to consider when deciding how to secure hardware, how to secure information databases in your network, how to conduct routine analysis, and how to respond to security incidents when they occur.

Securing Hardware

Your company's physical computing assets—the actual hardware devices that keep data flowing throughout the network—are the most obvious objects that need to be identified. You have to decide how you're going to protect your hardware. First, think about obvious kinds of physical protection, such as environmental controls to keep machines cool in hot temperatures and fire protection systems. Then consider whether you're going to lock up all hardware in your organization or use theft protection only for your database server and other servers. (Placing your servers in a room that can be locked with an alarm system so that unauthorized employees can't access them is critical; this equipment should never be left out in the open.)

Be sure to pay special attention to laptop computers in your organization. These machines can be lost or stolen easily, and any proprietary information on them could be compromised. These incidents happen regularly and often with serious consequences. Recent surveys have shown a steady increase in laptop theft all over the world. The 2004 CSI/FBI Computer Crime and Security Survey (*www.gocsi.com*) showed an increase of more than $6.7 million in laptop thefts. The 2005 Australian Computer Crime and Security Survey (*www.auscert.org. au/images/ACCSS2005.pdf*) reported that 59% of those who responded had experienced losses caused by laptop thefts.

To alleviate the problem of data on lost or stolen laptops being compromised, be sure to install startup passwords as well as screen saver passwords; experienced thieves can circumvent them, of course, but at least they make it more difficult to access files. In addition, you can encrypt files on your laptop with a program such as Pretty Good Privacy (PGP), which is available at *www.pgp.com*. For Windows-based computers, you should consider enabling Encrypting File System (EFS) on all company laptops.

Conducting a Hardware Inventory

Make a list of servers, routers, cables, computers, printers, and all other hardware the company owns. Be sure to include your company's **network assets**—the routers, cables, servers, and firewall hardware and software that enable employees to communicate with one another and other computers on the Internet. Make a topology map that shows how the devices are connected and includes an IP allocation register, such as the one in Figure 2-7. (In Hands-on Project 2-1 at the end of the chapter, you have an opportunity to create a software and hardware inventory.)

Ranking Resources To Be Protected

In listing physical, electronic, network, and system assets, assigning a value to each object is often helpful. The value can be an arbitrary number; what's important is to rank resources in order of importance so that you can focus your security efforts on the most critical resources first. The team that helps you prepare your security policy will probably determine that data is more important than the digital devices where they are stored.

TIP

The numbers you come up with might seem somewhat arbitrary; however, deriving your rankings with the cooperation of your organization's higher management is helpful. Developing a lengthy list of resources and rankings on your own without input from managers is likely to result in extensive revisions. You'll get better results if you submit a list of resources to management and ask them to develop their own rankings. Also, ask them to consider the cost to replace both software and computers you have listed. Suggest that they rank the assets on a scale of 1 to 10.

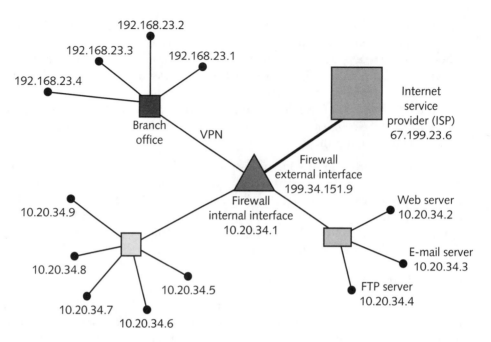

Figure 2-7   A topology map can supplement a hardware inventory

Securing Information

After you have decided on safeguards for your hardware, you need to determine how best to protect your company's **electronic assets**—the word processing, spreadsheet, Web page, and other documents on your network computers. Logical assets also include e-mail messages, any records of instant messaging conversations, and the log files compiled by your firewalls and IDSs. Data assets also include personnel, customer, and financial information that your company needs to protect.

Maintaining Customer and Employee Privacy

Many companies now conduct all or part of their business operations on the Internet. If your organization conducts e-commerce, you need to strike a balance between making it easy to find goods for sale and complete electronic transactions and keeping customer and business information confidential.

One way to protect the information your customers send via the Internet is to isolate that information from the Internet so that attackers can't gain access to it. In many high-profile attacks that have plagued Web sites recently, attackers manage to break into a site and gain access to credit card numbers and other data. You might want to spell out in your security policy that to minimize the risk of attackers stealing critical customer data, your company needs to move information from the directory where it's stored to a computer that's physically isolated from the Internet. You can configure backup software to save critical files in isolated locations automatically on a nightly or weekly basis. You can also use the following measures to protect information:

- *Encryption*—By encrypting data, you can protect it as it passes from one network to another so that it can't be read if it's intercepted or captured.

- *Message filtering*—This measure keeps potentially harmful messages from entering the network from the outside.

- *Data encapsulation*—The data in packets can be encrypted in such a way that the packets are encapsulated (or "wrapped") for extra protection.

- *Redundancy*—By providing redundancy through backup systems, you ensure that databases and other stores of information remain accessible if primary systems go offline.

- *Backups*—Systematic and periodic backups of information on the network are one of the most basic and important ways to protect that information.

TIP

You can separate your customer databases from your Web servers by using a hardware/software product called e-Gap by Whale Communications (*www.whalecommunications.com*). e-Gap uses a high-speed switch to keep data flowing between the external Web server and your internal database and other application servers. The switch means that at no time are application servers actually connected to Web servers—they're connected only to the switch.

Protecting Corporate Information

Do workers at your organization handle confidential, proprietary, or private information? If so, this information needs to be covered in the security policy as well. Safeguards are needed to inform these workers of their information protection duties and to tell them what they can and cannot do with sensitive information. You might decide to minimize risks by specifying the following measures in a security policy:

- Never leave company-owned laptops or handheld devices unattended.

- Always password-protect information on corporate devices.

- Encrypt any financial information.

- Password-protect all job records and customer information.

- Restrict all personnel information to human resources staff and/or upper management.

You then need to make sure all employees read and understand the policy. You might consider distributing the policy in the form of a manual issued to all new employees and published on the company Web site for current employees to review. Having employees sign a statement that they have read and understand their responsibilities is also a good idea.

Conducting Routine Analysis

Risk analysis is an ongoing operation. A company changes constantly in terms of the information it handles, its number of customers, the size of staff, and the number of computers on the network. Risk analysis should be done routinely despite common obstacles, such as indifference of IT staff and employees, heavy workload in critical areas (such as revenue generation), and lack of available personnel to do the evaluation.

Deciding how your organization performs routine analysis starts with the following questions:

- How often will a risk analysis be performed? Every year at budget time is a logical and consistent level of frequency. Note, however, that monthly or weekly reassessment is more effective because it enables you to keep up with new threats.

- Who will conduct the risk analysis? The same professionals who manage security for the organization are the ones who should participate, along with accounting or bookkeeping staff.

- Do all hardware and software resources need to be reviewed every time? You might not need to conduct a new risk analysis for every asset you have; you might decide that only assets that have increased or changed substantially should be reexamined.

The calculations and evaluations associated with risk analysis require subjective evaluations of how much an asset is "worth" and how "valuable" it is. Human emotions can influence evaluations, so many companies don't allow staff to perform these calculations manually. Because of the often complex calculations (levels of risk times assessed value, for instance), using risk analysis software can also be easier.

TIP   One of the best-known software tools for risk analysis, CRAMM, is available from Insight Solutions (*www.insight.co.uk/cramm*).

Handling Security Incidents

It's important to use the security policy to define how you will respond to security break-ins. You might want to fill out a form designed to record what happens during a break-in. You don't have to prepare this form from scratch; you can use one of the forms published on the Federal Agency Security Practices Web site of NIST. A sample form is shown in Figure 2-8.

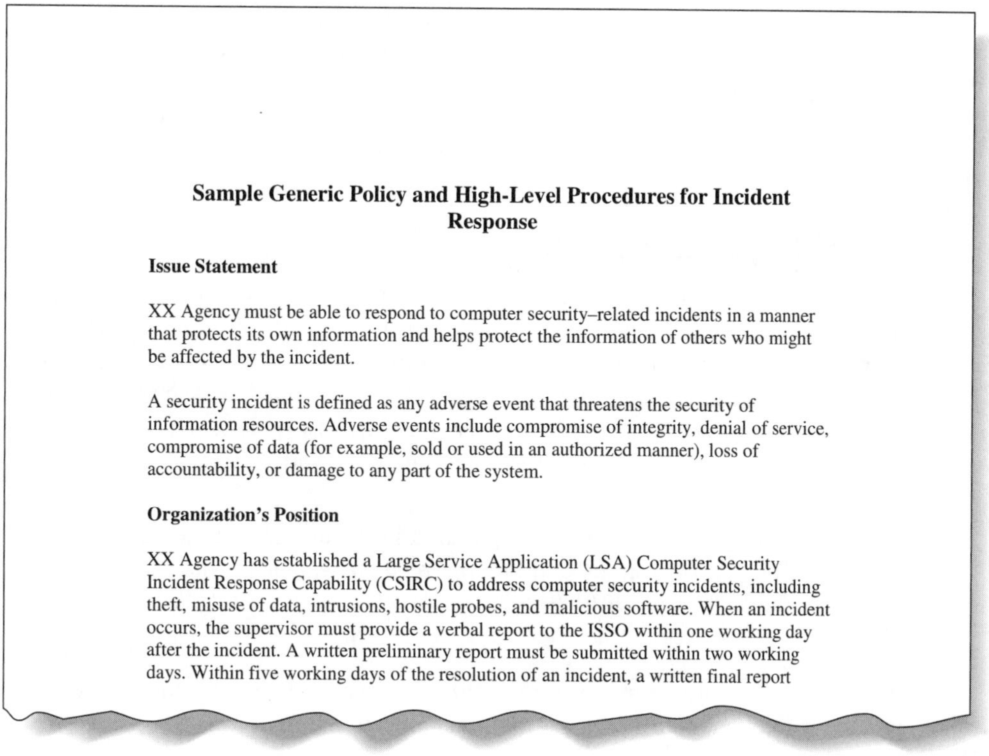

2

Sample Generic Policy and High-Level Procedures for Incident Response

Issue Statement

XX Agency must be able to respond to computer security–related incidents in a manner that protects its own information and helps protect the information of others who might be affected by the incident.

A security incident is defined as any adverse event that threatens the security of information resources. Adverse events include compromise of integrity, denial of service, compromise of data (for example, sold or used in an authorized manner), loss of accountability, or damage to any part of the system.

Organization's Position

XX Agency has established a Large Service Application (LSA) Computer Security Incident Response Capability (CSIRC) to address computer security incidents, including theft, misuse of data, intrusions, hostile probes, and malicious software. When an incident occurs, the supervisor must provide a verbal report to the ISSO within one working day after the incident. A written preliminary report must be submitted within two working days. Within five working days of the resolution of an incident, a written final report

---

Figure 2-8 A sample incident-handling form

Incident-Handling Procedures

In the course of formulating a security policy, it pays to describe in detail who will respond to security incidents, what needs to be done, and why these procedures need to happen. This part of a security policy is called the incident response section. You should begin by describing the need for careful and expeditious handling of an intrusion if it occurs. You might also describe the kinds of incidents that need to be addressed, such as:

- Alarms sent by intrusion detection systems
- Repeated unsuccessful logon attempts
- New user accounts that suddenly appear without explanation
- New files that appear on system servers with unfamiliar file names
- Unexplained changes to data or deletion of records
- System crashes
- Poor system performance

The incident-handling process should then be spelled out in the security policy. Tell employees to identify whether an intrusion has actually occurred. They can do this by auditing the system to see whether new files have been added. If so, they need to determine what resources have been compromised. The affected resources should then be contained, viruses or any other files introduced into the system should be eradicated, and resources should be recovered.

Assembling a Response Team

If an incident occurs, the security policy should spell out exactly which security staff in the organization needs to be notified. Include e-mail addresses and phone numbers. Also specify a location where team members should assemble in case they are unable to communicate. Teamwork is essential in responding to network security incidents successfully, and it's common for an organization to designate a **security incident response team (SIRT)**—a group of staff people designated to take countermeasures when an incident is reported.

NOTE   You might also see a SIRT referred to as a computer emergency response team (CERT), which can respond to any type of system failure, not just a security-related intrusion. SIRTs are covered in more detail in Chapter 8.

A SIRT is primarily intended to respond to security-related breaches and typically includes functions such as the following in its mission statement:

- Reacting to security breaches that originate from outside as well as inside the organization
- Isolating, reviewing, and interpreting information about security incidents
- Assessing the extent of damage of a security incident
- Determining the causes of intrusions and other incidents and recommending countermeasures to prevent them from reoccurring
- Monitoring the integrity of the organization's network on an ongoing basis

Typically, a SIRT contains IT operations and technical support staff, IT application staff, a chief security officer, and other information security specialists. In some large organizations, a special position called Incident Response Manager might be created; this person is primarily responsible for responding to incidents, doing an initial assessment, and summoning the SIRT and other staff people as needed. A SIRT can also include members from other areas of the organization, such as department management, public relations, and legal counsel. All staff involved in the SIRT should be identified in the security policy; if the primary contact person can't be found, another person on the list can be summoned.

Escalation Procedures

If an intrusion is found to have occurred and damage is more severe than originally thought—or if the intrusion is currently happening and files are being accessed at that time—the security policy should describe stages of response that escalate along with the incident's consequences. An **escalation procedure** is a set of roles, responsibilities, and measures taken in response to a security incident.

To determine how a response might escalate, you can come up with a system for ranking an incident's severity (for instance, using the same rankings listed in Table 2-5). Each ranking could then be mapped to an escalation chain—a hierarchy of staff members who should be involved in responding to incidents and making decisions. A possible mapping is shown in Table 2-5.

Table 2-5 Mapping an escalation chain to incident severity rankings

Incident Severity	Escalation Chain
Catastrophic	Business owner or manager, senior network administration staff, all department heads, public relations officer
Major	On-duty manager, on-duty network administration staff
Moderate	Immediate supervisor, help desk
Minor or insignificant	Immediate supervisor

Table 2-5 could be extended to spell out actions to be taken in response to incidents based on their severity. Incidents of minor to moderate severity might require a virus scan or log file review; major incidents might call for disconnecting the local network from the Internet or from other network segments while the response is ongoing.

Including Worst-case Scenarios

Worst-case scenarios are descriptions of the worst consequences that befall an organization if a threat happens. These scenarios might be unlikely, but they can help you determine the value of a resource at risk. Values are derived from reasonable consequences of files, computers, and databases being unavailable for specified periods of time. You might prepare scenarios that account for several time frames, such as a matter of minutes to a matter of several months.

CAUTION

Some security professionals don't recommend using this worst-case scenario approach to valuing assets because it can be extremely unlikely in the real world and can easily be used to distort a situation.

Another way to quantify the impact of financial loss or interruption of business activities is to assign a numeric value to an asset based on a range of dollar amounts. If the loss is estimated at $100 or less, the number 1 is assigned to that loss; if the loss is between $100 and $1,000, the number 2 is assigned, and so on.

CHAPTER SUMMARY

- Risk analysis plays a central role in formulating one of the most essential (and yet most overlooked) elements in an organization's overall network defense configuration: a security policy. Risks need to be calculated and security policies amended on an ongoing basis as a network configuration evolves and new threats emerge.

- Risk analysis covers a company's computer hardware, software, and informational assets. It lists the threats to those assets and the probability that those threats will actually occur. Vulnerabilities existing in the system are described as well as the consequences of a threat actually taking place.

- Your first task is to assess the level of risk to your network and its users. Risk analysis should be performed before *and* after a security policy is created. The ultimate goal is not to reduce risks to zero (which isn't possible) but to manage risk at reasonable levels on an ongoing basis.

- After you have assessed the level of risk to assets in your organization, you need to determine countermeasures for minimizing risk. You decide how to secure the physical computing assets in your company, the logical assets (your computer software, e-mail messages, and log file records), the data stored in your databases, your application software, and the personal assets of those who work in the organization. You then come up with a plan for conducting risk analysis on a routine basis and a plan for handling security incidents.

- You also assess threats to your network, such as attacks, power outages, and environmental disasters. Next, you determine the probability that those threats might happen and the safeguards and countermeasures that can reduce the chances that they will occur. First, however, you use the data you have assembled to perform a risk analysis, using an approach such as Survivable Network Analysis (SNA) or Threat and Risk Assessment (TRA). A risk analysis describes the level of risk to each asset in the organization as well as the economic impact should it be lost or damaged.

- After you have determined the level of risk to your network assets, you need to develop safeguards for managing that risk. You need to determine ways to secure your hardware assets, such as environmental controls, locks, or burglar alarms. Data on laptop computers can be protected through file encryption, for example, and corporate information can be protected by effective use of passwords and backup procedures.

KEY TERMS

assets — The hardware, software, and informational resources you need to protect by developing and implementing a comprehensive security policy.

cost–benefit analysis — A technique for comparing the costs of an investment with the benefits it proposes to return.

electronic assets — The word processing, spreadsheet, Web page, and other documents on your network computers.

2

escalation procedure — A set of roles, responsibilities, and measures taken in response to a security incident.

exposure — Vulnerability to loss resulting from the occurrence of a threat, such as accidental or intentional disclosure or destruction or modification of information resources. Exposure increases with the presence of multiple threat factors.

fault tolerance — The capability of an object or a system to continue operations despite a failure.

Monte Carlo simulation — An analytical method meant to simulate a real-life system by randomly generating values for variables.

network assets — The routers, cables, bastion hosts, servers, and firewall hardware and software that enable employees to communicate with one another and other computers on the Internet.

probability — The possibility that a threat will actually occur, influenced by geographic, physical, habitual, or other factors that increase or decrease the likelihood of occurrence.

residual risk — The risk remaining after countermeasures and defenses are implemented.

risk — The possibility of incurring damage or loss.

risk analysis — A process of analyzing the threats an organization faces, determining precisely what resources are at risk, and deciding the priority to give each asset.

risk management — The process of identifying, choosing, and setting up countermeasures justified by the risks you identify.

safeguards — Measures you can take to reduce threats, such as installing firewalls and intrusion detection systems, locking doors, and using passwords and encryption.

security incident response team (SIRT) — A group of staff people designated to take countermeasures when an incident is reported.

security policy — A statement that spells out exactly what defenses will be configured to block unauthorized access, what constitutes acceptable use of network resources, how the organization will respond to attacks, and how employees should safely handle the organization's resources to discourage loss of data or damage to files.

survivability — The capability to continue functioning in the presence of attacks or disasters.

Survivable Network Analysis (SNA) — A security process that starts with the assumption that a computer system will be attacked and follows a set of steps to build a system that can survive such an attack.

Threat and Risk Assessment (TRA) — An approach to risk analysis that starts from the standpoint of threats and accounts for risks to an organization's assets and the consequences of those threats and risks if they occur.

threats — Events and conditions that haven't occurred but could potentially occur; the presence of these events or conditions increases risk.

vulnerabilities — Situations or conditions that increase threat, which in turn increases risk.

worst-case scenarios — Descriptions of the worst consequences that befall an organization if a threat occurs.

REVIEW QUESTIONS

1. Which of the following should be done before formulating a security policy?

    a. intrusion handling plan

    b. risk analysis

    c. security review

    d. list of assets

2. Personnel records fit into which category of assets?

    a. personnel assets

    b. application software

    c. data assets

    d. physical assets

3. Survivable Network Analysis begins with what assumption?

    a. that you have laid the groundwork for a risk analysis

    b. that your network will be attacked

    c. that the probability of threats is increasing constantly

    d. that an effective security policy can reduce risk to zero

4. Survivable Network Analysis looks for which of the following in a network?

    a. failure points

    b. bottlenecks

    c. collisions of data

    d. software incompatibilities

5. What is an escalation procedure? (Choose all that apply.)

    a. It describes how network security can be improved in stages.

    b. It describes how a virus can multiply and affect more assets.

    c. It describes different levels of response based on incident severity.

    d. It describes staff members who should be involved in the response.

6. Name three factors that can increase the cost (beyond the actual sticker price) of replacing a piece of hardware that has been damaged or stolen.

7. List and describe the four steps of a Survivable Network Analysis in the order in which they should occur.

8. The hardware and software you need to protect can be valued more easily by following what approach?

    a. getting the most recent prices online

    b. keeping records of purchase costs

2

c. using your experience and expertise

d. interviewing support personnel

9. If an organization doesn't have a full-fledged security staff on duty, what should it do? (Choose all that apply.)

a. Hire a group such as CERT.

b. Designate IT staff to hold concurrent security positions.

c. Designate managers to fulfill security functions.

d. A standalone security staff is not needed.

10. When should an organization conduct a new round of risk analysis?

a. once every six months

b. once every three months

c. as frequently as possible

d. when equipment or staff change significantly

11. A risk analysis report should call attention to _____ .

a. all identified risks

b. the most urgent risks

c. the newest risks

d. the risks that are easiest to manage

12. _____ is the term for the process of identifying, choosing, and setting up countermeasures justified by the risks you identify.

a. Risk assessment

b. Risk identification

c. Threat management

d. Risk management

13. The ultimate goal of formulating a security policy is which of the following?

a. reduce the risks to zero

b. get the policy done right the first time so that it doesn't have to be rewritten constantly

c. convince management you deserve a raise

d. none of the above

14. What are the hardware, software, and informational resources you need to protect called?

a. threats

b. tangibles

c. assets

d. business holdings

15. Equipment and buildings in the organization are called _____ assets.
    a. facility
    b. tangible
    c. physical
    d. hard

16. Which of the following risk factors are events and conditions that haven't occurred but could happen?
    a. dangers
    b. disasters
    c. threats
    d. vulnerabilities

17. Documents on network computers, e-mail messages, log files compiled by firewalls and IDSs, and confidential information on personnel, customers, and finances are considered what type of asset?
    a. physical
    b. tangible
    c. electronic
    d. data

18. Ensuring that databases and other stores of information remain accessible if primary systems go offline is known as _____ .
    a. fault tolerance
    b. failover
    c. redundancy
    d. resiliency

19. The presence of one or more factors that increase threat probabilities increase your
    _____ .
    a. risk
    b. threats
    c. exposure
    d. consequences

20. The routers, cables, servers, and firewall hardware and software that enable employees to communicate with one another and other computers on the Internet are considered _____ assets.
    a. desktop
    b. server
    c. communications
    d. network

Hands-On Projects

Hands-On Project 2-1: Collecting Hardware and Software Inventory

Time Required: 15 minutes

Objective: Create a hardware and software inventory of your network and save it to a file.

Description: Making a complete hardware or software inventory of your network can be a daunting task. Luckily, several methods, from simple VBScripts to high-end software programs, can automate this chore. In this project, you use Network Asset Tracker from MIS Utilities to gather hardware and software data about your computer and save it to a file.

> **NOTE**
> At the time of this writing, the latest version of Network Asset Tracker was 2.8. If you download a more recent version, your screens might look slightly different from the figures shown in these steps.

1. Start your Web browser. Enter the URL for the Project Risk Analysis and Contingency Analysis page (**http://www.misutilities.com/download.html**), and then press **Enter**.

2. Scroll down and click the download link for **Network Asset Tracker**.

3. When you're prompted to open or save the Natracker.exe file, click **Save** and save it to a directory on your file system.

4. When the file download is finished, click **Close** in the Download Complete dialog box, and then close your Web browser.

5. Go to the directory where you downloaded the program, and double-click the **Natracker.exe** file. If necessary, when the Security Warning dialog box opens, click **Run**.

6. Click **Next** to accept the default setting of English (United States) in the Language Selection dialog box, as shown in Figure 2-9.

7. Click **Next** in the Welcome to the Installation Wizard window. Scroll through and read the Readme Information window, and then click **Next**.

8. Click to select the **Yes, I agree with all the terms of this license agreement** check box, and then click **Next**.

9. Click **Next** to accept the default installation directory and click **Next** in the Select Components window. Click **Next** two more times to start the installation, and then click **Finish**.

10. Click **Start**, point to **All Programs**, point to **Network Asset Tracker**, and click **Network Asset Tracker** to start the program. Click **Close** in the Tip of the Day message box.

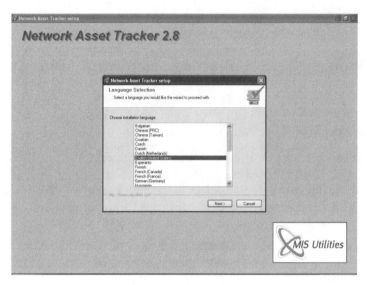

Figure 2-9   Network Asset Tracker setup

11. Right–click the **LOCALHOST** computer icon, and click **Get/Update Info**. A window similar to the one in Figure 2-10 is displayed with details about your system.

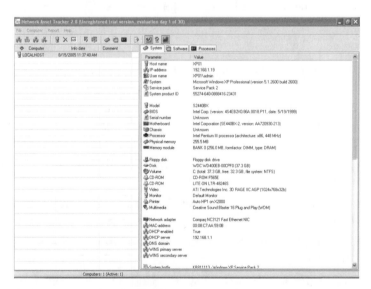

Figure 2-10   The Get/Update Info window

12. Click **Report**, **System Info** from the menu. Under Type of report, click to select the List option button, and then click **OK**.

13. Click **Export** and save the System Info file to a directory on your C: drive. Click **OK** in the Report exported successfully message box, and then click **Close**.

14. Navigate to the directory where you saved the System Info file, and double-click the **System Info.html** file. Read through the file to examine the information that was gathered. When you're finished, close the file.

15. Repeat Steps 12 through 14, substituting **Software Info** for **System Info**.

16. Click **File, Exit** from the menu to close the program.

CASE PROJECTS

Case Project 2-1: Conducting Risk Assessment and Analysis

Risk assessment can be as simple as noting an unlocked door or a password written on a note, or it can be a complex process requiring several team members and months to complete. A large enterprise environment probably has multiple locations, diverse activities, and a wide array of resources to evaluate. You don't need such a complex network, however, for your running case project; the main idea is to learn how to apply your knowledge in a methodical fashion to produce useful and accurate data. Approaching a task such as risk assessment without a strategy means repeating steps, wasting resources, and achieving mediocre results at best. Even worse, you might miss critical information.

You need the network and facility diagrams you completed in Chapter 1 for this project. Your instructor will provide documentation templates. Make additional copies as needed. In a real risk analysis process, one of the first steps is meeting with all department managers, upper management, employee representatives, workers in the production environment, human resources staff, and other staff members to get their input. Without input from the people actually doing the work, you might not think of essential factors. That isn't possible here, so direct any questions you have to your instructor, or do independent research to find your answers.

Remember that threats can affect multiple assets and vice versa, so the same asset might be listed more than once.

NOTE

1. First, identify the business processes that must continue for the organization to keep functioning—for example, collecting money from customers, receiving and processing sales, developing new products, and so on. Document major business processes that drive LedGrafix, using the Business Process column of the Business Process Identification Worksheet. (You need your imagination and some common sense for this step.) Assign a priority level to each process (using the priority rankings in the following list). Write down the department that performs the process, and leave the Assets Used column blank for now.

❒ *Critical*—Absolutely necessary for business operations to continue. Loss of a critical process halts business activities.

❒ *Necessary*—Contributes to smooth, efficient operations. Loss of a necessary process doesn't halt business operations but degrades working conditions, slows production, or contributes to errors.

❒ *Desirable*—Contributes to enhanced performance and productivity and helps create a more comfortable working environment, but loss of a desirable process doesn't halt or negatively affect operations.

2. Next, identify the organization's assets. Using the Asset Identification Worksheet your instructor provides, list each asset, its location, and approximate value, if known. (For multiple identical assets, describe the asset and list the quantity instead of listing each individual asset.) In organization-wide risk assessments, you would list all assets, including office furniture, industrial equipment, personnel, and other assets. For this project, stick to information technology assets, such as computers, servers, and networking equipment. The information you enter depends on the network design you completed in Chapter 1. All the equipment needed to build your network should be listed here as well as any cabling in the facility. (Assume the facility is already wired for a computer network with network drops available for each computer.) *Hint*: Remember to list items such as electricity and your Internet connection.

3. Next, determine which assets support each business process. On your Business Process Identification Worksheet, list the assets needed for each business process in the Assets Used column.

4. Each process should be documented and have a priority assigned to it. Next, transfer the priority rankings to your Asset Identification Worksheet. Now you know which assets are the most critical to restore and warrant the most expense and effort to secure. You also have the documentation to back up your security actions for each item.

5. The final step is assessing existing threats. Table 2-6 shows examples of ways to evaluate some types of threats and suggests ways to quantify them. On the Threat Identification and Assessment Worksheet, list each possible threat. Be sure to consider threats from geographic and physical factors, personnel, malicious attack or sabotage, and accidents. Also, examine the facility diagram you created for flaws in the facility layout or structure that could pose a threat, such as air-conditioning failure or loss of electrical service. Assess the probability of occurrence (POC) on a 1 to 10 scale, with 1 being the lowest and 10 the highest, and assign those ratings in the POC column for each threat.

Table 2-6 Threat evaluation and quantification methods

Type of threat	How to quantify
Severe rainstorm, tornado, hurricane, earthquake, wilderness fire, or flood	Collect data on frequency, severity, and proximity to facilities. Evaluate the past quality and speed of local and regional emergency response systems to determine whether they helped minimize loss.
Train derailment, auto/truck accident, toxic air pollution caused by accident, or plane crash	Collect data on the proximity of railroads, highways, and airports to facilities. Evaluate the construction quality of transportation systems and the rate of serious accidents on each system.
Building explosion or fire	Collect data on the frequency and severity of past incidents. Evaluate local emergency response to determine its effectiveness.
Militant group attacking facilities, riot, or civil unrest	Collect data on the political stability of the region where facilities are located. Compile and evaluate a list of groups that might have specific political or social issues with the organization.
Computer hack (external) or computer fraud (internal)	Examine data on the frequency and severity of past incidents. Evaluate the effectiveness of existing computer security measures.

6. Next, using the Asset Identification Worksheet, determine which assets would be affected by each threat. List those assets in the Assets Affected column of the Threat Identification and Assessment Worksheet. For an electrical outage, for example, list all assets requiring electricity to operate; for a hardware failure, list all assets a hardware failure would disrupt, damage, or destroy.

7. In the Consequence column, enter the consequences of the threat occurring, using the following designations:

   ◻ *Catastrophic (C)*—Total loss of business processes or functions for one week or more. Potential complete failure of business.

   ◻ *Severe (S)*—Business would be unable to continue functioning for 24 to 48 hours. Loss of revenue, damage to reputation or confidence, reduction of productivity, complete loss of critical data or systems.

   ◻ *Moderate (M)*—Business could continue after an interruption of no more than 4 hours. Some loss of productivity and damage or destruction of important information or systems.

   ◻ *Insignificant (I)*—Business could continue functioning without interruption. Some cost incurred for repairs or recovery. Minor equipment or facility damage. Minor productivity loss and little or no loss of important data.

8. Next, rate the severity of each threat in the Severity column, using the same designations as in the preceding list for consequences (C, S, M, or I). You derive these ratings by combining the probability of occurrence, the asset's priority ranking, and the potential consequences of a threat occurring. For example, if an asset has a Critical (C) priority ranking and a Catastrophic (C) consequence rating, it has a Catastrophic (C) severity rating. If you have mixed or contradictory ratings, you need to re-evaluate the asset and use common sense. A terrorist attack that destroys the facility and kills half the staff might have a probability of occurrence (POC) of only 1 (depending on your location), but if it happened, the consequences would definitely be catastrophic. Even so, because of the low POC, you wouldn't necessarily rank its severity as catastrophic.

9. Finally, on the Threat Mitigation Worksheet, list assets that are ranked as the most critical and threatened with the highest severity. In the Mitigation Techniques column, list recommendations for mitigating threats to those assets. For example, to mitigate the threat of an electrical outage damaging a critical server, you might suggest a high-end uninterruptible power supply (UPS).

10. Review your work, and submit it to your instructor.

3

SECURITY POLICY IMPLEMENTATION

> **After reading this chapter and completing the exercises, you will be able to:**
>
> ♦ Explain best practices in security policies
> ♦ Formulate a security policy and identify security policy categories
> ♦ Explain the importance of ongoing risk analysis and define incident-handling procedures

Computer crime is a continuing problem for businesses. The 2004 Annual CSI/FBI Computer Crime and Security Survey (*www.gocsi.com*) indicated that computer crimes and financial losses resulting from security incidents are on the decrease, which is good news for security professionals. Although it means a higher investment in security, many areas of business are beginning to integrate security as part of everyday business practices. Additionally, several areas of industry, most notably health care and financial services, are under new legislation that makes lack of security a major liability. That trend is likely to continue, and businesses must begin to consider security and its costs as part of daily operations. Information security is increasingly being addressed with a logical and structured methodology, and it's having a positive effect.

Progress has been made, but computer-related losses still happen and will continue to be a problem requiring ongoing management. Faced with these challenges, information security professionals and management need to evaluate the risks their organizations face and plan the deployment of standard methodologies to defend their systems. Armed with a detailed and accurate risk assessment, the next step is to develop a security policy—a statement that spells out exactly what defenses will be configured to block unauthorized access, how the organization will respond to attacks, and how employees should safely handle the organization's resources to discourage loss of data or damage to files.

What Makes a Good Security Policy?

Don't be surprised to be confronted at your organization with the question "Do we really need a security policy?" You need to be prepared with a response. You can begin by reminding skeptical fellow employees that a security policy is indeed necessary, particularly if your company falls into one of the following categories:

- If employees work with confidential or proprietary information
- If damage, theft, or corruption of systems or data would result in severe financial losses that could endanger business continuity
- If the organization holds trade secrets that are important to its goods or services
- If employees regularly access the Internet and use e-mail or other means of digital communication at risk of attack or infection
- If the company is in an industry regulated by emerging state and federal legislation on information security and privacy
- If the company uses Internet connections with partner businesses or application service providers (ASPs)—companies that provide Web-based services for a fee

To help your case, you can also convey examples that describe the sorts of public relations and human relations dilemmas that can occur if a clearly defined security policy is not in place. Here are some to consider:

- A copyeditor spent a lot of time surfing the Internet while on the job for personal pursuits as well as work-related research. Management was unable to discipline this employee because no policy was in effect that stated what constituted excessive personal use. The employee's supervisor later discovered that the copyeditor had downloaded a substantial amount of pornography; for this reason, the employee was fired. However, the employee subsequently appealed the dismissal with the Civil Service Board, claiming that he couldn't be fired because he had never been told he couldn't download pornography. After a hearing, the board ordered him to be reinstated with back pay.
- A clerk who was laid off because of downsizing at an insurance company was hired by a competing company. The former employer discovered that many of its customer files had been accessed and copied and that a number of its clients had switched to the competitor after they were offered lower insurance rates. The original company didn't have a policy for protecting its passwords or for switching passwords after employees left the company. The laid-off employee was easily able to access his former employer's network and steal files so that his new employer could market itself aggressively to potential customers.

3

The benefits of a security policy are wide ranging. In general, however, a security policy provides a foundation for an organization's overall security stance. A security policy not only gives employees guidelines on how to handle sensitive information and IT staff instructions on what defensive systems to configure, but also reduces the risk of legal liability for the company and its employees. It's common for employees who are fired or laid off to sue their previous employer or file a grievance, and in these cases, a well-defined security policy can make the difference between the company having to pay substantial damages and not being liable at all.

To protect overall security, it's important to formulate a clear policy that states what rights the employee has and how the employee should responsibly handle company resources. That policy should be signed by each employee when he or she is first hired. In some instances, having an employee who works with sensitive or proprietary information sign a nondisclosure or confidentiality agreement is also a wise precaution.

A good security policy is comprehensive and flexible; often, it's not a single document but a group of documents, each with its own specific emphasis. The next section discusses general best practices for security policies. Then, you examine major factors that result in an effective set of rules and procedures: the consideration of cyber risk insurance coverage; the need to base a policy on a thorough risk assessment; the need to teach employees about acceptable use of network resources; the need to specify what an employee's expected privacy rights are when on company property and equipment; the need to enable management to set priorities; the need to help administrators do their jobs; and the need to see a security policy as making subsequent risk analyses possible.

General Security Policy Best Practices

A security policy for a megacorporation might rival a metropolitan phone book in length and encompass every possible aspect of business, or it can be a simple document describing a few fundamental rules for a small company with only two computers and 11 employees. Whatever fits your organization's size, environment, and needs, there are a few basic concepts you need to understand about building an effective security policy:

- If it's too complex, no one will follow it. In fact, users might actively circumvent it.

- If it affects productivity negatively, it will fail.

- It should state clearly what can and can't be done on company equipment. Avoid jargon or complex descriptions, but be as thorough as possible.

- Include a generalized clause in statements, such as "Employees are not permitted to download games, screen savers, wallpaper, images, video clips, art, *or any other form of multimedia applications or files.*" The corporate attorney might need to tweak the wording, but the italicized clause covers anything not specifically mentioned.

- People need to know why a policy is important. They are more likely to accept it as necessary if they understand it.

- Involve representatives of all departments, including rank-and-file employees. The benefits are twofold:
  - You'll design a more accurate and appropriate policy if you tailor it to fit the needs of the people using the systems. You find out what those needs are by having input from the people who do the work.
  - By involving every level of the company, you have given employees a personal stake in the process. This encourages taking ownership, which leads to a more involved attitude and better morale—and that equals a more effective and enforceable security policy.
- The policy should contain a clause stating the specific consequences an employee could face for violating the policy.
- It must have support from the highest level of the company, and that support must flow down through the ranks. If management does not obey the policy, why should employees? No double standards, please.
- Although many companies hesitate to do this, have every employee sign a document acknowledging his or her understanding of the policy and agreement to abide by it. Some might think this practice denotes a lack of trust, but it's simply a sensible precaution and serves as an audit trail.
- Keep your security policy updated with current technologies. For example, include mobile device guidelines and regulate the use of portable storage devices. The point isn't to cover specific devices; it's to cover technology categories. For example, instead of listing "cell phones" or "USB drives," mention "wireless devices" or "portable storage devices." In addition, remove outdated material that no longer applies or has been integrated into another area. For example, the policy might have contained a clause about laptop or portable computers. When the policy is updated, laptops and portable computing devices are addressed in the section about mobile devices (cell phones, Palm pilots, wireless devices, and so on). To avoid conflicts, remove any other statements about laptops or portable computers.
- Make absolutely certain your policy directives are consistent with applicable laws. Retaining legal counsel to review your policy draft might be prudent to make sure all bases are covered and the policy doesn't violate civil rights or other laws. For example, it's illegal to forbid employees from publicly protesting a company's actions, unless they all agree to that provision. Even then, this clause could be challenged based on the First Amendment. Also, make sure the security policy doesn't conflict with other corporate policies.

Does this seem like an overwhelming task? It isn't as bad as it sounds. There are plenty of free resources with guidance on handling specific situations and templates you can customize to fit. One resource is the TechRepublic site, which has thousands of research documents, templates, checklists, and white papers, most of which are free and intended to help security professionals. You investigate this site in Activity 3-1.

ACTIVITY

Activity 3-1: Using Online Resources for Security Policy Development

Time Required: 20 minutes

Objective: Use a security policy template to guide the policy development process.

Description: For network administrators, security administrators, and IT staff, being understaffed and overworked with a less-than-adequate budget is more the rule than the exception. There are already too many things to do in a day, so tasks such as risk assessment and security policy drafting get pushed to the end of the line, when everything else is taken care of. Although you realize a security policy is crucial, how do you manage a full workload and still find time for yet another task? The answer is that you use whatever tools are available to lessen the time involved in drafting a security policy. One resource you can use is templates available on the Internet. In this activity, you sign up for a free membership to TechRepublic and then locate a security policy template.

1. From Windows XP, start your Web browser. Enter the URL **http://techrepublic.com/**, and press **Enter**.

2. Scroll down until you see the **Sign up for your free TechRepublic membership** dialog box. Enter your e-mail address as directed, and click **Join now**.

3. On the TechRepublic Registration page, enter the required registration information.

4. TechRepublic will send a confirmation e-mail to the address you entered in Step 2. Respond to the e-mail as instructed to complete your registration.

5. After your registration is completed, log in (if not already logged in) to TechRepublic. Enter the search term **security policy** in the Search box at the top, and click **Search**.

6. The results are categorized by resource types. Scroll down to the **Downloads** section, and click **More Downloads**.

7. In the Downloads section, click **Information Security Policy**. When the download dialog box opens, click the **Download Now** button.

8. When the File Download dialog box opens, click **Save**. Using the default file name, save the file to your desktop.

9. After the download is finished, double-click the **information_security_policy.zip** icon on your desktop. (The file is zipped, but Windows XP has a built-in utility that opens the file.)

10. Open the Microsoft Word document **information_security_policy.doc**. Take a few moments to read through the policy template.

11. Leaving the policy template open, close your Web browser.

You could modify this template to fit your organization. Keep this example in mind as you progress through the next sections, and refer back to the policy template to see how the following information relates to it.

Considering Cyber Risk Insurance

The dynamics of technology change business needs in some rather unexpected ways and can affect seemingly unrelated industries. Until a few years ago, **cyber risk insurance** wasn't available, but the insurance industry is beginning to find methods of evaluating coverage requirements and costs. Cyber risk insurance is simply an insurance policy, like your homeowner's or auto policy, that protects against losses to information assets. Policies are available that cover losses from cyber crime (such as break-ins that cause damage to, destruction of, or theft of sensitive data), malicious code damage (viruses, worms, and so on), and natural disasters. Industry is faced with a confusing array of losses and is trying to find methods of evaluating the true value of data. Determining the numbers is straightforward for hardware items, such as routers, switches, servers, and computers, but it gets tricky when insurance underwriters try to evaluate electronic assets accurately.

Insurers have begun to view requests for cyber risk coverage in a different light. Cyber risk insurance is being evaluated much like any other insurance. For your homeowner's policy, the insurance company wants to know certain things about your home, such as where it is and how much it cost. It also wants to know what security measures are used, such as a smoke alarm, carbon dioxide detector, and burglar alarm. Insurance companies also ask where the nearest police and fire services are located. They are beginning to apply the same tactics to cyber risk insurance. They want to know what losses are likely for your organization and what steps the organization is taking to prevent losses.

This approach should give you a good idea of how insurance and a security policy are related. Many answers to insurance application questions come directly from the security policy, and this policy could even earn your company a break on rates, much like a "good driver" discount. Because businesses are beginning to view information security as part of daily operations, concerns such as cyber risk insurance policies are also becoming part of day-to-day business and should be addressed in your security policy.

Most of the steps for developing a sound security policy play a prominent role in securing cyber risk insurance. Even the most thorough security mechanisms can't eliminate the risks an organization faces, so it makes sense that businesses would turn to insurance for protection against financial losses resulting from security incidents. That is noteworthy because auditing insurance coverage for IT systems is a task that naturally fits into the security policy development cycle.

NOTE

For more information on cyber risk insurance, go to the SANS reading room at *www.sans.org/rr/whitepapers/legal/1412.php*. In particular, read the seven-page questionnaire toward the end. By the end of this chapter, you'll be able to identify how many of these questions are actually part of your security policy or are included in the process you followed to develop it.

Activity 3-2: Investigating Cyber Risk Insurance

Time Required: 15 minutes

Objective: Learn how a company security policy can help in applying for cyber risk insurance coverage.

Description: In this activity, you search the Internet for companies offering cyber risk insurance.

1. From Windows XP, start your Web browser, and perform a search using the keywords **cyber risk insurance**.

2. In the list of results, click the first promising link you see. (*Note:* At the time of this writing, the first result was www.insuretrust.com.)

3. On your selected insurance site, locate an application document or form. On the Insuretrust site, the author selected Policies and Applications, then the **Complete one application form** link. (*Hint:* If your site doesn't offer an online application link, return to the search results and select another insurer's site.)

4. As shown in Figure 3-1, Insuretrust asks many questions related to computer security.

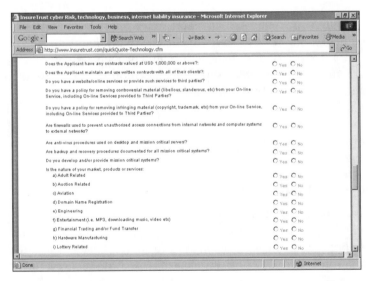

Figure 3-1   InsureTrust's online cyber risk insurance application

5. What information does the company request on its application form that would also be found in a security policy? Discuss this topic as a class or as specified by your instructor.

Developing Security Policies from Risk Assessment

If you're asked "Where do we start with a security policy?", you should be able to come up with an answer based on your review of Chapter 2 on risk analysis and what you learned in Activity 3-1. You start by identifying what needs to be protected. You then define the threats faced by the network, the probability that those threats will occur, and the consequences posed by each threat. You then propose safeguards and define how to respond to incidents.

The information you gather during the risk analysis phase should go into the security policy along with a statement of the policy's overall goals and the importance of employees actually reading and following its guidelines. In the document template you just reviewed, the penalties for violating the policy are stated prominently near the top. This is no accident; in litigation, the company attorney can argue that the employee could not have missed this section and so had to be aware that violating the policy could result in disciplinary action. Most policies state termination as a possible penalty, mainly to protect the company from wrongful termination lawsuits or similar grievances. A primary function of a security policy (for most companies) is to reduce legal liability. Defining security measures and specifying procedures are other important functions, but to upper management, the reduced liability factor is a major point in approving security policy development, implementation, and enforcement.

After the security policy is implemented, its effectiveness must be monitored. There's a difference between theory and practice, so it's reasonable to assume that some ideas might not work as planned. Like any large system with interdependencies between its parts, an organization-wide security policy requires periodic revision. Sometimes an immediate change is required in response to a problem, but other revisions can be done on a regular cycle. Remember that a security policy is a fluid document that must adapt to new circumstances to remain effective. Based on any problems, intrusions, or incidents that occur, you can update the policy as needed; the sequence of policy design, implementation, monitoring, and reassessment is an ongoing cycle.

Teaching Employees About Acceptable Use

The issue of trust is an integral part of a security policy. The policy needs to define who to trust and what level of trust should be placed in those people. It's easy to say that members of the organization should not be trusted at all, but you should clarify in writing how they should use system resources correctly so that acceptable use is no longer a matter of trust.

In reality, organizations have to achieve a balance between trust and issuing orders. You need to allow employees to use their computers to communicate and be productive. By placing too little trust in people and prescribing everything they should do in an excessively rigid fashion, you not only hamper their work, but also hurt morale and make it more likely that they'll attempt to circumvent your safeguards in some way. (Employee awareness is discussed in "Formulating a Security Policy" later in the chapter.)

Outlining Penalties for Violations

The cornerstone of many security policies is the acceptable use policy, which spells out how employees should make use of the organization's resources, including the Internet, e-mail, and software programs they use every day. More importantly, the policy should spell out what constitutes unacceptable use, such as downloading or viewing objectionable or offensive content, using company equipment for personal business, removing company property (including any digitized information) without specific permission, and other major usage problems. That doesn't mean employees should be fired for checking personal e-mail accounts two or three times a day, any more than they should be fired for calling home to check on their children.

Policy declarations exist to guide management and employees on the proper use of corporate resources. Penalty clauses exist mainly so that companies can discipline someone whose computer activities interfere with productivity. The policy should also contain guidelines for the penalty process so that employees who have read and agreed to the policy can't claim they didn't know they were violating it or didn't understand possible penalties. For example, the first offense can be a warning, the second offense could be a write-up or probation period, and the employee can be terminated for the third offense. Of course, if management views the violation as severe enough, the penalty could be immediate termination. In extenuating circumstances, an employee could be given another chance. The whole idea is to establish flexible methods of punishment that can be applied at management's discretion but protects the company from litigation if needed. Wrongful termination lawsuits are common and can result in significant costs for a company. Penalty clauses, if worded correctly, can protect companies from this type of lawsuit. Having legal counsel review any major corporate policies is usually a good idea, and a security policy is no exception.

Criminal Computer Offenses

So what happens if the security policy violation is a criminal offense, such as possessing child pornography? The situation becomes complicated: Law enforcement must be notified, and the investigation is turned over to them. There are some pitfalls to be aware of in this situation. After an investigation is turned over to the police, **Fourth Amendment** protections for search and seizure apply.

Your responsibilities as administrator for company systems that might contain evidence change when the public sector (police and government) is involved. Believe it or not, there's a tremendous burden of liability on you if you assist the police without being served with a **subpoena** or **search warrant**. A subpoena is an order issued by a court demanding that a person appear in court or produce some form of evidence (documents, papers, or other tangible items). A subpoena specifies what evidence is required, whether it's personal testimony, paper documents, or data files from the suspect's computer. A search warrant is similar to a subpoena, in that it's issued by the court and compels you to cooperate with law enforcement officers conducting an investigation. A search warrant also describes the place to be searched and specifies what evidence officers are allowed to search for.

The reasons for search warrants and subpoenas can be found in the Fourth Amendment, which grants the right to **due process** and protects U.S. residents against illegal search and seizure. Due process is the constitutional guarantee to a fair and impartial trial. The defendant in a case can sue you for violating his or her constitutional rights to due process if you provide evidence without being served with a warrant or subpoena. Providing assistance without being served is known as becoming a "de facto agent of law enforcement." This doesn't mean you are being paid by, or are employed by, law enforcement; it means you're acting under their direction and aiding them in an investigation, so you're bound by the same procedures and laws that bind public-sector investigators. When turning the case over to police officers, you can give them all the evidence you have gathered to that point, but you can't continue to investigate after that point unless you're ordered to do so. If you have been served with a subpoena or officers arrive to carry out a search warrant, you have no choice but to comply, thus removing any potential liability. Even if you want to help law enforcement, in a criminal case, you must not cooperate or turn over evidence unless you're ordered to do so.

Finally, there's the issue of an employee's expected right to privacy. The lines between Fourth Amendment protection and privacy expectations versus company-owned property can get blurry, unless you spell out what privacy an employee can expect while at work using company equipment. Your security policy must address this issue, stating clearly that company equipment and all digital information on it or accessed through it belong exclusively to the company, and the company reserves the right to search and inspect its property at any time. An employee has no expectation of privacy while using company resources. Unless this expectation is stated specifically, the company and anyone involved in an investigation could be liable if evidence is revealed that incriminates an employee. For example, if an employee is terminated for statements made in an e-mail, he could argue successfully argue that he didn't realize the company would be reading what he considered private e-mail and that he shouldn't be held accountable for what he said. Some companies might want to have employees sign a separate acknowledgement of this clause.

NOTE

For more information on the Fourth Amendment and Constitutional protections, visit *http://straylight.law.cornell.edu/constitution/.billofrights.html* for the text of the entire Bill of Rights and links to the full text of the Constitution. For more information on the Fourth Amendment, you can also visit *http://caselaw.lp.findlaw.com/data/constitution/amendment04/*.

ACTIVITY

Activity 3-3: Discovering the Rules of Criminal Search and Seizure of Electronic Evidence

Time Required: 30 minutes

Objective: Learn about federal rules for searching and seizing digital evidence in the workplace.

Description: In this activity, you read selected excerpts from the U.S. Department of Justice manual, *Searching and Seizing Computers and Obtaining Electronic Evidence in Criminal Investigations*. Although you might never need this information, if the situation ever comes up, you'll be thankful you have it.

1. From Windows XP, start your Web browser. Enter the URL **www.cybercrime.gov/s&smanual2002.htm**, and press **Enter**.

2. Take a moment to review the Table of Contents, and then click **D. Special Case: Workplace Searches**.

3. Read this section thoroughly, and answer the following questions:

   - How can an officer of law enforcement search a workplace without a warrant?

     _____

     _____

   - What is the difference between private-sector and public-sector searches?

     _____

     _____

   - What does the manual say about employer searches in private-sector workplaces? What segment of this statement relates to your involvement as an administrator cooperating with law enforcement?

     _____

     _____

4. Return to the Table of Contents. Scroll down and click **Appendix A** on network banner language. How do network banners affect a private-sector (nongovernmental) employee's reasonable expectations of privacy?

   _____

   _____

   _____

   _____

5. How should this information be incorporated into a security policy?

   _____

   _____

Enabling Management to Set Priorities

Security policies give employees guidelines they can follow during everyday work activities, but they are also helpful to management. They protect management in case disputes with employees happen or employees complain about security measures the organization uses.

Security policies do more than assist with dispute resolution, however. They provide a way for management to identify the most important security priorities facing the company. A security policy lists the network resources that managers find most valuable in the organization and that are most in need of protection. They spell out whether the organization's priority is to allow personnel to access the Internet or to restrict access to both the Internet and the internal corporate network. In addition, they describe the measures the company takes if resources are misused or if information is compromised by people outside or inside the company.

Helping Network Administrators Do Their Jobs

Network administrators responsible for instructing employees on how to access shared resources, change passwords, sort through e-mail, and other functions can gain considerable assistance from security policies. A security policy can spell out mundane but important information that an administrator would otherwise have to convey personally, such as:

- Users are not allowed to share accounts with other employees or with visitors or family members.

- Users are allowed to install only software programs that are in the Downloadables directory on the Shared Project server. Any other software is subject to approval.

- Users are not allowed to make copies of office-owned software.

- Users are required to use password-protected screen savers during the day and to shut down their computers each night.

- Only members of the IT staff are allowed to add hard drives or install networking devices on office computers.

- The network administrator needs to assign a user name and password to anyone who connects to the office network from a remote location. In addition, any remote PCs used to connect to the network need to be protected with firewall and antivirus software.

Administrators can be covered by a specific part of a security policy called a **privileged access policy**. This policy covers the access administrators can have to network resources and specifies whether they're allowed to run network-scanning tools, run password-checking software, and have root or domain administrator access.

TIP

To see an excellent model of a privileged access policy, visit *http://socrates. berkeley.edu:7015/proceds/access.html.*

3

Using Security Policies to Conduct Risk Analysis

After a security policy has been drafted, the work doesn't end there. After employees and managers are educated about the policy's requirements and provisions, the safeguards it prescribes are put in place. In addition to any information gathered by pre-existing security systems, such as log files, network traffic signatures, and peak traffic loads, further network monitoring after firewalls and other intrusion detection systems are installed can be helpful. You can use this information to determine how the network system is performing in terms of speed and loads and use the data in further rounds of risk analysis.

It's up to you to decide how often to do another round of risk analysis. The first time you analyze the level of risk might be after a fairly short period, such as a month or six weeks. After you make any needed adjustments to the security configuration as a result of threats that have come up, you might decide to conduct ongoing risk analysis every three months or every six months; there's no hard-and-fast rule. Conducting risk analysis after a major change occurs is important, such as when new equipment is installed or there's a lot of staff turnover. The risk analysis that occurs after the security policy is implemented involves the same steps as the initial round of risk analysis. The difference is that now you have real-world data on which to base your evaluations of risk and its consequences instead of being limited solely to "what if" situations.

FORMULATING A SECURITY POLICY

In the preceding sections, you learned that formulating a security policy begins with analyzing the level of risk to the organization's assets. You also learned that a security policy isn't always a single document; often, it contains many different component documents. After you know what assets are at risk and have come up with suggestions for safeguards, you can put these component documents together to form a security policy.

Additionally, you can assess what legal risks your company faces and the potential need for cyber risk insurance. These issues might seem unrelated to a security policy but are fast becoming important. Companies are always trying to find ways to protect themselves from the risks of doing business. A security policy can help do just that.

The following sections outline the steps in creating a security policy and offers tips and examples of specific types of policies you can create. When these different types of policies are put together, they form a complete security policy.

Seven Steps to Creating a Security Policy

After you have conducted a risk analysis, you should summarize your findings in the form of a report. The report should call attention to the most urgent risks the company needs to address. You might do this in an introductory paragraph or section. After the introduction, you could then present a grid that lists the most important assets in the company and the level of risk you have determined. An example is shown in Table 3-1.

Table 3-1   Risk analysis example

Asset	Threat	Probability	Consequences	Risk Assessment
Physical Assets	Low	Low	Significant	Medium
Data	Medium	Medium	Damaging	High
Software	Negligible	Minor	Minor	Low
Personal Assets	Low	Low	Significant	Medium
Hardware	High	Medium	Damaging	High

If your report lists types or groups of assets (for example, "Physical Assets" rather than specific items, such as buildings, desks, and telephones), include a set of definitions that explains what each group encompasses. Also, be sure to state who prepared the report and when it was conducted so that readers can verify that the information is current. You can add more weight to the assessment report by detailing the methodology for the assessment. Using a consistent, logical approach, as you did in the case project for Chapter 2, and providing careful documentation of the process, help verify the accuracy of results. It's important to use the same approach and document it so that others can verify your results, if needed. Management won't think much of your report or your recommendations if your results aren't sound and reproducible.

In the example in Table 3-1, you should explain why hardware and data assets are in a high-risk situation, which might not be obvious from looking at the grid to managers who read your analysis. The hardware risk might be high because servers are left in openly accessible work areas that are not protected by locks or any special environmental controls, so they can be easily stolen or damaged. The data assets in the company could be in a state of high risk because of a lack of virus protection in some servers, for instance.

After you have completed your risk analysis report, you should distribute it to the appropriate managers. When you have approval from top-level management, the CIO, or whoever is responsible for approving these projects, you would follow these steps to actually create the policy:

1. Call for the formation of a group that meets to formulate the security policy. Because of the political nature of security policies and the fact that they affect employees strongly, you shouldn't form the group on your own. Be sure to include a senior administrator, a member of your legal staff, some IT staff, and a representative of the rank-and-file employees.

2. Determine whether the organization's overall approach to security should be restrictive or permissive. A restrictive approach limits activity on the network to only a few authorized activities. A permissive approach allows traffic to flow freely and restricts only vulnerable ports, services, or computers.

3. Identify the assets you need to protect. You will have already done the groundwork for this step in the risk analysis phase.

4. Determine what needs to be logged and which network communications need to be audited. Then decide how often the results should be reviewed. **Auditing** is the process of reviewing records of activities of computers on the network; these records include who is connecting to a computer, what resources are being requested, and whether access was granted or blocked. This information is typically recorded in a log file.

5. List the security risks that need to be addressed.

6. Define acceptable use of the Internet, office computers, passwords, and other network resources.

7. Create the policy. The risks specified in the policy can be presented as individual sections within one long security policy document or as separate policies that, taken together, make up the organization's overall security policy.

Components of Security Policies

After the security policy committee has determined what should go into the security policy, the contents need to be written. Specific members or groups within the committee can be assigned the task of preparing different parts of the policy. A team approach ensures that all relevant points are covered. Many different kinds of policies can make up a policy; this section briefly describes the more common ones you are likely to need.

Acceptable Use

An **acceptable use policy** establishes what is acceptable use of company resources and usually offers some specifics on what's considered unacceptable use. An acceptable use policy might state the following:

"The following acceptable use policy covers the use of *Company Name* computers, network components, software applications, and other hardware. The term 'other hardware' includes, but is not limited to, personal computers, laptops, PDAs, floppy disks, CD-ROM drives and disks, servers, cables, routers, and tape backup systems. The term 'user' is defined as an individual who has an account to use *Company Name*'s network resources. All users of the *Company Name* network are expected to conduct themselves in a responsible, legal, non-threatening manner at all times, specifically:

- Users are not allowed to make unauthorized copies of copyrighted software except with the permission of the copyright holder.

- Users are responsible for storing their personal data on their computers. If they need assistance with storing data, they should consult the network administrator.

- Users are not permitted to engage in any activity, online or offline, that harasses, threatens, or abuses other users.

- E-mail accounts are for business use only; personal e-mail messages, as well as messages that might be judged obscene, harassing, or offensive, shall not be sent from or stored on *Company Name* systems.

Users who violate these policies will be reported to security staff. Offenses might result in loss of network privileges or termination of employment. If the offense warrants, the company may press civil or criminal charges against the user.

I have read and understand the *Company Name* acceptable use policy and agree to abide by it."

The signature of the user follows; some companies also include the signature of a witness and the date the policy was signed. These provisions are just a few examples of what can be included in an acceptable use policy. Your own policy can go into more detail on the use of network resources.

> The Virginia Department of Education offers some helpful tips and examples of creating acceptable use policies. You can find them at *www.pen.k12. va.us/go/VDOE/Technology/AUP/home.shtml*.

The acceptable use policy is usually stated at the beginning of a security policy because it affects the largest number of employees in an organization, and it can generate the highest degree of controversy. Because everyday work routines might be changed to comply with the new policy, gaining cooperation from all employees can be tough. The transition will be easier if upper management and direct supervisors begin an awareness campaign early in the process. Also, having a representative from the rank-and-file employees on the policy development committee is wise for a few reasons. First, employees' interests are represented. Second, having input on the many decisions that need to be made can help avoid making changes that negatively affect production. Finally, with an employee representative on the committee, managers and supervisors are more likely to talk to employees about the policy, why it is important, and why employees should support it can help prepare everyone for the changes. These discussions are called a **security user awareness program** (or something similar) and should be part of the implementation plan. Efforts should start as early as possible to get employees involved and excited about the policy.

The first step in an awareness effort could be posting informational memos on bulletin boards. Then supervisors might call departmental meetings to talk to their employees about the new policy and answer questions. A company can also post information about the policy on its internal Web site or devise games, such as brief quizzes asking basic questions about the security policy or giving scenarios for employees to "handle." Departments are awarded points for correct answers, and at the end of the game, the department with the most points wins a party or bonuses.

The point is to make sure a policy isn't just sprung on employees with a mandate to obey it. That approach would practically ensure failure because the policy depends on employees following it. An awareness program also needs to explain how the policy benefits the employees, such as increased revenue resulting in better pay or improved working conditions from using new technologies. However this task is approached, it must be consistently carried out before, during, and after security policy implementation.

Many companies require their employees to read and sign an acceptable use policy before they are given a user account or when they are first hired.

NOTE

3

Violations and Penalties

As mentioned earlier, many companies now include a section in their policies on what constitutes a violation and how violations are dealt with. These clauses vary in exact terminology and wording, but the meaning is usually the same. In large companies, legal counsel reviews and sometimes writes the corporate security policy to make sure it's legal and binding. Legal counsel also helps ensure that important points are clear, such as violations and penalty clauses.

Defining these points can help a company avoid legal problems. New employees are often required to sign a statement acknowledging their understanding of company policies, including any penalties resulting from violations of company policies.

Now would be a good time to refer to the policy template you have open from Activity 3-1. Note the passage on violations. In this policy template, the violations clause refers to the company policy. Because it's an information security policy, it's specific to computing resources.

NOTE

User Accounts and Password Protection

By creating a policy that guides how user accounts are to be used, you gain flexibility in developing and enforcing the security policy because you don't limit yourself to actual employees who work on-site. User accounts include employees and contractors who work at home and suppliers who connect to your network from their own facilities. Your security policy might specify user account policies, such as the following:

- Users are not permitted to attempt to gain access to an unauthorized resource.

- Users can't block an authorized user from gaining access to an authorized resource.

- Users can't give their account user names and passwords to others for any reason. If a password is lost or user account disabled, contact the administrator or help desk for assistance.

- Users must protect their user names and passwords in a secure location not visible on their desktops.

- Users must abide by the password policy of the company, specifically:

  - Passwords must meet complexity requirements: Strong passwords use a random combination of letters, numbers, and symbols and use both uppercase and lowercase characters.

  - Passwords must be at least eight characters.

- Passwords must not be words from the dictionary, names, dates, or other information that can be associated with the user or company.

- Passwords must be changed every 90 days. Users may not reuse old passwords for a period of one year.

Passwords represent a first line of defense (and possibly a second or even a third) for many organizations. Passwords not only allow users to gain access to e-mail messages, but they control access to the network from outside, to shared directories on servers, and much more. Often, companies require users to protect their computers or Web browsers by means of passwords so that other staff or visitors can't use them after hours.

Your company can use these guidelines or might have others suiting its needs and security goals. Whatever the case, a password policy should be established in the security policy and enforced by software means whenever possible.

Remote Access

More organizations use freelancers and consultants who work with them via broadband connections, e-mail, or VPN connections. Even now, however, a surprising number of workers still use dial-up connections. In addition, mobile workers often need to connect to the home office while on the road or at home, and business partners want to update their orders or view their account information by connecting directly to the company network.

These types of workers represent an opportunity for increased productivity but also increase security vulnerabilities. If a user who connects to the corporate network is working at a computer that's infected with a virus or has been compromised by a hacker, that hacker or virus can potentially gain access to the corporate network while the user is connected to it. Mobile devices can be stolen, and thieves can attempt to gain access to your network at their leisure.

A **remote access policy** spells out the use of **role-based authentication**, which gives users limited access based on the role they are assigned in the company and what resources that role is allowed to use. The sensitivity of those applications determines the type of authentication to be used, which can also be spelled out in the remote access policy. For example, access to applications or data sources that aren't considered confidential can be granted with a simple password; access to confidential resources can be secured with a smart card or token, a piece of hardware used with a password to provide **two-factor authentication**. This type of authentication combines something the owner *is* (finger-prints, signature, retina scan), *has* (a card or token), or *knows* (a password or PIN). Any two of these factors combined qualifies as two-factor authentication. The idea is to provide an extra layer of protection to authentication, so adding a second requirement effectively doubles the security. For example, if you simply had to insert your bank card to make purchases, that's all a thief would need (your card). Because you also have to enter a PIN code or sign the receipt, a thief has a harder time using your card to buy airline tickets to Acapulco. Using public or private keys for authentication would also work.

Another option for remote access that has become popular because of its effective and inexpensive nature is a virtual private network (VPN). VPNs create a tunnel to transport information through public communications media, such as regular phone lines. The data is kept safe by the use of **tunneling protocols** and encryption. You learn more about VPNs in Chapters 5 and 6.

Secure Use of the Internet and E-mail

An **Internet use policy** can be integrated with an acceptable use policy or with the overall security policy. However, because Internet use is becoming so integral to day-to-day work functions, it's worth creating a standalone security policy section that covers how employees can access and use the Internet.

A clear policy governing the use of e-mail is essential. Without this type of policy, the following incident is an example of what might occur: An employee receives a virus hoax sent by e-mail. The message indicates that if other users receive a message with the heading "You're a Winner!" they should not read it because it will erase all files on the user's hard disk. As a result, the employee broadcasts the e-mail to all other staff in the company. Many of those people send the same e-mail to other parts of the organization, thinking they are doing others a favor. Because no policy defined how they should handle these warnings, the company's mail servers are flooded with e-mail, and technical staff is called to diagnose the trouble, which wastes staff time and resources. E-mail hoaxes are more than nuisances. They can cause real problems on the network.

TIP   Visit *http://hoaxbusters.ciac.org/* or *www.snopes.com/* to investigate e-mail hoaxes.

An Internet use policy prohibits broadcasting any e-mail messages. Instead, users should be directed to contact the network administrator about suspicious mail messages. The policy should also spell out whether users are allowed to download software or streaming media from the Internet, and if so, specify the limits on size of file downloads. The policy could prohibit users from opening executable e-mail attachments that might contain viruses. It could also specify whether the company has blocked any objectionable Web sites and inform users how the company will protect their privacy with regard to e-mail.

LAN Security Policy

A **LAN security policy** should clearly define and establish responsibility for the protection of information that's processed, stored, and transmitted on the LAN and for the LAN itself. The primary responsibility can be with the data owner—the manager of the organization that creates the data and processes it. Secondary responsibility is then assigned to users in the organization who have access to the information. Primary responsibility means ensuring that policies and procedures to protect data are followed. The owner of the data (or the owner's representative, such as a department manager) has primary access to the data and grants access to others. Those granted access to data have the secondary responsibility of protecting it.

LAN management should clearly define the role of the people responsible for maintaining the LAN's availability. This policy should describe the following:

- *Applicability*—What constitutes the LAN environment and what parts, if any, are exempt from the policy

- *Evaluations*—The value of information stored on the LAN

- *Responsibilities*—Who is responsible for protecting information on the LAN

- *Commitment*—The organization's commitment to protecting information and the LAN

The sample LAN security policy that follows defines responsibilities for these employees:

- *Functional managers*—Employees who have primary responsibility

- *Users*—Employees who have secondary responsibility

- *Local administrators (LAs)*—Employees who are responsible for ensuring that end users have access to LAN resources on their servers

- *End users*—Any employees who have access to the organization's LAN (those responsible for using the LAN in accordance with the LAN security policy)

All users of data are responsible for complying with the security policy established by those with the primary responsibility for the security of the data and for reporting to management any suspected breach of security.

NOTE   The material in this section reflects the Federal Information Processing Standard (FIPS) 191, Guideline for the Analysis of LAN Security. The full text of FIPS 191 can be found at *www.itl.nist.gov/fipspubs/fip191.htm*. Reading the entire document is highly recommended.

The following is an excerpt of a sample LAN security policy developed by NIST in Federal Information Processing Standard (FIPS) 191, Guideline for the Analysis of LAN Security:

"A computer security incident is any adverse event whereby some aspect of computer security could be threatened: loss of data confidentiality, loss of data or system integrity, or disruption or denial of availability. In a LAN environment, the concept of a computer security incident can be extended to all areas of the LAN (hardware, software, data, transmissions, etc.), including the LAN itself.

Contingency plans in a LAN environment should be developed so that any LAN security incident can be handled in a timely manner, with minimal impact on the ability of the organization to process and transmit data. A contingency plan should consider: (1) incident response, (2) back-up operations, and (3) recovery.

The purpose of incident response is to mitigate the potentially serious effects of a severe LAN security problem. It requires not only the capability to react to incidents, but the resources to alert and inform the users, if necessary. It requires the cooperation of all users to ensure that incidents are reported and resolved and that future incidents are prevented. [NIST Special Publication 800-3, Establishing a Computer Security Incident Response Capability (CSIRC)] is recommended as guidance in developing an incident response capability.

Backup operation plans are prepared to ensure that essential tasks (as identified by a risk analysis) can be completed after the LAN environment is disrupted and continue until the LAN is sufficiently restored.

Recovery plans are made to permit smooth, rapid restoration of the LAN environment following interruption of LAN usage. Supporting documents should be developed and maintained that minimize the time required for recovery. Priority should be given to applications, services, and so forth that are deemed critical to the organization's functioning. Backup operation procedures should ensure that critical services and applications are available to users."

CONDUCTING ONGOING RISK ANALYSIS

After a security policy has been in place for a while, the security policy committee should decide on a routine reassessment of the risk to the company and its assets. You may or may not need to comprehensively examine every asset in the company each time this reassessment is done. You might decide to focus on only the most urgent security risks or any new risks that have cropped up as a result of changes in the company.

The following sections examine what you should keep in mind when re-evaluating the organization's security policy on an ongoing basis: the need to make these reviews routine; the need to work with management to accept the ongoing risk analysis/security policy cycle; the need to respond to security incidents as they occur; and the need to revise the security policy as a result of incidents and other identified risks.

Conducting Routine Security Reviews

An effective security policy not only describes the immediate steps to be taken when an intrusion is detected, but it can also look to the future and specify how often risk analyses should be conducted. A section of the policy that describes ongoing security reviews should begin by identifying the people who conduct the analysis on an ongoing basis. It should then describe the circumstances under which a new risk analysis is done. For instance, whenever a substantial purchase of new equipment is made, these people can be notified so that they can determine whether new security policy statements need to be written or whether new measures should be taken.

Even though the security policy might state that a risk analysis should be conducted routinely every six months or every year, the policy should be flexible enough to allow "emergency" reassessments as needed. For instance, any attacks to partner businesses or offices of employees who work off-site should prompt the security policy development team to reassess the risks facing the organization; in addition, news of any major security attacks on Internet servers or viruses circulating widely on the Internet should prompt risk reassessment.

Working with Management

This section offers hints for working with management after you're hired. When you prepare a project proposal for developing full-fledged security policies or for spending extensively on security-related hardware and software, you're likely to be asked what kind of return on investment (ROI) the company will realize.

As discussed in Chapter 2, ROI indicates how long before the savings caused by preventing security incidents pays back the investment. Tell your colleagues that they should think about the issue not only in terms of ROI, but also in terms of the cost of doing nothing. Large organizations with employees who connect remotely are far more vulnerable to security breaches than other businesses. They need to consider three factors:

- How much information systems and the data on them are worth
- Possible threats they've already encountered and will encounter
- The chances that those security threats will result in real losses of time and money

These days, security threats can originate from many different sources and have a wide variety of signatures, and no single solution can block them all. (Security measures, such as an IDS or antivirus software, use known signatures of attacks, viruses, and other malware to identify and block potentially harmful traffic. Chapter 4 discusses traffic signatures.) A comprehensive security plan is not just a return on investment, but also a way of protecting systems and customers' personal information. Ask management to quantify the future revenue lost when customers' credit card numbers are stolen by an attacker and posted on the Internet, which destroys the company's credibility. In addition, ask management to estimate the cost to the business if information is unavailable for weeks or months at a time. You should present these scenarios diplomatically, and you must have the statistics to back up your points. Nothing can make a proposal go down in flames as fast as anecdotal scare tactics, even if they're true. If you can't prove they are true, don't bring them up. Stick to the facts.

Stay away from making quantitative statements that can't be verified with precision because equipment depreciates and an office's environment changes. Businesses are usually dynamic in nature, so new employees, products, and technologies are constantly being added, and employees leave, old technologies are removed from service, and so on. Instead of trying to assign hard numbers to these items, get management to consider the following aspects of a business's activities that can be affected adversely by intrusions:

- Costs related to financial loss and disruption (includes cost of downtime and lost productivity, among others)
- Personnel safety
- Personal information

- Legal and regulatory obligations
- Commercial and economic interests
- Intangibles such as consumer trust and company image or reputation

Dealing with the Approval Process

Developing a security policy can take anywhere from several weeks to several months, depending on the organization. When you have cooperation from all relevant employees, preparing a security policy in two or three weeks is possible. Don't rush the process, however. Take the time to do it right and cover all bases. The only thing worse than no security policy is a bad security policy. If that happens, you can almost be guaranteed that management won't continue to back the project.

One aspect of development you have to address is the need for the security policy to be reviewed and approved by upper management, executives, and other stakeholders, if needed, and this process can take several weeks to several months. Don't be dismayed if the need to schedule and reschedule meetings, hold discussions, and get approval takes longer than you think. For a security policy to work, rank-and-file employees need to accept it. You might encounter resistance, which is natural with any policy that affects an entire organization. A security user awareness program, in which employees are instructed formally about the organization's security strategy, can help.

Feeding Security Information to the Security Policy Team

Any changes made to the organization's security configuration should be conveyed to the security policy team. This team can suggest changes to the policy; the policy then dictates whether new security tools need to be purchased or new security measures need to be taken.

The participation and backing of top-level management can help the process of amending the security policy. Encourage managers to inform employees that protecting company assets is everyone's responsibility. Provide training to users to make them aware of security issues, and explain why data collection and management should be conducted in a secure manner. Educate users so that they have the required knowledge to carry out their job in a secure manner. Listen to employees' concerns. Develop sensible security solutions that allow daily business to be conducted yet provide an acceptable level of protection against risks.

Responding to Security Incidents

As you learned in Chapter 2, a security policy should address the general steps to be followed when an intrusion is detected and what personnel should be notified. Often, members of the security policy team also serve as members of the incident response team, which consists of the key personnel notified in the event of an incident. These people assess the situation and determine whether additional personnel, such as the IT manager, should be notified. Remember that this chain of escalation is specified in the security policy so that there are clear guidelines on who to contact for an incident. Chapter 2 discussed the general escalation procedures that should be addressed in the policy.

The security policy's section on incident handling and escalation procedures spells out what happens when an alarm goes off. It also covers less dramatic situations that can, nevertheless, have serious implications, such as how an organization responds when an employee loses a password or when an employee's termination proceedings don't go smoothly.

Escalation Procedures

Escalation procedures, as explained in Chapter 2, describe how an organization increases its state of readiness when a threat arises or a security incident occurs. Levels of escalation in an organization are usually divided into three levels:

- Level One incidents are the least severe and typically must be managed within one working day from when they occur.
- Level Two incidents are of moderate seriousness. They should be managed the same day the event takes place—ideally, within four hours.
- Level Three incidents are the most serious; they must be handled immediately.

Escalation procedures also specify the staff members who handle each level. A large organization might have a full-fledged department whose members are assigned only to maintaining security and with titles such as security analyst, security architect, and chief security officer. Many organizations assign technical staff to these roles, which have to be performed in addition to their other responsibilities. In either case, the escalation procedures in a security policy spell out who needs to respond in statements, such as the following examples:

- A Level One incident requires notifying only the on-duty security analyst.
- A Level Two incident requires notifying the security architect.
- A Level Three incident requires notifying the chief security officer.

In addition, Level Two or Level Three incidents might require the participation of outside security groups, such as Computer Incident Advisory Capability (CIAC) or CERT. These highly regarded organizations keep records of serious security attacks; if your organization is hit by a new virus or an unusually strong distributed denial-of-service (DDoS) attack, it should let others on the Internet know about the attack.

Incident Handling

To determine how incidents should be escalated, the security policy's section on incident handling and escalation procedures should clearly define the types of incidents to watch out for and what level of escalation each one represents. Following are some examples:

Loss of password (Level One incident)—The on-duty supervisor should be notified within 24 hours. He or she will determine whether a change of password is necessary.

Burglary or other illegal building access (Level Two incident)—If an unauthorized person is discovered on the premises, notify your immediate supervisor. He or she will determine if police need to be notified and who the incident should be escalated to, if at all. If the incident is serious enough to warrant it, the supervisor will notify the appropriate people in the escalation chain, such as the CSO, IT manager, or security administrator (SA). The person should be escorted out of the building, either by the authority to whom the incident was reported or escalated or by police. The responsible party specified in the security policy then writes an incident report.

Property loss or theft (Level Two or Level Three incident)—If company property has been stolen, the human resources (HR) director or the on-duty supervisor should be notified immediately. They will escalate the incident to the CSO and local law enforcement, if needed.

Updating the Security Policy

Based on the security incidents reported as a result of your ongoing security monitoring and any new risks your company faces, you should update the security policy. Any changes to the policy should then be broadcast to the entire staff by e-mail or by posting the changes on the company's Web site or intranet.

The goal of changing the security policy is to change employees' habits so that they behave more responsibly. Ultimately, a security policy should result in actual physical changes to the organization's security configuration. A call for redundant systems in the security policy might result in major expenditures of a new firewall or server to act as a "failover" device, for instance. The need to review security logs on a daily basis, as prescribed in a security policy, might result in the company investing in log file analysis software to make the jobs of IT professionals easier. Better protection means fewer internal or external incidents (attacks, viruses, worms, intrusions, and so forth), which enables the company to focus on its primary mission.

CHAPTER SUMMARY

- The benefits of a security policy are wide ranging. In general, however, a security policy provides a foundation for an organization's overall security stance. A security policy gives employees guidelines on how to handle sensitive information and IT staff instructions on what defensive systems to configure; in addition, it reduces the risk of legal liability for the company and its employees.

- To protect overall security, it's important to formulate a clear policy that states what rights employees have and how they should handle company resources responsibly.

- Cyber risk insurance is becoming necessary for businesses. Because risk can't be eliminated, businesses are turning to insurance to offset losses. An organizational security policy can help with applying for insurance and with identifying what needs to be insured and from what threats.

❑ A good security policy is based on risk assessment, covers acceptable use of system resources, sets priorities for the most critical resources that need to be protected, and specifies the use of network resources by administrators and security staff.

❑ Legal liabilities should be covered in a security policy. Statements of acceptable and unacceptable use must be included, and guidelines for violations and punishments must be covered. This helps the company avoid litigation from employees fired for misuse of systems.

❑ If an incident turns out to be a criminal offense, it's important to understand your legal obligations and how to protect yourself from litigation. After an investigation is turned over to the police, Fourth Amendment protections for search and seizure apply, and failure to respect those protections can result in being named in a lawsuit. You must understand the implications of a criminal investigation, and aid police after you have been ordered to do so by the court in a subpoena or officers arrive to carry out a search warrant.

❑ Often, a security policy is formulated as a series of several specific policies rather than one long document. There are seven steps in creating a security policy: forming a security policy group; determining the overall security approach; identifying assets to protect; specifying auditing procedures; listing security risks, defining acceptable use; and finally, creating the specific policies, such as user account, password protection, and Internet use policies.

❑ You need to present the proposal to management and gain approval to proceed with the project. Part of this process involves explaining the expected ROI and calling attention to the other costs associated with security incidents, such as loss of productivity, loss of morale or customer confidence, and possible legal costs.

❑ A security policy's section on incident handling and escalation procedures defines the response and escalation for incidents of varying severity. It also contains contact information for anyone who might need to be notified of an incident.

❑ Security policies should be reviewed and updated regularly. They should be modified sooner than the regular review cycle if intrusion attempts or actual intrusions occur. They should also be modified to account for personnel changes and acquisition of new equipment.

Key Terms

acceptable use policy — This policy section establishes what constitutes acceptable use of company resources and usually offers some specifics about what's considered unacceptable use.

auditing — The process of reviewing records of activities of computers on the network; these records include who is connecting to a computer, what resources are being requested, and whether access is granted or blocked.

cyber risk insurance — Like business liability insurance, a cyber risk insurance policy protects businesses from losses resulting from attacks, viruses, worms, sabotage, and so on. Each policy has specific coverages and exclusions, as with any other insurance policy.

due process — A legal concept that ensures the government respects a person's rights or places limitations on legal proceedings to guarantee fundamental fairness, justice, and liberty.

Fourth Amendment — The Fourth Amendment is contained in the Bill of Rights and provides constitutional protection from illegal search and seizure and guarantees the right to due process. It is from the Fourth Amendment that an expected right of privacy is implied, even though no such right is stated specifically.

3

Internet use policy — A policy that defines how users can access and use the Internet and specifies what rules apply to e-mail and other communications. Internet use, e-mail use, and other forms of communication, such as instant messaging, can be included in a single section or addressed separately in an Internet use policy and a digital communications policy.

LAN security policy — This type of policy defines and establishes responsibility for the protection of the LAN itself and for information that is processed, stored, and transmitted on the LAN.

privileged access policy — A policy detailing additional access, functions, and responsibilities of users with privileged (administrative or root) access to resources.

remote access policy — A policy that defines what security measures need to be in place on a remote desktop before the user or that desktop can connect to the organization's network.

role-based authentication — A method of authentication that grants users limited access based on the role they are assigned in the company and defines what resources that role is allowed to use.

search warrant — A legal document issued by the court allowing a search of a specified place for specific evidence. The warrant must detail what the search is seeking and where law enforcement is permitted to look for it.

security user awareness program — A training program designed to educate users about security topics, answer their questions about security, and prepare users to accept changes made for security purposes.

subpoena — A legal document requiring a person to appear, provide testimony, or cooperate with law enforcement. Testimony consists of written or oral declaration of fact under penalty of law.

tunneling protocols — Network protocols that encapsulate (surround or envelope) one protocol or session inside another.

two-factor authentication — Authentication requiring at least two forms of verification from a user to be granted access. Verification requires something the user possesses, knows, and/or is.

REVIEW QUESTIONS

1. What general best practices should you follow when developing a security policy? List at least five guidelines discussed in this chapter in your own words.

2. What can occur if a security policy is so rigidly formulated that too little trust is placed in network users? (Choose all that apply.)

   a. Network resources can be compromised.

   b. Productivity can be reduced.

   c. Employees might quit and go to other companies.

   d. Employees will find ways to circumvent security systems.

3. The section of a security policy that affects the most people in an organization is the _____ .

   a. incident-handling policy

   b. privileged access policy

   c. acceptable use policy

   d. remote access policy

4. How do security policies help management? (Choose all that apply.)

   a. They can protect management in cases of wrongful termination disputes.

   b. They force employees to use company resources correctly.

   c. They state the company's most important security priorities.

   d. They circumvent the need to hire security professionals.

5. Having a security policy developed can help with what aspect of acquiring cyber risk insurance coverage?

   a. The security policy tells the insurance company how many employees you have.

   b. The security policy contains detailed information about safety records.

   c. Many of the security configurations specified in the security policy also provide information for insurance applications.

   d. Auditing network use provides information about hardware coverage needs.

6. Which of the following policies should contain the statement "Network administrators are the only staff authorized to have root or domain administrator status"?

   a. user account policy

   b. acceptable use policy

   c. privileged access policy

   d. Internet use policy

7. _____, if worded correctly, can protect companies from wrongful termination lawsuits.

   a. Nondisclosure clauses

   b. Acceptable use policies

   c. Penalty clauses

   d. Punishment clauses

8. A security policy can spell out mundane but important information that an administrator would otherwise have to convey personally, such as:

   a. Users are not allowed to share accounts with each other.

   b. Users are not allowed to use password-protected screen savers.

   c. Users may install software on their own computers.

   d. Users are authorized to make copies of office software to install on their home systems.

9. Why is an acceptable use policy usually listed first in a security policy? (Choose all that apply.)

   a. It can generate controversy.

   b. It affects the most employees.

   c. It can get employees in trouble.

   d. It is the basis for terminating troublemakers.

10. Why is it helpful to speak in terms of "user accounts" rather than "full-time employees" in a security policy? (Choose all that apply.)

   a. User accounts apply to all employees, not just full-time people.

   b. User accounts include freelancers and business partners.

   c. User accounts cover password use.

   d. User accounts are the most important aspect of network security.

11. A password policy might specify which of the following attributes for password selection?

   a. length requirements

   b. complexity requirements

   c. changing passwords

   d. all of the above

12. A password policy should be established in the _____ and enforced by _____ whenever possible.

   a. risk assessment process, management

   b. company Web site, network administrators

   c. security policy, software

   d. company employee handbook, security guards

13. Which of the following can be used to authenticate users for access to sensitive information? (Choose all that apply.)

    a. public or private keys

    b. password-based authentication

    c. role-based authentication

    d. two-factor authentication

14. E-mail hoaxes don't cause damage; they are only a nuisance. True or False?

15. Organizations with employees who connect remotely should consider which of the following security concerns?

    a. possibility of theft of mobile devices

    b. virus infections spreading from home and mobile systems or storage to corporate systems

    c. the use of up-to-date, effective antivirus and firewalls on mobile devices or home systems connecting to the network

    d. all of the above

16. A(n) _____ instructs employees formally about the organization's security strategy.

    a. acceptable use policy

    b. risk assessment

    c. strategy meeting

    d. security user awareness program

17. Loss of a password could constitute a Level _____ incident.

    a. Two

    b. Two or Three

    c. One

    d. One or Two

18. A good security policy is based on identifying the assets to be protected and then implementing steps to secure them. True or False?

19. How can you convince management to support a security policy?

    a. Tell them how a security policy can help reduce legal liabilities.

    b. Tell them it won't cost anything.

    c. Provide information about potential costs of doing nothing, such as loss of productivity or customer confidence or damage to the company's image in the event of a security incident.

    d. Reassure them that it won't be difficult or take much time.

20. What protects U.S. residents from illegal search and seizure?

    a. Fourth Amendment

    b. Smith and Wesson

    c. U.S. Patriot Act

    d. First Amendment

3

HANDS-ON PROJECTS

HANDS-ON PROJECTS

Hands-On Project 3-1: Conducting Security Policy Analysis

Time Required: 20 minutes

Objective: Evaluate security policy clauses, identify deficiencies, and update policies in response to events or changes.

Description: Security policies can and should be revised to address security breaches or new threats. In this project, you evaluate an incident involving theft of proprietary information and identify some obvious security policy deficiencies. Then, you recommend changes to the security policy to prevent similar incidents from occurring in the future.

Consider the following situation: A local branch office of a major national stock brokerage had no policy requiring the termination of user ID and password privileges after employees leave. A senior trader left the brokerage and was immediately hired by a competing brokerage. Shortly thereafter, the first brokerage lost two clients who said they were moving to a competing firm and whose personal data files disappeared mysteriously from the company's databases. In addition, a year-end recommendations report that the employee had been preparing was released two weeks earlier by the same competing firm. An investigation of the company's access logs revealed that the employee records file had been accessed by someone outside the company. The job records, however, did not reveal whether the report had been stolen because they had not been set up to record object accesses in a log.

The existing security policy states the following:

"On termination, employees shall surrender any laptops, disks, or computer manuals they have in their possession. They are no longer authorized to access the network, and they shall not take any hardware or software when they leave the office."

1. What changes would you make to the existing security policy so that it improves security after employees are terminated?

_____

_____

_____

_____

2. Brainstorm ideas for a security policy clause that covers access of company records and helps track when files are accessed.

_____

_____

_____

_____

CASE PROJECTS

CASE PROJECTS

Case Project 3-1: Mapping Risk Analysis to a Security Policy

Six months after a security policy has been formulated and put into place, your company decides to do a risk analysis. The data in Table 3-2 presents some of the findings. Suggest ways in which you would modify the security policy to cover the new threats.

Table 3-2   Modifying a security policy

Asset	Threat	Probability	Consequences	Risk Assessment	Change
Web server	High	Medium	Serious	Critical	Was medium; Web site went online during this period
Office computers	Low	Low	Significant	Medium	Unchanged
Customer data	Medium	High	Damaging	High	Was medium; two employees in customer service were laid off and expressed anger
Job records	High	High	Serious	Critical	Was medium; one laptop was lost or stolen while VP of marketing was in airport

Case Project 3-2: Drafting a Security Policy

In this running case project, you continue developing a secure network for LedGrafix, the video game development company for which you designed a network in Chapter 1 and performed a risk assessment in Chapter 2. Using the information in those projects and what you have learned in this chapter, produce a draft security policy for the company that contains the following:

- Title page
- Table of contents
- Introduction
- Scope and definitions
- Violations and penalties
- Acceptable use
- Unacceptable use
- Responsibilities (make up your own names and contact information) for the following:
  - Departmental (IT, Human Resources, and so on)
  - Management
  - Employee
- Internet and e-mail use
  - File downloads
  - Attachments
  - Objectionable content
  - Spyware, adware, and cookies
- Privileged access policy
- Remote access policy
- User accounts and passwords
- Physical security (*Hint*: Remember to use the facility diagram)
- Illegal activities
  - Spam
  - Objectionable content
  - Theft of intellectual property and copyright infringement
  - Unauthorized entry into systems, corporate or otherwise, from corporate equipment

- Contact information (again, make up your own names and contact information) for the following:
  - Incident response team
  - Escalation procedures
- Security user awareness program
  - Methods
  - Responsible parties
- Employee acknowledgement (signature page)
- Appendixes
  - Network diagram (from Chapter 1)
  - Facility blueprint (from Chapter 1)
  - Risk analysis reports and data (from Chapter 2)
- Change control and revision history
- References

This project might look like a tremendous task, but reviewing the information security policy document you downloaded from TechRepublic should be helpful. As you'll see, many sections of the policy are only a few sentences.

You can organize the information in whatever sequence you like and add items as needed. You can also use whatever resources you want, as long as you don't infringe copyrights and trademarks or violate your school's plagiarism policy. Any sections you don't understand can be clarified by running an Internet search. Using free templates (not copyrighted) and modifying them as needed is strongly recommended. In the real world, you wouldn't be required to write the policy from scratch, and saving time means saving money the company is paying you for this task. The only rule is to cite your sources. Your grade won't be affected by using a template.

Remember, this is a draft policy, meaning you'll be adding to it, changing items that don't work, and revising based on changes in the environment, just as you would in a real security policy development and management cycle. When you're finished, proofread your work carefully and turn it in to your instructor.

4

NETWORK TRAFFIC SIGNATURES

After reading this chapter and completing the exercises, you will be able to:

♦ Describe the concepts of signature analysis

♦ Detect normal and suspicious traffic signatures

♦ Identify suspicious events

♦ Explain the Common Vulnerabilities and Exposures (CVE) standard

At its most basic level, securing network traffic can be broken down to a simple principle: allowing the communications you want to pass through your network gateways and blocking all the traffic you don't want. The challenge is to separate the two types of network traffic. This is done by using a combination of firewalls, router access lists, intrusion detection system (IDS) filtering, antivirus software, and other security tools. For these devices to determine whether traffic is normal, administrators must tell them which is which. After a device can accurately tell the difference, it must then know how to respond, if it's capable of doing so.

This chapter examines some techniques for identifying what constitutes normal network traffic and what constitutes an attempt to gain unauthorized access (abnormal network traffic) to network resources. You begin by learning what signature analysis is and how it's used in network security. You learn how to capture packets for inspection and analyze traffic signatures, both normal and suspicious. You then identify and analyze common suspicious events. Last, you examine a standard for recording information on attack signatures: the Common Vulnerabilities and Exposures (CVE) standard.

Understanding Signature Analysis

A **signature** is a set of characteristics—such as IP numbers and options, TCP flags, and port numbers—used to define a type of network activity. Besides individual TCP/IP packet attributes, a signature can also consist of a sequence of packets or other events, such as logons to a network.

Some intrusion detection devices assemble databases of "normal" traffic signatures. As traffic is detected, it's compared to the database, and any deviations from normal signatures trigger an alarm. Other intrusion detection devices refer to a database of well-known attack signatures. Any traffic that matches one of the stored attack signatures triggers an alarm. Your understanding of both normal and suspicious traffic signatures enables you to configure IDSs to work more effectively—to minimize the number of false positives (false alarms) and maximize detection of genuine attacks. You will learn about false positives and false negatives in Chapter 7.

The following sections introduce you to understanding signature analysis. Then, you learn how to capture packets so that you can analyze them and review some common normal traffic signatures you're likely to encounter. Finally, you learn about suspicious traffic signatures that indicate a possible attempt to scan and gain unauthorized access to your network.

Understanding Signature Analysis

Signature analysis is the practice of analyzing and understanding TCP/IP communications to determine whether they are legitimate or suspicious. TCP/IP packets that are sent back and forth by a host and client and are judged to be suspicious fall into several categories: bad header information, suspicious data payload, single-packet attacks, or multiple-packet attacks.

Bad Header Information

A common way in which packets are altered is in their header information, and packet filters usually scan for these alterations. Suspicious signatures can include malformed data that affects some or all of the following:

- Source and destination IP address
- Source and destination port number
- IP options
- IP fragmentation flags, fragmentation offset, or fragment identification
- IP protocol
- IP, TCP, or UDP checksums

A checksum is a simple error-checking procedure for determining whether a message has been damaged or tampered with while in transit. The number of data bits in a message is processed by using a mathematical formula. A numeric value (the checksum) is then calculated. The receiving computer applies the same formula to the message; if a different checksum is found, the receiving computer determines that the message has been tampered with or corrupted in some way and drops it.

Attackers can use software for generating packets set to their specifications to forge IP addresses or other types of header information. For instance, a packet can be broken into chunks and sent in a series. The initial chunk in the series can be eliminated from the set, which makes the receiving computer unable to reassemble the packets and, therefore, circumvent a packet filter. More or fewer packets than indicated in the initial packet can be sent, which can disable a server that can't process more or fewer packets than it expected to receive.

Suspicious Data Payload

The payload (data) part of a packet is the actual data sent from an application on one computer to an application on another. Sometimes attacks can be detected by an IDS that matches a text string to a specific set of characters in the payload. For instance, a Trojan program called Hack'a'Tack sends a UDP packet that uses both source port 31790 and destination port 31789. Originally designed as a remote administration tool for Windows 9x systems, Hack'a'Tack can be used for a variety of attacks, such as installing other programs, logging passwords, and rebooting the system. The key to defending against this attack is detecting the string "A" in the payload part of the packet.

NOTE UDP ports 31791 and 31787 and TCP port 31785 are also known Hack'a'Tack ports. For more information on this Trojan program, run an Internet search. G-Lock Software (*www.glocksoft.com/trojan_list/Hack_a_Tack.htm*) provides technical details of Hack'a'Tack and has some helpful tools, such as the AAtools port scanner.

In another type of attack, the UNIX Sendmail program is exploited by adding codes to packet contents. Codes such as VRFY and EXPN are used to uncover account names on the Sendmail server. By adding the code EXPN DECODE in a packet's data payload, attackers attempt to establish a connection with an alias called "decode." If a connection is made, attackers can use it to place malicious files on the exploited system. To defend against this type of attack, a network administrator should remove the "decode" alias line, which is installed by default with many UNIX/Linux systems in the /etc/mail/aliases file.

TIP   Running an Internet search yields a wealth of tools and information, but be careful of downloading files. You might end up downloading the malicious software you're trying to avoid! Create a folder to store the files, unzip into that folder if necessary, and then run a virus scan on the folder. Any known malware signature will be recognized (provided you keep your antivirus software updated), and you can safely remove the files without harm in most cases. There's still a risk, but it can be reduced with some common sense and basic security protocols.

Single-Packet Attacks

A **single-packet attack** (also called an "atomic attack") can be completed by sending a single network packet from client to host. Because only a single packet is needed, a connection doesn't need to be established between the two computers involved. Many changes to IP option settings can cause a server to freeze up because it doesn't know how to handle these packets. The IP option settings are shown in Table 4-1.

Table 4-1   IP option settings

Option Number	Name of Option
0	End of Options
1	No Operation
2	Security
3	Loose Source and Record Routing
4	Internet Timestamp
7	Record Return Route
8	Option has been deprecated
9	Strict Source and Record Routing

As an example of IP options processing, suppose an ICMP echo request (or "ping") packet is sent from a host to a server with Option 7 set. The echo reply response from the server might spell out the route the request takes to return from the server, thus revealing the IP addresses of hosts or routers on the network that the attacker can then target. Option 4 can be used with Option 7 to record the time the echo reply packet spends between "hops" on the network. (A hop is the movement of a packet from one point on the network to another.) This information is valuable to attackers because it indicates how many routers are on the network.

Multiple-Packet Attacks

In contrast to single-packet attacks, **multiple-packet attacks** (also called "composite attacks") require a series of packets to be received and executed for the attack to be completed. These attacks are especially difficult to detect. They require a system, such as Cisco Secure IDS, to have multiple attack signatures on hand for reference. In addition, the sensor needs to maintain state information about a connection after it has been established, and it needs to keep that state information on hand for the entire length of an attack.

Denial-of-service (DoS) attacks are obvious examples of multiple-packet attacks. A type of DoS attack called an ICMP flood occurs when multiple ICMP packets are sent to a single host on a network. The result of this flood is that the server is so busy responding to the ICMP requests that other traffic cannot be processed.

Capturing Packets

4

A **packet sniffer** is software or hardware that monitors traffic going into or out of a network device. A packet sniffer captures information about each TCP/IP packet it detects. By using such an application yourself, you can study packets and identify characteristic features that tell you what type of connection is underway and whether the transmission is legitimate or suspicious.

Capturing packets and studying them can help you better understand what makes up a signature. Figure 4-1, for instance, shows a packet that was sent from one computer to another as part of a simple echo request.

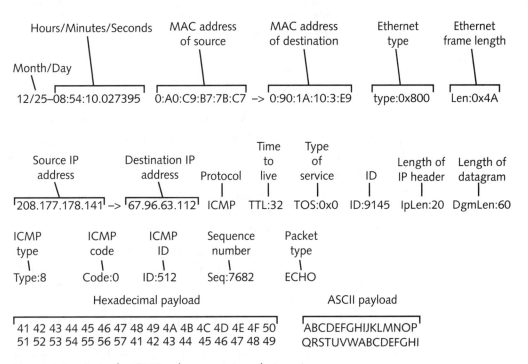

Figure 4-1   A single ICMP echo request packet capture

The lines of the packet capture have been separated so that they're easier to read and label. Normally, the lines are more crowded. The following list describes the elements in this ICMP packet:

- *Month/day*—The month and day the packet was captured; in this example, it's 12/25.

- *Hour:minute:second*—The hour, minute, and second the packet was captured. This packet-capturing software (Snort) breaks the seconds down into milliseconds, as you can see in the entry 08:54:10.027395; not all software does.

- *Media Access Control (MAC) address of source computer*—The MAC address (0:A0: C9:B7:7B:C7, in this example) of the source computer is used to identify a hardware device on a network.

- *Media Access Control (MAC) address of destination computer*—The MAC address of the computer being "pinged" (in this case, 0:90:1A:10:3:E9).

- *Ethernet type*—The type of Ethernet being used on this Internet connection. (*Note*: There are hundreds of Ethernet types. You can look up the type at *www.nswc.navy.mil/ISSEC/Docs/Ref/Networking/type.html*.)

- *Frame length*—Ethernet transmits data in fixed-length segments called frames. This value describes the length of the frame being used on this network.

- *Source IP*—The IP address of the computer that makes the connection request.

- *Destination IP*—The IP address of the computer being contacted.

- *Protocol*—The protocol used; in this case, it's Internet Control Message Protocol (ICMP), which is used to do IP error-checking and verify that computers are present on the network.

- *Time to live (TTL)*—The **time to live (TTL)** value in this example is 32 hops. Both 32 and 128 are values commonly used by Windows systems, so this TTL value indicates that the source computer is using Windows.

- *Type of service (TOS)*—The **type of service (TOS)** is a part of the packet header that can be used to express the packet's precedence—whether it should have low delay, whether it needs high reliability, and so on. No special precedence is being requested in this packet.

- *ID*—Every packet is assigned an identifying number when it is created. The **ID number** can be used to reassemble a packet in case it's divided into fragments. Looking at a sequence of packets to see how ID numbers increment from one to another can indicate the type of computer being used. ID numbers moving from packet to packet in an increment of one (from 9144 to 9155, for example) points to a Windows computer.

- *Length of IP header*—The IP length is set at 20 bytes, a length consistent with both Linux and Windows operating systems.

- *Length of datagram*—The length of the datagram (or packet) is 60 bytes, a value consistent with Windows systems. The minimum size is 21 bytes.

- *ICMP type*—ICMP has different types of messages (echo request, redirect, source quench, and so on). Type 8 indicates that this is an echo request packet.

- *ICMP code*—An 8-bit value that provides further information about some types of ICMP packets.

4

- *ID*—This is the ICMP ID number (as opposed to the packet ID number given earlier). It helps identify the ICMP packet so that the originating computer can make sure the response came from its original request.

- *Seq*—The ICMP sequence number is used to identify the ICMP packet in a sequence of packets.

- *ECHO*—This is the type of ICMP packet being sent, based on the ICMP type number.

- *Hexadecimal payload*—The **hexadecimal payload** is the actual data the packet is communicating, expressed in hexadecimal format.

- *ASCII payload*—The **ASCII payload** is the actual data part of the packet, given in ASCII format.

The information in a TCP packet contains elements that don't appear in an ICMP packet. The parts of a TCP packet that are different from the preceding ICMP packet are shown in Figure 4-2.

The following list describes the TCP-specific elements in the packet. Note that some values shown in Figure 4-2 are in hexadecimal format, such as the sequence and acknowledgement numbers.

- *Source IP address:port / Destination IP address:port*—In a TCP packet, the port being used appears after the IP address, separated by a colon.

- *Protocol*—The protocol used is TCP.

- *Flags*—In the packet shown in Figure 4-2, two TCP flags, ACK and PSH, are used together. The ACK (acknowledgement) flag indicates that a connection has been established. The PSH (push) flag indicates that data is being sent from a memory buffer to the destination computer. (The information isn't being held in a buffer—it's being sent immediately.)

- *4-byte sequence number*—This value gives the sequence number of the packet.

- *4-byte acknowledgement number*—This number acknowledges receipt of the previous packet in the sequence.

- *Window size*—This value indicates the size of the window (buffer size) on the source computer so that the recipient can determine how many packets can be sent at any one time.

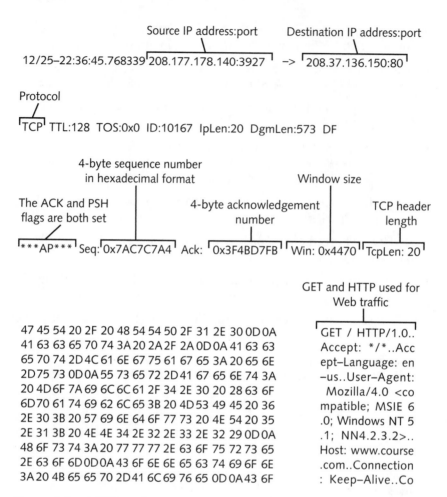

Figure 4-2   A TCP packet capture

- *TCP header length*—This value is the overall length of the TCP header plus options, if there are any.

- *GET and HTTP*—The GET method and the HTTP protocol in the ASCII payload of the data indicate that a Web server is being contacted. The HTTP headers Accept-Language, User-Agent, and Host also appear in the ASCII payload section.

The information in IDS signatures resembles the information in a packet capture. For instance, the Hack'a'Tack Trojan program mentioned previously corresponds to the signature shown in Figure 4-3. You can determine that the capture is a Trojan program because it's a recognized signature.

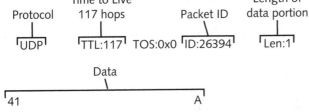

Figure 4-3   A Trojan program signature

The following list analyzes this information:

- *00/00*—A generic designation of the month and date the packet was captured.

- *23:23:23*—A generic designation of the hour, minute, and second the packet was captured. Additionally, some devices break seconds down into milliseconds.

- *attacker:31790—> target 31789*—The attacker uses port 31790 and targets the port 31789 on the destination computer.

- *UDP*—The protocol used.

- *TTL*—The TTL value represents the number of hops from one router or device to another.

- *TOS*—The type of service.

- *ID*—The ID number used by this packet; an attacker can manufacture an ID number along with other packet header information.

- *Len*—The length of the data part of the packet—only one byte, in this example.

The last line is the actual data part of the packet. In this case, the suspicious packet is distinguished by the presence of the string "A" in the payload.

A variety of software tools can be used to capture packets that pass through a computer's network interface card. In Chapter 1, you learned how to use a program called Ethereal, which is available in Windows and Linux versions. The IDS program Snort can also be used to capture packets in real time. Activity 4-1 walks you through downloading and installing Snort.

Activity 4-1: Downloading and Installing Snort

Time Required: 30 minutes

Objective: Download and install the open-source IDS program Snort.

Description: Snort is a freeware IDS program developed by Brian Caswell and Martin Roesch that's available for both Linux and Windows systems. In this activity, you download and set up the program on Windows XP. You use Snort in Activities 4-2 and 4-4 as a packet-capturing tool.

1. Start your Web browser, enter the URL **http://www.winsnort.com/modules. php?op=modload&name=Downloads&file=index&req =viewsdownload&sid=10**, and then press **Enter**.

2. Scroll down the list of files on the page, and click **Snort 2.0.0 Build 72 RELEASE Auto Installer** to download a simple version for Windows to your computer.

The Snort version you're downloading isn't the latest version, but a version that doesn't need to access a database program; in addition, it works with a GUI front-end program for testing purposes.

3. When the File Download-Security Warning dialog box opens, click **Save**. Create a folder called **Snort** at the top level of your disk drive (for example, C:\Snort or D:\Snort) where you can install the files and run them later. Then, click **Save** to begin the download.

4. When the download is finished, double-click the icon for the file you downloaded. The InstallShield Wizard starts.

5. If an Open File-Security Warning dialog box opens warning you that the publisher of this file could not be verified, click **Run** to proceed.

6. In the next window, read the license agreement, and then click **I Agree**.

7. In the Installation Options window, leave the defaults and click **Next**.

8. In the Choose Components window, accept the defaults, and then click **Next**.

9. In the Choose Install Location window, locate the Snort folder you created in Step 3, and then click **Next**.

10. When the installation is completed, click **Close** in the Installation Complete window. If you see a dialog box warning you that WinPcap is required, click **OK** and close any open windows. (*Note*: WinPcap was installed in Chapter 1.)

11. To test that the installation worked, click **Start**, point to **All Programs**, point to **Accessories**, and click **Command Prompt**.

12. At the command prompt, type **C:\Snort\bin\snort.exe –V** (substituting the path

to Snort.exe on your computer, if necessary), and press **Enter**. If the installation was successful, you see a message with the version and Snort author's name, similar to the following:

```
-*>Snort!<*- Version 2.2.2-ODBC-MySQL-WIN32 <Build 92>
By Martin Roesch...".
```

13. Leave your system running for the next activity.

4

When Snort starts, it begins to capture packets as they connect with your network interface card (NIC). When you stop the real-time packet capture by pressing Ctrl+C, the program displays a brief summary of what it found (see Figure 4-4).

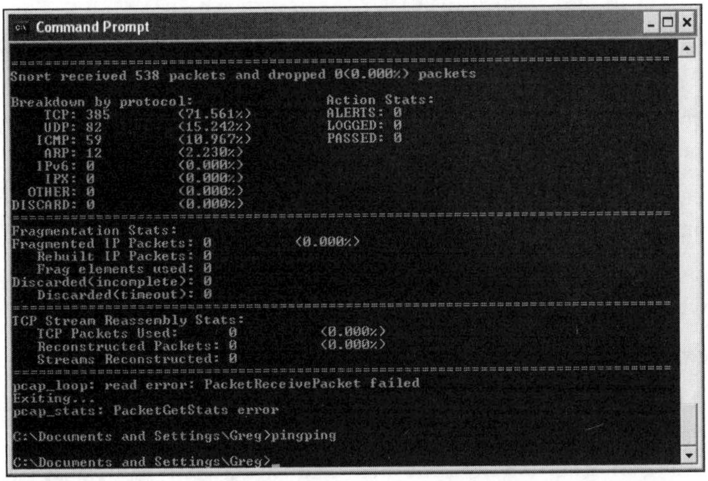

Figure 4-4 Using Snort to capture TCP and UDP packets

One problem with using Snort as a packet-capturing tool is that unless you have logging enabled, Snort doesn't retain more than a few dozen packets at a time. The packets come across the network interface so quickly that you can easily lose the opportunity to see them and, therefore, can't analyze them. Ethereal captures far more packets and stores them so that you can review them. The advantage of using Snort, however, is that you can set up intrusion alerts and block network traffic.

DETECTING TRAFFIC SIGNATURES

Now that you have learned the basics of packet captures, you need to be able to determine whether traffic is normal or suspicious. You're probably familiar with the concept of network baselining, which is the process of determining what's normal for your network before you can identify anomalies. The following sections explain how to tell the difference between normal traffic and suspicious activity.

Normal Traffic Signatures

To detect suspicious traffic signatures, being able to recognize normal traffic signatures is important. One aspect of normal TCP signatures that's easiest to identify is the use of TCP flags, as described in the following list:

- *SYN (synchronize) flag (0x2)*—This flag is sent from one computer to another when a connection is initiated; the two computers are attempting to synchronize a connection.

- *ACK (acknowledgement) flag (0x10)*—This flag is sent when the connection has been made.

- *PSH (push) flag (0x8)*—This flag indicates that immediate data delivery is required and to forward all the queued (stored in the buffer) data immediately to the destination.

- *URG (urgent) flag (0x20)*—This flag is used when urgent data is being sent from one computer to another.

- *RST (reset) flag (0x4)*—This flag is sent if one computer wants to stop the connection when there's a problem with it.

- *FIN (finished) flag (0x1)*—This flag lets one computer know that the other is finished when sending data.

- *The numbers 1 and 2*—These numbers are used for two reserved data bits.

The placement and use of these flags are definite and strictly defined, and deviations from normal use mean that the communication is suspicious. For instance, the SYN flag should appear at the beginning of a connection; the FIN flag should only appear at the end of a connection. Both the SYN and FIN flags appearing in the same packet indicates suspicious network activity. However, the ACK and PUSH flags can be used together when data is sent from one computer to another.

Ping Signatures

In the previous section, a single ICMP echo request packet was analyzed. The sequence of packets shown in Figure 4-5 shows a signature of ICMP echo request packets captured by Snort when packets are sent that "ping" two different target computers. If you examine the first line of each echo, you can see that all three packets were sent from the same computer. Two of the requests were sent to the same machine, and the third targeted a different machine. This is easy to determine from the MAC addresses of the sending (0:A0:C9:B7: 7B:C7) and receiving computers (0:90:1A:10:3:E9 and 0:10:B5:50:33:A2).

The echo request packets received did not cause a response to be sent, however. (The host computer had a firewall installed that prevented it from responding to echo request packets.) The packets exchanged when a computer *does* respond successfully to an echo request with echo reply packets are shown in Figure 4-6. Notice that both computers exchanging packets have a unique set of sequence numbers.

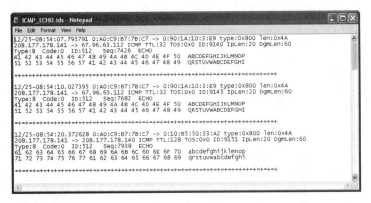

Figure 4-5   Normal signatures for ICMP echo requests

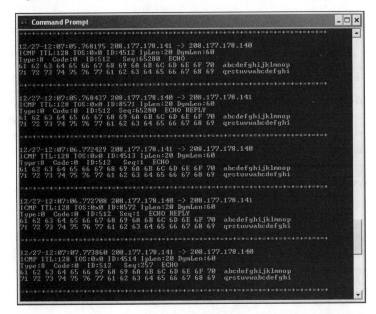

Figure 4-6   A successful exchange of ICMP echo request and echo reply packets

An analysis of the first four packets in Figure 4-6 shows the following:

1. The first packet shows the computer at IP address 208.177.178.141 sending an echo request packet (ICMP type 8) to 208.177.178.140 with the sequence number 4512 (shown in the figure as ID: 4512).

2. The second packet shows the computer at IP address 208.177.178.140 responding with an echo reply packet (ICMP type 0) with sequence number 8571.

3. The third packet shows the computer at IP address 208.177.178.141 responding with another echo request packet with sequence number 4513—only one number higher than the previous packet it sent.

4. The fourth packet shows the computer at IP address 208.177.178.140 responding with another echo reply packet with sequence number 8572.

You can also tell from examining the packets that two Windows computers are involved, as indicated by the TTL of 128, the IP length (IpLen) of 20, and the datagram length (DgmLen) of 60. A TTL of 64 and a datagram length of 84 are part of a Linux computer's signature. In addition, ICMP echo request packets start with a sequence number of 0 on a Linux computer.

TIP

The ASCII data payload section of an ICMP packet on a Windows computer consists of a sequence of alphabetic characters; in Linux, the data payload is a string of characters followed by the numerals 0 through 9 (for example, !"#$%&'()*+,-./ 0123456789).

ACTIVITY

Activity 4-2: Using Snort to Capture ICMP Packets

Time Required: 15 minutes

Objective: Use Snort to capture ICMP packets for examination.

Description: For this activity, you need two computers connected to one another through the same network or on the Internet. One student should sit at one computer with Snort installed (as described in Activity 4-1) to capture packets. The other should sit at the second computer to send echo request packets. Both computers can use Linux or Windows XP. Make sure no firewall rules are set up that block ICMP traffic (such as the ICMP rules applied by Windows XP's built-in Windows Firewall). Remember that switches are case-sensitive when using the command line.

NOTE

For the version of Snort used in these activities to work correctly, you must have WinPcap 3.0 installed before running Snort. If you have another version installed from Chapter 1, you need to uninstall it, and then locate install WinPcap 3.0. At the time of this writing, WinPcap 3.0 could be obtained at *www.winpcap.org/archive/*. Scroll down to the 3.0 WinPcap.exe link and click start the installation. Follow the instructions, accepting the defaults, to complete the installation.

1. Both students should open a command prompt window. In Windows, click **Start**, point to **All Programs**, point to **Accessories**, and click **Command Prompt**. In Linux, click the **Red Hat** icon, click **System Tools**, and click **Terminal**.

2. Both students should type **ipconfig** (**ifconfig** for Linux) at the command prompt, and then press **Enter**.

3. Each student should write down the IP address of his or her computer and exchange it with the other student.

4. Student 1 (at the computer with Snort installed) should locate the Snort.exe program and write down the path leading to it. (These steps use the path C:\Snort\bin\snort.exe as an example; replace it with your own directory path.)

5. At the command prompt, Student 1 should type **C:\Snort\bin\snort.exe –v –d** (substituting the path leading to Snort.exe on his or her computer, if necessary), and then press **Enter**. (*Note*: Be sure to leave a blank space before each hyphen in the command.)

6. Student 2 should make sure Student 1 is ready, and then type **ping *IP address of Student 1's computer***, and press **Enter**.

7. When packets begin to appear in the command prompt window, Student 1 should press **Ctrl+C** quickly to stop them. Ideally, Student 1 should stop the packet capture after only a few packets have crossed the network interface card so that they can be reviewed from the beginning. (*Note*: If packet captures do not appear, try removing and reinstalling WinPcap.)

8. If necessary, repeat Steps 6 and 7 to stop the packet capture near the beginning of the communication. What are the sequence numbers of the packets the two computers exchanged? Record your answer here:

9. Leave your system running for the next activity.

FTP Signatures

If your organization operates a public FTP server, you'll be called on to review the signatures of packets that attempt to access that server. You need to determine whether the computer making the connection attempt is actually allowed to access the server in accordance with your packet-filtering rules.

The signature of a normal connection between a client and an FTP server includes a three-way handshake. Three separate packets contain different TCP flags that enable you to keep track of the connection, as shown in Figure 4-7.

The packets shown in Figure 4-7 can be analyzed as follows:

1. In the first packet, the computer at IP address 208.177.178.140, port 3118 attempts to connect to the FTP server at 207.155.252.72, port 21. The third line shows that the packet has the SYN flag (S) set because a synchronization request is being made to the remote server. In the fourth line, the TCP option code 4 (maximum segment size, MSS) is set at 1460 bytes. This tells the FTP server the maximum IP packet size it can handle without fragmenting the packet.

2. In the second packet, the FTP server responds to the client by sending a packet with the ACK flag (A) as well as the SYN (S) set.

3. In the third packet, the client responds with a packet that has the ACK flag (A) set.

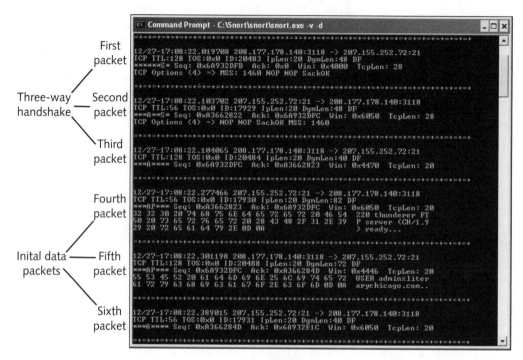

Figure 4-7 An FTP session's three-way handshake followed by initial data exchange packets

4. In the fourth packet, the ACK and PSH (A and P) flags are set, and client and server identify one another. In the packet's ASCII data payload section, the server identifies itself as ready.

5. In the fifth packet, the user's logon name appears in cleartext in the ASCII data payload section.

6. In the sixth packet, the FTP server responds with the ACK flag (A), and the connection is established.

The maximum segment size (MSS) is specified early in the handshake between client and server—specifically, as part of the SYN or SYN/ACK packets that are part of the three-way handshake. The MSS option in an ACK or ACK/PSH packet can be taken as a warning sign of a falsified packet. The NOP (no operation) TCP option provides several bytes worth of padding (in other words, unused space) around other options. A Selective Acknowledgement OK (SackOK) message follows at the end of line 4 of the packet. This means that **selective acknowledgements** (acknowledgements that certain packets in a sequence have been received) are permitted during this connection.

When data is actually exchanged between client and FTP server, the original ports are not used. In this case, the server port 21 and client port 3118 are ports that initiate a **control connection** (an initial FTP connection). The data is transferred over a new connection using server port 20 and a client port, such as 5005, as shown in Figure 4-8.

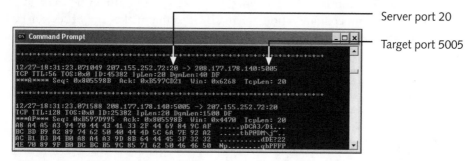

Server port 20

Target port 5005

Figure 4-8 An FTP data connection

NOTE

The options in FTP handshake packets are the same, but they are presented in a different order. That's not, however, an indication of a malformed packet; TCP options can be presented in any order.

ACTIVITY

Activity 4-3: Analyzing an Echo Request

Time Required: 15 minutes

Objective: Analyze captured echo request packets to determine information about the sending computer.

Description: Your firewall regularly receives a series of echo request packets from a computer at 67.118.23.141. You capture the packets with a packet-sniffing tool and notice the following characteristics: DgmLen 84, ID 0, TTL 64. Answer the following questions:

1. What kind of computer is being used to send echo requests to your network?

   _____

   _____

2. What other criteria could you use to identify the computer being used?

   _____

   _____

   _____

   _____

Web Signatures

Most of the signatures you see in log files you analyze are usually Web related. When a signature is Web related, that means it consists of packets sent back and forth from a Web browser to a Web server as a connection is made. A signature of a normal handshake between two Web browsers consists of a sequence of packets distinguished by their TCP flags. As mentioned in the preceding section, normal TCP traffic makes use of several TCP flags to control the connection. Being aware of these flags and where they're used can help you determine whether a signature is normal or part of a possible intrusion attempt.

In Figure 4-9, you see four packets that represent part of the handshake between the Web browser at IP address 208.177.178.140, using port 3927, and the Web server 208.37.136.150, using HTTP port 80.

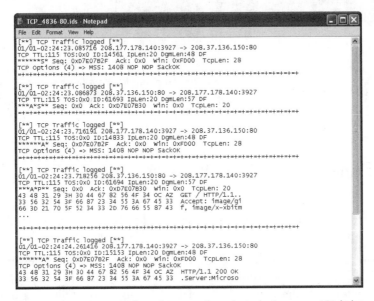

Figure 4-9   A normal exchange of packets between a Web browser and a Web server

The packets you see in Figure 4-9 can be broken down as follows:

1. The first packet has the SYN flag set (the S in the third line), as the browser asks to synchronize a session with the server.

2. The second packet has the ACK flag set, as the server acknowledges the connection with the browser. In addition, the SYN flag is sent back to the browser as the server seeks to synchronize the connection with the browser.

3. In the third packet, the ACK flag is exchanged to acknowledge that a connection has been made.

4. In the fourth packet, the PSH flag is used with the ACK flag to indicate that data is going to be sent (or pushed) from memory storage areas called buffers.

Activity 4-4: Capturing a Web Site Handshake

Time Required: 20 minutes

Objective: Use Snort to capture a Web site connection handshake for examination.

Description: Capturing the sequence of a Web site connection with Snort enables you to inspect the HTTP headers in each packet and the TCP flags exchanged during the handshake. You can use a Linux or Windows XP computer; this activity assumes that you have Snort installed and a Web browser and your lab computer is connected to the Internet.

1. In Windows, click **Start**, point to **All Programs**, point to **Accessories**, and click **Command Prompt**. In Linux, click the **Red Hat** icon, click **System Tools**, and click **Terminal**.

2. At the command prompt, type **C:\Snort\bin\snort.exe –v –d** (substituting the path leading to Snort.exe on your computer, if necessary), and then press **Enter**.

3. When you see a message stating that Snort is initializing, start your Web browser, enter the URL **http://www.course.com**, and press **Enter**.

4. Quickly switch back to the command prompt window and press **Ctrl+C** to stop the packets from being captured. Snort should display a brief report of the packets captured so far. Besides TCP packets, what sorts of packets were captured? Record your answer here:

   _____

   _____

5. Scroll to the top of the packets shown in the command prompt window, and look for the SYN, SYN/ACK, ACK three-way handshake. (If you don't see it, you might need to connect to a different Web site and repeat Steps 3 and 4.)

6. Close any open windows, and leave your system running for the next activity.

Now that you know something about capturing normal traffic, you can look at analyzing more suspicious signatures.

Suspicious Traffic Signatures

As IDS becomes more widespread and sophisticated, the techniques attackers use to circumvent them have multiplied and become more complex. Features such as illegal combinations of TCP flags and private IP addresses in packets are relatively easy to identify as abnormal compared with attacks that work by a range of packets. Suspicious traffic signatures can fall into one of these categories:

- *Informational*—This traffic might not be malicious but could be used to verify whether an attack has been successful. Examples include ICMP echo request packets or TCP packets sent to a specific port on a specific system.

- *Reconnaissance*—This traffic could represent an attacker's attempt to gain information about a network as a prelude to an attack. Examples include ping sweeps and port scans.

- *Unauthorized access*—This traffic might be caused by someone who has gained unauthorized access to a system and is attempting to retrieve data from it. Examples include the BackOrifice attack and the Internet Information Services Unicode attack.

- *Denial of service*—This traffic might be part of an attempt to slow or halt all connections on a network device, such as a Web server or mail server. Denial-of-service examples include the ping of death attack and Trinoo attack.

Some common examples of suspicious traffic—ping sweeps, port scans, random back door scans, and Trojan scans—are described in the following sections along with their signatures.

NOTE If you need to review specific attacks or attack methods, such as BackOrifice, Internet Information Services Unicode, sweeps, port scans, and ping of death attacks, run a search on your favorite Internet search engine. It's a good idea to review these attacks because variations of them surface from time to time.

Ping Sweeps

To gain access to specific resources on an internal network, a hacker needs to determine the location of a host. One way to do this is to conduct a **ping sweep** (also called an ICMP sweep)—to send a series of ICMP echo request packets in a range of IP addresses. Usually, the messages come in quick succession (multiple packets can be detected in a single second), indicating that an automated tool is being used. An example of a ping sweep is shown in Figure 4-10. Be sure to examine the PING times in the first line; this sweep took place over a period of about 14 seconds.

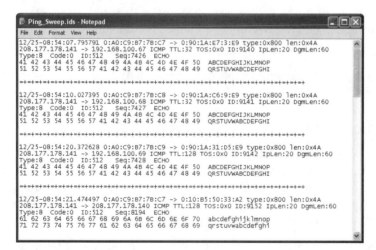

Figure 4-10 A log file record displaying the signature of an automated ping sweep

The ping sweep alone doesn't cause harm to computers on your network. The prudent response is to make note of the IP address used in the ping sweep to track further activity.

An IDS could be configured to transmit an alarm if the IP address in question attempts to connect to a specific host on the network, for instance.

Port Scans

If an attacker is able to determine any legitimate IP addresses on an internal network, the next step is to target one of those IP addresses and perform a **port scan**—an attempt to connect to a computer's ports to see whether any are active and listening. The signature of a port scan typically includes a SYN packet sent to each port on an IP address, one after another, as shown in Figure 4-11.

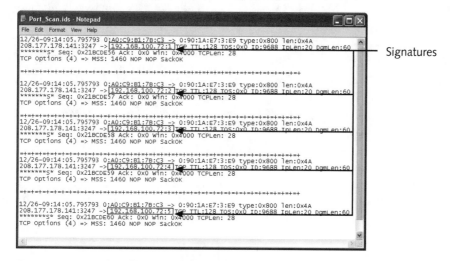

Figure 4-11   A log file record displaying the signatures of a port scan

In the example in Figure 4-11, the source port (3247) doesn't change from packet to packet. This indicates that the attacker isn't expecting the target computer to establish a full three-way connection but wants to find out whether the IP address is being used. In another type of port scan, the source *and* destination ports change with each packet because a full three-way connection is expected.

Random Back Door Scans

You can think of a port as a virtual door through which data can enter and leave a computer. In that context, a back door can be thought of as an undocumented or unauthorized hidden opening (such as a port) through which a computer, program, or other resource can be accessed. One type of port scan probes a computer to see if any ports are open and listening that are used by well-known Trojan programs—applications that seem to be harmless but can cause harm to a computer or its files.

Some Trojan programs are so well known that the "back door" ports on which they operate can be probed one after another to see whether any of those applications are already present.

For example, a random back door scan might target certain ports and subsequently seek to exploit the programs listed in Table 4-2.

Table 4-2 Well-known Trojan programs and ports

Trojan Horse Name	Port Used	Description
SubSeven	1243	Disables antivirus or firewall protection
NetBus	1245	Gives Trojan progam author remote access to the user's computer
Back Door	1999	Gives Trojan program author remote access to the user's computer
KeyLogger	12223	Copies user keystrokes and sends information about the user's OS and passwords back to Trojan program's sender
Whack-a-mole	12361	Gives Trojan program author remote access to the user's computer
Back Orifice	31337, 31338	A scanner that records keystrokes and sends passwords back to the Trojan program author; can also be used to run programs on a computer

A random **Trojan scan** involves an attacker searching for any Trojan programs present on a target computer to save the effort of installing these programs from scratch. Each SYN packet that's sent attempts to contact a different port used by a Trojan, such as the sequence of packets shown in Figure 4-12. (The ports being probed have been outlined in the figure for clarity.)

Figure 4-12 A log file record showing the signatures of a back door scan

If you see this type of scan in your log files, you need to take action quickly to block the source IP address because it's likely that specific attacks will take place in the near future. Blocking specific IP addresses, subnets, or address ranges is discussed in Chapters 9, 10, and 11.

Specific Trojan Scans

Port scans can be performed in several ways. In a **vanilla scan**, all ports from 0 to 65,535 are probed one after another. In another type of scan, sometimes called a **strobe scan**, an attacker scans only ports commonly used by specific programs in an attempt to see whether a certain program is present and can be used.

One common type of strobe scan searches IP addresses on a network for the presence of a specific Trojan program. If attackers can find a Trojan program that has already circumvented the firewall and IDS and is already operating, they can save the time and effort of installing a new Trojan program. For instance, in Figure 4-13, a series of IP addresses is being scanned on port 31337. This port is used by the notorious BackOrifice Trojan program as well as other Trojans, such as ADM worm, Back Fire, and BlitzNet.

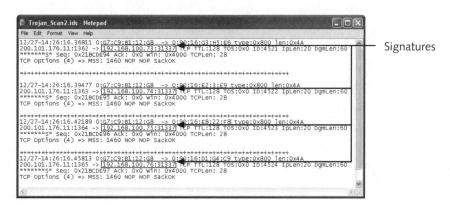

Signatures

Figure 4-13   A log file record indicating a scan for the BackOrifice Trojan program

The type of scan shown in Figure 4-13 is not necessarily dangerous, but it's worthy of some concern because it's so specific. Attackers typically start with a general scan of IP addresses and get progressively more specific as they look for ports, back doors, or individual applications. If an attacker has received an indication from another method (such as an exchange of e-mail messages) that the BackOrifice program might be present on the network, the attacker might locate BackOrifice, and an attack using the program could be imminent. You should immediately scan all computers on your network for viruses and Trojans and make sure the Trojan signatures your antivirus program, firewall, or IDS use are up to date.

Antivirus software and many IDSs share a commonality: They both look for known signatures, whether they're virus or attack signatures. In addition, both require up-to-date signature files to operate at peak efficiency.

NOTE

TIP

Another specific Trojan scan might target port 12345, which is used by the NetBus Trojan and, like port 31337, is familiar to security professionals because it appears so often in security alerts and lists of frequently used Trojan ports.

Nmap Scans

Network Mapper (Nmap) is a popular software tool for scanning networks, and you should be able to recognize the common types of scans it enables attackers to perform. With Nmap, attackers can send packets that circumvent the normal three-way handshakes two computers use to establish a connection. Nmap enables attackers to send packets for which an IDS might not be configured to send an alarm. The IDS might see a combination of TCP flags that it doesn't recognize, and because no rule exists for the combination, an alarm might not be triggered. Examples of Nmap scans include the following:

- *SYN scans*—The attacker sends a progression of packets with only the SYN flag set. The targeted computer responds with packets that have the ACK flag set, but the originating computer simply keeps sending SYN packets.

- *FIN scans*—The attacker sends only packets that have the FIN flag set; a SYN flag is never sent.

- *ACK scans*—The attacker sends only packets with the ACK flag set; a SYN or FIN flag is never sent.

- *Null scans*—The attacker sends a sequence of packets that have no flags set. An IDS is likely to ignore packets with no flags set.

In each case, a three-way handshake can never be established with the computer attempting to make a connection. It's likely the attacker is attempting to determine whether an application is active on a particular port: Each packet has an identical source port number and a seq (sequence) number that's set to zero and never changes, in violation of the standard rules of TCP communications. Figure 4-14 shows a FIN scan with the seq numbers, source port numbers, and F (FIN) flags enclosed in boxes to indicate the elements you should look for in this Nmap signature.

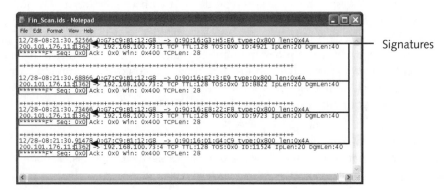

Figure 4-14 The signatures of a FIN scan conducted with Nmap

In this example, the constant source port numbers, seq numbers, and F flag in every packet point to the use of Nmap in crafting these packets.

Activity 4-5: Identifying an Nmap Scan

4

Time Required: 10 minutes

Objective: Analyze a scenario to identify the characteristics of an Nmap port scan.

Description: Normally, you review IDS logs for intrusion attempts by setting your IDS to log connection attempts that were blocked or for which an alarm was issued. By mistake, someone on your IT staff sets the IDS to log connection attempts that were allowed, too. The log file you need to review is huge, as a result. To reduce the file size, you sort out traffic from computers on your own network and from your DNS server. When you review the entries that are left, you notice by chance a series of hundreds of packets that were sent in sequence and have no flags set. The IDS didn't detect these packets because apparently they're of no value in making a network connection. Answer the following questions:

1. What clues would you look for in these packets to determine whether they're evidence that an attacker is attempting to gain information about open ports on your network?

   _____

   _____

2. What should you do if you determine that such an attempt has been made?

   _____

   _____

   _____

   _____

You can find out more about Nmap and how the program can be used to scan a network at *www.insecure.org/nmap*.

TIP

IDENTIFYING SUSPICIOUS EVENTS

The previous section described well-known attack signatures you might encounter when inspecting your IDS log files. Unfortunately, attackers often avoid launching such well-known attacks. Instead, they use more subtle means to try to gain unauthorized access to computers in your network. For instance, instead of the sequence of FIN packets described previously, you might see only a single FIN packet sent to a port on a computer. Other "orphaned" packets might follow, but only after an interval during which a substantial number of legitimate packets have passed through. The use of an interval acts as a distraction during which stages of the attack are separated from one another, so an administrator might not realize that they're part of the same attack.

These attacks can be extremely difficult to detect by reviewing log files manually. It's your responsibility to respond to alarms and determine what they mean, however, so the logs must be examined regularly. Log files can fill up quickly with so many entries that they are overwhelming to review, and you might miss important entries. Fortunately, there are ways around the tedious chore of poring through thousands of log entries looking for known attack signatures or other abnormal signatures. Instead, you need to depend on an extensive database of signatures that includes these events.

This section describes events and characteristics of network communications that you need to identify as suspicious events after your IDS has responded to them by transmitting an alarm. The discussion includes packet header discrepancies, advanced IDS attacks, and Remote Procedure Calls (RPC) abuses.

CAUTION IDS alarms for the suspicious events described in this section might indicate that your packet filter isn't working effectively (because it has let suspicious packets pass through to reach the IDS). As a result, the packet filter's rule base needs to be revised. You can also fine-tune how an IDS device responds to events. Advanced IDS configuration is covered in detail in Chapters 7 and 8.

Packet Header Discrepancies

Discrepancies you see in TCP, IP, ICMP, or UDP packet headers can provide warning signs indicating that an attacker has crafted the packet (in other words, purposely manufactured or altered it). However, instead of seeing these discrepancies on a well-defined and lengthy succession of packets, you might receive only a single packet with a falsified IP address, falsified port number, illegal TCP flags, TCP or IP options, or fragmentation abuses.

Falsified IP Address

Your IDS might send alarms for violations of IP header settings as specified in RFC 791, "Internet Protocol." For example, an IP address should not appear in one of the three reserved ranges (10.0.0.0 to 10.255.255.255, 172.16.0.0 to 172.31.255.255, and 192.168.0.0 to 192.168.255.255). The use of addresses in the reserved ranges is limited to private networks. If you do see one in a packet, the reason might be that a router or other device has been misconfigured or is malfunctioning. On the other hand, the packet might show one of the private addresses because an attacker has used **IP spoofing** (in other words, inserted a false address into the IP header to make the packet more difficult to trace back to its source).

TIP For more information about the correct use of private IP addresses, refer to RFC 1918, "Address Allocation for Private Internets," at *www.faqs.org/rfcs/rfc1918.html.*

A land attack is an example of a falsified IP address used to cause a server to malfunction. It occurs when an IP packet is detected that has an invalid IP address setting in which the source and destination IP/port addresses are the same. Another attack that uses an invalid IP address, the localhost source spoof, should trigger an alarm if the local host source address of 127.x.x.x occurs in a packet.

Falsified Port Number or Protocol

You already know that IP address information can be falsified in a packet, but protocol numbers might also be altered to elude an IDS. TCP and UDP headers should never have the source or destination port set to 0 because this number is reserved by IANA. IANA assigns protocol numbers in addition to port numbers. The Protocol field (IPv4; in IPv6, the field is called Next Header) is an 8-bit field used to specify the transport protocol, such as ICMP (#1), TCP (#6), or UDP (#17). Currently, the protocol number can't be set higher than 137. The numbers 138 to 252 are unassigned, 253 and 254 are used for experimentation and testing, and 255 is reserved. The use of undefined protocol numbers might indicate an attacker's attempt to establish a proprietary communications channel, which is a channel that's known to and used only by that person.

Illegal TCP Flags

As you learned in "Normal Traffic Signatures" earlier in this chapter, the TCP flags SYN and ACK are exchanged to establish a connection between two computers. The PSH flag is used when data is being sent, and the FIN flag is used when a connection is complete. Other normal TCP flag rules include the following:

- Every packet in a connection should have the ACK bit set, except for the initial SYN packet and possibly an RST packet used to terminate a connection.

- Packets during the "conversation" portion of the connection (after the three-way handshake but before the teardown or termination) contain only an ACK flag by default. Optionally, they can also contain PSH and/or URG flags.

- FIN/ACK and ACK are used during the normal teardown of an existing connection. PSH, FIN, and ACK might also be seen near the end of a connection.

- RST or RST/ACK can be used to terminate a connection immediately.

One of the most obvious ways to detect an abnormal packet signature is to look at the TCP flags for violations of normal usage. A packet with the SYN and FIN flags set should not exist in normal traffic; however, an attacker might set both flags to cause the destination computer to crash or freeze because it doesn't know how to respond. After the server is disabled, the attacker can then attack a computer on the internal network with an IP address that has been detected earlier through network scans.

The following list summarizes signatures of malformed packets that misuse the SYN and FIN flags:

- SYN/FIN is probably the best-known illegal combination. Because SYN is used to start a connection and FIN is used to end a connection, it doesn't make sense to include both flags together in a packet. Many scanning tools use SYN/FIN packets because in the past, many IDSs weren't configured to recognize or block them. However, most IDSs are configured to catch illegal combinations now. It's safe to assume that any SYN/FIN packets you see are created by attackers.

- SYN/FIN/PSH, SYN/FIN/RST, SYN/FIN/RST/PSH, and other variations on SYN/FIN exist, and their use is sometimes called an XMAS attack. These packets can be used by attackers who are aware that IDSs might be looking for packets with just the SYN and FIN bits set.

- Packets should never contain a FIN flag by itself. FIN packets are often used for port scans, network mapping, and other stealth activities.

- A SYN-only packet, which should occur only when a new connection is being initiated, shouldn't contain any data.

Null sessions were discussed in Chapter 1, and you might also encounter **null packets**—TCP packets with no flags set, which could cause a server to crash. It's a violation of TCP rules to use a packet with no flags set.

TCP or IP Options

TCP options in a packet can alert you to intrusion attempts and even enable you to identify the type of OS being used. For instance, only one MSS or window option should appear in a packet. MSS, NOP, and SackOK should appear only in packets that have the SYN and/or ACK flag set. Additionally, TCP packets have two "reserved bits." Any packet that uses either or both of the reserved bits is probably malicious. (RFC 793, the TCP Internet standard, says that the reserved field in the TCP header is for future use and must be zero.)

IP options were originally intended as ways to insert special handling instructions into packets that weren't dealt with in other header fields. However, attackers mostly use IP options now for attack attempts. Because of this vulnerability, many filters simply drop all packets with IP options set.

Fragmentation Abuses

Every type of computer network (for example, Ethernet, FDDI, or token ring) has its own **maximum transmission unit (MTU)**—the maximum packet size that can be transmitted. Packets larger than the MTU must be fragmented—broken into multiple segments small enough for the network to handle.

After a packet fragmented, each fragment receives its own IP header. However, only the initial packet in a set includes a header for higher-level protocols. Most filters need the information in the higher-level protocol header to make the decision to allow or deny. Accordingly, attackers send only secondary fragments (any fragment other than the initial one). These packets are often simply allowed past the IDS, and filter rules are applied to first fragments only.

Fragmentation can occur normally. However, an IDS should be configured to send an alarm if it encounters many fragmented packets. Several different types of fragmentation abuses can occur. Some of the more serious ones are described briefly in the following list:

- *Overlapping fragments*—Two fragments of the same packet have the same position in the packet, so the contents overlap. A correctly configured firewall should always drop this type of packet.

- *Fragments that are too long*—An IP packet can be no longer than 65,535 bytes. Packets that, when reassembled from their fragments, are larger than the maximum size might cause some systems to crash and could indicate a DoS attack.

- *Fragments overwriting data*—Some early fragments in a sequence are transmitted along with random data. Later fragments overwrite the random data. If the packet isn't reassembled correctly, the IDS can't detect the attack.

- *Fragments that are too small*—If any fragment other than the final fragment in a sequence is less than 400 bytes, it has probably been crafted intentionally. This small fragment is probably part of a DoS attack.

Advanced Attacks

Most attacks discussed so far have been protocol anomalies—violations of the protocol rules described in RFC statements. Some especially complex attacks use path names, hexadecimal codes, and obfuscated directory names to fool an IDS into letting the packet through without triggering an alarm. Some advanced IDS evasion techniques include the following:

- *Polymorphic buffer overflow attacks*—These attacks are as complicated as they sound. A tool called ADMutate is used to alter an attack's shell code in such a way that the code differs slightly from the known signatures many IDSs use. After attacking packets elude the IDS and reach their intended target, they reassemble into their original form.

- *Path obfuscation*—A directory path statement in the payload part of a packet is obfuscated by using multiple forward slashes. For example, /winnt/. /. /. / is essentially the same as /winnt. However, because the signatures don't match exactly, an IDS might be unable to detect this attack. Alternatively, to evade IDSs that have been configured to trigger alarms when they encounter multiple forward slashes, the Unicode equivalent of a forward slash, %co%af, is used.

- *CGI scripts*—A series of packets is sent to a series of well-known **Common Gateway Interface (CGI) scripts** (scripts used to process data submitted over the Internet). Examples include CGI scripts such as Count.cgi, FormMail, Any-Form, Php.cgi, TextCounter, and GuestBook. You can be certain someone is attempting to exploit your network if you don't actually have these files on your network, but packets attempt to locate them anyway. For more information on CGI scripts, visit *http://hoohoo.ncsa.uiuc.edu/cgi/overview.html*.

The only way to avoid these attacks is to keep your IDS signatures up to date and to watch your log files closely.

Remote Procedure Calls

Remote Procedure Calls (RPC) is a standard set of communication rules that allows one computer to request a service (in other words, a remote procedure) from another computer on a network. RPC uses the Portmapper service to maintain a record of each remotely accessible program and the port it uses; Portmapper converts RPC program numbers into TCP/IP port numbers. Because RPC can provide remote access to applications, attackers naturally attempt to use it to gain unauthorized access to those applications. Here are some examples of RPC-related events that should trigger IDS alarms:

- *RPC dump*—A targeted host receives an RPC dump request, which is a request to report the presence and port use of any RPC services that system provides.

- *RPC set spoof*—A targeted host receives an RPC set request from a source IP address of 127.x.x.x.

- *RPC NFS sweep*—A target host receives a series of requests for the Network File System (NFS) on a succession of different ports.

RPC services, such as Network Information System (NIS), use a four-byte service number because there are too many services to use a two-byte port number. When an RPC service starts, it allocates a random TCP or UDP port for itself. It then contacts Rpcbind or Portmapper and registers its service number and TCP/UDP port. Portmapper and Rpcbind always runs on port 111, for example. A client wanting to talk to a server contacts Portmapper first to get the port number, and then continues the exchange with the server directly. A client can bypass Portmapper and scan for services. There's no guarantee that a particular service will end up on a particular port.

NOTE

The Rpcbind daemon, a more recent implementation of Portmapper, includes all the functionality of Portmapper plus added features.

USING THE COMMON VULNERABILITIES AND EXPOSURES (CVE) STANDARD

One of the ways to prevent attacks is to make sure your security devices can share information and coordinate with one another. At the perimeter of any network, you're likely to have a variety of hardware and software devices that provide security and that need to work cooperatively with one another. You might have a router from one vendor, a firewall from another, and an IDS from a third. Unfortunately, the way they interpret signatures might differ. They probably address the same known attacks but give them different names and describe their characteristics differently. The **Common Vulnerabilities and Exposures (CVE)** standard enables these devices to share information about attack signatures and other vulnerabilities so that they can work together.

How the CVE Works

CVE enables hardware and security devices that support it to draw from the same databases of vulnerabilities, which are presented in the same standard format. For instance, a **scanner** (a device that scans a network for open ports or other potential vulnerabilities) that supports CVE compiles a report listing weak points in the system. When an alarm message is transmitted by an IDS that also supports CVE, the attack signature can be compared to the report of current vulnerabilities to see whether an attack has actually occurred (see Figure 4-15).

In Figure 4-15, the CVE standard has an impact on many different parts of a network:

1. A possible attack is detected by an IDS sensor.

2. The signature is checked against the database of known attack signatures available to the IDS to see whether a match is found. If the IDS being used is also CVE compliant, the report on the attack contains information on known network vulnerabilities associated with the attack signature.

3. The list of vulnerabilities is compared against a database of current vulnerable points in the system that have been compiled and stored by a CVE-compliant scanner to determine whether this possible attack can have an impact on the network.

4. Periodically, the list of vulnerabilities is updated with new entries from the CVE vulnerability Web site.

5. The manufacturers of CVE-compliant applications generate patches and updates in response to vulnerabilities, and those patches can then be applied to applications on the network.

Great benefits (such as stronger security and better performance) result from all the security devices on a network understanding and using information that complies with the CVE standard. If you're in a position to purchase IDSs or other equipment for your organization, you should make sure they support CVE.

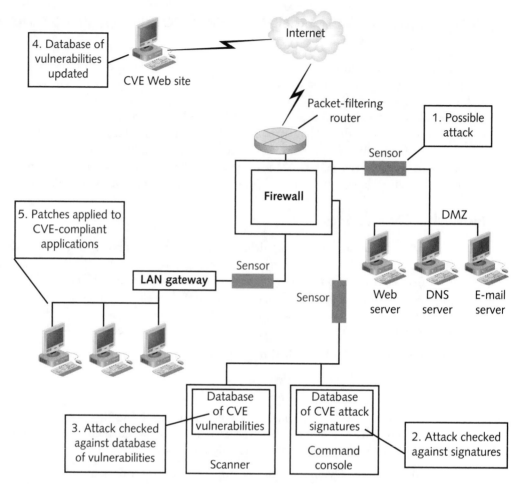

Figure 4-15   CVE enables multiple security devices to share information

The CVE standard is a cooperative effort. Mitre maintains the database of vulnerabilities at *www.cve.mitre.org*, which you should have bookmarked in Chapter 1.

NOTE

Scanning CVE Vulnerability Descriptions

You can go online to view current CVE vulnerabilities and even download the list so that you can review it at your convenience. Keep in mind, however, that as Mitre points out, the CVE list is not a vulnerability database that can be used with an IDS. It's simply an informational tool. CVE listings are brief and simply refer to listings in other databases; they don't contain IP addresses, protocol listings, or other characteristics of an event that qualify it as a signature. When you look at a CVE reference, you see the following:

- The name of the vulnerability
- A short description
- References to the event in other databases, such as BUGTRAQ

The number associated with a CVE listing tells you when the listing was made. For instance, CVE-2004-0221 tells you that this listing was made in 2004 and was number 221 for that year. The listing shown in Figure 4-16 was the 237th listing for 2004.

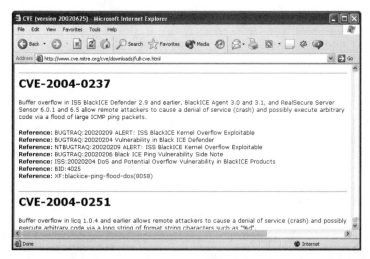

Figure 4-16   A CVE listing for a buffer overflow vulnerability that affects IDS software

The listing in Figure 4-16 indicates that vulnerabilities can affect IDS software, as well as other types of applications. A **CAN** is a candidate for inclusion in the CVE list and follows the same naming format as CVE. All CANs must be reviewed and accepted by the CVE Editorial Board before they can be added to CVE. The CVE numbering system was updated in October 2005 to replace the CAN prefix with a CVE prefix. The new numbering system includes a status line indicating whether the CVE name has a Candidate, Entry, or Deprecated status. Only the status line of a CVE is updated when new CVE versions are released. You can view vulnerability listings like the one in Figure 4-16 at *www.cve.mitre.org/cve/downloads/full-allitems.html*, or you can use CVE's search engine to look for specific vulnerabilities.

ACTIVITY

Activity 4-6: Discovering Traffic Signature Vulnerabilities

Time Required: 30 minutes

Objective: Use the CVE Web site to discover traffic signature vulnerabilities.

Description: In this activity, you search the CVE Web site for traffic signature vulnerabilities so that you can determine whether your traffic analysis is susceptible to flaws.

1. From your Windows XP Professional system, start your Web browser, type **www.cve.mitre.org** in the Address text box, and press **Enter**.

2. Scroll down the Common Vulnerabilities and Exposures (CVE) home page, and click the **search CVE** icon.

3. In the Search CVE dialog box, type **traffic signatures** in the Keyword(s) text box, and click **Search**. How many CVE entries did you find?

4. CVE-2000-0113 pertains to the SyGate Remote Management program. Click this entry and read the information. Should all SyGate users be concerned about this candidate?

5. Click the **Back** button on your browser to return to the page of entries, and click the **CAN-2004-0593** entry. What significance does it have, if any, for the internal network?

6. If time permits, read other CVE or CAN entries. When you're finished, close your Web browser.

CHAPTER SUMMARY

❏ Interpreting the signatures of normal and abnormal network traffic can help prevent network intrusions. Recognizing the characteristics of a possible intrusion makes it possible to interpret and react effectively to log files and alert messages.

❏ You can adjust filter rules to reduce the number of false alarms you receive from your IDS. More importantly, you can prevent intrusions before they occur or keep intrusions that are already underway from causing excessive damage.

❏ The analysis of traffic signatures is an integral aspect of intrusion prevention. A signature is a set of characteristics, such as IP addresses, port numbers, TCP flags, and options. Normal traffic makes valid use of these settings.

❏ Possible intrusions are marked by invalid settings. Invalid settings can include bad header information, suspicious contents in the data payload of packets, IP options settings, and a succession of packets, such as a denial-of-service attempt.

❏ You can set up the open-source IDS Snort as a packet sniffer to capture packets and study their contents. Parts of the packet header, such as the datagram length, can indicate whether a Windows or Linux system is being used. TCP flags are used in sequence to create a normal three-way handshake between two computers.

▫ By learning what normal traffic signatures look like, you can identify signatures of suspicious connection attempts. You can monitor suspicious events, such as ping sweeps, port scans, random back door scans, and Trojan scans. You should also be familiar with the characteristics of packets crafted with Nmap.

▫ You can identify a variety of other suspicious network events, including "orphaned" packets, land attacks (in which the source and destination IP/port addresses are the same), localhost source spoofs, falsified protocol numbers, and illegal combinations of TCP flags, such as SYN/FIN.

▫ Advanced attacks are especially difficult to detect without a database of intrusion signatures or user behaviors. Certain complex attacks, called polymorphic buffer overflow attacks, can be altered so that they don't match a known intrusion signature and elude the IDS. Others use confusing path names or other keywords in the data payload section of packets.

▫ Another advanced attack method might include attempts to connect with and abuse common CGI scripts that might be present or misuse Remote Procedure Calls that enable remote users to access services on a computer.

▫ Network security hardware and software should work cooperatively to share information. A standard called Common Vulnerabilities and Exposures (CVE) enables IDSs, firewalls, and other devices to share attack signatures and information about network vulnerabilities so that they can better protect networks. Mitre maintains a list of current vulnerabilities as an online database, and you can use the list to update your own CVE database and learn about new attacks.

Key Terms

ASCII payload — The actual data part of the packet, given in ASCII format.

CAN — A prefix the CVE Web site uses to identify candidate vulnerabilities. As of October 2005, this prefix was replaced with "CVE," and a vulnerability's status is noted as Entry, Candidate, or Deprecated.

Common Gateway Interface (CGI) scripts — Scripts used to process data submitted over the Internet.

Common Vulnerabilities and Exposures (CVE) — A standard that enables security devices to share information about attack signatures and other vulnerabilities so that they can work together to provide network protection.

control connection — An initial FTP connection between client and server.

hexadecimal payload — The actual data the packet is communicating, expressed in hexadecimal format.

ID number — For packets in general, it's an identifying number that can be used to reassemble a packet in case it's divided into fragments. For ICMP packets, it identifies the ICMP packet so that the originating computer can make sure the response came from its original request.

IP spoofing — The process of inserting a false address into the IP header to make the packet more difficult to trace back to its source.

maximum transmission unit (MTU) — The maximum packet size that can be transmitted over a type of computer network, such as an Ethernet network.

multiple-packet attacks — Attacks that require a series of packets to be transmitted for the attack to be completed.

null packets — TCP packets with no flags set.

packet sniffer — Software or hardware that monitors traffic going into or out of a network device and captures information about each TCP/IP packet it detects.

ping sweep — The act of sending a series of ICMP echo request packets in a range of IP addresses to see whether any computers respond.

port scan — An attempt to connect to a computer's ports to see if any are active and listening.

Remote Procedure Calls (RPC) — A standard set of communication rules that allows one computer to request a service from another computer on a network.

scanner — A device that scans a network for open ports or other potential vulnerabilities.

selective acknowledgements — Acknowledgements that selected packets in a sequence have been received; this process is in contrast to having to acknowledge every packet.

signature — A set of characteristics—such as IP numbers and options, TCP flags, and port numbers—used to define a type of network activity.

signature analysis — The practice of analyzing and understanding TCP/IP communications to determine whether traffic is legitimate or suspicious.

single-packet attack — An attack that can be completed by sending a single network packet from client to host.

strobe scan — A type of port scan that probes ports that are commonly used by specific programs, in an attempt to see if such a program is presented and can be utilized.

time to live (TTL) — An instruction that tells a router how long a packet should remain on the network before it's discarded.

Trojan scan — A type of port scan that looks for active Trojan programs that have already circumvented security measures and are running on the scanned system. If attackers can find one already installed, they can use it instead of having to install a new one.

type of service (TOS) — The part of a packet header that can be used to express a packet's precedence—whether it should have low delay, whether it needs high reliability, and so on.

vanilla scan — A type of port scan in which all ports from 0 to 65,535 are probed, one after another.

REVIEW QUESTIONS

1. Security devices on a network process digital information, such as text files and Web pages, the same way. However, which of the following information might they handle differently?

   a. protocols

   b. TCP/IP headers

   c. attack signatures

   d. port numbers

2. In which of the following can CVE improve the coordination of intrusion information on a network? (Choose all that apply.)

   a. Attack signatures can be compared to the lists of known attack signatures published on the CVE Web site.

   b. Attack signatures can be compared to current network topology.

   c. Installing application patches can thwart an attack report.

   d. Current network vulnerabilities can be used to generate application patches.

3. Which of the following can be included in a network traffic signature? (Choose all that apply.)

   a. logon attempts

   b. message digest

   c. TCP options

   d. Ethernet interface number

4. What is the name of an error-checking procedure that uses a formula to calculate a numeric value?

   a. check string

   b. one-way hash

   c. hexadecimal code

   d. checksum

5. How do attackers use fragmentation to circumvent network defenses? (Choose all that apply.)

   a. Fragments are too large or too small.

   b. The initial packet is missing.

   c. Multiple initial packets are sent.

   d. The final fragment sent is less than 400 bytes long.

4

6. Which of the following packets should never have a data payload?

   a. one with SYN/ACK flags set

   b. one with the ACK flag set

   c. one with the SYN flag set

   d. one with ACK/PSH flags set

7. Which of the following is not required for a single-packet attack? (Choose all that apply.)

   a. a source IP address

   b. a destination IP address

   c. an ICMP echo request

   d. an established connection

8. Which of the following is an example of a multiple-packet attack? (Choose all that apply.)

   a. ping of death

   b. ICMP flood

   c. false Internet timestamp

   d. a packet with SYN/FIN/ACK flags set

9. Which of the following time to live (TTL) values is commonly used by Windows computers? (Choose all that apply.)

   a. 128

   b. 64

   c. 32

   d. 60

10. What is the purpose of the 4-byte acknowledgement number in a TCP header?

    a. It acknowledges receipt of the previous packet in the sequence.

    b. It acknowledges that a connection has been made.

    c. It verifies that the source and destination IP addresses are correct.

    d. It acknowledges the ID number the packet is using.

11. Which of the following is the correct order in which TCP flags appear in the course of a normal connection?

    a. SYN, ACK, FIN, RST

    b. SYN, PSH, ACK, RST

    c. SYN, ACK, ACK/PSH, FIN

    d. SYN, PSH, ACK, FIN

12. Which OS typically has the following as part of its signature: DgmLen 84, TTL 64, initial sequence number 0?

13. Which OS typically has alphabetic characters in its ASCII data payload?

14. Which protocol uses different port numbers to establish a connection and to transfer data?

    a. TCP/IP

    b. FTP

    c. HTTP

    d. ICMP

15. Which of the following is an example of a reconnaissance traffic signature?

    a. Trojan program

    b. ping sweep

    c. denial of service

    d. ping of death

16. A BackOrifice attack falls into what category of suspicious traffic signatures?

    a. information

    b. reconnaissance

    c. denial of service

    d. unauthorized access

17. Which program keeps track of services and ports made available through Remote Procedure Calls?

    a. Network Information System

    b. Network File System

    c. Network File Sharing

    d. Portmapper

18. What does the ASCII data payload section of an ICMP packet in Linux contain?

19. The maximum packet size that can be transmitted on a type of computer network (Ethernet, for example) is known as which of the following?

    a. maximum fragment threshold

    b. maximum packet limit

    c. mandatory transmission unit

    d. maximum transmission unit

20. To avoid attacks that use advanced evasion techniques, such as path names, hexadecimal codes, and CGI scripts, you must do which of the following? (Choose all that apply.)

    a. Watch your log files closely.

    b. Install additional IDS sensors.

    c. Keep your antivirus software updated.

    d. Keep your IDS signature files updated.

HANDS-ON PROJECTS

HANDS-ON PROJECTS

Hands-On Project 4-1: Researching the TCP and IP RFCs

Time Required: 45 minutes

Objective: Research RFCs to find specific, accurate technical protocol details.

Description: All too often, network administrators receive alerts from IDSs but don't know how to interpret the data. This chapter has given you some tips for analyzing normal and abnormal traffic signatures, but you should also make sure you have a solid foundation in the specifications for TCP, IP, UDP, and ICMP traffic so that you know exactly what constitutes a possible intrusion. In this activity, you look up the original RFC documents for TCP and IP traffic but with an emphasis on possible intrusions.

> Although this book refers to the discrete "chunks" that make up TCP/IP communications collectively as "packets," be aware that details of the individual protocols you're about to examine refer to these chunks differently. This is because each protocol depends on higher- or lower-level protocols for certain services. For example, TCP relies on IP for fragmentation and reassembly, so the details of how they happen isn't a concern of the TCP protocol. In TCP, the chunks of data are called "segments," and IP calls them "datagrams." RFC 793 (TCP) also explains this concept in its introduction.

1. Start your Web browser, enter the URL **http://www.ietf.org/rfc.html**, and press **Enter**.

2. In the RFC number text box, enter **793** and click **go**.

3. Read the RFC for TCP packets closely. The MSS size must appear only in a TCP packet with which flag set? Record your answer here:

   _____

4. Look at Figure 6 in this RFC. Which flags does it indicate might appear together? Record your answer here:

   _____

5. Read page 27 of the RFC. What is being synchronized when a packet with the SYN flag is sent? Record your answer here:

_____

6. Go back to **http://www.ietf.org/rfc.html**. Enter **791** in the RFC number text box and click **go**.

7. In the original specification for Internet Protocol, scroll down to the part of the document titled "Fragmentation and Reassembly." How big should packet fragments be, and how many fragments can be in a packet? Record your answer here:

_____

8. Go to page 12 of the RFC. In the section on flags, you see an explanation of DF, which appears in many packet headers. What does DF stand for? Record your answer here:

_____

9. Close any open windows, and shut down your system.

CASE PROJECTS

Case Project 4-1: Filtering Out Common Scans

You have determined that an Nmap null scan has been launched against a computer on your network, as described in Activity 4-5. You suspect that other scans might take place. What sorts of filter rules should you establish so that your IDS can send an alarm when one is detected?

Case Project 4-2: Researching Security Products

In Chapter 2's running case project, you drafted an initial security policy for LedGrafix. During the remainder of the book, you'll be adding to that document. As in real life, technology systems and the businesses they support seldom remain static, and your policies must adapt with the changes in the environment. You must also keep up with changes and do your research. Believe it or not, one of your main challenges will be keeping up with new technologies, threats, and products. You'll spend countless hours researching tools, utilities, devices, and applications that you can use to meet new threats that emerge daily. Information security is a dynamic field, to say the least.

You already know that network security devices and software exist to enforce and support your security policies. By establishing a complete plan for each segment of your network and documenting that plan, you are laying the groundwork for effective and consistent security management practices.

The chapter has covered some important information you'll use to secure networks. In particular, you learned that you must review and monitor traffic logs for signs of intrusion or attack. Reviewing logs has some disadvantages, however. Even minimal logging can generate thousands of entries daily, and examining those entries manually is time-consuming and tedious, and spending all day reviewing logs doesn't allow you the time you need to secure your network. Reviewing log files manually is also prone to errors, and log entries show you only what happened in the past, so they aren't useful for real-time monitoring. Finally, log files have a size limit, so when they reach that limit, they overwrite older entries, possibly deleting important information.

Fortunately, tools that monitor logs on a real-time basis are available. Most can send an alert if suspicious activity is detected, and some can even mount a defense under certain conditions indicating an attack. Your task for this chapter is to research these log analysis tools. Using the Tool Comparison Chart from your instructor, locate several tools for analyzing logs, and record the required information about them. Many tools also perform other tasks. If you can find an all-in-one tool that fits, that's great from a budget standpoint. There are several factors to consider:

- *Compatibility*—Is the tool compatible with your existing systems? You need to refer to the hardware and software inventory you completed in Chapter 1 to answer this question. Check the platform the tool runs on, programming languages required for the tool, and hardware the tool supports, such as IDS, firewalls, servers, routers, and so on.

- *Scalability*—Can the tool support the company's projected growth for the next five years? Ten years? Can the tool be upgraded or updated to keep up with new threats, attack signatures, and so forth?

- *Cost*—How much will the tool cost to set up? To maintain?

- *Vendor*—Is the vendor reputable and stable? What kind of long-term support can you expect?

- *Portability*—Can the tool be used for (ported to) different platforms or products?

- *Tracking*—Does the tool offer reverse DNS lookup, WHOIS, and other capabilities for tracing attacks and connections?

- *Report format*—How does the tool organize and display reports? GUI or command-line interface?

- *Response and alerts*—Can the tool send alerts? Can you customize alerts (specify alert-triggering conditions and people to send the alert to) and configure a response if certain conditions are met?

- *Security flaws*—Does the tool have any known security flaws? For example, older versions of AWStats (a tool listed as an example on Tool Comparison Matrix) that use the CGI feature can allow attackers to run arbitrary commands by using the permissions of your Web server user, usually nobody or wwwroot. Keep in mind that software is code, and code can have flaws.

- *Management and configuration*—How is the tool managed? Centrally? Remotely? Does configuration require one or many files to edit? Does it use a GUI or command-line interface? Does the tool require knowledge of a particular programming language, script, or platform unfamiliar to support personnel?

You won't be selecting any of these tools just yet. You still need to learn about VPNs, IDSs, and firewalls in subsequent chapters. As you progress through this book, keep these tools in mind and be thinking about how to integrate log file analysis, auditing, and ongoing maintenance and monitoring into your security policy and procedures.

Use Internet search engines, your library, and other resources to find tool examples, and compile your list in a report to submit to your instructor. Remember to cite your sources and avoid plagiarism and copyright and trademark infringement.

5

VIRTUAL PRIVATE NETWORK (VPN) CONCEPTS

After reading this chapter and completing the exercises, you will be able to:

♦ Explain basic VPN concepts

♦ Describe encapsulation in VPNs

♦ Describe encryption in VPNs

♦ Describe authentication in VPNs

♦ Summarize the advantages and disadvantages of VPNs

A virtual private network (VPN) combines two factors that represent essential elements of a network defense strategy: security and connectivity. VPNs play important roles in businesses that rely on the Internet for critical communications. For businesses, VPNs are attractive because of their low cost and efficiency. As travel and other costs of doing business rise, companies need to reduce costs while maintaining productivity.

In the past, companies that wanted to conduct secure electronic transactions used leased lines—private connections rented from telecommunications companies, using technologies such as frame relay or Integrated Services Digital Network (ISDN). Leased lines form a secure connection between two networks, but the rental cost can quickly reach thousands of dollars per month. A VPN is a cost-effective way for two or more networks to make a secure connection through the public Internet, thus avoiding the cost of leased lines.

A VPN is said to be "virtual" because the connection between networks doesn't use a dedicated line. Rather, it uses the same public Internet connections used by millions of other people. Users who make VPN connections gain privacy via a variety of technologies, such as encryption and authentication. In this chapter, you learn what VPNs are, why they are growing in popularity, and how they ensure private communication between networks. This chapter also explains the different protocols that create a secure "virtual tunnel" between computers and describes encryption methods that are integral to maintaining the privacy and integrity of VPN communications.

UNDERSTANDING VPN CONCEPTS

A **virtual private network (VPN)** provides a way for two computers or computer networks to communicate securely by using the same public communication channels available on the Internet, where millions of computers and networks exchange data. To better understand what VPNs do, consider how baseball players communicate with each other and their coaches during a game. The catcher uses signals to indicate what pitch the pitcher should throw. The pitcher signals his agreement, and the pitch is thrown. The batter hits a single to right field. Meanwhile, there are runners on first and second base. The opposing team's third base coach signals the runner on second to advance to third and proceed to home. The batter, meanwhile, is out at first, and the runner on first base advances to second, where the base coach signals him to stay. All this communication takes place by using complex codes the teams have developed. The information being exchanged is coded so that no one else can understand it and is "transmitted" in plain view of the public. In a sense, the team's communications are "tunneled" through the public, protected by a form of "encryption." This analogy begins to describe what VPNs do: They enable computers to exchange private encrypted messages that others can't decipher. The following sections give you an overview of how VPNs work; you learn what VPNs are, why your organization might establish a VPN, and how to configure VPNs.

What VPNs Are

To understand what VPNs are, consider how the regular mail works. Because you don't want your correspondence traveling in the open (you want it kept private), you place it in a sealed envelope (encapsulation). You need to tell the mail carrier where to deliver the envelope and exactly who is supposed to receive it, so you place a destination name and address on the outside (the destination address information). If your envelope can't be delivered to the correct person or address, you put a return address on the envelope (the source address) so that the mail carrier can bring it back to you. You don't necessarily know what route your message takes, whether it's processed through the St. Louis or Denver mail center or through another processing hub. As on the public Internet, it can take several paths to its destination. This is the "virtual" part of VPN. Finally, the mail is processed through many different sorting centers, air and ground transportation systems, and post offices that form the United States Postal Service (USPS) "network," just as the Internet is a conglomeration of private LANs, public transmission lines, and other systems forming a giant mesh network. If you're concerned about the possibility of your message being intercepted and read by someone else, you could even write it in code (encryption), but you would need a way to let the receiver decrypt it, which could be considered a "key exchange."

Specified computers, users, or network gateways are identified as endpoints of the VPN connection, which is called a **tunnel**, and only those designated computers, users, or gateways can participate in the VPN (see Figure 5-1). Finally, a VPN is a network because it connects computers and extends an organization's network beyond its current boundaries.

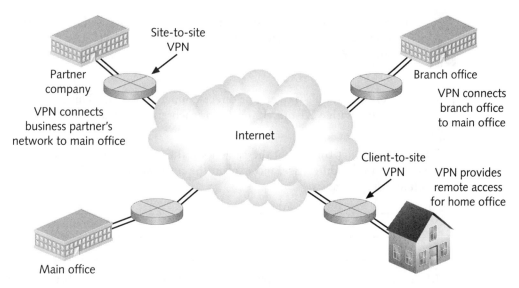

Figure 5-1   Establishing connections with a VPN

A VPN, then, is a virtual network connection that uses the Internet to establish a secure connection. The following sections describe the VPN components that enable the connection to be made and the VPN core activities that ensure security.

The VPN endpoints represent extensions of the participating networks. Those endpoints must be secured by a firewall, or they could give intruders a way to access the network. Unless your VPN client software incorporates its own firewall, you need to make sure that any remote computers that connect to your organization's VPN are equipped with their own desktop firewalls.

Activity 5-1: Direct-Connecting Two Lab Computers

Time Required: 15 minutes

Objective: Connect two lab computers with a null-modem/crossover cable.

Description: In this activity, you direct-connect two computers in your lab so that you can create a VPN between them in subsequent activities. You need two computers running Windows. However, you can also connect a laptop or other computer running Windows 95, 98, or Me as the client computer to a server that runs Windows 2000 or XP, or you could connect two Windows 2000 or XP computers to one another.

NOTE

These steps are written to describe one computer functioning as the VPN host running Windows XP and one computer functioning as the VPN guest running Windows 2000.

1. Obtain a crossover, null-modem, or direct-connection cable. This is a specially designed cable with a 25-pin connector at each end. (A 9-pin null modem cable also works.)

2. The connectors at the end of the cable look the same, but they are not. Inspect them, explain the difference, and explain the purpose of this cable, using the following lines for your answers.

   _____

   _____

   _____

3. Make sure the computers are physically close to one another so that the cable can reach easily.

4. Plug the cable into the serial port of each computer you want to connect.

5. On both Windows XP and Windows 2000 computers, open Control Panel.

6. In Windows XP in Category View, click **Printers and Other Hardware**, and then click **Phone and Modem Options**. In Windows 2000 and Windows XP in Classic View, double-click **Phone and Modem Options**. If the **Location Information** dialog box opens, specify the local area code and click **OK**.

7. In the Phone and Modem Options dialog box, click the **Modems** tab, and then click **Add**.

8. Click the **Don't detect my modem; I will select it from a list** option, and then click **Next**.

9. In the Manufacturers list, verify that Standard Modem Types is selected. In the Model list, click **Communications cable between two computers**, and then click **Next**.

10. Click **COM1** or **COM2**, and then click **Next**.

11. Click **Finish**.

12. Click **OK** to close the Phone and Modem Options dialog box, and close any open windows. Leave your system running for the next activity.

Why Establish a VPN?

The need to keep business transactions private drives an increasing number of organizations to adopt VPNs. The popularity of e-commerce is an incentive as well. In addition, government and military agencies need to share information more than ever to provide effective homeland security (the protection of U.S. citizens from terrorist attacks and the damage they cause). A VPN is an excellent solution for an organization that needs to follow a budget while maintaining security. The following sections examine the business incentives driving VPN adoption and the advantages and disadvantages of using VPNs.

Business Incentives Driving VPN Adoption

Budgetary considerations have always made VPNs an attractive business proposition. When you implement a VPN, you are essentially spreading the cost of its operation over many users, which makes it cost-effective.

In addition, many companies employ remote contractors who need to access the corporate network from their homes or offices. Employees who travel for business reasons need to check e-mail and transfer files with colleagues in the central office. Accordingly, secure remote access represents an essential requirement for businesses and is an important incentive for establishing a VPN. Another incentive for creating a VPN is the need to establish a secure means of access for partners, suppliers, contractors, and others outside the company.

VPN Components

VPNs can be assembled by using a variety of components. However, all VPNs contain a set of essential elements that enable the data to be transmitted securely from one point to another:

- *VPN server or host*—A **VPN server** is configured to accept connections from clients who connect via dial-up or broadband.

- *VPN client or guest*—A **VPN client** can be a router that serves as the endpoint of a site-to-site VPN connection, which uses hardware to connect two networks. It can also be an OS that can be configured to function as an endpoint in a VPN, such as Windows 9x or later, Linux, UNIX, and other OSs.

- *Tunnel*—The connection through which data is sent.

- *VPN protocols*—**VPN protocols** are sets of standardized communication settings that software and hardware use to encrypt data sent along the VPN. They include Internet Protocol Security (IPSec), Point-to-Point Tunneling Protocol (PPTP), and Layer 2 Tunneling Protocol (L2TP).

The number of components in a VPN depends on the number of networks in its configuration. For instance, if a VPN contains four networks, it has at least four separate servers and four tunnels; multiple clients from each endpoint can participate in any of the VPN tunnels they have permission and credentials to access.

In general, you can set up two different types of VPNs. The first type links two or more networks and is called a **site-to-site VPN** (or a gateway-to-gateway VPN). The second type makes a network accessible to remote users who need dial-in access and is called a **client-to-site VPN** (or a remote access VPN). The two types of VPNs aren't mutually exclusive. For example, many large corporations link the central office to one or more

5

branch locations or business partners by using site-to-site VPNs, and they also provide dial-in access to the central office by means of a client-to-site VPN.

Hardware Versus Software VPNs

The components you choose to establish a VPN depend on whether you want to use existing hardware or software. Creating a VPN with new components increases IT costs but has the benefit of reducing the load on the other network security components (such as firewalls).

Hardware-based VPNs connect one gateway to another. Typically, the VPN hardware is a router at each network gateway that encrypts outbound packets and decrypts inbound packets. Another hardware option involves a **VPN appliance**, a hardware device designed to serve as the VPN endpoint and join multiple LANs (see Figure 5-2).

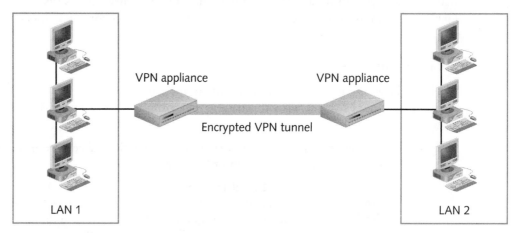

Figure 5-2   VPN appliances create secure connections between two or more LANs

NOTE   VPN appliances can permit connections between large numbers of users or multiple networks, but they don't provide other services, such as file sharing and printing.

In general, hardware products such as routers that are dedicated to the operation of VPNs tend to handle more network traffic than software products. As a result, they are more **scalable** (capable of maintaining a consistent level of operation as a network grows) than software VPNs. They can also be more secure than software VPNs, because they are designed from the ground up for a specific purpose and don't depend on an underlying OS that might have security flaws. Hardware VPNs should be the first choice for fast-growing networks that need to encrypt all traffic passing through the VPN device. They are also a good choice when VPN endpoints use the same type of routers and are controlled by the same organizations. Table 5-1 lists some examples of hardware VPN devices.

Table 5-1   Hardware VPN products

Manufacturer	Product Name	Web Site
Cisco Systems	VPN 3000 series concentrators, VPN 3002 Hardware Clients, 7600 series WebVPN Services Module, and 7600 series routers, among others	www.cisco.com
SonicWALL	SonicWALL PRO 5060, 4060, 3060, 2040, 1260	www.sonicwall.com
Nokia	Nokia 50s, 60s, 100s, 500s, 5i, 10i, 50i, 100i, 500i	www.nokia.com
Juniper Networks	NetScreen 5000 series, ISG series, NetScreen 500/200 series, Secure Access 6000/4000 series	www.juniper.net
WatchGuard	WatchGuard Firebox X series	www.watchguard.com

TIP   Another kind of hardware device audits inbound connections that pass through the VPN appliance before they reach the internal network to verify that they conform with the organization's security policy. For example, CyberGatekeeper Remote Policy Enforcer by InfoExpress, Inc. ensures that you won't encounter viruses or intrusions from your own remote access VPN users. This product functions as its own host computer and includes policy manager software. You can find out more about this product at *www.infoexpress.com*.

Most software-based VPNs are integrated with firewalls and are more cost-effective than hardware VPN devices. They also increase network security because they are integrated with functions that a firewall already performs, such as packet filtering and Network Address Translation (NAT). Software-based VPNs are appropriate when the networks participating in the VPN use different routers and firewalls or when the endpoints are controlled by totally different organizations and network administrators. The reason for using software VPNs to link networks is that software VPN solutions offer maximum flexibility. They can, for instance, be configured to enable traffic based on domain name, protocol, or IP address. These restrictions prove useful when only some, but not all, of the traffic passing through the VPN is meant to be encrypted and sent through the tunnel. Because software VPNs often rely on the OS they are installed on, they have another layer of complexity in configuring and implementing them, however. Table 5-2 lists some examples of VPN software solutions.

Table 5-2   Software VPN products

Manufacturer	Product Name	Web Site
CheckPoint	VPN-1 VSX, VPN-1 Pro, VPN-1 Edge, Firewall-1, Safe@Office	www.checkpoint.com
NETGEAR	ProSafe VPN	www.netgear.com
3Com Corporation	OfficeConnect Upgrade for Internet Firewall	www.3com.com

Table 5-2 Software VPN products (continued)

Manufacturer	Product Name	Web Site
Symantec Corporation	Symantec Enterprise Firewall, Norton Personal Firewall for Macintosh	www.symantec.com
Astaro Internet Security	Astaro VPN Gateway	www.astaro.com

VPN Combinations

VPN installations need to be flexible to keep up with changing network needs. By combining VPN hardware or software with other hardware or software, you add layers of network security. One useful combination is a VPN bundled with a firewall. VPNs don't eliminate the need for firewalls. In fact, firewalls are essential to ensure that VPN traffic passes through the network gateway to the destination and non-VPN traffic is filtered according to the organization's security policy.

Product combinations for VPNs are as versatile as the businesses VPNs serve. Each installation can be designed to fit with the company's current and future needs. Some points to consider when selecting VPN hardware and software include the following:

- *Compatibility*—You need to consider whether the products you want to use are compatible with your existing infrastructure or if another product will integrate better.

- *Scalability*—The VPN configuration you choose must be able to grow with the needs of the business.

- *Security*—The level of security needed (specified in your organization's security policy) contributes to your choice of products and the configurations you choose for encapsulation, encryption, and authentication.

- *Cost*—As always, budget is a major factor when selecting equipment.

- *Vendor support*—Most hardware or software eventually requires patches, updates, repair, or other forms of support, which is usually the vendor's responsibility. The product support options the vendor offers are important points to consider when planning your purchases.

NOTE A VPN combination makes use of VPN hardware and software in the same device. The Cisco VPN 3002 device, for instance, gives users the choice of operating in one of two modes: client mode and network extension mode. In client mode, the VPN 3002 acts as a software client, enabling users to connect to another remote network via a VPN. In network extension mode, the VPN 3002 provides a secure site-to-site VPN connection. Both modes can be scaled to hundreds or even thousands of VPN users. For more on the Cisco VPN 3002 device, visit www.cisco.com and run a search on "VPN 3002."

VPN Core Activity 1: Encapsulation

VPNs can use public Internet connections and still provide a high level of security because they perform a core set of activities: encapsulation, encryption, and authentication. Together, these activities tunnel data from one network to another using the infrastructure of the Internet.

First, VPNs perform **encapsulation** of data: They enclose a packet within another packet that has different IP source and destination information for a high degree of protection. Encapsulation protects the integrity of data sent along the VPN tunnel; the source and destination information of the actual data packets (the ones being encapsulated) are completely hidden. The VPN encapsulates the actual data packets within packets that use the source and destination addresses of the VPN gateway, as shown in Figure 5-3. The gateway might be a router that uses Internet Protocol Security (IPSec), a VPN appliance, or a firewall that functions as a VPN and has a gateway set up.

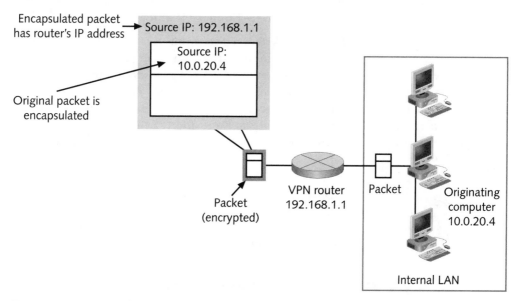

Figure 5-3   Encapsulating data to conceal source and destination information

When a VPN tunnel is in place, the source and destination IP addresses of the actual data packets (the ones that have been encapsulated) can be in the private reserved blocks that aren't routable over the Internet, such as the 10.0.0.0/8 addresses or the 192.168.0.0/16 reserved network blocks.

Understanding Tunneling Protocols

Because VPNs link networks and gateways that might have different OSs or hardware platforms, standard sets of instructions, called protocols, need to be established so that communications can take place.

When you configure a device to function as a VPN host, you need to choose the protocol you want to use. For instance, IPSec with Internet Key Exchange (IPSec/IKE) is fast becoming the protocol of choice among VPNs. However, if remote users need to dial in to your main office network, you should use a dial-in protocol, such as Point-to-Point Tunneling Protocol. A variety of VPN protocols are discussed in the following sections.

Point-to-Point Tunneling Protocol (PPTP)

IPSec and Secure Shell provide VPN security in many circumstances, but they aren't appropriate for every application. Users who need to dial in to a server with a modem connection on a computer running an older OS might need to connect to VPN servers that have been configured to use **Point-to-Point Tunneling Protocol (PPTP)**.

PPTP encapsulates a TCP/IP packet. The header information that encloses the packet and that appears on the network contains only the information needed to route the data from the VPN client to the VPN server, or vice versa. PPTP uses a proprietary technology called Microsoft Point-to-Point Encryption (MPPE) to encrypt data that passes between the remote computer and the remote access server. In contrast, the newer L2TP protocol uses IPSec encryption, which is more secure and more widely supported. PPTP is useful, however, if your dial-in users need to connect from computers running Windows 95, 98, or NT 4.0.

Vulnerabilities related to MPPE and Microsoft Challenge/Response Authentication Protocol (MS-CHAP) make PPTP a poor choice for high-performance networks with a large number of hosts. Use PPTP only for a small-scale VPN that needs to support mobile users.

Activity 5-2: Setting Up a Remote Access Server

Time Required: 30 minutes

Objective: Configure a computer as a remote access/VPN server.

Description: In this activity, you configure Routing and Remote Access Services (RRAS) on one of the two computers you connected directly (the one running Windows XP) so that it can accept incoming VPN connections. Then, you can use it to set up a direct VPN connection or a dial-up connection using PPTP or L2TP. This activity requires you to have a direct connection between two computers, as described in Activity 5-1.

1. Open Control Panel, and click the **Network and Internet Connections** icon.

2. Click the **Network Connections** icon, and under Network Tasks on the left, click **Create a new connection**.

3. When the New Connection Wizard starts, click **Next**.

4. Click **Set up an advanced connection**, and then click **Next**.

5. Verify that the Accept incoming connections option is selected, and then click **Next**.

6. If necessary, click **Communications cable between two computers**, and then click **Next**.

7. Verify that the Allow virtual private connections option is selected, and then click **Next**.

8. In the User Permissions dialog box, click the box next to the user(s) to whom you want to grant access to your computer. If your lab partner doesn't have a user name, click **Add** and create a user name and password in the New User dialog box. When you're done, click **Next**.

9. In the Networking Software dialog box, verify that Internet Protocol (TCP/IP) and File and printer sharing for Microsoft Networks are selected. Click **Internet Protocol (TCP/IP)**, and then click **Properties**.

10. Verify that the Allow callers to access my local area network check box is selected, and then click **Specify TCP/IP addresses**.

11. In the From and To text boxes, specify a range of IP addresses for the VPN server to allocate. For this example, enter **192.168.1.1** in the From text box and **192.168.1.254** in the To text box. Click **OK**.

12. Click **Next**, and then click **Finish**. Close any open windows, and leave your system running for the next activity.

Layer 2 Tunneling Protocol (L2TP)

As mentioned in the preceding section, **Layer 2 Tunneling Protocol (L2TP)** provides a higher level of security through its support for IPSec. Introduced with the release of Windows 2000, the L2TP/IPSec VPN protocol is a more secure alternative to PPTP. IPSec enables L2TP to perform authentication and encapsulation as well as encryption. Using L2TP, a host machine can make a connection to a modem and then have its PPP data packets forwarded to another, separate remote access server. When the data reaches the remote access server, its payload is unpacked and forwarded to the destination host on the internal network. To support down-level clients (Windows 98, Me, and NT 4.0 Workstation), you need to install the Microsoft L2TP/IPSec VPN Client software on those machines. (To download the client software, go to *www.microsoft.com* and search for "L2TP/IPSec VPN Client." Click the download link, download the software, and then follow the instructions to install it.) Table 5-3 indicates which protocols are supported by which OSs.

Table 5-3 Support for PPTP and L2TP

Protocol	Windows 95	Windows 98	Windows NT 4.0	Windows 2000	Windows XP	Red Hat Linux
PPTP	Yes	Yes	Yes	Yes	Yes	Yes
L2TP	No	No	No	Yes	Yes	Yes

L2TP also works with non-VPN connections, such as frame relay or Asynchronous Transfer Mode (ATM) networks.

NOTE

PPTP and L2TP client downloads are available for Windows 9x and NT 4.0 at *www.microsoft.com*. Search for "L2TP/PPTP Client" to find the download.

TIP

Activity 5-3: Setting Up a Direct Client Connection

ACTIVITY

Time Required: 25 minutes

Objective: Configure a computer to act as a VPN client to the remote access server configured in Activity 5-2.

Description: After installing a null-modem cable between two computers, you can configure the second computer (the Windows 2000 computer) to function as the client. This activity assumes you have installed a null-modem cable as described in Activity 5-1 and created a user name and password as instructed in Activity 5-2.

1. Open Control Panel.

2. Double-click **Network and Dial-up Connections**, and double-click **Make New Connection.**

3. In the first window of the Network Connection Wizard, click **Next**.

4. Click **Connect directly to another computer**, and then click **Next**.

5. Click **Guest**, and then click **Next**.

6. In the Select a device drop-down list, click the port where you installed your null-modem cable in Activity 5-1, and then click **Next**.

7. If necessary, click **For all users**, and then click **Next**.

8. Click **Finish**. The Connect Direct dialog box opens.

9. Enter the user name and password you created in Activity 5-2, and then click **Connect**.

10. A dialog box opens stating that the connection is being made. In a few seconds, a second dialog box should appear, stating that the connection has been established. Verify this by switching to the Windows XP computer and opening the Network Connections dialog box. An icon showing the connection should be displayed. Click **OK** to close the Connection Complete dialog box.

11. Close any open windows, and leave your system running for the next activity.

Secure Shell (SSH)

Like IPSec, **Secure Shell (SSH)** provides authentication and encryption of TCP/IP packets over a VPN or other connection. SSH works with UNIX-based systems, such as Red Hat Linux, to create a secure transport layer connection between participating computers. Versions for Windows are also available. SSH also makes use of public-key cryptography (discussed later in the chapter in "VPN Core Activity 2: Encryption").

When a client initiates an SSH connection, the two computers exchange keys and negotiate the algorithms to be used for authentication and encryption to create a secure connection at the transport layer. The user name and password transmitted to the server are encrypted. All data that is sent subsequently is also encrypted. SSH is available free via the OpenSSH package of applications (*www.openssh.org*).

Socks V. 5

The **Socks** protocol is normally used as a way to provide proxy services for applications that don't usually support proxying. Socks version 5 adds encrypted authentication and support for User Datagram Protocol (UDP). With these new features, Socks v .5 can enable applications to set up a secure tunnel by using encryption and authentication.

NOTE

Both SSH and Socks v. 5 are not widely supported by VPNs, so they aren't covered extensively in this chapter. If you're interested in learning more about SSH, try *www.openssh.com* or *www.ssh.com*. Another good starting point for learning more about the Socks protocol is *www.socks.permeo.com*.

ACTIVITY

Activity 5-4: Establishing a VPN Connection

Time Required: 15 minutes

Objective: Establish a VPN connection using the VPN server and client configured in previous activities.

Description: After you have established a direct connection between your two lab computers, you can then establish a VPN connection on top of the direct connection. The VPN connection uses the direct connection you already established and adds authentication and encryption. This activity assumes you have completed Activities 5-1, 5-2, and 5-3.

1. On the host computer, open a command prompt window.

2. Type **ipconfig** and then press **Enter**. Details about your computer's IP addresses are displayed. How many connections do you have listed? What is the IP address for the first connection listed? Write down the IP addresses here:

_____

_____

3. Switch to the client computer, and open a command prompt window. Type **ipconfig** and then press **Enter**. Write down your PPP adapter IP address.

_____

4. If necessary, open the Network and Dial-up Connections dialog box from Control Panel. On the following line, write the name of the icon representing the direct connection you made to the other lab computer (probably the generic name Direct Connection unless you changed it to something else).

_____

5. Right-click any other network connections that might be active (such as Local Area Connection, if you use it to connect to the Internet), and then click **Disable**.

6. Double-click **Make New Connection**. When the Network Connection Wizard starts, click **Next**.

7. Click **Connect to a private network through the Internet**, and then click **Next**.

8. In the Public Network window, click **Automatically dial this initial connection**.

9. In the drop-down list, click the direct connection you made to the other lab computer, and then click **Next**.

10. In the Destination Address window, type the IP address of the Windows XP host computer that you entered in Step 2, and then click **Next**.

11. In the next window, verify that the For all users option is selected, and then click **Next**. In the Internet Connection Sharing window, click **Next**.

12. In the final window, change the default name of the connection (Virtual Private Connection) if you like, and then click **Finish**.

13. When the Connect Virtual Private Connection dialog box opens, enter the network user name and password you created in Activity 5-2, and then click **Connect**. A dialog box opens, notifying you of the progress of the connection. After a few seconds, a second dialog box should appear, notifying you that you're connected. Close any open windows, and leave your system running for the next activity.

NOTE

If you see an error message stating that the port is not connected, make sure all firewall software is disabled on both the client and server. In case another program is using the port, restart the client, which forces the port to close correctly.

IPSec/IKE

Internet Protocol Security (IPSec) is a set of standard procedures that the Internet Engineering Task Force (IETF) developed for enabling secure communications on the Internet. IPSec has become the standard set of protocols for VPN security for a number of reasons:

- IPSec works at layer 3 (the network layer) of the OSI model of network communications and, therefore, provides a type of security not available with other protocols, which work at layer 2 (the data link layer).

- IPSec can encrypt an entire TCP/IP packet—the data portion as well as the source and destination IP addresses in the header. Other protocols encrypt only the data portion of a packet.

- IPSec was originally developed for use with IPv6, although it can also work with the current version, IPv4. Other protocols can work only with IPv4.

- IPSec provides authentication of source and destination computers before the data is encrypted or transmitted. In other words, its components combine authentication, strong encryption, and key management. Other protocols provide for authentication or encryption, not both.

Perhaps the biggest advantage of using IPSec is that it has gone through the process of standardization and is supported by a wide variety of VPN hardware and software devices. Operating systems such as Windows 2000 and XP enable you to set up an IPSec connection with another Windows computer that has IPSec enabled. In fact, you add IPSec security policy support as a snap-in to the Microsoft Management Console. (You perform this task in Activity 5-5.)

TIP If you want more background on IPSec and its related technologies, you'll find links to the original RFC papers for those technologies on the IETF Web site (*www.ietf.org/rfc/rfc2401.txt*).

When an IPSec connection is established between two computers, the computers authenticate one another and then establish the **Security Association (SA)** settings they use to communicate. An SA is a relationship between two or more entities that describes how they will use security services to communicate. Each IPSec connection can perform encryption, encapsulation, authentication, or any combination of the three. When determining which services to use, the parties in a connection must agree on the details, such as what algorithm to use for encryption. After that transaction is complete, the entities must then share session keys. An SA is the method IPSec uses to track all the particulars of a communications session. SAs are unidirectional, meaning that an SA is set up in each direction of a communication, forming 2 one-way SAs between the peers.

These transactions take place in the background. However, in an OS environment, you need to decide whether IPSec is required for all connections to the host machine, or whether the host requests an IPSec connection for computers or other devices that support it. If IPSec is not supported on the client machine, it won't be used. You also have the option of requiring a secure connection to another computer over a VPN. If you want to connect to another computer while requiring IPSec, you need to adjust the packet-filtering rules; otherwise, your IPSec-enabled computer blocks all other connections by default.

Activity 5-5: Activating IPSec and Specifying a Policy

ACTIVITY

Time Required: 30 minutes

Objective: Using the two lab computers connected via a VPN, configure the host (VPN server) to use IPSec.

Description: After you have two computers connected via a VPN, you can configure them to use IPSec to talk to one another. You can also set up a tunnel using L2TP or PPTP as the tunneling protocol. Follow these steps on the Windows XP computer that serves as the host for your VPN connection. This activity requires you to have established a virtual private connection, as described in Activity 5-4.

1. Click **Start**, **Run**. In the Open text box, type **MMC**, and then click **OK**.

2. A Microsoft Management Console window opens, labeled Console1. Click **File**, **Add/Remove Snap-in** from the menu. In the Add/Remove Snap-in dialog box, click **Add**.

3. Click **IP Security Policy Management** (see Figure 5-4), and then click **Add**.

Figure 5-4   Adding the IPSec snap-in

4. When the Select Computer or Domain dialog box opens, verify that Local computer is selected, and then click **Finish**.

5. Click **IP Security Monitor** in the Add Standalone Snap-in dialog box, and then click **Add**.

6. Click **Close** to close the Add Standalone Snap-in dialog box, and then click **OK** to close the Add/Remove Snap-in dialog box.

7. In the left pane of the MMC, click **IP Security Policies on Local Computer**.

8. In the right pane of the MMC, right-click **Secure Server (Require Security)**, and then click **Assign**.

9. Right-click **Secure Server (Require Security)** a second time, and click **Properties**.

10. In the Secure Server (Require Security) Properties dialog box, click **All ICMP Traffic**, and then click the **Edit** button.

11. Click **All IP Traffic**, and click **Edit** to open the IP Filter List dialog box, as shown in Figure 5-5. In the Description text box, you can read that the rule blocks all IP traffic to and from the local computer that doesn't use IP security. You need to create a less restrictive rule—one that sets up a tunnel between the host computer and your VPN guest.

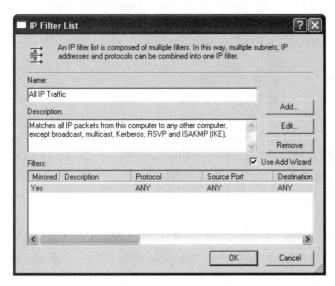

Figure 5-5   Viewing packet-filtering rules for an IPSec VPN connection

12. Click the **Edit** button. In the Filter Properties dialog box, click **A specific IP Address** in the Destination address drop-down list, and then enter the IP address of the client computer that's direct-connected to this host computer. Click **OK**.

13. Click **OK** to close the IP Filter List dialog box.

14. Click **All ICMP Traffic**, and then click **Edit**.

15. Repeat Steps 12 and 13 to set up an ICMP traffic rule for the same IP address you entered in Step 12.

16. Click **Apply** and then click **OK** to close the Edit Rule Properties dialog box, and click **Close** to close the Secure Server (Require Security) Properties dialog box.

17. Click **File**, **Exit** to close the MMC window. When prompted to save your changes, click **Yes**, and then click **Save**. Close any other open windows, and leave your system running for the next activity.

IPSec's many components provide for encryption, encapsulation, key exchange, and authentication. These components include the following:

- *Internet Security Association Key Management Protocol*—**Internet Security Association Key Management Protocol (ISAKMP)**, an IPSec-related protocol, enables two computers to agree on security settings and establish a Security Association (SA) so that they can then exchange keys using Internet Key Exchange.

- *Internet Key Exchange (IKE)*—This protocol enables two computers that establish an IPSec connection to exchange keys to make a Security Association. IKE uses UDP port 500 on both the client and server computers.

- *Oakley*—This protocol enables IPSec to use the Diffie-Hellman encryption algorithm to create keys. (You can find out more about Diffie-Hellman encryption at *www.ietf.org/rfc/rfc2631.txt.*)

- *IPSecurity Policy Management*—This service runs on Windows computers. It retrieves IPSec security policy settings from Active Directory and applies them to computers in the domain that use IPSec.

- *IPSec driver*—An **IPSec driver** is software that handles the actual tasks of encrypting, authenticating, decrypting, and checking packets.

Suppose you have configured a VPN connection between two computers and you want that connection to make use of IPSec. When one IPSec-compliant computer connects to the other, the following events occur:

1. The IPSec driver and the ISAKMP retrieve the IPSec policy settings.

2. ISAKMP negotiates between hosts, based on their policy settings, and builds a Security Association (SA) between them.

3. The Oakley protocol generates a master key used to secure IPSec communications.

4. Based on the security policy established for the session, the IPSec driver monitors, filters, and secures the network traffic.

IPSec isn't foolproof. For instance, if the machine that runs IPSec-compliant software has already been compromised, no communication from that machine, including IPSec communications, can be trusted. IPSec isn't a substitute for firewall, antivirus, and intrusion detection software.

The two core IPSec components are the ones that protect the TCP/IP packets exchanged in the VPN: Authentication Header (AH) and Encapsulating Security Payload (ESP), discussed in the following sections.

Authentication Header (AH)

As its name suggests, **Authentication Header (AH)** is an IPSec component that provides authentication of TCP/IP packets to ensure data integrity. With AH, packets are signed with a block of encoded data called a digital signature. The signature indicates to other IPSec-compliant devices that the packet contains accurate IP header information because it originated from a computer using IPSec. Digitally signing a packet indicates that it hasn't been tampered with or that the IP information in the header hasn't been spoofed. It preserves integrity but doesn't ensure confidentiality.

To authenticate all or part of a datagram's contents, AH adds a header calculated by the values in the datagram (the IP header and the data), essentially creating a message digest of the datagram. (This process works in much the same way that a checksum works for error detection.) Security is achieved by calculating the values with a special hashing algorithm and a specific key known only to the entities in the transaction. (Remember that the IPSec particulars, including keys, are negotiated and exchanged when the SA is set up.) Because only the authorized parties in the transaction have the keys, only they know how to run the computation to see whether the data has been tampered with. If the computation is the same, the message's authenticity is considered intact.

An AH header doesn't change the contents of a message, it simply adds a field following the IP header. The field contains the computed value of the IP header (except any fields that change in transit, such as the time to live [TTL] field) and the data, as shown in Figure 5-6.

AH works a little differently in the two IPSec modes: tunnel and transport (see Figure 5-7). In tunnel mode, AH authenticates the entire original header and builds a new IP header placed at the front of the entire datagram. The only fields not authenticated by AH in tunnel mode are the fields in the new IP header that can change in transit. In transport mode, AH authenticates the data payload and the original IP header, except the fields that change in transit.

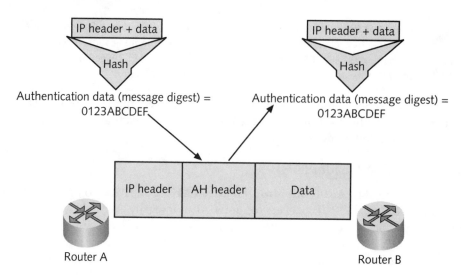

Figure 5-6 AH message exchange

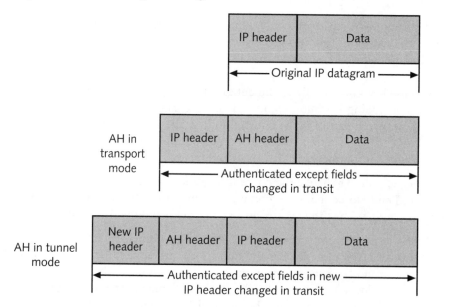

Figure 5-7 AH in tunnel and transport modes

Encapsulating Security Payload (ESP)

AH provides authentication and integrity for messages but does not provide confidentiality. The confidentiality of data transmitted through a VPN tunnel using IPSec is ensured by means of **Encapsulating Security Payload (ESP)**. ESP encrypts different parts of a TCP/IP packet, depending on whether IPSec is being used in transport mode or tunnel mode.

In tunnel mode, ESP encrypts both the header and data parts of each packet. This encryption protects data, but because the IP header is encrypted, the data can't pass through a firewall that uses NAT. The data won't pass because the firewall doesn't know how to interpret the IP source and destination information in its encrypted form.

In transport mode, only the data portion of the packet is encrypted. As a result, if the VPN is to be used with a firewall that performs NAT, IPSec should be configured to work in transport mode. Figure 5-8 illustrates the difference the IPSec mode makes to ESP.

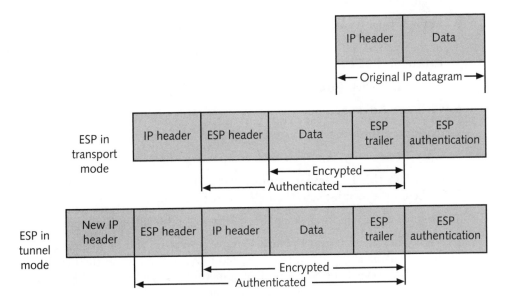

Figure 5-8 ESP in tunnel and transport modes

 NOTE You don't need to use AH and ESP together. Using them together offers additional security, but you might not want to use ESP if another device or application is already providing encryption. ESP, like other forms of encryption, requires a substantial amount of processing resources and can slow the rate of data transfer through a VPN.

Activity 5-6: Configuring the Client VPN Tunnel with IPSec

Time Required: 15 minutes

Objective: Configure the VPN client computer to use IPSec.

Description: After you have set up the host computer in your VPN connection to require IPSec, you need to configure the client computer to use IPSec as well. This activity assumes that you have directly connected two lab computers as described in Activities 5-1 and 5-2, configured a VPN client connection as described in Activity 5-3, and set up IPSec on the host computer as described in Activity 5-4. It requires a Windows 2000 computer as the client.

1. Open Control Panel, and double-click the **Network and Dial-up Connections** icon.

2. Right-click the **VPN** icon, and then click **Properties**.

3. In the Virtual Private Connection Properties dialog box, click the **Networking** tab.

4. In the Type of VPN server I am calling drop-down list, click **Layer-2 Tunneling Protocol (L2TP)**.

5. If necessary, click **Internet Protocol (TCP/IP)**, and then click **Properties**.

6. Click the **Advanced** button.

7. Click the **Options** tab.

8. Click **IP security**, and then click **Properties**.

9. Click **Use this IP security policy**. Verify that Client (Respond Only) is selected in the drop-down list, and then click **OK** four times.

10. Close all open windows except the Network and Dial-up Connections window.

11. Right-click the **Virtual Private Connection** icon, and then click **Connect**. Enter the user name and password you created in Activity 5-2, and then click **Connect**. A dialog box, opens notifying you that something is needed to make the connection. What is it? When you're finished, close all open windows.

NOTE Multiprotocol Label Switching (MPLS) is an IETF initiative that provides efficient routing, forwarding, switching, and designation of traffic. It's independent of layer 2 and 3 protocols and provides a means to map IP addressing information into a simple, fixed-length label. MPLS labels contain information based on routing tables, IP headers (source address), socket numbers, and services. After a packet has been labeled, it's routed by label switching. MPLS shows promise for reducing latency and easing strained Internet backbone infrastructures and does not rely on encapsulation or encryption for security. Although MPLS is beyond the scope of this book, it's worth learning more about this technology. You can read more about MPLS (RFC 3031) at *www.faqs.org/rfcs/rfc3031. html*. For a great tutorial at the International Engineering Consortium, go to *www.iec.org/online/tutorials/*, scroll down the list of tutorials, and select Multiprotocol Label Switching (MPLS).

VPN Core Activity 2: Encryption

Encryption is the process of rendering information unreadable by all but the intended recipient. The encryption process is carried out by means of a mathematical formula called an algorithm, which generates an encoded block of data called a **key**. The key is part of an electronic document called a **digital certificate**, which is obtained from a **certification authority (CA)**, a trusted organization that issues keys. (A quick search on any Internet search engine returns pages of results for CAs.) The key is then used to process data that the VPN transmits from one point to another; it encrypts data at the originating endpoint and decrypts it at the destination endpoint, as shown in Figure 5-9.

To perform encryption at both endpoints of the VPN, the keys must be exchanged by participants who have a Security Association (SA). The exchange can be performed using a variety of encryption methods. In one method, **symmetric cryptography**, the same key is exchanged by sender and recipient. In **asymmetric cryptography** (also called "public key cryptography"), two different keys are used—a public key and a private key. When a person or an organization obtains a digital certificate from a CA, an encryption algorithm is used to generate a private key. This key is never exchanged but is maintained securely by the certificate holder. The private key is used to generate a public key, which can be exchanged freely among VPN participants.

Another type of key exchange method, **Internet Key Exchange (IKE)**, uses **tunnel method encryption** to encrypt both the header and data parts of a packet and encapsulate the packet within a new packet that has a different header. IKE is increasingly popular because it provides a high level of security, which outweighs the degradation in network performance that results from complex encryption.

Other key exchange methods, such as FWZ, a proprietary protocol developed for the Check Point NG firewall, use **transport method encryption**, in which only the data portion of a packet is encrypted, not the header. Because the packet's original TCP/IP headers are left in place, performance is improved. However, transport method encryption doesn't offer as

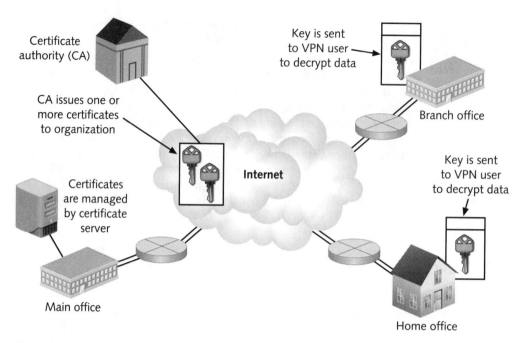

Figure 5-9   VPN endpoints encrypt and decrypt data by exchanging keys

much security as tunnel method encryption because the original IP header source and destination addresses could be intercepted, potentially revealing information about the organization's internal LAN configuration to attackers.

Encryption Schemes Used by VPNs

One advantage of a VPN is the capability to extend a wide area network (WAN) to multiple locations by using the Internet. However, the openness of the Internet creates security risks that need to be addressed by encryption. Encryption is one of the most important aspects of a firewall because it's how a VPN achieves its primary goal of preventing unauthorized users from reading the data payload.

Encryption schemes don't ensure a uniform level of security, however. Most older encryption algorithms, such as Data Encryption Standard (DES), have been cracked. The reason for this is simple: As computers have grown faster and more powerful, more processing power could be brought to bear on cracking an algorithm. The approach is usually brute force, meaning all possible keys are tried. Generally, the longer the key, the more difficult the cipher is to crack. So algorithms had to become more complex and use longer keys and more rounds of iteration (applications of the cipher to blocks of data). Some encryption schemes provide strong encryption that makes use of long (for instance, 128-bit) keys or multiple keys. The following sections describe encryption methods frequently used in VPNs.

Encryption and cryptography are fascinating if you enjoy math. Even if you don't, learning how some of these ciphers work is a good idea. For more information, try DES first, as it's a well-known algorithm, and there are thousands of helpful papers for every knowledge level. If you find DES interesting, you might want to check out Advanced Encryption Standard (AES), the new standard approved for the U.S. government (specified in FIPS 197). AES uses the Rjindael (arguably pronounced *Rhine*-dahl) symmetric encryption algorithm. You can find details on AES at *www.faqs.org/rfcs/rfc3268.html*.

5

Triple Data Encryption Standard (3DES)

Most VPN software or hardware makes use of **Triple Data Encryption Standard (3DES)** encryption. 3DES is a variation on **Data Encryption Standard (DES)**, which was developed by IBM in the mid-1970s and adopted as an encryption standard in 1977. Comparatively speaking, DES is not a secure encryption method; it has been cracked, although it requires multiple computers working on the problem solidly for many hours. 3DES is a far more secure protocol because it uses three separate 64-bit keys to process data. The same bit of unencrypted text is processed by the three keys in turn: The first key encrypts it, the second key decrypts it, and the third key encrypts it again, as shown in Figure 5-10.

3DES encryption

Figure 5-10   Most VPNs use 3DES encryption

Although the use of three keys in Figure 5-10 makes for a strong level of encryption, the problem is the time and resources needed to encrypt the information. It takes three times as long compared to using the original or "regular" version of DES, which uses only a single key. It's also more processing intensive, making its use a tradeoff. Although most modern computers are capable of using stronger encryption without intolerable performance degradation, encryption must be selected and managed carefully. Use stronger encryption to ensure confidentiality where needed and other forms of security, such as digital certificates, for authentication or integrity. In short, deploy what's needed without going into overkill; if you don't need to encrypt everything, don't.

NOTE

The National Institute of Standards and Technology (NIST) has developed a new encryption standard, Advanced Encryption Standard (AES), to replace 3DES. AES is stronger than 3DES and has the advantage of working faster. As of this writing, no successful attacks against AES have been recognized. For more information about AES, see *www.csrc.nist.gov/publications/fips/fips197/fips-197.pdf*.

Secure Sockets Layer (SSL)

A growing number of VPNs are using **Secure Sockets Layer (SSL)** to encrypt tunneled information via the Web. SSL was developed by Netscape Communications Corporation as a way of enabling Web servers and browsers to exchange encrypted information. SSL gets its name from the following:

- It uses public and private key encryption to create secure communications.

- It uses the sockets method of communication between servers and clients. (As you'll recall from previous networking courses, a socket is simply a combination of an IP address and a port number, such as 210.45.73.28/443.)

- It operates at the network layer (layer 3) of the OSI model of network communications. However, it can still provide a level of security that works between TCP and HTTP.

SSL is widely used on the Web; in fact, VPNs that use SSL can support only data that's exchanged by Web-enabled applications. For this reason, SSL is unlikely to replace IPSec as a security standard for VPNs, but it can be a useful adjunct to IPSec when Web browsers and Web servers need to connect securely.

An SSL session makes use of both symmetric and asymmetric keys. The asymmetric keys are used to start an SSL session, but symmetric keys are then generated dynamically for most of the transfer. It works like this:

1. The client connects to Web server using SSL protocol.

2. The two machines arrange a "handshake" during which they authenticate each other and determine what formulas and protocols will be used to encrypt and exchange information. The client sends the server its preferences for encryption method, the SSL version number, and a randomly generated number to be used later.

3. The server responds with the SSL version number, its own cipher preferences, and its digital certificate. The digital certificate tells the client who issued it, a data range, and the server's public key. The server can ask the client for its own digital certificate at this point.

4. The client verifies that the date and other information on the digital certificate are valid. The domain name on the digital certificate is checked to verify whether it matches the server's domain name. If it matches, the client generates

a "pre-master" code and sends it to the server using the server's public key. The client's digital certificate is also sent, if the server requested one.

5. The server uses its private key to decode the pre-master code that the client sent. The server then generates a master secret key that both client and server use to generate session keys—symmetric keys that are used to encrypt and decrypt information exchanged during the SSL session and to verify the integrity of data exchanged.

6. The server and client then exchange messages to the effect that future messages will be encrypted with the session key, and both send the other a separate, encrypted message that their side of the handshake is complete.

7. The handshake is completed, and the SSL session begins. Either side can renegotiate the connection at any time, and the process repeats (which could happen because of a lost connection, timeout, or user intervention, such as logging out).

SSL is a secure way to transmit data on the Web, such as credit card numbers used for online purchases. However, SSL can cause problems for firewalls that can't interpret SSL data, in much the same way that firewalls can have trouble interpreting IPSec data that use tunnel mode encryption.

NOTE Transport Layer Security (TLS) is the protocol the IETF is currently working on to replace SSL. Although it's not an official Internet standard yet, it's likely to become a prominent figure on the Web in the future. You can find out more about how TLS can be used to secure HTTP connections at *www.ietf.org/rfc/rfc2818.txt* or by running a search on the keyword TLS. The major RFCs on TLS are RFC 2818 and RFC 2246.

VPN Core Activity 3: Authentication

The third core activity VPNs perform to ensure the security of tunneled communications is authentication—the process of identifying a user or computer as being authorized to access and use network resources. Authentication is essential because network hosts that receive VPN communications need to know that the originator of the communication is an approved user of the VPN.

The type of authentication used in a VPN depends on the tunneling protocol. A growing number of networks use IPSec to authenticate users; the participants in a VPN establish a Security Association (SA) and exchange keys to authenticate one another. PPTP, which is used for dial-in access to a remote server, uses MS-CHAP, in which both computers exchange authentication packets and authenticate one another.

VPNs use digital certificates to authenticate users and use encryption to ensure that, even if communication is intercepted in transit, it can't be read. The VPN core activities of encapsulation, encryption, and authentication are shown in Figure 5-11.

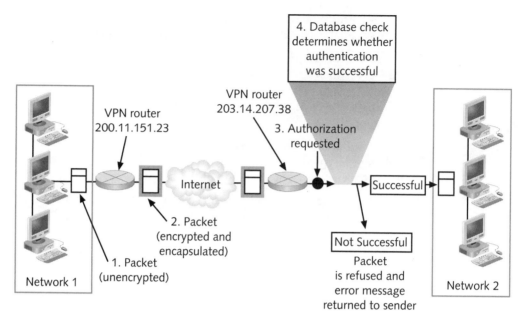

Figure 5-11 VPN core activities

In Figure 5-11, the following are the basic steps in the authentication process:

1. The source computer transmits the unencrypted packet on internal network 1.

2. After the VPN router at 200.11.151.23 encrypts and encapsulates the packet, the packet passes through the gateway into the Internet.

3. The VPN router at internal network 2 requests authentication.

4. A database check determines whether authentication is successful. If it is, the packet is allowed to reach its destination. If it's not, an error message is returned.

Kerberos

Kerberos is an authentication system developed at the Massachusetts Institute of Technology (MIT). The name refers to the three-headed dog in Greek mythology that was said to guard the gates of Hades. Kerberos authenticates the identity of network users by using a simple method called "authentication by assertion." In this method, the computer that connects to a server and requests services asserts that it's acting on behalf of an approved user of those services.

Although this method sounds simple, the process by which computers communicate the assertion and response is not. Figure 5-12 illustrates how Kerberos works.

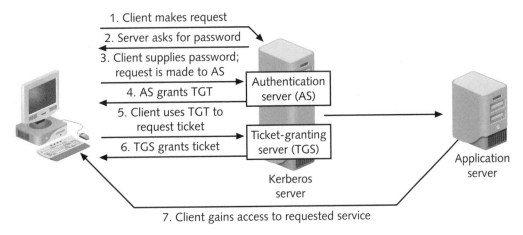

Figure 5-12   The authentication process using Kerberos

In Figure 5-12, the following list outlines what happens at each step:

1. A client requests a file or other service.

2. The server prompts the client for a user name and password (user account credentials).

3. The client submits the credentials, and the request is sent to an authentication server (AS) that's part of the Kerberos system. The Kerberos AS is known as the **Key Distribution Center (KDC)**. A domain controller can also serve as the authentication server in Windows 2000 or XP.

4. The AS creates an encrypted code called a session key, based on the client's password plus a random number associated with the service being requested. This session key is called a **ticket-granting ticket (TGT)**.

5. The AS grants the TGT.

6. The client presents the TGT to the **ticket-granting server (TGS)**. The TGS is also part of the Kerberos system but may or may not be the same server as the AS.

7. The TGS grants the session ticket and forwards the session ticket to the server holding the requested file or service on behalf of the requesting client.

8. The client gains access to the requested service or file.

This process sounds complex and it is, but this transaction takes place in the background, so it isn't noticeable to users. A major advantage of Kerberos is that passwords aren't stored on the system, so they can't be intercepted. A ticket is specific to a particular user and typically expires after a set period of time (usually eight hours). Kerberos does allow postdated tickets and renewable tickets, but users can't manipulate tickets directly; they must request these flags when requesting their tickets.

In addition, Kerberos has a lower "network overhead" than a Public Key Infrastructure (PKI), which means you don't need to install a central server and perform as many management tasks as you might with a PKI. This is especially true in a small internal network where only a few users need access to shared resources. Kerberos is also handy for single sign-on (SSO), in which a user signs on once but is allowed access to multiple resources. Instead of having to sign on to each resource and keep track of all those user account names and passwords, the user simply signs on to the Kerberos authentication services and has access to all resources he or she has permission to access.

There is a major concern with Kerberos, however. The AS (KDC) is a single point of failure for Kerberos. If the AS goes down (and there are no backup servers that can take over this role), no one is able to be authenticated. Administrators using a single AS should take measures to ensure that authentication services can continue to function in the event of an AS failure.

NOTE   Kerberos is defined in RFC 1510. If you want more information on Kerberos, the RFC is a great place to get accurate, detailed information. Be wary of your research sources; remember, they might not always be accurate, so getting your information directly from the source is often better. Make sure you're looking at the currently valid document, however, because standards change or become obsolete.

Advantages and Disadvantages of VPNs

VPNs offer a high level of security—provided network administrators address their inherent challenges. For instance, if a VPN device is configured incorrectly or a remote user at a VPN endpoint disables his or her firewall by mistake and lets in an attacker, the protection the VPN normally provides can be undone. In addition, VPNs can be complex to configure, and the hardware and software can represent a substantial investment. You should be aware of the advantages and disadvantages of VPNs. Table 5-4 summarizes some of the important ones.

Table 5-4   Some advantages and disadvantages of VPNs

Advantages	Disadvantages
Far less expensive than leased lines	Can be complex to configure
Many elements working together provide strong security	Can result in slower data transfer rates than a leased line
Standards and protocols used in VPNs are well developed and widely used	Depends on the often unpredictable Internet; if your ISP or other parts of the Internet go down, your VPN goes down
Can result in less overall complexity in an organization's network	Requires administrator to install VPN client software on remote computers
Can make use of a company's existing broadband connection	VPN hardware and software from different vendors might prove incompatible because they use different protocols

By focusing on Internet-based technologies, VPNs simplify a network. You have only one Internet connection to manage instead of an Internet connection plus one or more leased lines. In addition, running a VPN means you have even more ways to maximize your **network uptime** (the amount of time a network, such as the Internet or a corporate LAN, is available to users). Downtime (the time your network resources are unavailable to users) is expensive. In addition to the actual hard cost of repairs, downtime costs administrators time to troubleshoot and repair the problem and results in lost productivity for users. If your network is up and running smoothly, you don't need to spend time troubleshooting and making repairs.

TIP Some companies that maintain VPNs with partner organizations benefit by using the same ISP as those partners for their Internet connection. Positioning the participants in the VPN on the same part of the Internet backbone can make the VPN run more smoothly and reliably.

CHAPTER SUMMARY

- VPNs are virtual in that they do not make use of dedicated leased lines. Instead, they connect computers and networks through the public Internet.

- VPNs are private because they send data through a secure tunnel that leads from one endpoint to another. Only the endpoints are static; tunnels are established as needed and torn down when no longer needed. Each endpoint is terminated by VPN hardware or software that encrypts and encapsulates the data.

- VPNs are networks that connect one network to one or more networks, one computer to another, or one computer to a network.

- Because VPNs can be complex to configure, the reasons for establishing them should be understood. The need to keep critical business communications private and secure drives adoption of VPNs. The cost-effectiveness of using the Internet for VPN communications also makes VPNs attractive. On the other hand, encryption performed by VPNs can slow down data transfer rates. Reliance on the Internet, which is often unpredictable, can result in the VPN going down along with ISP connections.

- VPNs consist of various components. They include VPN servers, which are configured to accept connections from client computers; VPN clients, the tunnels through which data passes; and protocols that determine how the tunneled data is to be encrypted, such as Internet Protocol Security (IPSec). A site-to-site VPN uses these components to connect to networks. A client-to-site VPN connects a remote user to a network. VPN endpoints can be terminated by VPN hardware, VPN software, or a combination of both.

- VPN encapsulation encloses one packet of digital information within another to conceal the original packet's source and destination IP address and to protect the contents.

- VPNs make use of standard sets of instructions called protocols that secure tunneled communications between endpoints. Secure Shell is a protocol used to authenticate and encrypt packets in a UNIX-based environment. Version 5 of the Socks protocol can also provide security for VPN transactions, but it's not widely used. Point-to-Point Protocol Tunneling (PPTP) and Layer 2 Tunneling Protocol (L2TP) enable remote users to dial in to a computer over a secure VPN connection.

❑ Internet Protocol Security (IPSec) combined with Internet Key Exchange (IKE) is one of the most popular protocols because of its wide support in the industry and high degree of security through Authentication Header (AH) authentication and Encapsulating Security Payload (ESP) encryption.

❑ Encryption makes the contents of the packet—not only its data, but also its header information—unreadable by all but the intended recipient. Encryption is one of the technologies that make VPNs possible. Most VPNs today use 3DES encryption, a variation of Data Encryption Standard (DES) in which three separate keys are used to process information. However, some VPNs use Secure Sockets Layer (SSL) encryption when Web-based applications need to be connected securely. Digital certificates, symmetric and asymmetric cryptography, and Internet Key Exchange (IKE) are also used to encrypt VPN transmissions.

❑ Authentication ensures that the computers participating in a VPN are authorized users. The authentication method used by VPNs depends on the tunneling protocol and can include IPSec, key exchanges, MS-CHAP, and digital certificates.

❑ Another strong authentication/encryption system, Kerberos, is used in Windows and other operating systems to give employees access to network resources for relatively short periods by issuing "tickets."

❑ VPNs have several advantages: They offer a high level of security, low cost, and great flexibility for remote access and establishing extranets. They can simplify network management and maximize network uptime. VPNs have their disadvantages, too. If they're configured incorrectly, they can introduce serious security risks. Encryption can slow performance, and reliance on the Internet means your VPN is down if your Internet connection or ISP is down. Remote machines must have the VPN client software installed, and there are compatibility issues between different VPN products.

KEY TERMS

asymmetric cryptography — A type of encryption in which two different keys are used; also called public key cryptography. A private key is kept by the certificate holder and never shared; a public key is shared among users to encrypt and decrypt communications. *See also* symmetric cryptography.

Authentication Header (AH) — An IPSec protocol that provides authentication of TCP/IP packets to ensure data integrity.

certification authority (CA) — A trusted organization that issues digital certificates that can be used to generate keys. *See also* digital certificate.

client-to-site VPN — A type of VPN connection that makes a network accessible to remote users requiring dial-in access; also called a remote access VPN.

Data Encryption Standard (DES) — An encryption scheme developed by IBM in the mid-1970s that was adopted as an encryption standard in 1977.

digital certificate — An electronic document issued by a certification authority that contains information about the certificate holder and can be used to exchange public and private keys. *See also* certification authority (CA).

Encapsulating Security Payload (ESP) — An IPSec protocol that encrypts both the header and data parts of each TCP/IP packet.

encapsulation — The process of enclosing a packet within another one that has different IP source and destination information to ensure a high degree of protection.

encryption — The process of rendering information unreadable by all but the intended recipient.

Internet Key Exchange (IKE) — A form of key exchange used to encrypt and decrypt data as it passes through a VPN tunnel. IKE uses tunnel method encryption to encrypt and then encapsulate packets for extra security. *See also* tunnel method encryption.

Internet Protocol Security (IPSec) — A set of standard procedures that the Internet Engineering Task Force (IETF) developed for enabling secure communications on the Internet.

Internet Security Association Key Management Protocol (ISAKMP) — An IPSec-related protocol that enables two computers to agree on security settings and establish a Security Association so that they can exchange keys using Internet Key Exchange. *See also* Internet Key Exchange (IKE) *and* Security Association (SA).

IPSec driver — Software that handles the actual tasks of encrypting, authenticating, decrypting, and checking packets in an IPSec connection.

Kerberos — An IETF standard for secure authentication of requests for resource access. Kerberos is defined in RFC 1510.

key — An encoded block of data generated by an algorithm and used to encrypt and decrypt data.

Key Distribution Center (KDC) — A Kerberos component that holds secret keys for users, applications, services, or resources that use Kerberos; creates and distributes session keys by using symmetric cryptography.

network uptime — The amount of time a network is available for users to connect successfully and access resources.

Point-to-Point Tunneling Protocol (PPTP) — A tunneling protocol used for dial-up access to a remote server.

scalable — The capability to maintain a consistent level of operation as a network grows.

Secure Sockets Layer (SSL) — A protocol developed by Netscape Communications Corporation as a way of enabling Web servers and browsers to exchange encrypted information.

Secure Shell (SSH) — A VPN authentication that works with UNIX-based systems to create a secure transport layer connection between participating computers; SSH makes use of public key cryptography.

Security Association (SA) — A designation for users, computers, or gateways that can participate in a VPN and encrypt and decrypt data using keys.

site-to-site VPN — A VPN that uses hardware devices, such as routers, to connect two networks; also called a gateway-to-gateway VPN.

Socks — A communications protocol that provides proxy services for applications that don't normally support proxying and enables applications to set up a secure tunnel using encryption and authentication.

symmetric cryptography — A type of encryption in which the sender and recipient exchange the same key. *See also* asymmetric cryptography.

ticket-granting server (TGS) — The part of the KDC that creates and distributes session keys clients use to access resources. *See also* Key Distribution Center (KDC).

ticket-granting ticket (TGT) — The TGT is essentially a digital token sent from the Authentication Server to the client. The client presents the TGT to the TGS to obtain a session key to access the resource. *See also* Key Distribution Center (KDC) *and* Ticket-Granting Server (TGS).

transport method encryption — A method of encryption in which only the data portion of a packet is encrypted, not the header. This method results in improved performance.

Triple Data Encryption Standard (3DES) — A stronger variation of DES that uses three separate 64-bit keys to process data, making the encryption much harder to break.

tunnel — The connection between two endpoints in a VPN.

tunnel method encryption — A method of key exchange that encrypts both the header and data parts of a packet and encapsulates the packet within a new packet that has a different header.

virtual private network (VPN) — A set of technologies that provides a cost-effective way for two or more networks to make a secure private connection using public connections, usually the Internet. VPN endpoints establish connections (tunnels) to transmit and receive data, and then tear the connections down when they're no longer needed. Combinations of encryption, authentication, and encapsulation help ensure confidentiality, privacy, and integrity of transmitted information.

VPN appliance — A hardware device designed to terminate VPNs and join multiple LANs.

VPN client — A router or an operating system that initiates a connection to a VPN server.

VPN protocols — Sets of standardized communication settings that software and hardware use to encrypt data that's sent through a VPN.

VPN server — A computer configured to accept VPN connections from clients.

REVIEW QUESTIONS

5

1. A VPN is said to be virtual because the connections are _____ .
   (Choose all that apply.)

   a. established permanently

   b. circuit-switched

   c. transient

   d. set up and torn down as needed

2. VPNs differ from leased lines in that they use which of the following to make connections?

   a. hardware or software

   b. the public Internet

   c. operating systems

   d. all of the above

3. The VPN connection through which data passes from one endpoint to another is called a(n) _____ .

   a. gateway

   b. extranet

   c. tunnel

   d. transport

4. Under what circumstances does a firewall need to be installed at the endpoint of a VPN connection, and why?

5. A VPN that uses hardware to connect two networks is called which of the following? (Choose all that apply.)

   a. gateway-to-gateway VPN

   b. hub-and-spoke arrangement

   c. tunnel

   d. site-to-site VPN

6. What term describes a set of procedures for enabling a VPN to encrypt traffic?

   a. public key cryptography

   b. protocol

   c. encapsulation

   d. digital certificate

7. _____ protects the integrity of data sent along the VPN tunnel; the source and destination information of the actual data packets is completely hidden.

   a. Encryption

   b. A VPN appliance

   c. IPSec

   d. Encapsulation

8. PPTP uses a proprietary technology called _____ to encrypt data that passes between the remote computer and the remote access server.

   a. Layer 2 Tunneling Protocol (L2TP)

   b. Microsoft Point-to-Point Encryption (MPPE)

   c. MS-CHAP

   d. IPSec

9. What type of VPN is used to provide remote users with dial-up access to a central office?

   a. client-to-site

   b. site-to-site

   c. gateway-to-gateway

   d. mesh configuration

10. A group of authentication and encryption settings that two computers negotiate to set up a secure VPN connection is called which of the following?

    a. protocol

    b. Security Association (SA)

    c. handshake

    d. key exchange

11. Computers in a VPN authenticate one another by means of which encryption-related component?

    a. public key

    b. challenge/response

    c. digital certificate

    d. user name/password

12. What makes a VPN such a cost-effective option?

    a. Computers can use the same hardware and software.

    b. It requires no administrative configuration to set up or maintain.

    c. Many VPN applications are available as shareware or freeware.

    d. VPNs use public Internet and ISP connections.

13. _____ provides authentication and encryption of TCP/IP packets over a VPN or other connection and is used primarily on UNIX-based systems.

  a. SSL

  b. SSH

  c. MPPE

  d. PPTP

14. Companies that maintain VPNs with business partners often benefit by using the same _____ . (Choose all that apply.)

  a. VPN hardware

  b. IP address range

  c. Internet service provider (ISP)

  d. certification authority (CA)

15. IPSec provides for what security activity to take place before data is encrypted or transmitted?

  a. encapsulation

  b. authentication

  c. establishment of a Security Association (SA)

  d. application of security policy settings

16. To access an application protected by Kerberos, which of the following is required?

  a. certificate

  b. key

  c. user name/password

  d. ticket

17. Which of the following adds encrypted authentication and support for User Datagram Protocol (UDP)?

  a. SSH

  b. Kerberos

  c. Socks v. 5

  d. ESP

18. Internet Key Exchange (IKE) uses which of the following to encrypt a packet's header and data?

  a. asymmetric cryptography

  b. public key cryptography

  c. transport method encryption

  d. tunnel method encryption

19. If a VPN is to be used with a firewall that performs NAT, IPSec should be configured to work in which mode?

    a. tunnel

    b. transport

    c. pass-through

    d. encapsulation

20. To perform encryption at both endpoints of a VPN, the keys must be exchanged by participants who have a(n) _____ .

    a. Symmetric Association

    b. Internet Key Exchange tunnel

    c. certificate

    d. Security Association

HANDS-ON PROJECTS

HANDS-ON PROJECTS

Hands-On Project 5-1: Combining a VPN with a Firewall

Time Required: 15 minutes

Objective: Troubleshoot a problem scenario and propose solutions to correct the problem.

Description: You configured a VPN to use IPSec in its most secure mode—using ESP with tunnel mode. However, you encounter problems with the firewall, which is positioned between the VPN and the internal LAN. The firewall ends up dropping a substantial percentage of the packets that are terminated by the VPN device. Troubleshoot the situation by answering the following questions:

1. What could be causing the firewall to fail to process VPN traffic?

   _____

   _____

2. How could you solve the problem?

   _____

   _____

   _____

   _____

Hands-On Project 5-2: Adjusting a VPN for Scalability

Time Required: 15 minutes

Objective: Analyze a problem scenario to determine possible solutions.

Description: Your security policy calls for your network defenses to provide maximum security, as well as compatibility with other systems. Accordingly, you configure your organization's VPN to use both AH authentication and ESP encryption. You perform a network audit after a week and notice that performance has slowed dramatically. You have received user complaints about it and need to make adjustments. Use the following lines to summarize your options:

_____

_____

_____

_____

_____

CASE PROJECTS

Case Project 5-1: Planning Remote Access

In this book's previous running case projects, you have designed a basic network, conducted a risk assessment, and drafted an initial security policy for LedGrafix. Since then, you have researched log analysis tools and started to think about how to handle ongoing network management.

In a recent progress meeting, the vice president of LedGrafix brought up some points of concern. In the video game business, salespeople often travel to promote and demonstrate products, and marketing representatives must travel occasionally to explore market demand for new products and to visit retailers to expand the company's market. In addition, several game developers have approached the VP about working from home part-time and attending development seminars.

Because the VP's concerns are valid, the president has asked you to provide a way for traveling workers to connect to resources on the company LAN and for remote workers to access development materials and resources from home securely. You have met with all department heads to determine remote access needs and have compiled a list of requirements. The company president and VP have reviewed your list and approved it. Now you must revise your network plan to satisfy these additional requirements:

1. All personnel must be able to access their work email accounts and personal folders remotely.

2. No personal folders can contain documents deemed confidential, and any data of this type must be secured in transit.

3. Sales personnel must be able to access their personal folders and do the following from any location:

   a. Access order-processing systems to enter new orders, check order status, or modify orders.

   b. Access customer account data to enter payment information, check debt status, or adjust pricing for orders.

   c. Access company brochures, flyers, demonstrations, presentation programs, and other sales materials.

4. Marketing personnel must be able to do the following:

   a. Connect to customer account data to enter new information and update information on existing customers.

   b. Access company marketing materials, brochures, and presentations.

   c. Develop new marketing materials while traveling and upload new materials for review by upper management.

5. Accounting data and payroll must be remotely accessible only to Bostern Accounting and Tax Services, the company handling bookkeeping services for LedGrafix. No accounting and payroll files can be e-mailed outside the company LAN or accessible (internally or externally) to any employees other than upper management and the Accounting Department.

6. The Shipping and Receiving Department must be able to track outgoing and incoming shipments.

7. An outside vendor produces, packages, and distributes LedGrafix game software. This vendor must be able to connect to the ordering system to get new orders, update order status, and record shipping details of completed orders.

Additionally, you must address the following concerns:

- The system must be scalable to meet the company's needs for the next three years.

- Budget is a concern. The company is doing well financially but has limited capital to work with currently, so you must propose a solution that costs as little as possible up front.

You have two vendors who need remote access and up to 25 company employees who might need remote access to the corporate LAN. Develop a remote access plan that meets the requirements described so far. Your design must include the following:

1. A complete list of the hardware and software needed

2. A cost breakdown for any expenditure your design requires (including any fees for ISPs, dedicated lines, and so on)

3. An estimate of ongoing maintenance costs, including support personnel, employee training, possible repairs, updates, and upgrades

4. Other costs, if applicable

5. Complete information about support options, costs, contact information, and warrantees

6. A plan for testing the new systems

7. An updated network diagram that shows the physical and logical layout of the network with the remote access solution

8. Any other information relevant to your design, such as dial-up numbers, encryption techniques, authentication and access controls, how client machines should be configured, and so on

Submit your design proposal, cost breakdown, and updated diagrams to your instructor.

CASE PROJECTS

Case Project 5-2: Determining the True Cost of Downtime

Many companies judge their network administrator's success or failure based on network uptime: The higher the ratio of uptime to downtime, the "better" the administrator is thought to be. Downtime includes planned outages for maintenance and upgrades, as well as unplanned outages caused by attacks, equipment failures, disasters, and so on. Calculating the true cost of downtime is difficult because intangibles are part of the equation. You must include the obvious costs of repairs, such as replacement equipment, and the time to install equipment, restore configurations and data, test the replacement, and deploy it. Other costs might not be as easy to quantify. Placing a dollar amount on lost productivity, loss of consumer confidence, and loss of staff morale can be difficult.

For this project, locate methods of calculating the cost of downtime. Begin by conducting an Internet search on the term "cost of downtime." This search should produce useful results. What are some common costs associated with downtime? How are some of these costs calculated? Are any utilities available? How accurate do you think they are? Write a report summarizing your findings.

6

VPN IMPLEMENTATION

After reading this chapter and completing the exercises, you will be able to:

♦ Explain design considerations for a VPN

♦ Describe options for VPN configuration

♦ Explain how to set up VPNs with firewalls

♦ Explain how to adjust packet-filtering rules for VPNs

♦ Describe guidelines for auditing VPNs and VPN policies

A virtual private network (VPN) combines two of the three tenets representing essential elements of a network defense strategy: confidentiality and integrity. (Refer to the CIA triad discussed in Chapter 1.) Designed and deployed correctly, a VPN is a secure, cost-effective way for remote users to access corporate resources, for remote sites to connect to one another or the central office, and for partners or vendors to share resources. Designed or deployed incorrectly, a VPN creates a potentially disastrous security liability. Although it's no laughing matter, an improperly configured VPN can be compared to the proverbial "screen door on a submarine"—it's there, but it does little good.

This chapter builds on the concepts you learned in Chapter 5. Using those concepts, you learn the process of designing, testing, and deploying a VPN to meet an organization's needs. Like most technologies, VPNs exist to support business processes. You need to know about the business and its goals, needs, and plans before you can design an effective and secure VPN strategy. First, you assess the business, its existing infrastructure, and connectivity needs. After you have a clear picture of what's needed and the resources you have to work with, you can decide where and how to place the VPN server and how to configure and control access.

You also learn the importance of using a VPN with a firewall and how packet filtering is used to further secure your VPN. Finally, the importance of auditing and reviewing your VPN security policy is discussed.

Designing a VPN

Like so many other tasks in information technology, designing a VPN first requires a thorough assessment of an organization's needs and goals. Considering the type of business, how many employees it has, what infrastructure is already in place, and the security required for its data gives you the basis for planning VPN deployment. Perhaps the most difficult aspect of the design process is enforcing security on the client side of the VPN tunnel. For example, many telecommuters use their personal computers to work from home. If these computers are compromised somehow, the internal network will be at risk. Client-side issues to consider when designing your VPN strategy include whether to require the client to use a firewall (hardware or software) and intrusion detection system (IDS) software and whether policies should be enforced on client computers before allowing remote users to authenticate to the internal LAN.

Business Needs

As with most technologies, your business processes determine the manner in which you implement a VPN strategy. The nature of the business, its employees, current and projected growth, and locations are helpful in determining what configuration you use and what hardware you need. A careful analysis of the existing infrastructure helps you integrate the VPN with minimal disruption, and testing the planned deployment carefully helps you avoid unexpected and undesirable outcomes. You also need to review the company security policy for guidance on existing security goals and procedures.

As you learned in Chapter 5, functionally speaking, VPNs can be classified as site-to-site or client-to-site. They can be used together or separately to offer cost-effective, secure connectivity to other offices or partners or to give employees, vendors, and others inexpensive access to corporate resources. The key to remember is that a VPN extends the corporate network by using public communications channels. When it's set up and configured correctly, a VPN can supply inexpensive, secure access; set up incorrectly, a VPN is a tremendous security liability that can give intruders full access to your network. There are also legal implications to failing to secure access to a remote network. If your VPN connects to partner or vendor networks, and an intruder gains access to their network through your poorly configured VPN, your company could face litigation for any damages resulting from the breach. This scenario probably isn't likely, but it isn't impossible. The point is that you must consider the security implications of any extension of your network.

Nature of the Business

First, consider the nature of the business. What does it do? What product or service does it sell and who are its customers? These questions might seem unrelated, but they're an important part of planning and deployment. You need to know who you're providing access for and where they're located. Analyzing the computing systems in place helps you determine how and where to place the VPN systems. The network administrator might have accurate and current documentation that can help, but the task of documenting a network is usually neglected.

Cost is usually a key factor and narrows down the choices of hardware and software. Beware of "bleeding edge" technology that could become outdated or unsupported just weeks after you purchase it. Also, be aware that having unlimited funds can cause almost as many problems as not having enough funds. Having the authority to use the most expensive components and configurations doesn't mean your design will be foolproof. Regardless of your budgetary restrictions (or lack of them), your design must integrate with existing technology and provide services without failure. In other words, don't redesign the wheel if it isn't necessary. For example, if you're installing VPN services on a network that uses older firewalls on the perimeter network, consider configuring the existing firewalls to provide VPN services before deciding to replace the firewalls with newer versions. If the firewalls provide the necessary services with acceptable performance and security and offer adequate scalability, upgrading probably isn't necessary. Of course, if the CIO instructs you otherwise, buy the brand-new high-end solution and deploy it.

For a VPN design, there are no hard-and-fast rules. As you learned in Chapter 5, VPNs can be implemented through OS software or hardware devices or supported by routers or firewalls. VPNs are as diverse as the needs they support. When you have a clear picture of the organization and its users, you can begin planning the configuration, testing, and deployment. A secure VPN design should address the following factors:

- Secure connectivity
- Availability
- Authentication
- Secure management
- Reliability
- Scalability
- Performance

Client Security

There are several ways to increase VPN client security, from network configuration settings to third-party software solutions. When a Windows client connects to the VPN server, the Use default gateway on remote network check box is selected (see Activity 6-1). This option prevents split tunneling by the client. **Split tunneling** is the term used to describe multiple paths. One path goes to the VPN server and is secured, but an unauthorized and unsecured path permits users to connect to the Internet or some other network while still connected to the corporate VPN (see Figure 6-1). Split tunneling leaves the VPN server and internal LAN vulnerable to attack.

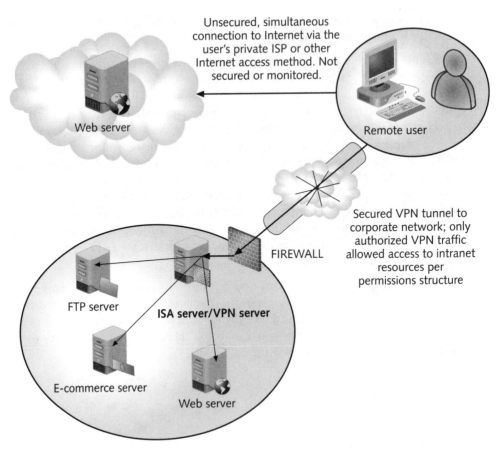

Figure 6-1 Split tunneling opens a security risk in your network

Small organizations without the resources to enforce total control over the client should at least require users to sign an acceptable use agreement. Remote users should be required to maintain an Internet firewall and current virus protection on the client computer and to secure the computer against unauthorized use and should be prevented from enabling split tunneling while connected to the company's LAN.

Activity 6-1: Setting the Default Gateway on a Client Computer

Time Required: 15 minutes

Objective: Prevent split tunneling on a VPN client computer.

Description: Using the VPN connection you established on the Windows 2000 computer in Chapter 5, you enable the Use default gateway on remote network option on the client computer's VPN dial-up connection.

1. On the Windows 2000 computer, open Control Panel and double-click **Network Connections**.

2. Right-click the VPN connection you want to change, and then click **Properties**.

3. Click the **Networking** tab, click **Internet Protocol (TCP/IP)** in the Components checked are used by this connection list, and then click **Properties**.

4. Click the **Advanced** button, and then click the **Use default gateway on remote network** check box (see Figure 6-2).

5. Click **OK** three times and close any open windows.

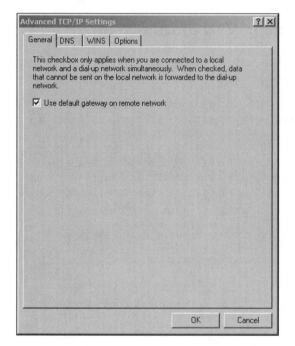

Figure 6-2   Preventing split tunneling

Planning VPN Deployment

Now that you have a clear picture of the business, you can begin planning the VPN deployment. The first consideration is the existing infrastructure. If the network administrator has an accurate network map, your job is fairly easy. This is rarely the case, however, so you might need to examine the network and make your own map. It doesn't need to be complex. It just needs to accurately reflect the configuration into which you're integrating VPN services.

After you decide on the placement of VPN servers, you can begin researching the hardware or software to use. You can determine whether reconfiguring the existing firewall or a server in the perimeter network to support VPN connections will work, or if you need to purchase a VPN appliance, server, firewall, or router to do the job. This task is highly subjective, and the architectures vary so widely that listing all the options is nearly impossible. Your research into the business and assessment of its needs and existing infrastructure will guide you, and vendors are always happy to assist potential buyers. Use their knowledge to help you decide what's going to meet your needs, offer sufficient scalability, fall within budgetary constraints, and integrate with existing systems. You might want to develop a list of requirements when meeting with vendors to ensure nothing is overlooked. Remember to follow security policy guidelines, however, when giving out network information. Some information, such as trade secrets or business processes that give your company a competitive advantage, must remain confidential.

ACTIVITY

Activity 6-2: Recommending VPN Procurement

Time Required: 30 minutes

Objective: Research and recommend hardware to meet a specific VPN solution.

Description: In this activity, you assess the following scenario and research different ways to meet the requirements. Your instructor might have you present your recommendations to the class or ask you for a written report.

Scenario: You manage all parts of an extranet that comprises several different subnets. Because you are the administrator for these subnets, you have control over what equipment each part of the network uses. You're expecting heavy traffic needs and have been assigned to recommend VPN equipment.

1. What kind of VPN components would make sense in this situation?

   _____

   _____

2. What kind of topology would be the easiest for you to configure and maintain?

   _____

   _____

CONFIGURING VPNS

To set up a VPN, you need to define a **VPN domain**: a set of one or more computers that VPN hardware and software handle as a single entity. The computers in a VPN domain use the VPN to communicate with another domain. With a firewall program, such as Check Point NG, a domain might be a set of networked computers grouped under a name—Local_Net or Office_Net, for example. If you set up Windows to function as a VPN host, you can designate a set of IP addresses for accessing that host (see Figure 6-3).

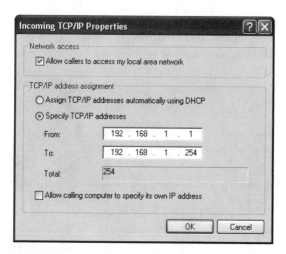

Figure 6-3   Enabling a Windows-based VPN host to work with a set of IP addresses

Single and Multiple Entry Point Configurations

In addition to defining a VPN domain, you need to determine whether the network gateway will be included in that domain. Including the network gateway, in turn, depends on whether your network has a site-to-site or client-to-site VPN configuration (as explained in Chapter 5). Small networks that use VPNs typically have only site-to-site connections and often have **single entry point configurations**: All traffic to and from the network passes through a single gateway, such as a router or firewall (or both). In a single entry point configuration, the gateway must be a member of the VPN domain. In the configuration shown in Figure 6-4, the VPN domain includes a group of computers in the internal LAN as well as the gateway itself.

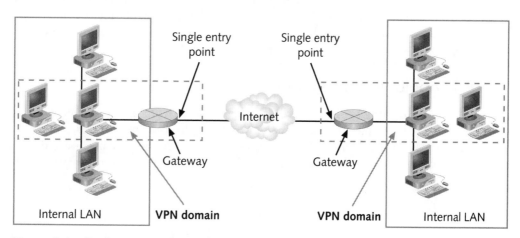

Figure 6-4   Single entry point configuration

In contrast, many large organizations have networks with several client-to-site connections. These connections require **multiple entry point configurations** in which multiple gateways are used, each with a VPN tunnel connecting a different location (see Figure 6-5).

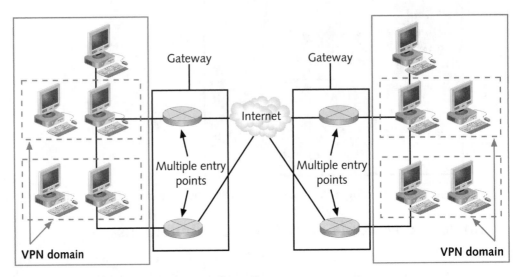

Figure 6-5   Multiple entry point configuration

In a multiple entry point configuration, excluding the gateway from the VPN domain is important. If you don't exclude the gateway, all traffic to and from each gateway in the internal network is encrypted. This encryption would reduce performance unnecessarily because you need to encrypt only the traffic from gateway to gateway. It's also important to prevent VPN domains from overlapping; having multiple routes in routing tables could cause some traffic to be routed incorrectly or not at all because of repeated IP addresses. If a router has multiple paths for directing packets, it might not respond correctly. This problem is easily corrected by configuring routing tables correctly; however, this topic is beyond the scope of the SCNP certification and this book.

VPN Topology Configurations

A VPN's **topology**—the way components in a network are connected physically to one another—determines how gateways, networks, and clients are related to each other. As explained in the following sections, VPN topologies correspond to the basic physical and logical topologies of any network. The three basic configurations are mesh, star, and hybrid VPNs.

Mesh Topology

In a **mesh configuration**, all participants in the VPN have Security Associations (SAs) with one another. (Refer to Chapter 5 for a review of SAs.) Two types of mesh arrangements are possible:

- *Full mesh*—Every subnetwork is connected to all other subnets in the VPN (see Figure 6-6). This topology is complex to manage and is best used with small VPNs.

- *Partial mesh*—Any subnet in the VPN may or may not be connected to the other subnets. This configuration offers more flexibility than a full mesh arrangement.

6

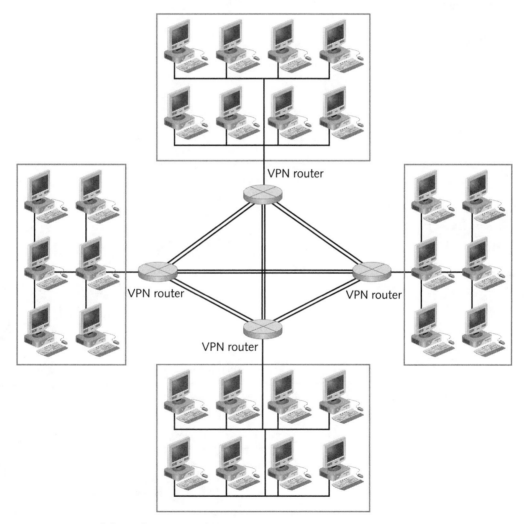

Figure 6-6   A full mesh VPN configuration

The advantage of a mesh configuration is that each participant can establish VPN communications with all the other participants. However, if a new LAN is added to the VPN, all other VPN devices have to be updated to include information about new users in the LAN. The problem with mesh VPNs is the difficulty in expanding the network and updating every VPN device whenever a host is added.

Star Topology

In a **star configuration** (also known as a hub-and-spoke configuration), the VPN gateway is the hub, and other networks that participate in the VPN are called rim subnetworks (see Figure 6-7).

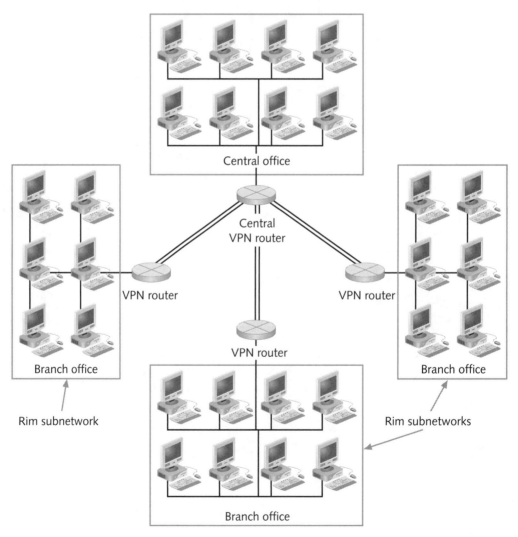

Figure 6-7   A star VPN configuration

Separate SAs are made between the hubs of each rim subnetwork in the star configuration. The central VPN router is at the organization's central office because most star VPNs have all communications go through the central office where the main IT staff is located. Any LANs or computers that want to participate in the VPN need to connect only to the central server, not to any other machines in the VPN. This setup makes it easy to increase the VPN's size when more branch offices or computers are added. On the other hand, in star configurations, all communications flow into and out of a central router. This setup creates a single point of failure at the central router and can also slow communication, especially if branch offices are far apart, such as on different continents.

Hybrid Topology

As organizations with VPNs grow to include new computers and new branch offices, they naturally evolve from a mesh or star configuration into a **hybrid configuration** that combines two different network topologies (see Figure 6-8). Because mesh configurations tend to operate more efficiently, the central core linking the most important branches of the network should probably be a mesh configuration. However, as branch offices are added, they can be added as spokes that connect to a central VPN router at the central office. A hybrid setup that combines the two configurations benefits from the strengths of each one—the scalability of the star configuration and the speed of the mesh configuration.

Activity 6-3: Designing a VPN Topology

Time Required: 30 minutes

Objective: Recommend a strategy for a VPN solution for a company.

Description: Discuss the following scenario in class or research it individually. You might want to use Microsoft Paint or another drawing program to demonstrate the specifics of your design and help in your assessment. Evaluate the requirements, and present your recommendations in writing or orally, as directed by your instructor.

Scenario: You manage a network that connects via a VPN to a combination of branch offices and remote workers. Four branch offices and one central office need to communicate with one another securely to transfer files, especially confidential budget data. In addition, three remote workers need to communicate with the network by using a VPN, but they don't need to talk to one another because they work in different areas of the company.

1. Describe a VPN configuration that would serve all parts of the extended corporate network.

   _____

   _____

2. What are your recommendations for securing remote users' connections? How would you enforce those recommendations?

   _____

   _____

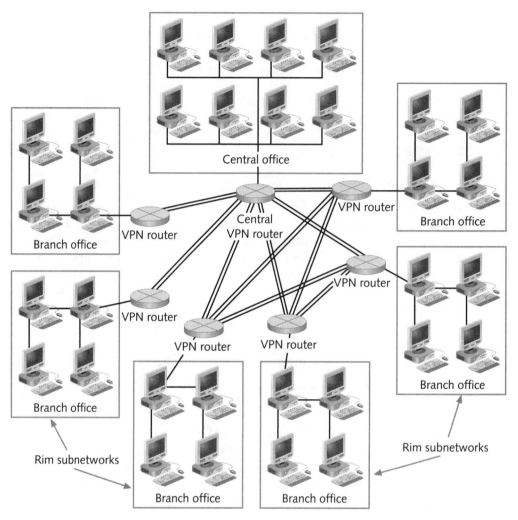

Figure 6-8   A hybrid VPN configuration

USING VPNS WITH FIREWALLS

Having a VPN doesn't reduce the need for a correctly configured firewall. You should always use a firewall as part of your VPN security design. Using a VPN with a firewall, however, requires careful planning and configuration. Several different configurations are possible, and each configuration option has advantages and disadvantages, as explained in this section. One option is to install VPN software on the firewall itself. Several commercial firewalls include VPN components as an added option. As you can see in Figure 6-9, this configuration has a single point of entry into the network:

- The firewall allows outbound access to the Internet.

- The firewall prevents inbound access from the Internet.

- The VPN service encrypts traffic to remote clients or networks.

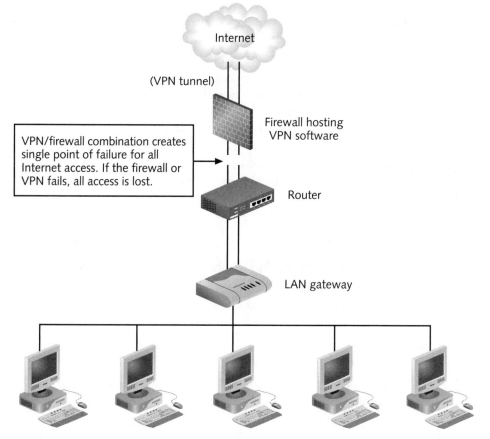

Figure 6-9   The VPN server on a firewall

The advantages of putting the VPN on a firewall include the following:

- You can control all network access security from one server.

- There are fewer computers to manage, meaning less chance of configuration mistakes.

- You can create and manage rules that apply to your VPN traffic with the same tools you already use to manage your firewall.

The disadvantages of installing the VPN on a firewall include the following:

- You have one server controlling all network access security. Any errors in configuring the VPN or firewall could leave your network open to attack.

- You must make sure to configure routes carefully so that traffic goes through the correct interfaces.

- Incorrect configuration of the firewall or VPN rules could allow traffic from the Internet to get past your security.

- Internet access and VPN traffic compete for resources on the server, so a more powerful computer might be necessary.

Another configuration is to set up the VPN parallel to your firewall inside the demilitarized zone (DMZ). Internal client computers continue to point to the firewall as their default gateway and are unaware of the VPN connection. The firewall has a route to any networks accessible via the VPN server and instructs clients to send packets to the VPN server when appropriate. Figure 6-10 shows this type of configuration.

NOTE   A DMZ can also be called a screened subnet or a perimeter network. If used for sharing files and access to company data with a business partner, the perimeter network is often referred to as an extranet.

These are the advantages of putting the VPN server parallel to the firewall:

- VPN traffic is not going through the firewall, so there's no need to modify firewall settings to support VPN traffic.

- This configuration can be scaled more easily. New VPN servers can be added without having to reconfigure the firewall.

- If the VPN server becomes too congested, you can add another server and distribute the load.

The disadvantages of a VPN parallel to a firewall include the following:

- The VPN server is connected directly to the Internet, making it an ideal target for attackers.

- If the VPN server becomes compromised, the attacker will have direct access to your internal network.

- The cost of supporting a VPN increases with the addition of new servers and extra support staff.

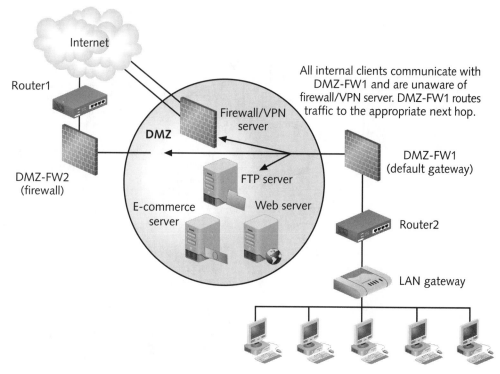

Figure 6-10   The VPN server parallel to a firewall

Another location for the VPN server is behind the firewall connected to the internal network. As shown in Figure 6-11, the VPN server isn't directly accessible from the Internet. All packets must go through the firewall to reach the VPN server. As with the parallel configuration, you need to add a route to the firewall that redirects VPN traffic from internal computers to the VPN server. You also need to configure the firewall to pass encrypted VPN traffic directly to the VPN server.

Putting the VPN server behind the firewall has some advantages:

- The VPN server is completely protected from the Internet by the firewall.

- The firewall is the only device controlling access to and from the Internet.

- Network restrictions for VPN traffic are configured only on the VPN server, making it easier to create rule sets.

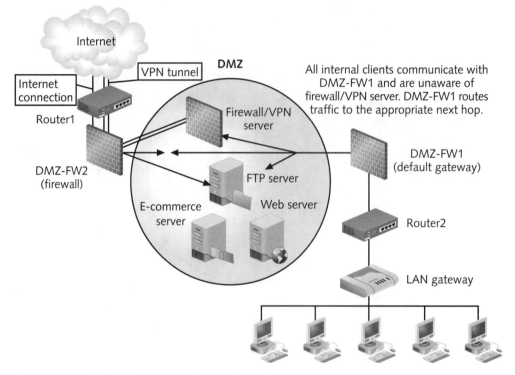

Figure 6-11   The VPN server behind a firewall

The disadvantages of putting the VPN server behind the firewall include the following:

- All VPN traffic must travel through the firewall, which adds congestion and latency.

- The firewall must handle VPN traffic from the Internet to the VPN server directly. Getting the firewall to pass encrypted VPN traffic to the VPN server could require advanced configuration.

- The firewall might not know what to do with IP protocols other than ICMP, TCP, and UDP. Supporting VPNs that use IP protocols, such as ESP packets for IPSec or Generic Routing Encapsulation packets for PPTP, might be difficult or even impossible.

NOTE   If you terminate the VPN connection in front of the firewall, VPN traffic will be on the unprotected external network for a brief period before it passes through the firewall.

Activity 6-4: Setting up a VPN with a Firewall

Time Required: 30 minutes

Objective: Explore the placement of a VPN in relation to a firewall.

Description: There's more to planning and deploying network resources than technical details. Ultimately, "soft skills" are what earn you recognition, promotions, raises, and respect in your job. Soft skills include written and oral communication skills, critical thinking, problem solving, collaboration, initiative, and creativity, among many others. Don't underestimate the power of these skills!

In this activity, you explore where to place a VPN in relation to a firewall. Care must be taken to ensure correct placement and configuration. In groups or individually, read the following scenarios and answer the questions. Your instructor might want you to present your recommendations to the class. Remember that effective communication and presentation skills are vital soft skills.

Scenario 1: You configured a VPN to use IPSec in its most secure mode—using ESP with tunnel mode. However, you encounter problems with the firewall, which is positioned between the VPN and the internal LAN. The firewall ends up dropping a substantial percentage of the packets that are terminated by the VPN device.

1. Troubleshoot the situation: What could be causing the firewall to fail to process VPN traffic? How could you solve the problem?

   _____

   _____

Scenario 2: You need to determine whether you should put the VPN server in front of the firewall where it's exposed to the Internet or in the DMZ behind the firewall. Your organization's security policy calls for the firewall to implement NAT. In addition, the VPN needs to connect to only a single gateway. Members of the IT staff are in disagreement about where the firewall should be placed. One group argues that there's a security risk in putting the VPN in the DMZ because it creates two points of entry to the LAN (the firewall and the VPN device). Another group argues that placing the VPN in front of the firewall means that the firewall needs to be configured carefully to let traffic through from the VPN without giving attackers a point of entry.

1. You are asked to resolve the disagreement. What recommendation would you make?

   _____

   _____

6

ADJUSTING PACKET-FILTERING RULES FOR VPNS

A perimeter firewall is configured with rules that filter packets the VPN sends or receives. These rules control intranet traffic to and from VPN clients and should be based on your organization's security policies. Packet filtering is based on the header fields of inbound and outbound packets. However you choose to configure your VPN and firewall combination, you need to set up packet-filtering rules that allow VPN traffic to pass through as needed. Packet filtering makes use of three IP packet header fields in particular:

- The source address is the 32-bit IP address of the host that sent the packet and generated the information in it.

- The destination address is the 32-bit IP address of the intended destination host expected to receive the packet and the information it carries.

- The protocol identifier (protocol ID) is a number indicating to which upper-level protocol the data in the packet belongs.

You can conduct packet filtering based on any or all of these header fields. Using the source or destination address, for example, you can block all packets from an address or set of addresses, and you can route to a set of addresses the packets you allow to enter. The protocol ID field can be used to refer to many protocols, such as:

- ICMP, protocol ID 1

- TCP, protocol ID 6

- UDP, protocol ID 17

- **Generic Routing Encapsulation (GRE)**, an encapsulation protocol used commonly in VPNs, protocol ID 47

- ESP, protocol ID 50

- AH, protocol ID 51

The Internet Assigned Numbers Authority (IANA) maintains a list of all protocol IDs at *www.iana.org/assignments/protocol-numbers*. RFCs 1701 and 1702 define GRE standards.

TIP

PPTP Filters

PPTP, the first widely supported VPN protocol, supports legacy authentication methods, does not require a PKI, and provides automated configuration. PPTP might be the only option when VPN connections must pass through a NAT server or firewall. NAT changes the internal computer's IP address to the address of the NAT device. For this reason, NAT is not compatible with most IPSec implementations. The problem comes from the Internet Key Exchange (IKE) protocol used by IPSec. IKE embeds the sending computer's IP address in its payload, and because the embedded address doesn't match the source address of the IKE packet (which is the address of the NAT device), the receiving computer drops the packet.

NOTE The IPSec working group of the IEEE has created standards for NAT Traversal (NAT-T) defined in RFCs 3947 and 3948. NAT-T is designed to solve the problems of using IPSec with NAT.

6

PPTP often comes into play when older clients need to connect to a network through a VPN or when a tunnel must pass through a firewall that performs NAT. For PPTP traffic to pass through the firewall, you need to set up packet-filtering rules that permit this communication. PPTP uses two protocols: TCP and GRE. A VPN server that has been configured to receive PPTP traffic listens for incoming connections arriving on TCP port 1723. It also needs to receive GRE packets (identified by protocol ID 47). Table 6-1 shows the filtering rules you would use for your own gateway, if it had an IP address of 205.43.1.78 and a remote gateway with an IP address of 77.127.39.2.

Table 6-1 PPTP packet-filtering rules

Rule	Source IP	Destination IP	Protocol	Source Port	Destination Port	Action
1	Any	205.43.1.78	TCP	Any	1723	Allow
2	Any	205.43.1.78	Protocol ID 47	Any	Any	Allow

In Table 6-1, two rules are established. Rule 1 allows incoming PPTP connections from any computer to be received at the VPN server at 205.43.1.78 via port 1723. Rule 2 allows incoming traffic that uses protocol ID 47 (incoming traffic consisting of GRE packets).

TIP For increased security, in the Action column, you could specify an option such as "Drop all packets except those that meet this criteria" or something similar, if your firewall enables you to make these distinctions. In your rule base, you must configure this option as any other rule, specifying source, destination, protocol, the action to take (Deny, in this case), and so forth.

L2TP and IPSec Filters

If you use L2TP, you need to set up rules that permit IPSec traffic. You have to account for IKE using protocol ID 171 and UDP on port 500. ESP uses protocol ID 50, and AH uses protocol ID 51. Table 6-2 shows the filter rules you would use for your own gateway, if it has an IP address of 205.43.1.78 and a remote gateway with an IP address of 77.127.39.2.

Table 6-2   L2TP packet-filtering rules

Rule	Source IP	Destination IP	Protocol	Transport Protocol	Source Port	Destination Port	Action
1	Any	205.43.1.78	IKE	UDP	500	500	Allow
2	Any	205.43.1.78	ESP	Protocol ID 50	Any	Any	Allow
3	Any	205.43.1.78	AH	Protocol ID 51	Any	Any	Allow

In Table 6-2, Rule 1 covers inbound IKE traffic, which uses UDP port 500. Rule 2 allows traffic if you decide to use ESP, which requires a filter rule that enables protocol ID 50 packets. Rule 3 allows traffic if you use AH, which requires a rule for protocol ID 51. As with the filters for PPTP, you achieve a higher level of security if, in the Action column, you specify an option such as "Drop all packets except those that meet this criteria" or something similar.

AUDITING VPNS AND VPN POLICIES

Auditing must be carried out to make sure organizations have a well-defined VPN policy in place and that the policy is enforced and followed by anyone who connects to the internal LAN. The organization's VPN or remote access policy defines standards for connecting to the company network from any host or remote system. As you can guess, these policies must be integrated tightly with the company's overall security policies. Enforcing these policies can be difficult when you have remote users working from their own computers. Policies should be defined for different levels of restriction, such as what time of day access is allowed. You might want to define tighter controls for business partners than you do for company employees working from home. Controls for administrators might be less restrictive; however, their access should be defined by other security policies that require administrators to have more secure passwords and change them more often.

VPN endpoints are vulnerable to many of the same viruses, Trojans, and spyware as internal network computers. Any infected remote computer can spread viruses or malicious code to any computer on the internal network. Your security policy should require that remote computers connecting to the network have good antivirus software installed along with some type of firewall. This software should run at all times but especially during VPN connections.

After you have installed and configured your VPN, you need to test each client that will connect to the corporate LAN to help prevent network threats. Unless you have strict policies on client-side OSs, configuration, and VPN client software, you have a lot of work ahead of you. Each remote user's computer has to be configured, often over the phone with the help of tech support. This process can be frustrating and time consuming. One approach to this problem is to standardize the VPN client for remote users. That way, tech support staff need to learn how to support only one application, so there's less chance of errors. Many companies use third-party solutions, such as the Cisco Secure VPN Client, Nokia VPN Client, and SonicWALL VPN Client.

After all the bugs are worked out and remote users can access the corporate LAN, it's time to verify that everything is working according to the organization's policies and procedures. Remote users' connections should be monitored for performance, as well as capability to connect. Is the connection maintained during file transfers? How long does a normal file transfer take? Is an idle connection terminated after a specified time? You should work with a knowledgeable remote user to assist in determining a baseline for future auditing, testing, and troubleshooting.

CHAPTER SUMMARY

6

- The business, its existing infrastructure, and its security policy help determine what configuration you use and what hardware you need.

- Client-side issues to consider when designing your VPN strategy include whether to require the client to use a firewall (hardware or software) and intrusion detection system (IDS) software and whether policies should be enforced on the client before allowing remote users to authenticate to the internal LAN.

- After you decide on the placement of VPN servers, you can begin researching the hardware or software to use. You can determine whether reconfiguring the existing firewall or a server on the perimeter network to support VPN connections will work, or if you need to purchase a VPN appliance, server, firewall, or router to do the job.

- A VPN is often configured by establishing a VPN domain, a group of computers handled as one entity, which eases management and enhances security. You also need to determine whether the network gateway is included in that domain, depending on whether your network has a site-to-site or client-to-site VPN configuration.

- Networks that use VPNs can have single entry point configurations, in which all traffic to and from the network passes through a single gateway. Some VPNs are part of multiple entry point configurations, in which more than one gateway is used. Whether single or multiple entry points are used in a network, that network can be connected to other VPN participants by using a mesh, star, or hybrid configuration.

- VPNs need to be used with firewalls. For the two devices to work together, packet-filtering rules need to be set up. Packet filtering makes use of three IP packet header fields in particular: the source address, the destination address, and the protocol ID. The protocol ID field can be used to refer to many protocols.

- Packet-filtering rules cover such protocols as PPTP, L2TP, and IPSec, with the goal of filtering packets so that only traffic to and from VPN endpoints passes through the VPN, and other traffic is filtered by the firewall to reach specific destinations on the network.

❏ After you have installed and configured your VPN, you need to test clients. Each remote user's computer has to be configured, which can be a frustrating and time-consuming process. One approach to this problem is to standardize the VPN client.

❏ After all the bugs are worked out and remote users can access the corporate LAN, you should work with a knowledgeable remote user to assist in determining a baseline for future auditing, testing, and troubleshooting.

KEY TERMS

Generic Routing Encapsulation (GRE) — An encapsulation protocol (protocol ID 47) commonly used in VPNs.

hybrid configuration — A VPN configuration that combines characteristics of the mesh and star configurations.

mesh configuration — A VPN configuration in which all participants in the VPN are connected to one another. This configuration is commonly arranged as a full mesh or partial mesh setup.

multiple entry point configuration — A type of VPN configuration in which multiple gateways are used, each with a VPN tunnel connecting a different location.

single entry point configuration — A VPN configuration in which all traffic to and from the network passes through a single gateway, such as a router or firewall.

split tunneling — The term used to describe multiple paths. One path goes to the VPN server and is secured, but an unauthorized and unsecured path permits the user to connect to the Internet or some other network while still connected to the corporate VPN.

star configuration — A VPN configuration in which a single gateway is the "hub" and other networks that participate in the VPN are considered "rim" networks.

topology — The way in which participants in a network are connected physically to one another.

VPN domain — A group of one or more computers that the VPN hardware and software handle as a single entity. This group uses the VPN to communicate with another domain.

REVIEW QUESTIONS

1. Under what circumstances does a firewall need to be installed at the endpoint of a VPN connection, and why?

2. A VPN domain is a group of computers that _____ .

   a. share the same domain name

   b. are in the same subnet

   c. are handled as a single entity

   d. make up a VPN

3. In what type of VPN configuration must a router belong to the VPN domain?

   a. gateway-to-gateway VPN

   b. multiple entry point

   c. single entry point

   d. partial mesh

4. Which of the following is an advantage of using a mesh VPN configuration?

   a. You need to configure only the central office's VPN server.

   b. All participants can communicate securely with all other participants.

   c. All participants can exchange encrypted communication.

   d. The VPN can be scaled along with the organization.

5. Which of the following is an advantage of using a star VPN configuration?

   a. Fewer connections with ISPs need to be made.

   b. Fewer VPN hardware or software devices need to be used.

   c. Only the VPN server at the center or "hub" needs to be updated.

   d. All participants can communicate with all other participants.

6. Briefly describe split tunneling.

7. What client-side issues do you need to consider when designing your VPN? (Choose all that apply.)

   a. whether to require the client to use a firewall

   b. the organization's current growth rate

   c. how policies should be enforced on the client computer

   d. cost of equipment employees need to buy

8. To set up a VPN, new hardware or software must always be purchased. True or False?

9. Determining whether the network gateway is included in the VPN domain depends on whether your network has a _____ VPN configuration.

   a. site-to-site

   b. client-to-gateway

   c. gateway-to-domain

   d. client-to-client

10. In a multiple entry point configuration, you should exclude the _____ from the domain.

   a. perimeter network

   b. site

   c. gateway

   d. VPN server

6

11. Which of the following terms describes multiple routes in routing tables that could cause some traffic to be routed incorrectly?

    a. duplicate routes

    b. static routes

    c. path topology

    d. overlapping

12. In a mesh topology, all participants in the VPN have _____ with one another.

    a. tunnels

    b. SAs

    c. static routes

    d. trusts

13. What is a main disadvantage of mesh VPNs?

    a. They are not reliable.

    b. There is a lack of confidentiality among peers.

    c. They are difficult to enlarge or change.

    d. The equipment must be the same at all sites.

14. What is a main disadvantage of star VPNs? (Choose all that apply.)

    a. Changes are hard to make.

    b. The central hub is a single point of failure.

    c. Performance can degrade, especially if sites are geographically dispersed.

    d. Communication is easy to intercept.

15. Putting a VPN on the firewall has which of the following disadvantages? (Choose all that apply.)

    a. There are more computers to manage.

    b. Only one server controls security, so any configuration errors leave the network open to attack.

    c. Internet access and VPN traffic compete for resources on the server.

    d. VPN traffic isn't encrypted.

16. A VPN server configured to receive PPTP traffic listens for incoming connections on port _____ and needs to receive GRE traffic identified by protocol ID _____ .

    a. UDP 1443, 17

    b. TCP 1723, 47

    c. UDP 3349, 443

    d. UDP 1723, 47

17. Which protocols and ports do you need to allow to pass when using L2TP and IPSec? (Choose all that apply.)

 a. protocol ID 50

 b. UDP 500

 c. TCP 50

 d. protocol ID 171

18. _____ might be the only option when NAT traffic must pass through a firewall.

 a. IPSec

 b. PPP

 c. L2TP

 d. PPTP

19. There's no need to set up packet-filtering rules on the perimeter firewall for VPN traffic. True or False?

20. AH uses protocol ID _____ .

 a. 50

 b. 171

 c. 500

 d. 51

6

HANDS-ON PROJECTS

HANDS-ON PROJECTS

Hands-On Project 6-1: Configuring L2TP Packet-Filtering Rules

Time Required: 10 minutes

Objective: Configure access for remote user VPN connections.

Description: In this project, you configure a set of packet-filtering rules that enable a remote user to connect to your VPN gateway at 101.26.111.8 from the user's gateway, which is assigned an IP address dynamically and uses L2TP. The packet-filtering rules should enable the VPN traffic to pass through your firewall.

1. Write down the UDP source and destination ports that L2TP uses. (*Hint:* Refer to the "L2TP and IPSec Filters" section earlier in this chapter.)

   _____

2. Write two rules for inbound traffic. What are the two options you could specify as the action for these rules?

   _____

   _____

3. Write two rules for outbound traffic.

   _____

   _____

CASE PROJECTS

CASE PROJECTS

Case Project 6-1: Implementing Your Remote Access Solution

The security policy you drafted for LedGrafix in Chapter 3 should be reviewed and updated, if needed, with each change in your network design. Now that you have designed remote access resources for the company, you must conduct another risk assessment and update your security policy. In Chapter 5, you should have documented your remote access solution, including a complete list of equipment and software needed and a cost breakdown for the additions. You should also have revised your network diagram so that you know the logical and physical layout. This documentation provides a good deal of information you can use to reevaluate risks. As always, you can use any available templates or resources, as long as you adhere to academic honesty guidelines and respect all copyrights and related laws.

Complete the following tasks to update your security policy:

1. Conduct a risk assessment of your revised design. (Refer back to Chapter 2 if you need a refresher on the risk assessment process, and remember that reevaluating every aspect of the design might not be necessary. If an area of the network is unaffected by your remote access design, it might not need to be changed.)

2. Next, integrate this information into your security policy. Place the revised risk assessment documents in the appendix of your security policy, and be sure to include revision information. (Don't forget to do the same with the updated diagrams, remote access design proposal, and cost information you completed in Chapter 5.)

3. Based on your risk assessment, what areas of the security policy need revision? (*Hint:* Look at your Security Policy Table of Contents to review sections.) Revise the sections of the security policy affected by the addition of your remote access solution.

4. After you have updated your security policy, employees and vendors affected by the change must be told about the new resources and how to use them. Write a brief memo (one to two pages) to all employees explaining the remote access solution, what it does for them, and how to use it. Be sure to include new security protocols.

5. Write a memo to vendors who will be using the remote access solution to advise them of changes and updates for security protocols. You might also consider drafting an agreement for vendors to sign, stating that they accept responsibility for any data in their care and will maintain their own information security at a level equal to or above that of LedGrafix.

Examine your revisions to be sure you haven't overlooked any changes, and submit your revised policy and accompanying documentation to your instructor. Remember to proof-read and submit a well-written, professional report.

6

7

INTRUSION DETECTION SYSTEM CONCEPTS

After reading this chapter and completing the exercises, you will be able to:

♦ Identify the components of an intrusion detection system

♦ Explain the steps of intrusion detection

♦ Describe options for implementing intrusion detection systems

♦ Evaluate different types of IDS products

Your security policy is the basis for securing an organization's network. An intrusion detection system (IDS) adds a supplementary level of defense to firewalls, VPNs, and other security devices. Like a burglar alarm, an IDS has sensors to detect when unauthorized users attempt to gain access and notifies you if someone is trying to break in so that you can take countermeasures. Unlike a burglar alarm, however, some IDS devices can be configured to respond in a way that can actually stop an attack.

Intrusion detection involves monitoring network traffic, detecting attempts to gain unauthorized access to a system or resource, and notifying the appropriate professionals so that countermeasures can be taken. This chapter introduces the subject of intrusion detection by discussing IDS components and then examining step by step how those components operate together to protect a network. Next, you learn about the options for designing an IDS by distributing its components at critical locations. Finally, you investigate real-world IDS products that take different approaches to intrusion detection.

Examining Intrusion Detection System Components

A network **intrusion** is an attempt to gain unauthorized access to network resources. The term "intrusion" is a polite way of saying "attack," and often an attack is launched with the intention of compromising the integrity and confidentiality of network data or users' privacy. An **intrusion detection system (IDS)** consists of more than one application or hardware device and incorporates more than just detection. **Intrusion detection** involves three network defense functions—prevention, detection, and response. As shown in Figure 7-1, firewalls perform the prevention function, IDSs provide the detection function, and network administrators carry out the response function.

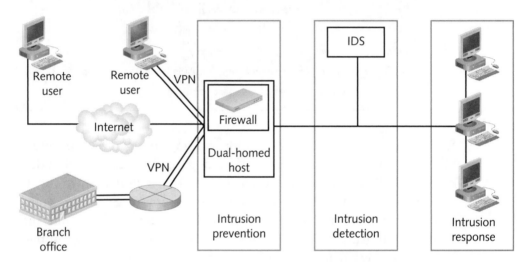

Figure 7-1   The role of intrusion detection in network defense

The following sections describe the components that make up an IDS:

- Network sensors that detect suspicious packets
- Alert systems that notify you of those packets
- The command console on which you view alerts
- The response system that can take countermeasures automatically when possible intrusions occur
- The database of attack signatures or behaviors that an IDS uses to identify potentially suspicious traffic

Network Sensors

A **sensor** functions as the electronic "eyes" of an IDS. In a burglar alarm, a sensor is a switch attached to a door or metal tape that adheres to a glass window. When the door is opened or the glass breaks, the alarm goes off (unless the owner has disabled the system or turned it off). In a network IDS, a network sensor is hardware or software that monitors traffic passing into and out of the network in real time. (You can visit *www.enterasys.com/products/ids/* for a look at a network sensor.) When a sensor detects an event it considers suspicious, an alarm is triggered. Attacks detected by an IDS sensor can take one of two forms:

- Single-session attacks, in which an intruder makes a single isolated attempt to locate a computer on the internal network or gain access by other means

- Multiple-session attacks, such as port scans or network scans, that take place over a period of time and are made up of multiple events

An IDS installed on an individual host computer (called a host-based IDS) has its sensor built in to the IDS software. An IDS that checks for intrusions on a network (called a network-based IDS) might have one or more hardware sensors placed at strategic locations. (These two IDS configurations are discussed later in "Options for Implementing Intrusion Detection Systems.") Sensors should be placed at common entry points into the network, such as:

- Internet gateways

- Connections between one LAN and another or between parts of a LAN separated from each other by a switch

- A remote access server that receives dial-up connections from remote users

- Virtual private network (VPN) devices that connect a LAN to the LAN of a business partner

NOTE   In some IDS configurations, software called a network sensor collects data from a hardware device called a network tap. The network tap actually collects data from network traffic, and the sensor determines whether an event is suspicious by comparing the event's characteristics to a set of user behaviors or rules or a database of known attack characteristics.

In a sophisticated IDS security product, a management program controls one or more sensors. The options for sensor placement are shown in Figure 7-2.

If a firewall is used to protect the LAN, sensors could be positioned on either side of the firewall. However, if the sensor is placed outside the firewall at a point exposed to the Internet, the sensor itself could become the subject of an attack. A more secure location is behind the firewall in the demilitarized zone (DMZ), as shown in Figure 7-3.

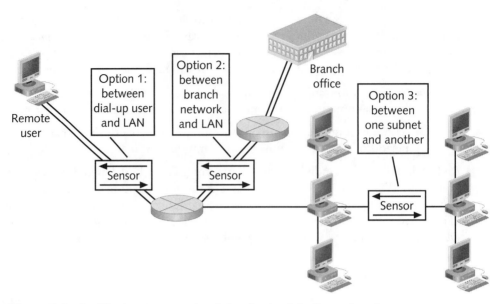

Figure 7-2   Positioning sensors at points of entry into the network

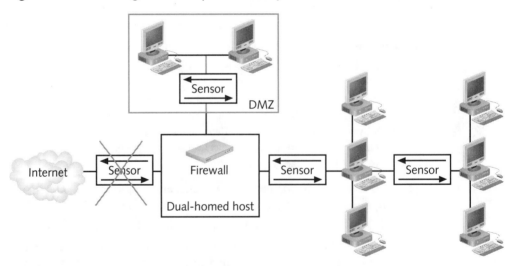

Figure 7-3   Positioning sensors inside the firewall in the DMZ

Alert Systems

A home burglar alarm system is configured to emit a sound if a particular event occurs, such as a window breaking or a door opening. An IDS operates in much the same way—it sends an alert when it encounters packets or traffic patterns that seem suspicious. In response to these events, the IDS uses a **trigger**—a set of circumstances that causes an alert message to be sent. Alert messages can take many forms, such as a pop-up window, an e-mail message, a sound, or a message sent to a pager.

Alerts can result from two general types of triggers (discussed in more detail in the following sections):

- *Detection of an anomaly*—The system sends an alarm when it detects an event that deviates from behavior defined as "normal." Anomaly detection is sometimes called "profile-based detection" because it compares current network traffic to profiles of normal network use. You might use anomaly detection if you're especially concerned with misuse from inside the organization, or if you want to monitor all traffic heading into and out of your e-mail, Web, and FTP servers.

- *Detection of misuse*—An IDS configured to send an alarm in response to misuse makes use of signatures, which are sets of characteristics that match known examples of attacks. You might select misuse detection if you have the time and ability (and perhaps the software) to make sense of the large amounts of log file data this system generates. Organizations that want a basic IDS and are concerned primarily with known attacks from intruders trying to access hosts from the Internet should choose a misuse-based IDS and update the system's signatures regularly.

Anomaly Detection

An **anomaly detection** system requires you to make use of **profiles** for each authorized user or group on the system. These profiles are sets of characteristics that describe the services and resources a user normally accesses on the network. (Another concept you might associate with profiles is a network baseline.) Some IDSs can create user profiles during a "training period"—a period of time in which the IDS monitors network traffic to observe what constitutes "normal" network behavior. Otherwise, you need to create the profiles yourself. Because a large-scale corporate network might consist of hundreds or even thousands of users divided into multiple groups, profile configuration can be a lot of work.

The accuracy of profiles has a direct impact on how effectively an IDS detects anomalies. If the profiles are accurate, the IDS sends alarms only for genuine attacks. If the profiles are incomplete or inaccurate, the IDS sends alarms that turn out to be **false positives**, alarms generated by legitimate network traffic rather than actual attacks. False positives waste valuable time and resources and can cause unnecessary alarm among IT employees, who might not take these alarms seriously if they occur often. You need to configure an anomaly-based IDS with accurate profiles to minimize or even eliminate false positives. You also need to configure an IDS accurately enough to avoid **false negatives**, genuine attacks that aren't detected by an IDS because no profiles exist for them. **True negatives** are legitimate communications that don't set off an alarm. The term **true positive** is sometimes used to describe a genuine attack.

An anomaly-based detection system can also generate false positives caused by changes in user habits; after all, people don't use computer systems the same way all the time. When users vary a pattern (by attempting to access a database they've never used before, for instance), a false positive is likely.

Misuse Detection

In contrast to anomaly-based detection, which triggers alarms based on deviations from "normal" network behavior by users or groups in an organization, **misuse detection** triggers alarms based on characteristic signatures of known attacks from outside the organization. Network engineers who configure an IDS research well-known attacks and record the rules associated with each signature. A database of these signatures is then made available to the IDS. Because the IDS comes equipped with a set of signatures, it can begin to protect the network immediately after installation. An anomaly-based IDS, on the other hand, must be trained to recognize "normal" network traffic before it can begin to protect the network. Anomaly detection and misuse detection have their advantages and disadvantages, as summarized in Table 7-1.

Table 7-1   Advantages and disadvantages of IDS triggering mechanisms

Trigger	Advantages	Disadvantages
Anomaly detection	Because an anomaly detection system is based on profiles that the administrator creates, an attacker cannot test the IDS beforehand and cannot anticipate what will trigger an alarm.	A substantial amount of time is required to configure the IDS to use profiles of network users and groups.
	As new users and groups are created, IDS profiles can be changed to keep up with the new arrangements.	As new users and groups are created, profiles available to the IDS must be updated to remain effective.
	Because an anomaly detection system does not rely on published signatures, it can detect new attacks.	The definition of what constitutes "normal" traffic changes constantly; the IDS must be reconfigured continually to keep up.
	The system can effectively detect attacks from inside the network by employees or attackers who have stolen employee accounts.	After installation, the IDS must be "trained" for days or weeks at a time to recognize normal traffic.
Misuse detection	This approach makes use of signatures of well-known attacks.	The database of signatures must be updated to maintain the effectiveness of the IDS.
	The IDS can begin working immediately after installation.	New types of attacks might not be included in the database.
	The IDS is easy to understand and is less difficult to configure than an anomaly-based system.	By making minor alterations to the attack, attackers can avoid matching one of the signatures in the database.
	Each signature in the database is assigned a number and name so that the administrator can identify the attacks that need to set off an alarm.	Because a misuse-based system makes use of a database, a considerable amount of disk storage space might be needed.

A misuse-detection IDS has another potential weakness you should keep in mind: the need to maintain **state information** (information about a connection) on a possible attack. When an IDS receives a packet, information about the connection between the host and remote computer is compared to entries in the state table. A state table maintains a record of connections between computers. This information includes the source IP address and port, destination IP address and port, and protocol. Furthermore, the IDS needs to maintain state information for the entire length of the attack, which is called the **event horizon**. Maintaining this information might require an IDS to review many packets of data; for long attacks, such as those that last from user logon to user logoff, the IDS might not be able to maintain the state information long enough, and the attack could circumvent the system.

Besides misuse and anomaly detection, an IDS can detect suspicious packets in other ways, including:

7

- *Traffic rate monitoring*—If a sudden and dramatic increase in traffic is detected, such as that caused by a denial-of-service attack, the IDS can stop and reset all TCP traffic.

- *Protocol state tracking (stateful packet filtering)*—Some IDSs can go a step beyond matching packet signatures by performing firewall-like stateful packet filtering. The IDS maintains a record of the connection's state and allows packets to pass through to the internal network only if a connection has been established already.

- *IP packet reassembly*—Some IDSs can reassemble IP packets that have been fragmented to prevent individual fragments from passing through to the internal network.

Other IDS products, such as neuSecure by Guarded Net (*www.guarded.net/prod.html*), are combination systems that perform both anomaly and misuse detection while gathering data from many different sensors in a single interface.

NOTE

IDS rules are discussed in Chapter 8, and packet filtering is addressed in detail in Chapters 9 and 10.

ACTIVITY

Activity 7-1: Analyzing Anomalies in User Behavior

Time Required: 30 minutes

Objective: Analyze a user's behavior to determine whether an event is normal or a possible intrusion.

Description: In anomaly-based intrusion detection, the network administrator must determine whether an anomaly deviates from "normal" behavior severely enough to warrant investigation. For this activity, you use the information in Table 7-2 gathered from an anomaly-based IDS to answer the following questions.

Table 7-2   User profile analysis

User	Behavior	Date	Time
Bob	Network login	M-F	8:00 a.m. – 9:00 a.m.
	Log in to e-mail account	M-F	8:30 a.m. – 5:00 p.m.
	Log in to file server	M-F	8:30 a.m. – 5:00 p.m.

1. Describe how you would respond to receiving an alert notifying you that Bob logged in at 2 p.m. on a Friday and logged off at 7 p.m.

   _____

   _____

   _____

2. Describe two possible causes (one legitimate, one suspicious) for this series of events: You receive an alert stating that on Tuesday, Bob logged on at 2 a.m., logged off at 7 a.m., logged on again at 8:30 a.m., and logged off at 5 p.m.

   _____

   _____

   _____

3. Describe a suitable response to discovering that the scenario in Step 2 was repeated every day during the previous week.

   _____

   _____

   _____

Command Console

A **command console** is software that provides a graphical front-end interface to an IDS. It enables administrators to receive and analyze alert messages and manage log files. In large-scale networks with more than one IDS deployed, a single console gives administrators a way to keep up with a large volume of events so that they can respond and take countermeasures quickly. A program such as Symantec Network Security (run a search at *http://enterprisesecurity.symantec.com*) provides a single interface for viewing security events or looking up past alerts or intrusion attempts for comparison.

An IDS can collect information from security devices throughout a network, which are connected to the command console where they can be reviewed and evaluated. The command console shouldn't be slow to respond because its host computer is busy backing up files or performing firewall functions when a suspicious event is detected, so typically, a command console is installed on a computer dedicated solely to the IDS to maximize the speed of response.

Response System

As mentioned, some sophisticated IDS devices can be set up to take some countermeasures, such as resetting all network connections when an intrusion is detected. This type of system shouldn't be considered a substitute for a network administrator taking appropriate countermeasures, however. An administrator can use his or her judgment to determine whether an alarm is being triggered by a false positive or a genuine attack. If the attack is genuine, administrators can use their judgment to gauge the severity of an attack and determine whether the response should be **escalated**—increased to a higher level.

Database of Attack Signatures or Behaviors

IDSs don't have the capability to use judgment, so network administrators should exercise their own judgment when evaluating security alerts. However, IDSs can make use of a source of information for comparing the traffic they monitor. Misuse-detection IDSs reference a database of known attack signatures; if a sensor detects a packet or a sequence of packets that matches one of the signatures, it sends an alert. The SecurityFocus online database (*http://online.securityfocus.com/bid*) of known vulnerabilities (shown in Figure 7-4) is updated frequently, and you can search it online for a particular type of attack to find more information.

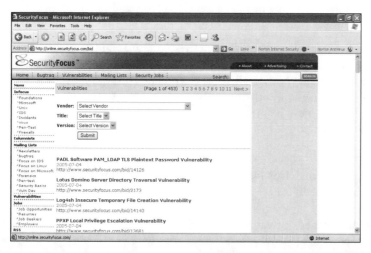

Figure 7-4   The SecurityFocus online database of known vulnerabilities

The key to attack signature databases is to keep them up to date; a new type of attack that hasn't been added to the system's available signatures can defeat an IDS quickly. An IDS vendor that uses attack signatures should include a way to download new entries and add them to the database. The problem with systems that depend solely on signatures is that they are passive: They monitor traffic, compare it to the database, and send alerts whenever a packet matches an available signature, which can result in many false positives. With most

IDSs, however, administrators can address this passive system by adding their own custom rules to the database of signatures to reduce the number of false alarms.

An anomaly-based IDS also makes use of a database of stored information against which network traffic is compared. For example, SecurVantage by Securify (*www.securify.com*) examines network traffic over a period of time and takes a snapshot of what's considered "normal." SecurVantage develops a set of policies that describe who can normally use a network device and how the device can be used. Any deviations from the accumulated set of policies trigger an alarm. Check for the latest version at the Securify Web site to learn about new or deleted features.

ACTIVITY

Activity 7-2: Categorizing IDS Packages

Time Required: 30 minutes

Objective: Evaluate IDS vendors and categorize them by the detection method they use.

Description: Most IDSs perform anomaly detection, misuse detection, or a combination (hybrid), but they aren't always described in terms of these categories on vendors' Web sites or in media reviews. Sometimes IDS packages are described as offering a "new" technology that's actually one of the aforementioned approaches. Having a firm idea of which detection method a product uses (anomaly, misuse, or hybrid) can help you make the right purchase for your organization. In the following steps, you do some online "shopping" for IDSs and divide them into categories.

1. Start your Web browser, enter the URL **http://www.eweek.com**, and press **Enter**. If an ad appears, click **Go Directly to eWEEK.com** to bypass it. At the eWeek site, search for the article "New IDS Tools Automate Response." As you read the article, pay attention to the evaluation of Securify's SecurVantage 3.0, which is described as having a "new feature" called Automatic Policy Generation. What detection method that you learned about earlier does this system actually use?

2. Visit the Web sites of the IDSs listed in Table 7-3 and categorize them as anomaly-based, misuse-based, or hybrid. Write the answers in the Method column.

Table 7-3   Detection methods of various IDS products

IDS	URL	Method
Sentinel 5	www.esecurityinc.com	
StealthWatch	www.lancope.com	
IDP	www.juniper.net/products/intrusion/	
Entercept Management System	www.networkassociates.com/us/products/ mcafee/host_ips/category.htm	

EXAMINING INTRUSION DETECTION STEP BY STEP

IDSs operate in different ways, depending on whether they are configured to react to anomalies (deviations from normal network behavior) or misuse (characteristic signatures of known attacks). Despite differences in operation, the process of network intrusion detection can be divided into general steps, shown in Figure 7–5, that apply to virtually all IDSs. These steps are described in the following sections.

The SANS Institute maintains a useful FAQ on intrusion detection at *www.sans.org/resources/idfaq.*

7

Step 1: Installing the IDS Database

The first step in the intrusion detection process occurs before the first packet is ever detected on the network. The database of signatures or user profiles needs to be installed along with the IDS software and hardware. This database enables the IDS to have a set of criteria against which it can compare packets as they pass through the sensor.

In an anomaly-based system, installing the database can take as much as a week after installation of the IDS devices. The extra time is required so that the IDS can observe network traffic and compile a baseline set of data that describes normal network use. Some data can take a week to be recorded because it occurs over a period of days—for example, a series of daily logons to the network.

In a misuse-based IDS, you can install the database of attack signatures included with the software, or you can add your own custom rule base to account for new attacks or special situations that have caused the IDS to generate false positives.

Step 2: Gathering Data

After the IDS and database are installed, network sensors can gather data by reading packets. Sensors installed on individual hosts observe packets as they enter and leave that host. Sensors placed on network segments read packets as they pass into and out of those segments.

Sensors need to be positioned where they can capture all packets entering and leaving a host or network segment. Sensors placed on network segments can't always capture every packet if the traffic level becomes too heavy, however. Repositioning the sensors on each network host improves accuracy, even though the expense of purchasing new sensors and the effort of installing them can be considerable. What's important is to be able to capture all packets so that none can potentially circumvent the IDS.

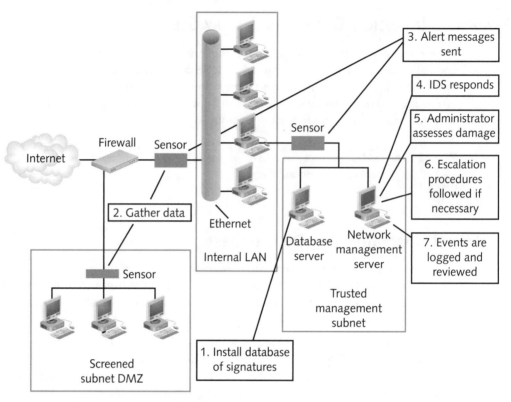

Figure 7-5   Steps in intrusion detection

Step 3: Sending Alert Messages

The sensor's detection software compares the packets it observes with the signatures of normal behavior patterns stored in its database. An alert message is transmitted when a packet matches an attack signature or deviates from normal network use. The alert message goes to the IDS command console, where the network administrator can evaluate it.

Step 4: The IDS Responds

When the command console receives an alert message, it notifies the administrator in one of several ways that the administrator has configured beforehand. The console might display a pop-up window or send an e-mail message, for instance.

Besides the automated response sent to the command console, the IDS can be configured to take action when a suspicious packet is received and an alert message is sent. These are the typical actions:

- *Alarm*—An alert message is sent to the command console.

- *Drop*—The packet is dropped without an error message being sent to the originating computer.

- *Reset*—The IDS is instructed to stop and restart network traffic, thus halting especially severe attacks.

NOTE   An IDS stops TCP traffic by sending a TCP packet with the RST (reset) flag set, which terminates the connection with the computer that's attempting to attack the system. Resetting TCP traffic doesn't affect UDP traffic, however.

Step 5: The Administrator Assesses Damage

An automated response sent by an IDS is like a call to action. It's the network administrator's responsibility to monitor alerts and determine whether countermeasures need to be taken. When an IDS is first installed, it might receive many alerts that are actually false positives, depending on the accuracy of the information the IDS is working with in its database. An administrator can anticipate having to fine-tune the database to account for situations that seem to the IDS to be intrusions but that are actually legitimate traffic.

In an anomaly-based system, for example, an adjustment might be needed for an employee who logs on over the weekend instead of during the standard Monday through Friday work week. In a misuse-based system, an adjustment can be made to enable traffic that the firewall might otherwise determine to be suspicious, such as a vulnerability scan performed by a scanning device at a particular IP address. The IDS could be configured to add a rule that changes the action it takes in response to traffic from that IP address from alarm to drop. The dividing line between acceptable and unacceptable use of the network is shown in Figure 7-6.

The line that divides acceptable from unacceptable network use isn't always clear, however. In Figure 7-6, for example, the box indicating the use of a network printer is shown as overlapping because acceptable use of this resource depends on its purpose. Printing office-related documents constitutes acceptable use, but printing personal photos, for example, probably falls onto the unacceptable side of the line.

The goal of adjusting the IDS database is not to avoid false positives because, almost inevitably, they will occur. False positives do consume an administrator's time and energy, but they don't compromise the security of the network being protected. The goal is avoiding false negatives—incidents that should cause an alarm to be sent to the command console but do not. False negatives occur without anyone's knowledge and represent a potentially serious breach of security for a network. Although false positives are often seen as nuisances, they are far better to have than false negatives.

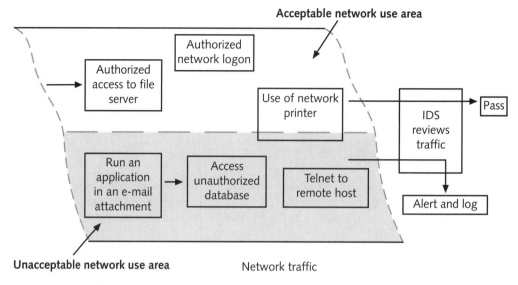

Figure 7-6   Differentiating acceptable and unacceptable network use

Step 6: Following Escalation Procedures

Escalation procedures are a set of actions to be followed if the IDS detects a true positive (a legitimate attack). As you learned in Chapters 2 and 3, escalation procedures for security incidents should be spelled out in the organization's security policy. These procedures vary, depending on the severity of the security incident. A Level One incident might be managed quickly with only a single security professional, a Level Two incident represents a more serious threat and must be escalated to include involvement by a security professional with more authority, and a Level Three incident represents the highest degree of threat.

Step 7: Logging and Reviewing the Event

After an IDS has sent an alert to the command console and responded as necessary, the event that caused the alert is entered in the IDS log file. The event can also be sent directly to a database file, where it can be reviewed along with other previous alerts. Reviewing a number of alerts sent over a period of time enables an administrator to determine whether patterns of misuse have been occurring. This review also gives an administrator the opportunity to spot a gradual attack, such as a series of logons that occur only once every few days or a series of ping sweeps (attempts to solicit a response from a series of IP addresses inside an internal network) that might take place once a week over a few months.

An IDS should also provide **accountability**—the capability to track an attempted attack or intrusion back to the responsible party. Some systems have a built-in tracing feature that attempts to locate the IP address associated with an event. Although it isn't an IDS per se, Symantec Personal Firewall enables users to trace a source IP in a log file entry. To do this, open the log file, right-click the source IP address, and click BackTrace, as shown in Figure 7-7.

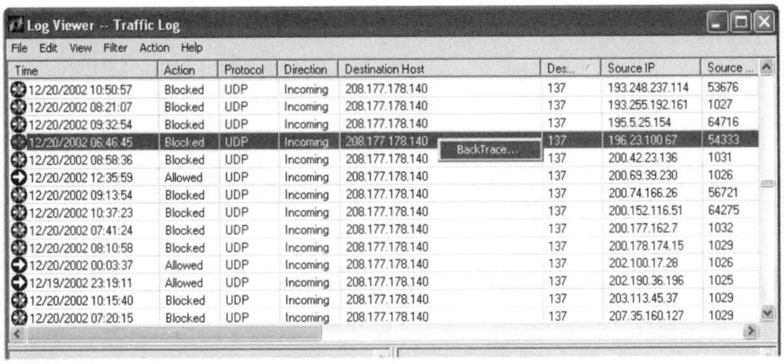

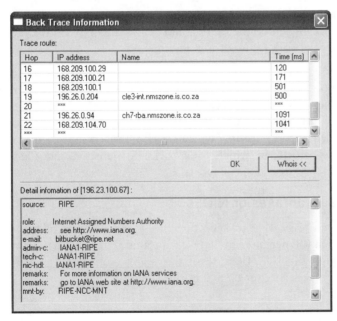

Figure 7-7 Tracing an IP address

Notice that in the log file in Figure 7-7, the IP address being traced is an anomaly: It differs dramatically from typical network traffic in its IP address and source port, which is in the upper reaches of the list of dynamic port numbers. (Recall from Chapter 4 that IANA assigns port numbers to services; well-known port numbers are in the range 0 to 1023, registered port numbers are 1024 to 49151, and dynamic ports are 49152 to 65535.) When the BackTrace option is selected, an Information dialog box opens showing the IP address being traced from the user's computer back to its source (see Figure 7-8).

Figure 7-8 Investigating an IP address to assist with identification

Identifying the person who used the source computer can be quite difficult, but a trace can at least provide a starting point for identifying an attacker.

OPTIONS FOR IMPLEMENTING INTRUSION DETECTION SYSTEMS

The preceding sections described different ways that IDSs detect suspicious events and send alarms. In this section, you examine another way to describe IDSs: by their position on the network and how their position affects their activities. In the following sections, you examine network-based IDSs, host-based IDSs, and hybrid IDSs.

Network-Based Intrusion Detection Systems

The following sections cover these aspects of network-based intrusion detection systems:

- Locating them on the network
- Compiling known data about intruders
- Logging intrusion attempts
- Sending alert messages
- Advantages and disadvantages of a network-based configuration

Locating an NIDS on the Network

A **network-based IDS (NIDS)** is a set of components that includes a command console and sensors positioned at locations where they can monitor network traffic. Three common locations for NIDS sensors are behind the firewall and before the LAN, between the firewall and the DMZ, or on any network segment (see Figure 7-9).

An NIDS typically has its primary management and analysis software installed on a **dedicated computer** (a computer used solely for running intrusion detection software and logging traffic). Positioning sensors at the network perimeter is ideal for enabling the IDS to **sniff** packets—in other words, to receive and analyze packets as they pass into the network. Each IDS sensor is also equipped with its own network interface card so that it can sniff packets in **promiscuous mode**, in which each packet is detected and analyzed in its entirety.

Advantages and Disadvantages of NIDSs

NIDS configurations need to be able to keep up with a large volume of network traffic because of their position at the perimeter, where all inbound traffic that has passed through the firewall passes through the IDS. Because of the high volume of traffic, a dedicated hardware appliance IDS makes a better choice in this situation.

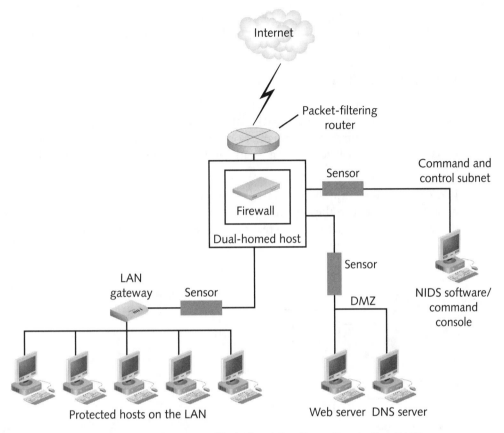

Figure 7-9   An NIDS monitoring traffic behind the firewall or in the DMZ

Host-Based Intrusion Detection Systems

In contrast to an NIDS on the network perimeter, a **host-based IDS (HIDS)** is deployed on a host in the LAN that's protected by the firewall. The host could be a printer, Web server, computer, firewall, switch, router, or any combination. Packets generated by the host are monitored and evaluated by the IDS. The data is gathered from operating system and application logs on the host. An HIDS gathers system variables such as the following:

- System processes
- CPU use
- File accesses

System events that match the signatures of known attacks reach the IDS on the host computer, which sends an alert message to users or the network administrator. An HIDS doesn't sniff packets as they enter the LAN. Instead, it monitors log file entries and user activity and is highly effective at tracking misuse of resources by internal users. HIDSs are generally deployed only on sensitive or mission-critical hosts because placing one on each host in the network would be cost prohibitive. (Remember that the cost of software and licensing is a factor to consider.)

Configuring an HIDS

An HIDS can have two configurations: centralized or distributed. In a centralized configuration, the HIDS sends all data that's gathered to a central location (the command console) for analysis. In a distributed configuration, the data analysis is distributed among individual hosts; each host analyzes the data and sends only alert messages (not the data) to the command console.

In a centralized design, the host's level of performance is unaffected by the IDS. However, because data is sent to the command console where it must be analyzed, any alert messages that are generated don't occur in real time. The detection process in a centralized configuration is shown in Figure 7-10.

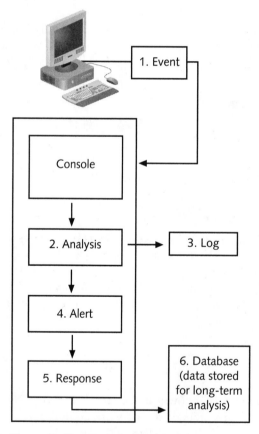

Figure 7-10 A centralized HIDS

The process in Figure 7-10 is as follows:

1. An event is generated on the host.

2. The data gathered by the IDS sensor (a software program running on the host) is transmitted to the command console, where the analysis is performed.

3. A log file entry is created.

4. If necessary, an alert is generated.

5. The IDS responds.

6. Finally, the data is stored in a database where long-term analysis can be performed.

In a distributed HIDS configuration, the processing of event data is distributed between the host and command console. The host generates the data and analyzes it in real time. As a result, the analysis can be performed without a delay, but the tradeoff is a performance reduction on the host computer. The host processes all data, whether alerts are required or not. Data is then transmitted to the command console in the form of alert messages, as shown in Figure 7-11.

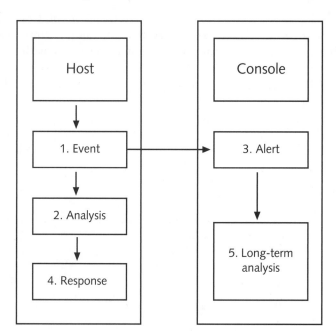

Figure 7-11   Processing event data from an HIDS

Choosing the Host Computer

The available RAM, hard disk memory, and processor speed required on the host computer depend on the type of HIDS that's used. In a centralized configuration, the processing is performed on the command console, so the performance requirement on the host in terms of the IDS is minimal. However, in a distributed configuration, the host is called on not only to gather intrusion data, but also to analyze it in real time, so the host should be equipped with the maximum memory and processor speed available. Check the vendor's IDS requirements for recommended configurations.

Advantages and Disadvantages of HIDSs

An HIDS can tell you whether an attack attempt on the host was actually successful. An NIDS, on the other hand, provides alerts on suspicious network activity, but it doesn't tell you whether an attack attempt actually reached the targeted host and whether an intrusion actually occurred. HIDSs can easily catch attacks that would otherwise get past an NIDS. For example, fragmentation, out of sequence, or other masking techniques might bypass firewalls and NIDSs as legitimate traffic. HIDSs are also more effective in switched networks than in NIDSs. Because a switch isolates traffic on the network, it requires an NIDS on each subnet.

On the other hand, an HIDS provides only the data pertaining to the host on which it's installed, not the network as a whole. An HIDS can't detect an intrusion attempt that targets the entire network, such as a port scan on a range of computers in succession. If you use an HIDS, you need to install it on several hosts on the network, which takes time and can be more expensive than an NIDS. The following lists summarize the advantages and disadvantages of HIDSs:

Advantages

- Can detect events on host systems and attacks that might evade an NIDS
- Encrypted traffic is decrypted on the host and available for processing
- Not affected by use of switched network protocols
- Can compare records stored in audit logs to detect inconsistencies in how applications and systems programs are used

Disadvantages

- More management issues
- Vulnerable to direct attacks and attacks against host OSs
- Susceptible to some denial-of-service attacks
- Can use large amounts of disk space
- Could cause increased performance overhead on host systems

Hybrid IDS Implementations

A **hybrid IDS** combines the features of HIDSs and NIDSs to gain flexibility and increase security. The challenge in implementing a hybrid system is getting the various components to work together. Variations of hybrid IDS implementations—combined IDS sensor locations, combined IDS detection methods, shim IDSs, and distributed IDSs—are described in the following sections.

Combining IDS Sensor Locations

One type of IDS hybrid implementation combines host-based and network-based systems. The combination enables sensors to be positioned on both network segments and individual hosts. As a result, the network can report on attacks aimed at particular network segments or the network as a whole. In addition, individual computers containing confidential information, such as databases of job records, can be protected with an HIDS. An IDS on the host (especially one with a distributed configuration) can analyze the data in real time and send an alert immediately that notifies the administrator of a possible unauthorized access attempt.

7

Combining IDS Detection Methods

Another IDS hybrid results from the combined use of anomaly and misuse detection. The combination helps overcome the limitations of each detection method in the following ways:

- Having a database of known attack signatures enables the system to get up and running immediately and effectively repels most well-known external attack methods.

- Having an anomaly-based system keeps the alert system flexible and capable of detecting internal misuse that deviates from normal use patterns.

A hybrid IDS that combines anomaly with misuse detection can respond to the latest, previously unreported attacks. It has the capability to respond to attacks from both external and internal sources. A drawback is that the administrator has more configuration and coordination work to do. The data from multiple sources must be collected in a central location, where it can be reviewed and analyzed.

Shim IDS

A **shim IDS** acts like a type of NIDS because it involves sensors being distributed around a network, and data is collected at the packet level from those sensors and sent to a centralized command console. However, the sensors are installed in selected hosts as well as network segments. Unlike an HIDS, the sensors don't have to be installed on every host in the network. They need to be installed only on hosts that require special protection, such as databases of proprietary product information.

Distributed IDS

Quick response is enhanced by a **distributed IDS (DIDS)**, in which multiple IDS devices are deployed on a network to monitor traffic and report suspicious events. By using multiple IDSs rather than a single IDS, patterns develop that enable administrators to distinguish between harmless anomalies and genuine attacks. Two popular DIDSs are myNetWatchman (*www.mynetwatchman.com*) and DShield (*www.dshield.org*). The DShield Web site shown in Figure 7-12 tracks attacks from all over the globe and gathers data submitted voluntarily by Internet users. The more data that's assembled, the more accurate the patterns that develop. DShield notifies you if the log files you submit contain patterns of intrusion so that you can configure your IDS software to block the intruder.

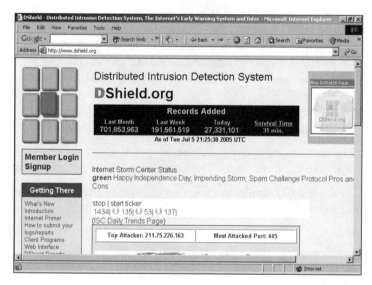

Figure 7-12   DShield provides a DIDS

Advantages and Disadvantages of Hybrid IDSs

Hybrid IDSs have the advantage of being able to combine aspects of NIDS and HIDS configurations. You can monitor the network as a whole with network-based sensors and monitor attacks that reach individual computers with host-based sensors. The drawback of a hybrid arrangement is the need to get disparate systems to work in a coordinated fashion. The data gathered from multiple systems can also be difficult to absorb and analyze easily.

Activity 7-3: Redistributing Network Sensors

Time Required: 15 minutes

Objective: Optimize sensor placement and discuss the pros and cons of the change.

Description: You have installed an NIDS in a traditional design: A sensor is placed on each segment of the network, and alarms are transmitted to the command console where you can review and evaluate them. A comparison of firewall logs with IDS alarms indicates that the sensors can't capture every packet that passes into and out of the network. Based on this situation, answer the following questions:

1. Describe how you would troubleshoot this configuration by rearranging the sensors.

   _____

   _____

   _____

2. What are the pros and cons of making the change?

   _____

   _____

7

EVALUATING INTRUSION DETECTION SYSTEMS

You should select an IDS only after surveying available products and matching them to your needs. Most enterprise-level IDS packages consist of multiple hardware or software components, and many cost thousands of dollars, depending on the number of users.

To make an informed decision, your first step is to review the topology of your own network, paying particular attention to those parts of the network that would have direct interaction with the IDS, such as:

- The number of entry points into the network, including dial-up and VPN connections
- The use of firewalls on the network
- Whether your network consists of a single segment or is divided into separate segments, each with a distinct purpose

Evaluating IDSs can be time consuming. Many packages aren't available in trial versions you can simply download and install. Some are hardware appliances that don't offer a "try before you buy" policy. The following sections aren't meant to be comprehensive, but they give you an overview of a few IDSs you can choose from: freeware programs, commercial host-based programs, and IDS hardware appliances.

ACTIVITY

Activity 7-4: Designing an IDS

Time Required: 45 minutes

Objective: Prepare a report on an IDS for your network and create a topology map to aid in your IDS design.

Description: Before you install and configure an IDS, you'll probably be asked to prepare a report explaining what an IDS is and how to create one for your network. In this project, you prepare this report. You can use any computer connected to the Internet and need a word processing file or lab notebook to answer the following questions and draw diagrams.

1. To describe your lab network, use the following lines to list the number of computers and indicate the OSs running on them. (If you don't have access to a lab network, assume you're working in a lab with 10 computers, 8 running Windows XP and 2 running any version of Fedora Core.)

   _____

   _____

2. Draw a topology map of your network. (*Tip:* If you don't have access to Visio or some type of drawing program, you can download a freeware network-diagramming program at *www.networknotepad.com*.)

3. List the components needed to create an IDS.

   _____

   _____

4. Position an NIDS in a distributed configuration on your topology map.

5. Map out the IDS process in steps that include the following:
   a. Packet detected
   b. Detection engine processes packet
   c. Alert transmitted
   d. Notification sent
   e. Alert logged
   f. Analysis and countermeasures performed

Freeware NIDS: Snort

Snort (which you installed in Chapter 4) is a freeware IDS created by Martin Roesch and Brian Caswell. It doesn't consume extensive system resources and is ideal for monitoring traffic on a small network or an individual host. Snort is intended for installation on a computer positioned at the network perimeter. It can also function on a dedicated computer on a home or small business network.

Snort comes with a collection of rule files customized for different types of network traffic and are activated in the overall configuration file Snort.conf. Separate rules exist for port scans, back door attacks, Web attacks, and many other kinds of potential intrusions. The rule files are text-based; you open them in a text editor and review and edit them to conform to your own network. For example, Figure 7-13 shows the preset rules for access attempts on the NetBIOS port 139.

Figure 7-13   Snort comes with an extensive set of preconfigured rules

The configuration files are easy to edit and can be customized to fit a variety of other events. In addition, other configuration files contain variables that enable you to protect the SMTP, HTTP, and SQL servers on your network, which can otherwise cause false alarms because of the amount of traffic that passes through them. A variety of GUI interfaces for Snort are available, such as IDScenter or SnortSnarf. (You will install IDScenter in Chapter 8.)

Commercial HIDS: Norton Internet Security

Norton Internet Security by Symantec Corp. is a personal firewall program designed to protect a home-based standalone computer or a computer on a small network. However, the program also contains a limited number of intrusion detection features. These features are specifically designed to block port scans and block attack attempts on ports used by known Trojan programs. If an attack is detected, a feature called AutoBlock (Figure 7-14 shows its setup) stops communication from the intruder to your computer for 30 minutes to 48 hours. In that time, the intruder is likely to switch to another computer to attempt an attack. If the intruder attempts the same attack on your computer, communication is blocked again.

Norton Internet Security, like other personal firewall programs, can "learn" what constitutes normal network use and what is a deviation from that use. It also enables users to establish rules blocking communication that deviates from normal use. Pop-up alert messages appear when encountering traffic that represents a possible intrusion. However, the program lacks the capability of setting up user profiles and doesn't make use of a set of attack signatures, other than the port scans and Trojan attacks mentioned earlier.

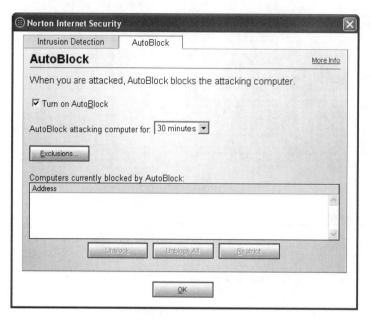

Figure 7-14   IDS features in personal firewall programs, such as Norton Internet Security

IDS Hardware Appliances

IDS hardware appliances, like firewall hardware appliances, can handle more network traffic and have better scalability than software IDS packages. Plug-and-play capability counts as one of the biggest advantage of IDS hardware options. A hardware device doesn't have to be configured to work with a particular OS and isn't affected by any vulnerabilities that might be present in an OS. Hardware IDS devices are becoming more common; the following are just a few examples:

- iForce IDS appliance by Sun and Symantec (run a search on "iForce IDS" at *www.symantec.com*)

- Intrusion SecureNet by Intrusion Inc. (*www.intrusion.com*)

- StealthWatch G1 by Lancope (*www.lancope.com*)

IDS hardware manufacturers sometimes claim that the devices simply need to be plugged in to a network to begin protecting it. However, you should take the time to create a custom configuration, which prevents false positives and blocks new attacks as they're created. In addition, hardware devices, like software programs, need to be updated periodically to remain effective. Updating the OS and/or IDS software on the appliance is fairly simple. Updating the appliance to keep up with a growing network can be an expensive proposition, so it pays to buy a more powerful device than you think you'll need at first.

NOTE

Remember that you need to document all your configurations fully and keep backups. No backup means no recovery, which means you better start searching for a new job!

CHAPTER SUMMARY

❑ Intrusion detection systems (IDSs) add a supplementary line of defense behind firewalls and antivirus software. Some IDSs can go a step beyond transmitting alarms and actually respond to an event.

❑ All IDSs use similar components. A network sensor should be placed at entry points to the network and on individual network segments. An alert message is sent in response to a trigger, which can result from anomaly detection, misuse detection, or a combination of both. The alert message is sent to a command console, which acts as a single interface to data the IDS gathers. A response system built in to the IDS instructs it to drop packets or reset traffic if attacks are detected. To remain accurate and avoid false positives (false alarms), the IDS database of signatures or user profiles must remain current.

❑ Intrusion detection begins with installing a set of attack signatures (if misuse detection is used) or normal network use profiles (if anomaly detection is used). Next, sensors monitor packets. Specified actions, such as sending alerts or responding to the incident, are taken when a packet matches an attack signature or deviates from normal network use.

❑ False positives are highly likely and require administrators to fine-tune the system to allow legitimate traffic to pass through without an alarm. If the intrusion is found to be a legitimate attack, escalation procedures should be followed, if necessary. The IDS also logs each alarmed event so that it can be reviewed later.

❑ An IDS can be implemented in several ways. A network-based intrusion detection system (NIDS) makes use of sensors positioned around the network perimeter or on network segments. A host-based intrusion detection system (HIDS) deploys sensors on each host on the LAN that needs to be protected and uses data generated by each host. A hybrid IDS combines aspects of network-based or host-based IDS configurations. It can also combine anomaly-based and misuse-based detection.

❑ Shim IDSs and distributed IDSs (DIDSs) are two common types of hybrid arrangements. A shim IDS makes use of sensors installed on both network segments and individual hosts, and a DIDS collects data gathered from multiple IDS devices and firewall logs to analyze data across a wide area.

❑ There are several different types of IDS products. The best-known open-source IDS is Snort, which uses a set of predetermined rules and is designed for small-scale networks. Commercial firewall programs, such as Norton Internet Security, include limited sets of IDS features. IDS hardware appliances can handle a higher traffic load than software programs and offer plug-and-play functionality.

KEY TERMS

accountability — The capability to track an attempted attack or intrusion back to the responsible party.

anomaly detection — A type of intrusion detection that causes an alarm to be sent when an IDS detects an event that deviates from behavior defined as "normal"; also called profile-based detection.

command console — Software that provides a graphical front-end interface to an IDS.

dedicated computer — A computer used solely for running IDS software and logging traffic.

distributed IDS (DIDS) — A type of hybrid IDS that uses multiple IDS devices deployed on a network to monitor traffic and report suspicious events.

escalated — The process of increasing the response to an intrusion to a higher level.

event horizon — The entire length of an attack, from the first packet the IDS receives to the last packet needed to complete the attack signature.

false negatives — Attacks that occur but aren't detected by the IDS.

false positives — Alarms generated by legitimate network traffic rather than actual attacks.

host-based IDS (HIDS) — An IDS deployed on each host in the LAN that's protected by the firewall.

hybrid IDS — An IDS implementation that combines the features of HIDSs and NIDSs to gain flexibility and increase security.

intrusion — An attempt to gain unauthorized access to network resources and to compromise the integrity and confidentiality of network data or users' privacy.

intrusion detection — The process of monitoring network traffic to detect attempts to gain unauthorized access to a system or resource and notifying the appropriate professionals so that countermeasures can be taken.

intrusion detection system (IDS) — A network security measure that can consist of multiple applications and hardware devices deployed on the network, hosts, or both to prevent, detect, and respond to traffic interpreted as an intrusion.

misuse detection — A type of intrusion detection in which an IDS is configured to send an alarm in response to sets of characteristics that match known examples of attacks.

network-based IDS (NIDS) — A set of components that includes a command console and sensors positioned at locations where they can monitor network traffic.

profiles — Sets of characteristics that describe the services and resources a user normally accesses on the network.

promiscuous mode — A mode of operation in which an IDS or packet sniffer detects and analyzes each packet in its entirety.

sensor — A component of the IDS (hardware, software, or combination of the two) that monitors a host or network segment for misuse or attacks.

shim IDS — A type of hybrid IDS in which sensors are installed on selected hosts as well as network segments.

sniff— The process of receiving and analyzing packets as they pass into and out of the network; sniffing is carried out by packet-sniffing programs, network traffic analyzers, or IDSs.

state information — Information about a network connection, which is typically kept in a state table.

trigger — A set of circumstances that causes an IDS to send an alert message.

true negatives — Legitimate communications that don't cause an IDS to set off an alarm.

true positive — A genuine attack detected successfully by an IDS, in contrast to a true negative or a false positive.

REVIEW QUESTIONS

7

1. How can the data gained from intrusion detection be used to improve network security? (Choose all that apply.)

   a. It can be used to prevent future attacks.

   b. It can be used to route traffic more efficiently.

   c. It can be used to shield IP addresses on the LAN.

   d. It can help determine how to respond to security incidents.

2. Name the three network defense functions in intrusion detection.

3. Which of the following is an example of a multiple-session attack? (Choose all that apply.)

   a. fragmented packets

   b. IP address spoofing

   c. port scans

   d. network scans

4. Network sensors should be positioned at what locations on the network?

   a. external or internal interfaces

   b. points of entry

   c. before the firewall

   d. between the DMZ and the LAN

5. Advanced network sensors can perform which of the following advanced security functions?

   a. monitoring inbound and outbound traffic

   b. maintaining state information

   c. resetting TCP traffic

   d. updating access control lists

6. Anomaly-based detection makes use of which feature of network traffic?

   a. profiles

   b. signatures

   c. state tables

   d. access control lists

7. Misuse detection is based on which feature of network traffic?

   a. profiles

   b. normal traffic

   c. signatures

   d. user accounts

8. An anomaly-based IDS can be circumvented in which of the following ways?

   a. new attacks

   b. changes in user habits

   c. changes in published signatures

   d. minor changes in attack methods that don't match known signatures

9. A misuse-detection IDS can be circumvented in which of the following ways?

   a. changes in attack methods

   b. a stolen user account

   c. making traffic appear normal

   d. attacks made during the IDS training period

10. Which intrusion detection method can begin protecting a network immediately after installation?

11. Which intrusion detection method is almost impossible for intruders to test before attempting an attack?

12. Which activity performed by an IDS could detect a denial-of-service attack?

   a. protocol state tracking

   b. misuse detection

   c. traffic flow monitoring

   d. IP packet reassembly

13. Which IDS component enables administrators to consolidate and track a large volume of events?

   a. log file analyzer

   b. database

   c. response system

   d. command console

14. Which of the following events has the most serious security implications?
    a. true positive
    b. true negative
    c. false positive
    d. false negative

15. Which of the following is a characteristic of a firewall rule base that isn't shared by an IDS database? (Choose all that apply.)
    a. It can be custom-configured by an administrator.
    b. It should be as short and simple as possible.
    c. It starts by blocking all traffic by default and ends with a cleanup rule.
    d. It needs to be updated regularly.

16. An HIDS can detect an intrusion attempt that targets the entire network, such as a port scan on a range of computers in succession. True or False?

17. An IDS can respond to a possible attack. Which actions can it take?
    a. alarm, drop, reset
    b. deny, alarm, reset
    c. allow, reset, alarm
    d. alarm, log, drop

18. Which of the following is almost inevitable and should be expected after an IDS is installed? (Choose all that apply.)
    a. false negatives
    b. huge log files
    c. signatures that become outdated
    d. false positives

19. What is the value of reviewing an IDS log file, especially when you already have firewall and system log files to review?
    a. You can identify events that occur too quickly for the sensor to detect.
    b. You can identify attacks that occur over a long period.
    c. You can identify ranges of vulnerable IP addresses.
    d. You can trace IP addresses that are trying to gain unauthorized access.

20. A device that detects and analyzes each packet in its entirety is said to operate in which mode?
    a. network-based
    b. host-based
    c. promiscuous
    d. real-time

HANDS-ON PROJECTS

Hands-On Project 7-1: Configuring Windows Firewall

Time Required: 15 minutes

Objective: Configure the Windows XP built-in firewall, Windows Firewall, and set up logging.

Description: Before you can understand how a distributed IDS such as DShield (used in Hands-on Project 7-2) can help you secure your network, you should have a firewall configured and running. Windows XP Professional has a built-in firewall called Windows Firewall (previously Internet Connection Firewall), which is active by default when Service Pack 2 (SP2) is installed. If you aren't running SP2 or your Windows Firewall is disabled, you need to install SP2 or configure Windows to use Windows Firewall. In this project, you configure Windows Firewall and learn how to adjust settings and enable logging. You can use any Windows XP Professional computer connected to the Internet for this project.

1. Click **Start**, **Control Panel**. Make sure Control Panel is in Category View.

2. Click **Security Center**, and then click **Windows Firewall** to open the Windows Firewall dialog box. If necessary, click the **General** tab.

3. Windows Firewall has three settings: On (recommended), On with the Don't allow exceptions check box selected, and Off (not recommended). Click the **On (recommended)** option button, if it's not already selected.

4. There are requests that you'll want to allow, so click the **Exceptions** tab to configure them. What programs are already added to the exceptions list by default?

   _____

5. To add programs and services you want to allow, click their corresponding check boxes in the Programs and Services list.

6. To add programs or services that aren't listed, click the **Add Program** button. For ports, click the **Add Ports** button. To change the default handling of a program or service, click the **Edit** button.

7. Click the **Advanced** tab, and then click the **Settings** button in the Security Logging section (see Figure 7-15). Click the **Log dropped packets** and **Log successful connections** check boxes, if necessary. Write down the location of your log file (for example, C:\Windows\Pfirewall.log). Then, click **OK** to close the Log Settings dialog box and **OK** to close the Windows Firewall dialog box.

8. Close any open windows, and leave your system running for the next project.

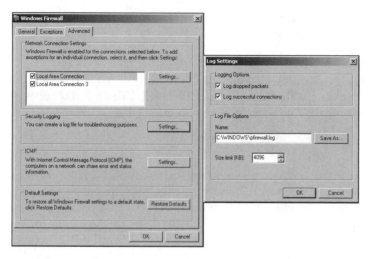

Figure 7-15   The Advanced tab and the Log Settings dialog box

Hands-On Project 7-2: Installing Distributed IDS Software

Time Required: 30 minutes

Objective: Download and install software to enable existing firewall log files to be submitted to DShield.

Description: In this project, you download and install software that works with existing firewall log files to submit log data to DShield. This project requires a Windows XP computer and a file-archiving utility, such as WinZip. The following steps show how to configure software to submit logs compiled by Windows Firewall.

1. Start your Web browser, enter the URL **www.dshield.org/windows_clients.php**, and then press **Enter**.

2. Scroll down the DShield - Windows Clients page and click the **CVTWIN-SETUP.EXE** link.

3. When the File Download dialog box opens, click **Save** and save the file to a location on your hard disk.

4. When the download is finished, double-click the **cvtwin-setup.exe** file you just downloaded. If you see the Open File Security warning box, click **Run** to proceed.

5. When the DShield CVTWIN Install Files Self-Extractor dialog box opens, click **OK**.

6. If you used WinZip and a WinZip Self-Extractor dialog box opens, click **Setup**.

7. When the DShield Universal Firewall Client Setup dialog box opens, click **OK**.

8. In the next dialog box, select an installation location, if necessary. Then, click the computer icon button to begin setup.

9. Click **Continue** when prompted to choose a program group.

10. You might be prompted to overwrite existing files with older versions. In all cases, click **Yes** to retain the current file version.

11. Click **OK** when you see a dialog box stating that the installation is complete.

12. Start the CVTWIN client by clicking **Start**, pointing to **All Programs**, pointing to **DShield**, and clicking **DShield Universal Firewall Client**, or by double-clicking the program's icon in the directory where you installed it.

13. When the DShield Universal Firewall Client window is displayed, click **Edit**, **Configure** from the menu.

14. In the Configure dialog box, enter your e-mail address, your SMTP e-mail server name, and the other required information. Be sure to select your firewall name in the Firewall drop-down list; for this example, click **Windows XP ICF** (this selection might change to Windows Firewall in later versions). Also, be sure to locate the log file for Windows Firewall, which you wrote down in Hands-on Project 7-1. Click **OK**.

15. Click **Edit**, **Edit Source IP Filters** from the menu to open the text file SourceIP.flt.

16. At the bottom of the list of IP addresses to exclude, enter the IP address of your own computer and any others you want the log files to ignore. Close the text file, and then click **Yes** when prompted.

17. Click **Edit**, **Edit Target IP Filters** from the menu. In the text file that opens, enter the IP addresses of any destination computers you want the log files to ignore. Close the text file, and then click **Yes**.

18. Click **File**, **Convert Windows XP ICF** from the menu. A set of conversion data is displayed in the program window.

19. Click **File**, **E-mail test to [your e-mail address]** to send yourself a test log file. Open the e-mail message. Were any connections reported from possible intruders? Write the answer on the following lines. (For the "e-mail test to" menu option to be available, DShield Universal Firewall Client must have actually converted some log file data. If you had no log file data to convert, make sure Windows Firewall is operating and logging data as described in Hands-on Project 7-1. If it's running, your data format might be incorrect. Click **Help**, **Troubleshooting** from the menu to troubleshoot the data conversion problem.)

   _____

   _____

20. Click **File**, **E-mail to report@dshield.org** to send your log file to DShield. (If the "e-mail to" option is not available, troubleshoot as described in Step 19.)

21. Close any open windows, and leave your system running for the next project.

**HANDS-ON
PROJECTS**

Hands-On Project 7-3: Using Distributed IDS Attack Information

Time Required: 15 minutes

Objective: Assess potential security risks to your computer by using the DShield list of Top Ten Target Ports.

Description: DShield gathers log files from users around the world and prepares reports that those users can analyze to determine whether their networks have encountered intrusion attempts. You can view reports on the DShield site and apply them to your own firewall or IDS.

1. Start your Web browser, enter the URL **www.dshield.org/reports.php**, and then press **Enter**.

2. Click the **Top 10 Ports** link to view the DShield – Top 10 Target Ports Web page.

3. Make a list of the most frequently targeted ports. (Does the list include port 137?)

   _____

   _____

   _____

4. To determine whether your computer currently has connections open on UDP port 137 with computers outside your network, you can open a command prompt window and use the **netstat –a** command to view a list of open network connections.

5. Note how many connections have been on destination port 137, which is used for NetBIOS traffic. How many are computers in your own domain? How many are not? Write down the IP addresses of any computers outside your domain.

   _____

   _____

   _____

6. Enter the URL **www.dshield.org/ipinfo.php** and press **Enter** to connect to the DShield IP Address page. Enter the IP address you wrote down in Step 5 in the Check another IP address text box, and then click **Submit**. Where is the remote computer located?

   _____

7. When you're finished, close any open windows, and leave your system running for the next project.

7

Hands-On Project 7-4: Analyzing a Suspicious Signature

Time Required: 20 minutes

Objective: Analyze an attack signature to determine details about the intrusion, identify the type of attack taking place, and suggest methods to prevent these attacks.

Description: An IDS that depends on a database of known attack signatures is vulnerable to attacks that aren't already included in its database. Systems that enable the administrator to create custom rules depend on the administrator to analyze attack signatures.

1. Review the data in Figure 7-16. In particular, note the destination IP addresses and ports.

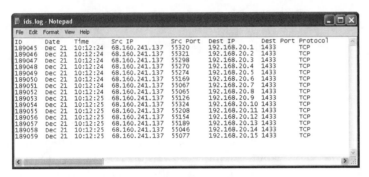

Figure 7-16   Destination IP addresses and ports

2. Identify the possible intruder. How would you trace the intruder and determine whether this person has been responsible for any other attacks? (*Hint:* Review preceding activities and projects in this chapter.) Record your answer here:

_____

_____

_____

_____

3. Where is the source IP computer located? Is the computer known to have been involved in any other attacks?

_____

_____

4. Describe what kind of event is happening in Figure 7-16:

_____

_____

_____

_____

5. Suggest how you could prevent similar intrusion attempts from succeeding in the future:

_____

_____

_____

_____

CASE PROJECTS

7

CASE PROJECTS

Case Project 7-1: Providing a Two-Tiered IDS Response

You administer a network configured with two separate subnets: 10.8.1.1/16 and 10.9.1.1/16. You add a new subnet, 10.10.1.1/16, to the network. Each internal subnet now has a separate Ethernet interface on the firewall/IDS device (designated by e0, e1, and e2). The firewall IDS also has an external interface on the Internet (designated by s0) at IP address 210.10.1.1. Because your network has expanded, you need to configure the IDS. You don't want the IDS to interfere with traffic originating from the interfaces e0, e1, and e2 by resetting the TCP connections if a packet matches the database and an alarm is sent. On the other hand, you *do* want the IDS to send an alarm and reset TCP connections if a suspicious packet reaches the external interface s0. How could you accommodate both types of responses?

CASE PROJECTS

Case Project 7-2: Using an IDS to Trace Internal Misuse

An IDS can be used to detect and track unauthorized access attempts that come from inside the organizations' network as well as outside. For example, your SMTP server's event log files indicate that the server has been sending hundreds of e-mail messages every Monday morning at 8:00 a.m. for the past three weeks. You suspect that the company's SMTP server is being used to distribute mass e-mails by an employee who manages an e-mail newsletter. How could you verify this by using the IDS?

CASE PROJECTS

Case Project 7-3: Designing an IDS for LedGrafix

For this running case project, you need your log file analysis tool research from Chapter 4, your revised network diagram from Chapter 5, and your updated security policy and risk analysis data from Chapter 6. You have designed LedGrafix's network using a distributed and layered security approach. You have also followed accepted best practices and performed important steps that are often overlooked, such as risk assessment and creation of a security policy. Your security policy will continue to provide guidance as you work through this book's running case projects. Using your updated security policy that incorporates a remote access solution, in this project you develop an intrusion detection solution for LedGrafix's network resources.

There are several decisions you must make to design an effective IDS solution. First, you must decide what the goals are for the IDS. Next, you must determine where sensors should be deployed. Do you need a centralized or distributed design? Then you must decide what administrative tools you need and begin investigating products that provide services you need. Follow these general steps to create your design:

You might want to do some research and find sample IDS designs to help you in this project. Cisco's SAFE Blueprint is a great place to start. You can find its IDS deployment documents by running a search for "IDS deployment" at *www. cisco.com*. At the time of this writing, the *SAFE: IDS Deployment, Tuning and Logging in Depth [SAFE Blueprint]* paper was listed first in the results.

TIP

Remember that some steps might not apply, and you might have to add others not listed here, depending on your design.

NOTE

1. Determine the goals for your IDS. Does it need to examine all traffic into or out of the network or only traffic on specific segments? Should each host be monitored or only servers or machines hosting confidential data or applications? Refer to your risk analysis documentation to determine what areas are most critical to protect or most at risk of intrusion. After you have defined your goals for the IDS, you can decide where sensors should be deployed.

2. Review your current network diagram to locate all points of entry into your network. Don't forget to include remote access, dial-up, VPN, and even any deliberate administrative "back doors" you have integrated. Using a copy of your diagram, mark points of entry.

3. Locate any internal hosts that are particularly critical, such as research and development servers, database servers containing customer or employee information, domain controllers, global catalog servers, and so forth. Mark them on your diagram.

4. Determine which segments, switches, or routers provide access to the internal hosts noted in Step 3 and any others that serve critical or confidential areas. Mark these hosts on your diagram.

5. Use your updated network diagram to determine optimum placement of sensors. The goal is to place as few sensors as possible (to reduce deployment cost and minimize installation and administrative effort) yet still provide coverage of all critical areas. These areas warrant additional expense. Mark the locations for sensor deployment on your diagram. Be sure to check them to make sure you haven't missed anything.

NOTE Consider having a classmate review your design at this point. A fresh pair of eyes often spots overlooked problems and can offer unbiased insight. Never underestimate the value of peer review!

6. Remember to look for alert and response capabilities, and don't forget signature files and updating.

7. Now you have the information to decide on administrative tools you need. Look at your diagram again. Is there a secure server where you can install the IDS administrative application? Do you need to purchase additional hardware for IDS administration and logging?

8. Next, make a list of your needs. How many sensors do you need? How many hosts require software? What type of administrative software will you use?

9. Using the Internet or other resources, find an IDS product that meets your needs. Be sure to consider the vendor's stability and reputation, available support options, cost, and scalability.

10. In Chapter 4, you researched a number of log file analysis tools. Review that research to determine whether you already have a suitable product for analyzing log files. If you don't, you need to do further research to find an effective tool, unless your IDS product provides log file analysis and management.

11. Document your configuration. Update your network diagram to reflect the final design, locations of sensors, hosts the product is installed on, server configuration, log file storage, alerts and analysis, and so on. Establish how and where signature files are obtained and how software will be updated.

12. Update your security policy to reflect any changes to the network configuration and relevant policies, such as incident response. List contact information for the vendor and support staff and note escalation procedures, if necessary.

13. Place your updated diagrams and details on new software and hardware in an appendix to your policy. Submit a management summary of the design, a copy of your current network design showing your IDS deployment, and supporting documentation of the product and configuration to your instructor. Specifically, your submission should include:

   - A summary of the deployment stating what it is, where it's deployed, and how it's intended to work. Include a brief statement of how this deployment supports the standards and requirements set forth in your security policy, if applicable. This management summary should be written for a nontechnical audience and give an overview of the system.

   - A network diagram showing locations of software and hardware deployments

   - Product details, including alert and response capabilities, scalability potential, vendor and support options, and specific configuration on your network

- Log file storage and analysis techniques

- Signature file availability and updating and any other update issues for the software or hardware IDS

- Optional: Write a report on factors affecting employees that would normally be included in the security policy, such as incident response instructions, escalation procedures, and updates for management and network administration. This information will be reviewed and updated in Chapter 8. You might also want to include ideas for testing the new IDS, as well as change techniques and management for signatures and handling false positives, false negatives, and so on.

8

INTRUSION DETECTION: INCIDENT RESPONSE

> **After reading this chapter and completing the exercises, you will be able to:**
>
> ♦ Configure an IDS and develop filter rules
> ♦ Develop a security incident response team for your organization
> ♦ Explain the six-step incident response process
> ♦ Describe how to respond to false alarms to reduce reoccurrences
> ♦ Explain options for dealing with legitimate security alerts

In previous chapters, you learned how to interpret signatures of legitimate traffic and known attack attempts and how to install an intrusion detection system (IDS). After you have installed and configured an IDS, you need to know how to respond to the alert messages it generates and develop filter rules. Without a doubt, you'll receive false alarms from an IDS, but you'll also receive legitimate attack alerts. It's essential to know how to respond to both events in a way that doesn't alarm your staff, that minimizes damage, and that prevents intrusions from happening in the future.

"Incident response" is the term for the actions taken after a computer security incident occurs to determine what happened and what countermeasures need to be carried out to ensure the network's continued security. The incident response process follows a set of well-defined steps that must be described clearly enough so that anyone authorized to perform incident response can follow them.

This chapter begins by examining IDS filter rules, installing a GUI editor for the Snort rule base, and reviewing the approaches to responding to intrusion alerts. You also learn how to develop a security incident response team (SIRT), how to respond to an incident, how to respond to false alarms (otherwise known as false positives), and how to respond to legitimate alarms (true positives).

Developing IDS Filter Rules

An intrusion detection system's effectiveness depends on how complete and up to date the signatures or user profiles in its database are. If the IDS command console receives alarms from well-known intrusion signatures or suspicious events, such as those described in Chapter 4, you should respond by:

- Adjusting packet-filtering rules
- Creating rules on the IDS

An IDS, like a firewall or packet-filtering router, can have its own rules that you should edit in response to network scans and attacks. It can do more than simply reacting to undetected attacks as a second line of defense and relying on firewalls and proxy servers to filter out packets. An IDS can be used proactively to block attacks and move from intrusion detection to intrusion prevention. The following sections examine ways of configuring an IDS to filter out potentially harmful traffic: specifying rule actions and rule data to apply and using rule options.

Rule Actions

The problem with a traditional IDS is its passive and reactive nature. By configuring an IDS to take actions other than simply triggering an alarm when it encounters a suspicious packet, you gain another layer of network defense. You have more control over how attacks are recorded and handled, and you can reduce false positives after you have worked out all the bugs. Finally, you also help the IDS handle new intrusion attempts that attackers develop.

Most IDS products include documentation about rule writing. Because some actions, options, or data can differ between platforms, referring to the product documentation for help in rule writing is best. Customizing rules can also increase false positives during the learning process, so be aware that your customizations might not help the situation. Fortunately, if you can develop a test lab that mimics your production environment, you can develop and test rules before applying them. Often, thorough testing can save you many headaches by allowing you to work out bugs in a new product or configuration without any undesirable outcomes on your live network.

The freeware IDS Snort gives you an idea of the kinds of actions a rule can take when it encounters a packet matching one of its rules. Actions are set in the Snort.conf file, which you can edit with a text editor. (You can also create a custom rules file and have Snort refer to it.) These are the available actions for rules:

- *Alert*—Sends an alert message that you define ahead of time when setting up the IDS.
- *Log*—Records the packet in the log files.
- *Pass*—Allows the packet to pass through to the internal network.

- *Activate*—Creates an alert message along with a dynamic rule, one that covers subsequent logging.

- *Dynamic*—Enables Snort to continue logging subsequent packets when a certain packet is detected. For instance, if a port scan packet is detected, you could call a dynamic rule that tells Snort to log the next 100 packets.

Other IDSs also give you the option to terminate the originating computer's TCP connection if an attack is detected.

Rule Data

After you specify the action you want Snort to perform when it encounters a match with one of its signatures, you specify the rest of the data that applies to the rule, which includes the following:

- *Protocol*—Snort supports IP, TCP, UDP, and ICMP.

- *Source and destination IP addresses*—You can use the word "any" to specify any IP address or the netmask format for specifying a subnet mask. A Class A IP address uses the 255.0.0.0 netmask, a Class B address uses the 255.255.0.0 netmask, and a Class C address uses the 255.255.255.0 netmask.

- *Port number*—You can specify an individual port or use the word "any."

- *Direction*—The direction from the source computer and port to the destination computer and port is specified with the -> characters. For rules that affect traffic heading in both directions, use <>.

For instance, a rule that logs traffic from any computer to a computer at 192.168.10.1 on port 23 would look like the following:

```
Log tcp any any -> 192.168.10.1 23
```

A rule that logs traffic in both directions between two subnets would look like this:

```
Log tcp 10.1.20.0/24 any <> 200.156.15.0/24 any
```

More specific attributes, such as ACK flags, are covered by the rule options, which follow the rule action and data.

Rule Options

Snort rules become more precise when you add rule options. Options are enclosed in parentheses, placed after the rule data, and separated from the data by a blank space. Each option is separated from other options enclosed in parentheses by a semicolon and a blank space, as shown in this example:

```
Alert tcp any any -> 192.168.10.0/24 any (msg: "SYN-FIN
scan packet"; flags: SF;)
```

This rule contains two options. The msg option prints the specified text message along with the alert message and the data recorded in log files. The flags option causes the rule to trigger a specified action when the indicated flags are detected in a packet—in the preceding example, the SYN and FIN flags (SF) are used together.

The most useful options that Snort can implement include the following:

- *msg*—Tells the logging and alerting engine what message to print along with a packet dump or an alert.

- *ttl*—Tells Snort to match the time to live (TTL) value in a packet's IP header.

- *id*—Tells Snort to match a packet's fragment ID number.

- *flags*—Tells Snort to match specified TCP flags set in a packet.

- *ack*—Tells Snort to match the ACK flag in a packet.

- *content*—Tells Snort to match a defined string in the packet's data payload.

- *logto*—Tells Snort to log files to a specified file name instead of the default log files.

TIP

More options are available for Snort rules; you can find a complete list at *www.snort.org/docs/writing_rules/*.

The TCP flags that form an important part of signatures are usually designated in Snort rules by a single character, as shown in the following list:

- F (FIN)
- S (SYN)
- R (RST)
- P (PSH)
- A (ACK)
- U (URG)
- 2—Reserved bit 2
- 1—Reserved bit 1
- 0—No TCP flags set
- + ALL flag—Matches all specified flags plus any others
- * ANY flag—Matches any of the specified flags
- !—Matches all flags except the flag you specify

After you understand the available options, you can set up a proactive set of rules that cover many of the suspicious traffic signatures described in Chapter 4. The rule base for an IDS is different from a packet-filtering rule base. The IDS rule base assumes that packets are already being filtered by firewalls or routers. Therefore, any traffic that gets through the packet filter and matches a signature on the IDS should be logged. That way, you can analyze what traffic is getting through the filter so that you can adjust the filter rules. The initial rules might be dramatically different from those for a packet filter.

Examine the following sample rules:

```
log tcp any any -> any any (msg: "TCP traffic log";)
log udp any any -> any any (msg: "UDP traffic log";)
alert icmp any any -> any any (msg: "ICMP traffic alert";)
```

The first two rules tell Snort to log any TCP and UDP traffic that reaches the IDS. The third rule sends an alert if any ICMP echo request packets or other ICMP packets also reach the IDS. After you set up these general rules, you can create rules for specific traffic signatures, as shown in the following examples.

This rule sends an alert if a packet with the SYN, FIN, and ACK flags is detected:

```
alert tcp any any -> 192.168.1.0/24 any (flags: SFA; msg:
"SYN-FIN-ACK packet detected";)
```

On the other hand, the following rule sends an alert if a packet is detected that doesn't have any flags set:

```
alert tcp any any -> 192.168.1.0/24 any (flags: 0; msg:
"null packet detected";)
```

The following two rules send an alert if any packets are detected that have the two most frequently watched for IP options: **loose source and record routing (lsrr)** and **strict source and record routing (ssrr)**. (Only one IP option can be specified per rule.)

```
alert tcp any any -> 192.168.1.0/24 any (ipopts: ssrr; msg:
"strict source routing packet";)
alert tcp any any -> 192.168.1.0/24 any (ipopts: lsrr; msg:
"loose source routing packet";)
```

The following rule sends an alert if the word "Password" is detected in a packet's data payload:

```
alert tcp any any -> any any (content: "Password"; msg:
"password transmitted?";)
```

The following rule is intended to address the path obfuscation attack mentioned in "Advanced Attacks" in Chapter 4:

```
alert tcp any any -> any 80 (content: "/. /. /. /"; msg:
"possible Web URL path obfuscation";)
```

Activity 8-1: Configuring a GUI Editor for the Snort Rule Base

Time Required: 30 minutes

Objective: Install IDS Policy Manager to view and edit Snort's rule base.

Description: One way to block intrusions is to update the rule base your IDS refers to so that you can determine when to send alerts, drop packets, and log events. Snort, which you installed in Chapter 4, uses a set of text files with the .rules extension as its rule base. Reviewing and editing these files can be difficult with a text editor, but a program called IDS Policy Manager enables you to view and edit the rule files easily. In this activity, you download, install, and configure IDS Policy Manager. You need a Windows XP computer. This activity assumes you have WinZip and Snort installed, as described in Activity 4-1.

1. Start your Web browser, enter the URL **www.activeworx.org/downloads/index.htm**, and press **Enter**.

2. Scroll down the page to IDS Policy Manager, and click the **idspm.v1.7.0.msi** link.

3. When prompted, save the file to your hard disk or folder as directed by your instructor. Close your Web browser.

4. When the download is finished, double-click the **idspm.v1.7.0.msi** file you downloaded. When the Open File - Security Warning dialog box opens, click **Run**.

5. When the Welcome to the IDS Policy Manager Installation Wizard starts (see Figure 8-1), click **Next**.

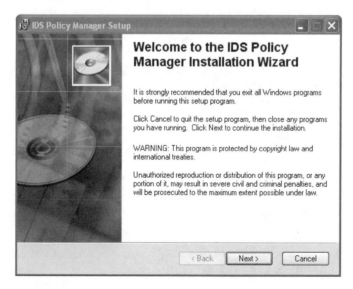

Figure 8-1   The IDS Policy Manager Installation Wizard

6. Accept the default installation folder, and then click **Next** twice to begin the installation. Click **Finish**.

7. Navigate to the C:\Program Files\Activeworx\IDSPolMan folder (the path for default installations). Double-click the **IDSPolicyMan.exe** file, and if asked whether you would like to auto check for updates on startup, click **No**.

8. When the Policy Manager window opens, click the **Policy Manager** tab near the bottom (see Figure 8-2).

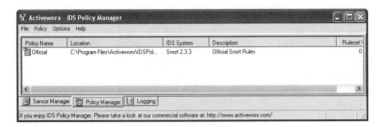

Figure 8-2 The Policy Manager tab

9. Right-click **Official** in the Policy Name column, and then click **Open in Policy Editor**.

10. The Policy Editor opens and displays Snort's default set of rules. For the purpose of this activity, if a dialog box opens asking whether you want to check for new rules, click **No**. (*Note:* Normally, you would make checking for new rules part of your regular duties.) If the dialog box Check for new Bleeding Snort Rules opens, click **No**.

11. If the Add Variable dialog box opens, click **OK**. Click **OK** to each new Add Variable dialog box that opens. If a dialog box opens stating how many new rules have been added to the default Snort rule base, click **OK**.

12. Click the **Settings** tab (see Figure 8-3).

13. Make sure the **HOME_NET** variable matches the IP address range of your own network. If you're working in a lab with its own subnet, such as 10.1.0.0/16, click the line with the name HOME_NET and the value 10.1.1.0/24. If your network contains only one or two IP addresses, click the check box next to HOME_NET that has the value (10.1.1.0,192.168.1.0/24).

14. Click the **Edit** button in the Variables section. In the Edit Variable dialog box, replace the default values in the Value text box with the IP address or addresses that apply to your network. For instance, if you're working on a two-computer network with the IP addresses 192.168.20.1 and 192.168.20.2, replace the default values in the Value text box with those IP addresses. Click **OK** to close the dialog box.

15. Click **File**, **Exit** from the menu to close IDS Policy Manager. If you're prompted to save your changes, click **Yes**. Leave your system running for the next activity.

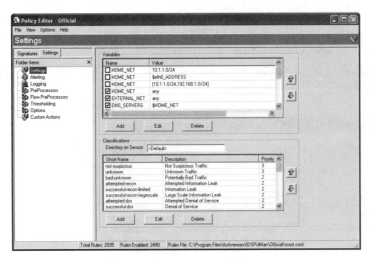

Figure 8-3   The Policy Editor Settings tab

As you can see, editing the rule base is much easier with a GUI editor. IDS Policy Manager makes maintaining your rule base easier, and in the following activity, you install and work with IDScenter, a GUI interface for Snort that is much easier to work with than using the command line.

Activity 8-2: Installing a GUI for Snort

Time Required: 35 minutes

Objective: Install a GUI interface for Snort.

Description: Snort works well as a command-line program, but with a GUI, it's far easier to configure. In this activity, you download and configure a GUI front-end interface designed especially for Snort called IDScenter. This activity assumes you have WinZip and Snort installed, as described in Activity 4-1.

1. Start your Web browser, enter the URL **http://www.snort.org/dl/contrib/front_ends** for a Web page containing links to GUIs for Snort, and press **Enter**.

2. Click **ids_center/**, and then click the **idscenter.zip** link to download the IDS Center for Snort.

3. When the File Download dialog box opens, click **Open** to download the program. Extract the Setup.exe file to a folder where you can find it. Close WinZip and your Web browser.

4. Double-click the **setup.exe** file. If necessary, click **Run** in the Open File - Security Warning dialog box. In the first Snort IDScenter 2001 setup window (see Figure 8-4), click **Next**.

Figure 8-4   The setup wizard for Snort IDScenter 2001

5. Follow the instructions in subsequent windows to set up the program on your computer.

6. When a window is displayed notifying you that the setup is finished, leave the View info.txt check box selected, and then click **Finish**. Read the info.txt file, and then close the file.

7. Double-click the **IDScente**r icon on your Windows desktop.

8. Double-click the **IDScenter** icon in the Windows taskbar to start the program.

9. When the IDScenter window opens, click the **General setup** button to make sure you're viewing the General setup window (see Figure 8-5).

10. To begin configuring the program, click the browse button (labeled with three dots) in the Snort setup section of the General setup window.

11. When the IDScenter 2001 dialog box opens, click the **Look in** list arrow to locate the folder where you installed Snort. Open folders until you locate the Snort.exe file (Snort\bin by default). Click **Snort.exe**, and then click **Open**. The path leading to the Snort program file should appear in the Snort file text box in the General setup window.

12. In the Home network text box, enter the IP address for your computer.

13. In the Network interface text box, enter the network interface number for your computer. (If you're working on a standalone computer, enter **1**. Otherwise, ask your network administrator for the network interface number.)

14. Click the **IDS rules** button at the left to open the window shown in Figure 8-6.

15. In the Snort IDS ruleset / Filters section, click the browse button.

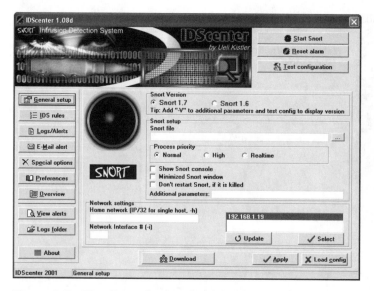

Figure 8-5   The General setup window

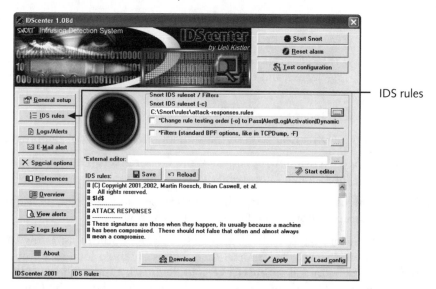

IDS rules

Figure 8-6   Configuring IDS rules in IDScenter

16. In the IDScenter 2001 dialog box, locate the Snort\rules folder, which should contain a number of predefined rules files for use with Snort. Click the **attack-responses.rules** file, and then click **Open**. The path leading to this file is then displayed in the Snort IDS ruleset text box.

17. Click the **Load config** button at the bottom.

18. Click **Save**. When a message box asks you to confirm whether you want to save changes, click **Ja**.

19. Click **Apply**. The message "script successfully generated" should appear at the bottom of the window.

20. Click the **Logs/Alerts** button at the left.

21. In the Logs & Alerts section, click the browse button next to Set directory for Snort log files.

22. In the Logs&Alerts directory dialog box, click the plus sign (**+**) next to the hard disk containing Snort, and keep expanding folders until you locate the log folder. Click the **log** folder, and then click **OK**. If an Information dialog box opens, click **OK**. The path leading to the log folder should appear in the text box under Set directory for Snort log files.

23. Click all check boxes under Specific packet infos and Other options.

24. Click **Apply**. The message "Script successfully generated" appears in the status bar.

25. Click **Start Snort**. The Start Snort button should change to Stop Snort to indicate that the program is running. Close the IDScenter window, and leave your system running for the next activity.

IDScenter and IDS Policy Manager help you manage your IDS more effectively. With the help of these add-ons, your job is simpler and less prone to errors. This doesn't mean you don't have to learn more about IDSs; it just means you can manage them and your valuable time more effectively.

ACTIVITY

Activity 8-3: Viewing Security Alert Options

Time Required: 10 minutes

Objective: Configure alert notifications in IDScenter.

Description: Any IDS needs to alert a network administrator when an intrusion attempt is detected. Most intrusion detection software gives you options for notification. Although some programs offer elaborate types of notification, such as sending a message to your pager, the basic alert methods are e-mail, sound, and graphics. The following activity assumes you have installed Snort and IDScenter on your Windows XP computer.

1. Right-click the **IDScenter** icon in the taskbar, and then click the **Settings** tab.

2. In the main IDScenter window, click the **Special options** button at the left.

3. In the Alarm sound section, click the option button next to one of the alarm sounds.

4. Notice that in the External program section, you can click the browse button to start a program when an alert is received. (You might choose to start your e-mail program, for example, so that you can e-mail other security personnel or staff that an intrusion has taken place.)

5. Click the **E-mail alert** button at the left of the IDScenter window. In the window that's displayed, click the **E-mail alert** check box, as shown in Figure 8-7.

Figure 8-7 Configuring e-mail alerts in IDScenter

6. In the SMTP server text box, type **smtp.***EmailServer* (substituting the name of your organization's e-mail server for *EmailServer*). In the From text box, type the name you want to appear in the e-mail's From line. For this example, type the legitimate e-mail address of someone in your classroom.

7. In the To text box, enter your own e-mail address. In the Message text box, type the standard alert message you want to receive; for this example, type **You have received an alert from the Snort IDS.** Click the **Apply** button.

8. Click **Stop Snort**, if necessary, and then click **Test AlertMail**. In a few minutes, check your e-mail inbox to see whether you received a message.

9. Close IDScenter. If you like, you can leave your system running for the hands-on projects at the end of the chapter.

After you have configured a rule base, your IDS can begin monitoring your network for suspicious activity. The next step in protecting your organization is developing response procedures. Because you can't be there around the clock to monitor the system for alerts and respond to incidents, you need to organize a security incident response team, as described in the following section, to take action should an incident occur.

DEVELOPING A SECURITY INCIDENT RESPONSE TEAM (SIRT)

You can respond to a security incident in a number of different ways, such as taking countermeasures designed to block intrusions, making corrections to packet-filtering rules and proxy servers to block intrusions an IDS has detected, and modifying security policies to cover new vulnerabilities when they're detected. Developing a security incident response team gives your organization the flexibility to carry out these response options.

You need to establish a framework in which intrusion detection and response can take place. The following sections examine one aspect of that framework—establishing a security incident response team. You learn how to establish goals and expectations for this team, review the responsibilities of team members, see when to notify public response teams, and discover when to consider outsourcing incident response.

Goals of a Security Incident Response Team (SIRT)

A security incident response team (SIRT), also known as a computer incident response team (CIRT), is a group of people assigned to respond effectively to security breaches. The team's primary functions consist of six steps:

1. *Preparation*—Begin with a risk analysis and security policy, and create the SIRT.

2. *Notification*—Monitor the integrity of the computing environment to uncover security vulnerabilities; receive notification from your IDS or firewall.

3. *Response*—React to internal and external security breaches and policy violations; determine who to notify; determine whether the attack is legitimate or a false alarm; assess the level of damage.

4. *Countermeasures*—Contain the damage and eradicate any harmful or unauthorized files that have been introduced. These countermeasures are strategies and approaches that address threats to network security. Also, take corrective measures to prevent recurrence.

5. *Recovery*—Restore damaged files and compromised resources.

6. *Follow-up*—Record what happened; conduct a forensic examination, if necessary; decide whether to prosecute offenders; adjust security policies as needed. (Forensics is discussed briefly in "Gathering Data for Prosecution" later in this chapter, but computer forensics techniques are beyond the scope of this text and the SCNP exam.)

The six steps of **incident response** are part of a larger workflow that encompasses everything from initial risk analysis to the reevaluation of security policies and procedures after an event occurs. The incident response process isn't a separate series of events but an ongoing process, as shown in Figure 8-8. The six primary functions of a SIRT are described in more detail in "How to Respond: The Incident Response Process" later in this chapter.

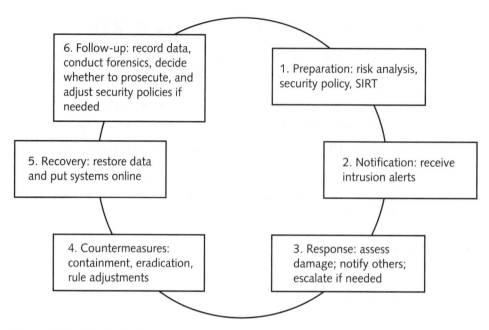

Figure 8-8   The intrusion response process

Responsibilities of Team Members

Often, it makes sense to look within the organization for SIRT members. Employees who are already in-house are familiar with the personnel and the organization's procedures and rules. They have gained the trust of their fellow employees and, in organizations such as government agencies, have the necessary level of security clearance.

Employees who become part of a SIRT need to be able to stop any work they have underway to respond to a security incident when it happens. They should also be given enough authority to make decisions if the organization's overall security calls for it. These decisions might range from ordering employees to change their network passwords if one has been stolen to shutting down the company's firewall and disconnecting the network from the Internet if the incident is judged to be serious. The following sections discuss aspects of assembling the response team: deciding what roles members will assume, staffing and training team members, and the value of staging "fire drills."

Deciding What Roles Team Members Will Assume

The SIRT should contain a range of employees representing a cross-section of the organization to ensure that all parts of the organization are represented in the process of responding to incidents. Each member can then report back to his or her department in the organization and describe any security concerns or incidents that might require changes in how personnel go about their daily business. Having all branches of the company represented in the SIRT reduces the chances of conflict or finger pointing that can result if files are lost or resources damaged. Typically, SIRT members are drawn from the following departments:

- *Management*—At least one member of the SIRT should be upper-level management from the organization. Decisions might need to be made that affect the entire company, such as shutting down the company's Web server or e-mail service if it's attacked, taking the network offline, restricting access to confidential resources, or other response measures. Someone with the authority to make these decisions needs to be on the SIRT.

- *Legal*—One of the attorneys in the company's Legal Department should be part of the SIRT to give advice if the company needs to take legal action against an intruder.

- *Information Technology (IT)*—At least one member of the IT staff should be on the SIRT. IT staff know where the affected data is located and what parts of the network should be off limits to unauthorized users. Having several IT staff members on the SIRT enables them to perform "first response" functions when incidents occur; each member can be assigned to respond on a different shift within the day.

- *Physical Security*—The personnel who physically guard a company and its resources should be involved if an incident involves physical damage to computer resources.

- *Information Security Services (ISS)*—ISS staff are specially trained to handle computer- and network-related security incidents. They will probably form the nucleus of the SIRT.

- *Human Resources (HR)*—Many security incidents originate from within the company. If employees are identified as being involved, disciplinary action is required. HR staff might not need to be involved at every stage of an intrusion. However, if an intrusion originates from inside, HR should be notified so that they can be well informed about the incident and take appropriate disciplinary measures.

- *Public Relations (PR)*—For well-known companies with a public profile, security incidents can affect business directly. Most companies prefer to keep security breaches out of the public eye, but this isn't always possible, especially if a high-traffic Web site goes down because of an attack. A PR person on the SIRT can convey accurate information to the media and the public.

- *Finance/Accounting*—Placing a dollar amount on a security incident might be required for insurance purposes, and having someone from the organization's financial staff on board can make the process go more smoothly.

All these people need not be available at once when an incident occurs. Because security breaches can occur any time of the day or night, you need to have at least one person on staff at all times who has been trained in responding to security incidents and who can summon members of the SIRT with a higher level of authority in the organization if decisions need to be made. The exact team organization and response procedures should be worked out at an initial meeting that includes all SIRT members. The SIRT should, however, include one person designated as the leader who calls other members to meetings and communicates SIRT activities to others in the organization.

You might also want to call in people from outside the company who can contribute to the SIRT. You can gain expertise and perspective by including outside security consultants, as well as law enforcement officers, who can give advice if needed.

Serious consequences can result if you fail to include enough people in the SIRT. For instance, suppose you fail to include someone from your IT staff. You might find that after a possible attack, the IT staff simply replaces all data on a database with a backup copy rather than reporting it to the SIRT for proper handling. Similarly, not having a HR person on the SIRT can cause legal problems if employees are accused without evidence.

Staffing and Training

A **virtual team** consists of employees with other jobs to perform during regular business hours, so the team exists only during meetings or when an incident becomes serious enough. This type of team tends to get out of touch and need retraining. In contrast, a team devoted solely to incident response full-time can stay on top of technical issues as part of its normal activities. All team members need training periodically, however. You can have senior staff train junior members by mentoring them. You can encourage self-study and recommend that team members subscribe to trade publications and become members in industry organizations, such as IEEE. Many companies are happy to pay for these publications and memberships to show due diligence.

Two trade publications focus solely on incident response: *Homeland Response News* (*www.respondersafety.net*) and *Homeland Protection Professional* (*www.hppmag.com*).

The speed and thoroughness with which your organization can respond to security alerts depends largely on the number of employees involved and how many other duties they are called on to perform in the organization. If your budget allows, you can assemble a group of employees whose sole responsibility is incident response or other security-related matters, such as configuring firewalls and IDSs. However, this arrangement might be economically feasible only for large corporations. Small companies might need to assign people to handle incident response in addition to networking or other responsibilities. A permanent, dedicated security officer or team of people who perform only security tasks results in the best level of response.

Staging Fire Drills

After the SIRT has held an initial organizational meeting and completed training, you need to conduct a security drill not unlike the fire drills in schools. Because of the staff time involved, you might need to convince upper management that this drill is necessary. However, drills can pay off in the long run by making response more effective and coordinated.

You don't need someone to actually attack your network. Instead, pick a time for the drill, and then follow a scenario in which you assume that an attack has occurred. Drills can be scheduled beforehand or can be unscheduled. Team members should be contacted when the "attack" takes place and should respond as they would to a real incident. Test the notification process to make sure all phone and pager numbers are correct. Next, test the response process by assembling the team and giving them a scenario.

Drills are intended to identify any holes in security procedures and to make sure everyone on the SIRT knows his or her duties and responsibilities. All procedures carried out during the drill should be documented, and after the drill, hold a meeting to discuss how the drill went and whether any procedures should be handled differently to respond more quickly or effectively. You might want to conduct subsequent drills periodically (such as once every quarter or twice a year) to reevaluate how well the response procedures work.

Public Resource Teams

A number of teams around the world have been assembled to publish notices and articles about serious security incidents. You can notify such a team if you encounter a significant security event to benefit from the group's expertise and ability to coordinate resources. These groups also provide training for response team members. Consider contacting groups such as the CERT Coordination Center (*www.cert.org*) in the United States or DFN-CERT in Germany (*www.cert.dfn.de/eng*).

TIP

The Forum of Incident Response and Security Teams (FIRST) holds periodic Technical Colloquia at which members exchange technical data about attacks and practical experiences with security software and hardware. Member teams are open to discussing their successes and failures dealing with security issues. To find out how to join FIRST, visit the organization's Web site at *www.first.org*.

Outsourcing Incident Response

Because of staff or budget constraints, you might need to outsource your incident response activities. In other words, you might need to hire a company that monitors your network and IDS sensors and tells you whether an intrusion has occurred.

Outsourcing has its advantages and disadvantages. On one hand, you might find that hiring an outside incident response team results in lower overall costs because the team has to deal only with actual incidents instead of managing firewalls, reviewing log files, and changing passwords and user accounts. On the downside, outsourcing systems or security functions could leave your organization at a disadvantage when it comes to timely, effective incident response procedures. Your network might be attacked at the same time as your contractor's other customers, which makes it unlikely that you'll get priority assistance.

Be sure to get references from current and former customers before you hire an incident response service. Yahoo! has a lengthy list of companies that can monitor your firewall and IDS and respond to incidents for you at *http://dir.yahoo.com/Business_and_Economy/ Business_to_Business/Computers/Security_and_Encryption/Consulting*.

How to Respond: The Incident Response Process

The process of intrusion response doesn't need to be a huge undertaking. In fact, you should be able to clearly describe your own process in a short document of perhaps five or six pages that SIRT members can refer to if an event occurs and they need to know how to proceed. The process is usually divided into a series of steps that cover the most important actions: determining exactly what happened, notifying the appropriate people, and taking the appropriate countermeasures to prevent events from happening again. If this process sounds familiar, it should. Incident response was first covered in Chapters 2 and 3. This section focuses more on handling intrusions or attacks the IDS detects; a security "incident," as you'll recall from those previous chapters, could be something as simple as a lost password. The following sections cover the six-step intrusion response sequence described earlier: preparation, notification, response, countermeasures, recovery, and follow-up.

Step 1: Preparation

As you learned in Chapter 2, risk analysis is the process of determining the possibility of damage or loss in a particular situation or environment. A security policy is a statement that describes how network defenses will be configured to block unauthorized access, how the organization will respond to attacks, and how employees should handle the organization's resources safely to prevent loss of data or damage to files. In the context of incident response, a security policy should include the following directives:

- A statement to the effect that incident response is mandatory for the organization

- The objectives of incident response

- The limits of incident response, including privacy violations and other issues that are prohibited, such as retaliation against an attacker

- The relationship of the SIRT to the law enforcement community—in other words, when law enforcement officers should be brought in to the incident response process

CAUTION

Setting limits on intrusion response activities is important to help avoid lawsuits. Disgruntled employees or employees who contend they have been wrongly accused can file suit and force the company to respond in court and possibly pay damages.

Using Risk Analysis to Prepare Your Response

As described in Chapter 2, risk analysis identifies an organization's logical, physical, and other assets and assigns values to each one to determine the impact if that asset is lost or damaged. Risk analysis is used to prepare a security policy, which describes how the organization should respond to intrusions—who should be on the SIRT, when incidents should be escalated, and when prosecution should be pursued. You should use the security policy as a guideline when responding to incidents. Many security policies contain a section on incident response; others note the location of current incident response protocols. Wherever this information is located, everyone involved in incident response should know where and how to get the current response guidelines quickly.

Active Network Monitoring

Monitoring the network for suspicious traffic is an essential activity. In a large organization, SIRT members might be dedicated to this task; in small networks, the network administrator monitors the network, or several people might take turns. This approach to monitoring can be considered proactive. In a passive approach to network monitoring, the IDS is set up to send alerts if activity is detected that warrants it, and traffic isn't monitored continuously. Although a proactive approach is best, many organizations don't have the resources for it.

By taking a proactive approach to monitoring rather than the passive approach of waiting for the IDS or firewall to detect trouble, you can prevent incidents from occurring. Screening possible attacks makes it more likely that the SIRT responds to legitimate events rather than false positives. You can be more certain that events that actually reach the IDS are worthy of serious attention, in many cases. If a passive approach is the best your organization can do, log file review becomes more critical because you're less likely to catch an attack in progress. You can, however, find evidence of attacks in log files and edit your IDS rule base to prevent future incidents. You can then examine your network to detect, assess, and repair any damage that occurred.

Monitoring involves actively testing your network to see how it reacts to scans and other events. You do this by means of a network vulnerability analyzer—software that doesn't just detect packets as they pass through a gateway, but that actively scans the network and sends packets to computers to see whether vulnerabilities exist. You can download software, such as the Security Administrator's Integrated Network Tool (SAINT), that scans your own network much as an attacker would. By scanning your own network, you learn about any open ports on your network's computers or any IP addresses that respond to echo request packets and, therefore, are vulnerable to attack. A convenient way to analyze a single host or a network is to use a Web-based network vulnerability scanner, such as WebSAINT (see Figure 8-9). One of the most popular open-source vulnerability scanners is Nessus (*www.nessus.org*), used by an estimated 75,000 companies and endorsed by the SysAdmin, Audit, Network, Security (SANS) Institute.

8

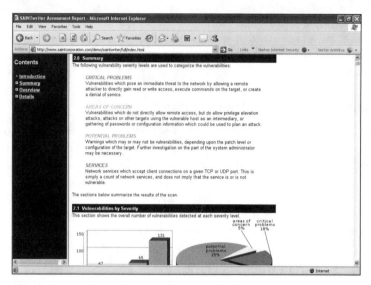

Figure 8-9 The Web-based service WebSAINT can scan your network

  WebSAINT is available at *www.saintcorporation.com/websaint/index.html*.

TIP

Step 2: Notification

Notification is the process by which SIRT members receive news about security incidents. Notifications can come from the firewall or IDS, from other SIRT members, or from a network administrator who detects suspicious network activity. In addition, employees should be instructed to notify the security team member on call when they detect a virus, find oddly named files on their file systems, or notice other signs that a security breach has occurred.

After the initial response—documenting what happened and capturing information about the event—you need to assess the level of damage, if any. Determining the incident's scope and severity tells you whether to escalate the incident (call in a wider group of security professionals and take immediate countermeasures). Your evaluation should answer questions such as the following:

- How many hosts on your network were affected?

- How many networks or subnets were involved?

- What level of privileges did the intruder gain? (If root or administrator privileges were gained, the attack becomes serious immediately.)

- What assets were at risk?

- How many different types of attacks were involved?

You don't necessarily need to call in all members of the SIRT every time an incident happens. First, you need to assess how serious the damage is. You might want to assign different levels of impact to each event. You can designate beforehand who is to be summoned if a Level One (not serious, probably a false alarm) incident occurs, a Level Two (moderately serious) incident occurs, and so on. As the level of impact grows more serious, a wider range of people are called in to respond. (Escalation policies and procedures were covered in Chapters 2 and 3.)

Step 3: Response

After the appropriate SIRT members have been notified that an incident has happened, the measures taken in response need to be systematic and thorough. When an intrusion occurs, SIRT members should keep the following principles in mind:

- Don't panic.
- Follow established procedures.

First, take time to analyze all reported events. Don't simply react to the first event you encounter. Make sure auditing is enabled so that you can capture the necessary data. Begin to document everything that happens.

An important aspect of response is having effective escalation procedures spelled out clearly. Planning how to handle incidents is the key to efficient response, and risk analysis of the sort described in Chapter 2 comes in handy during this step. When you conduct risk analysis, you identify the most critical network resources and assign values to them. When an intrusion occurs, you check ratings in the risk analysis to evaluate the value of the asset that has been compromised. The higher the value, the more urgent and stronger your response needs to be. To determine the different ways you can respond to intrusions based on the value of the assets involved, you need to answer questions such as the following:

- What are you trying to accomplish by your response? Determine whether you're interested primarily in protecting company data, recovering lost information, or maintaining a good reputation so that consumers have faith in your company and its products.
- How quickly can you respond consistently?
- Can you call in law enforcement or take legal action against offenders without exceeding your available budget?

Establish standard procedures in the form of a short, easy-to-read set of incident response instructions. The instructions might look similar to Figure 8-10.

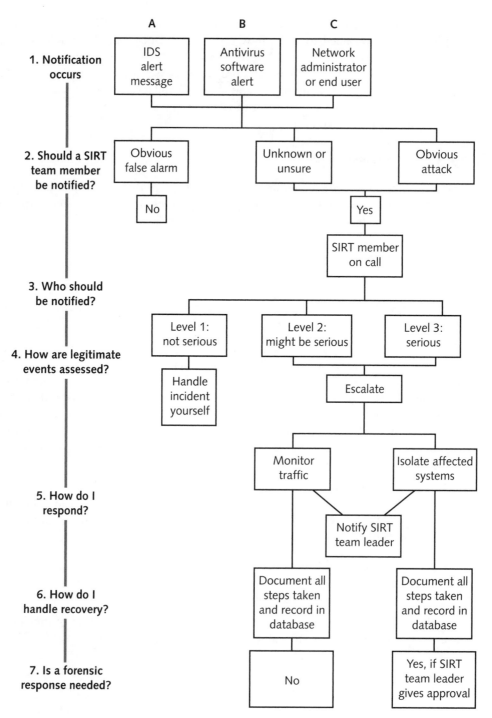

Figure 8-10 A sample diagram of incident response instructions

A diagram of instructions like the one in Figure 8-10 is called a flowchart. Although a flowchart can be quite complex, for the purpose of incident response instructions, it should be kept as simple as possible. Using a flowchart is simple: Starting at the top, an action occurs, and then a number of choices are available. Each level has actions, decisions, and subsequent actions based on those decisions. Following the flowchart in Figure 8-10, after notification occurs, you must decide whether to notify a SIRT member. Three possibilities determine the answer: obvious false alarm, unknown or unsure, and obvious attack. For an obvious false alarm, a SIRT member isn't notified. For the other two possibilities, the incident is escalated to the SIRT member on call. The process flows down the chart, top to bottom, in this fashion until the incident is resolved or escalated to the highest response level. In addition to the flowchart, instructions should supply details, such as contact information for SIRT members, as well as different types of incidents and their corresponding levels of severity.

Determining the Need for Escalation

After you have determined exactly what has happened and how severe the event is, you need to determine whether the event should be escalated or whether you can handle the incident yourself. If the incident is obviously a false alarm and no damage has occurred, you need to analyze what happened, adjust rules and procedures to prevent false alarms in the future, document what occurred, and move on.

If the incident is a legitimate attack, other members of the SIRT should be notified. You need to determine:

- What needs to be reported
- Who needs to know it
- How quickly you need to do the reporting

As far as what to report, you should provide the basic facts surrounding the incident—what type of event occurred, the OS on the affected computer, when the event took place, and whether it's still ongoing. The consequences of the attack should also be described—what systems have been accessed, what level of access privileges the attacker used, and any changes that have been made to the targeted system. You might want to create a form for this report similar to the one in Table 8-1.

Table 8-1   Incident reporting form

Element	Description
Incident Number	
Date	
Time	
Your Name	
Description of Event	
Origin	
Target(s)	
Data Lost	
Current Status	

You also need to figure out how people are going to be notified in case of attack, including **out-of-band notification**, that occurs not on a computer network but another communication device, such as a pager, cell phone, or telephone. If a natural disaster, such as a flood or tornado, knocks out power to your facility, you might be forced to use cell phones that don't rely on regular communication methods, such as telephone or cable lines.

If you encounter a serious security incident, consider informing the Current Activity section of the CERT Coordination Center (*www.us-cert.gov/current/current_activity.html*) so that other security professionals are alerted to the possibility of similar attacks to their networks.

ACTIVITY

Activity 8-4: Keeping the User Community Informed

Time Required: 30 minutes

Objective: Analyze incident scenarios and determine notification procedures.

Description: Keeping employees in your organization informed about security incidents when they occur and in their aftermath is important. However, not all employees should be asked to respond to every security incident, or they will become unduly alarmed or stop taking notifications seriously. In this activity, you analyze some common situations and answer questions about how to handle them.

1. Suppose someone gains access to your Web server, which hosts the company Web site and is used to sell goods and services. You realize you have to disconnect the Web server from the Internet while you respond. Name four different user groups in your organization who should be notified in this situation.

   _____

   _____

2. A password was used, apparently by someone in the company, to gain access to a file server containing financial data for the company. Which user groups should get full information about the incident? What information would you convey to rank-and-file employees while you attempt to determine who's responsible for the unauthorized access to the server?

   _____

   _____

   _____

   _____

Following Standard Response Procedures

Avoid contacting everyone by e-mail so that if the intruder has control of your e-mail server, he or she won't be alerted to your response. That way, team members can be reached at any time. You might also want to do the following:

- *Set up a hotline*—Employees and SIRT members can call this number if someone isn't available immediately and an incident occurs.

- *Set up a list of people to contact*—Determine whether the team leader should be contacted first, and then the leader can decide who else needs to be contacted based on the situation's severity.

You don't want to overreact to intrusions, however. For instance, you might receive an alarm that someone has broken into the company's Web server on the DMZ. If you respond immediately by disconnecting the server from the Internet, you might be causing more problems than you're solving. You'll be taking your Web site offline and interrupting any sales (if you run an e-commerce site); you'll be upsetting your employees; and the media might even find out and make inquiries, which can hurt your company's public relations. It's more prudent to determine first whether any files have been damaged and consult with fellow SIRT members—especially those in upper management—who have the authority to make such important decisions.

On the other hand, if an intrusion is occurring and files have been compromised, you need to have procedures in place that clearly tell you to shut down a server, if necessary. The time to work out these questions is at an initial meeting of the SIRT when rules and procedures should be discussed. All members should understand their roles and know what kinds of tasks they should carry out in case an incident happens.

Step 4: Countermeasures

After the appropriate team members have been notified and the initial assessment has taken place, countermeasures should be taken to control any damage that has occurred. Two general types of **countermeasures** can be carried out: containment and eradication.

Containment of Damage

Containment is the process of preventing a malicious file, intruder, or compromised medium from spreading to other resources on the network. If the problem can be contained so that it affects only a single disk or computer, the attacker's efforts will be curtailed or even thwarted. You might consider doing the following:

- Shut down the affected system.

- Disable user and group accounts.

- Disable services that were exploited.

- Make backups of affected systems to protect the originals as evidence.

SIRT members who are assigned to contain affected systems need to be prepared with backup media, such as hard disks, removable drives, CDs, and floppy disks. They should take care to adhere to a well-defined set of containment procedures recorded in an incident response instruction sheet (like the flowchart you examined in Figure 8-10). These instructions tell them to keep records of who performed each task and remind them to analyze the backup of the affected system while locking away the original media for safekeeping. Continue to record everything you do on a handheld device or in a notebook. Tell users of the attacked system what has happened, whether data has been lost, and how long data will be offline.

Eradication of Data Introduced by an Intrusion

Eradication involves removing any files or programs that resulted from the intrusion, including malicious code, Registry keys, unnecessary executable files, viruses, worms, or files created by worms. Eradication usually follows containment. The process of eradicating these files can be tedious and time consuming, but it should not be rushed. For instance, if the cause of an incident is a worm that was delivered to a computer on the network via an e-mail attachment, SIRT members should do research on sites such as Symantec Security Response (*securityresponse.symantec.com*) to discover what files, if any, the worm creates. Affected systems should then be scanned and any such files should be eradicated. In addition, SIRT members should do the following:

- Check user accounts to make sure no additional (and unauthorized) users have been added.
- Check services.
- Check .dll files and the Windows Registry.
- Make sure any files created during the time of the attack are legitimate.

In many cases, the affected system simply has to be rebuilt or replaced using the most recent clean backup file. Note that removing programs that attackers install or that viruses produce doesn't prevent the problem from occurring again. Any back doors that the attacker exploited to gain access to the system should be closed.

Step 5: Recovery

Recovery is the process of putting media, programs, or computers that have been compromised by intrusions back in service so that they can function on the network again. Don't simply plug machines or disk drives back in to the network and leave them to their users, however. Instead, you need to monitor restored devices for at least 24 hours to make sure the network is operating properly.

SIRT members might even have the machine's user sign a statement agreeing that the computer has been serviced and returned and is in working order. This statement might seem like excessive detail, but it's part of the process of documenting every step of the intrusion response so that other team members and management can handle similar situations in the future. Monitoring the machine closely for one or more days ensures that no undetected vulnerabilities remain. In addition, IT staff should adjust packet-filtering rules to block communications to or from any Web sites involved in the attack.

Step 6: Follow-Up

Follow-up is the process of documenting what took place after an intrusion was detected and a response occurred. The goal of this documentation is to prevent similar intrusions from reoccurring. By recording what happened in a file such as a database, information is stored where future SIRT members can review it.

Follow-up can be one of the most tedious parts of intrusion response. When an incident is over, your impulse is to move on to the next task. You aren't inclined to record what happened in a database. However, you'll see the value of this documentation if you need to refer to the database when, for instance, a Trojan program infects a computer. Referring to the database might well reveal that another Trojan program victimized the same machine the previous year through the same port, for example. Following the steps that were documented during the previous incident can make handling the new incident much less time consuming.

Recordkeeping

Recordkeeping is the process of recording all events associated with a security incident. This documentation has many goals. SIRT members who encounter events similar to the ones you have encountered will benefit enormously from your notes. The organization's legal representatives can also use the information in court.

Even though you do all your work on computers and computers are involved in the security incidents you encounter, recording the notes in electronic format might not be the best option. If the power goes out and your network is down, hand-held devices or a pad and pen are your only options. After the incident is resolved, you might want to transfer the notes to a centralized database where all team members can access it conveniently.

Documentation is essential if you intend to prosecute offenders. In that case, your log files, hard drives, and alert messages are all parts of a trail of evidence that plays a key role in legal procedures. Something that isn't well documented can mean that attackers or employees who steal resources go free because you can't provide the burden of proof.

Reevaluating Policies

Any recommendations for changes in security policies or procedures as a result of security incidents should be included in the follow-up database. If an attacker managed to steal a password by sending a fraudulent e-mail pretending to be a network administrator, for instance, you should note that in the database and notify employees so that they can detect this trick in the future.

Your organization's security policy might specify that details on security incidents are for internal use only, not for public consumption. Keeping information in-house ensures that your company won't suffer from bad public relations as a result of the event. It also keeps attackers from discovering that your network has fallen victim to an attack.

8

ACTIVITY

Activity 8-5: Responding to an Intrusion Alert

Time Required: 30 minutes

Objective: Evaluate an alert scenario and explain the correct response.

Description: You get an alert from the IDS telling you that a Trojan attack has been detected on port 31337 of the computer at 192.168.3.33. You run an antivirus program on the affected computer and find that the Trojan program is indeed present. While you're sitting at the computer, Outlook Express opens without prompting and begins sending e-mails. Follow these steps to indicate how you would respond:

1. Describe what your mental approach to these events should be.

   _____

2. Explain what you should do to isolate the affected computer.

   _____

   _____

   _____

   _____

3. After the computer is isolated, describe what should be investigated next.

   _____

   _____

4. List people who should be notified.

   _____

   _____

5. Describe what you could learn by a subsequent review of the firewall and IDS logs.

   _____

   _____

   _____

   _____

DEALING WITH FALSE ALARMS

An essential part of managing an IDS is minimizing the number of false positives and false negatives (attacks that occurred but that didn't set off an alarm). False positives are the bane of many IDS administrators and probably the main complaint people have about using IDSs. The problem is that as you tune the system in an effort to eliminate false positives and false negatives, its performance can become severely degraded and you can slow down the network significantly. Suppose you create a new firewall or IDS rule for every false positive. Before long, your rule base will be so long and unwieldy that network traffic slows down while each rule in the rule base is checked, one after another. It's much better to adjust existing rules if needed and create new rules only if absolutely necessary.

Filtering Alerts

8

When you get false alarms, you should adjust the rules used by your firewall, packet filter, or IDS to reduce them in the future. Many legitimate Web sites send echo request packets to determine whether a client computer that's making a request is actually on the network, for instance. You need to create rules that permit this traffic to pass through the filter without setting off an alarm.

One way to reduce the number of alerts is to exclude a specific signature from connecting to a selected host or IP address. (This topic is covered in more detail in "Disabling Signatures" later in this chapter.) If you exclude a signature, it neither generates an alarm nor creates a log record when it originates from the specified hosts or IP addresses. The addresses you exclude don't need to come from external hosts.

For instance, a command console or management computer on your own network might perform a ping sweep periodically (a series of echo request packets sent to each computer on your network in succession to verify that they're on the network). This event would cause the IDS to trigger an alarm unless you exclude the management computer from a ping sweep or an ICMP echo request signature that your IDS uses. You can extend this principle to encompass an entire subnet or network. You need to specify only a host subnet mask or a range of IP addresses, such as 10.0.0.0/8.

Disabling Signatures

In some cases, you might want to disable entire signatures from triggering an alarm. If you're testing your network and doing a port scan, for instance, you want to disable any signatures that would be matched if the IDS detected a port scan. (Traffic signatures were covered in detail in Chapter 4.) Even if a particular incident is a false alarm, you should still record it on a tracking chart that includes information, as shown in Table 8-2.

Table 8-2 Incident tracking form

Incident Number	Type of Incident	Location	Priority	Status	Last Update	Team Lead	Alternate Team Lead
28	Port scan	192.168.20.1 through 255	Moderate	Inactive	5/25	JB	MK
29	Trojan horse	192.168.20.39	High	Active	5/26	JB	GH

You might also want to exclude a signature on one IDS in the interest of efficiency if another IDS contains the same signature. By reducing the number of duplicated signatures, each device can operate more efficiently.

DEALING WITH LEGITIMATE SECURITY ALERTS

Suppose you get an alert from your IDS. How do you know the attack is legitimate? This section examines Step 3 of the six-step intrusion response process—response.

Initially, you need to determine whether the attack is a false alarm (false positive) or a legitimate intrusion (true positive). Look for indications such as the following:

- You notice system crashes.
- New user accounts suddenly appear on the network.
- Accounts that normally have only sporadic use suddenly have heavy activity.
- New files appear, often with strange file names.
- A series of unsuccessful logon attempts occurs.

If the event turns out to be a legitimate intrusion attempt, you need to respond calmly and follow procedures spelled out in the security policy. To some extent, the way you respond to a legitimate attack depends on your organization's size and the nature of its activities. For a small company with fewer than a dozen employees, disconnecting the Web site from the Internet for a day or two might not have a big impact on sales. For a large retail company that depends on Internet sales for 10% to 20% of its revenues and receives thousands of Web site visits per day, the response needs to be more measured—more people need to be involved, you should only take the Web site offline if absolutely necessary, and you should get it up and running as soon as possible.

You might remember a major attack on January 25, 2003, that caused traffic throughout the Internet to slow and even stop in some cases. Attackers used the MSSQL Slammer worm (also known as the Sapphire worm) to infect computers running unpatched versions of Microsoft SQL Server. The infected computers then flooded other computers with requests at UDP port 1434. The repeated requests caused a denial of service. The first defense called for configuring firewalls and packet filters to block all traffic to and from UDP port 1434.

This attack required affected systems to be disconnected for patches and service packs to be installed, if needed.

Government agencies or organizations in the public sector can call on law enforcement personnel to handle intrusion incidents, if necessary. Companies in the private sector will find it more difficult to call in the police or other authorities. Even if law enforcement personnel are called on to investigate, locating and prosecuting intruders can be time consuming and difficult. One of the most notorious hackers, Kevin Mitnick, was tracked by the FBI and U.S. marshals for two years and wasn't apprehended until 1995 after a security expert located him. His prosecution was lengthy, and he wasn't convicted until 1999. (You can read more about his case at *www.takedown.com*.)

Assessing the Impact

After you have determined that an incident is not a false alarm, you need to find out whether any host computers on your network were compromised. If an intruder did get into your systems, determine the extent of the damage. Many viruses and Trojan programs operate by creating files or renaming existing ones on an infected system. Some that infect Windows-based systems also change settings in the Registry so that the malicious code executable runs automatically whenever the computer is restarted. Your task is to locate any files that were added to network computers and which files were changed, if any. A software tool such as Tripwire (*www.tripwire.com*) enables you to document any changes to the file system since the program last ran a baseline test of the system.

Determine the scope and impact of the problem: Was one site affected or several different ones? How many computers were involved? There's no easy way to determine this information other than checking each computer, running virus scans, and examining firewall logs for suspicious activity, such as a flood of e-mail messages sent from one machine or tens of thousands of connection attempts from a single host to a computer on a remote network in another country.

If your firewall was compromised, any computer on the network could be accessed. The firewall must be reconstructed from scratch, which means the network will be down for a while. Then, all host computers need to be checked for software consistency—making sure software on those computers hasn't been altered. This process, however, is only in response to the most serious intrusions that occur, including unauthorized access to a critical database resulting in copies of confidential files being stolen; a virus attack resulting in harmful code erasing, corrupting, or otherwise modifying critical data; or physical theft of a file server containing mission-critical data. Your response depends on the event's seriousness.

Developing an Action Plan

Many SIRTs like to develop an action plan—a series of steps to be followed when a legitimate attack occurs. Writing down the steps to be followed might seem obvious. Individual steps such as "disconnect the computer from the network" are easy to think of, after all. However, in the heat of the moment, having the list at hand can be a valuable aid to a nervous responder. The action plan might involve the following steps:

1. Assess the seriousness of the attack.

2. If a serious incident is involved, notify the team leader immediately. Determine whether a forensic investigation is required.

3. Begin to document all actions, including who performed them and when they occurred.

4. Contain the threat by disconnecting the computer from the network.

5. Determine the extent of the damage. Were passwords compromised? Files accessed? New files added? Are Trojans present?

6. If you plan to prosecute, make a complete bit-stream backup of the media. A bit-stream backup copies every bit on the entire disk, including free space, slack space (the space left over between file clusters), and deleted files, essentially creating an exact duplicate. A straightforward copy doesn't copy deleted files, slack space, or free space. Often, evidence is hidden in these places deliberately, so making a bit-stream backup is important. Be sure to keep the original data for evidence, but never perform any analysis on the original. The original should be stored securely.

7. Eradicate the problem.

8. Restore the system or media and monitor it for integrity.

9. Record a summary of the incident. Send a memo to the CEO and Legal Department describing what happened.

After you have determined that an attack has actually occurred, you need to understand exactly how the attack was conducted so that you can configure countermeasures to prevent this event from happening again in the future. For some network security analysts, the most effective tool for conducting attack analysis is one that can perform **attack visualization**, which is the process of replaying the attack so that you can see what the attacker viewed.

Handling Internal Versus External Incidents

Intrusions and security breaches often originate from inside an organization. When you suspect that an employee is involved, your response needs to be more measured than if an attacker is compromising one of your computers. You might want to avoid notifying the entire staff, for instance, so as not to alert the offender.

Until you're sure who is involved, you might even want to keep affected computers online to keep the intruder from knowing that you're on his or her trail. The Human Resources and Legal departments should be made aware when you have identified the intruder so that they can begin considering disciplinary action. Notify the entire staff only when they need to know that something serious happened and when they need to change passwords or take active steps toward preventing future incidents.

TIP   Employees suspected of causing security breaches should be interviewed by trained, authorized personnel. The interviewers should explain that placing blame and administering punishment isn't the ultimate purpose of the incident investigation; instead, organizational security is. This explanation tends to put employees more at ease so that they will provide information.

Taking Corrective Measures to Prevent Reoccurrence

After you have contained and eradicated the problem, you need to take steps to prevent it from occurring again. For instance, if a password was intercepted because an attacker planted a Trojan program on a network computer that sniffed network passwords in transit, you need to track the following:

- Where the Trojan came from
- Who transmitted the password

In response, you should download signatures of known Trojan programs that your IDS does not already include. You should also set up an intrusion rule that sends an alarm whenever a password is submitted without being encrypted.

At times, you need to notify others on the Internet about your attack. Informing others that you have been hit by malicious code assists everyone else in the industry by allowing them to block incoming attacks and spread the workload of definition resolution. (In a nutshell, "definition resolution" is analyzing and defining the malicious code to develop patches, antivirus signature updates, and removal tools to solve the problem.)

Working Under Pressure

In an ideal world, security incidents would occur one at a time and take place slowly enough that security professionals could respond effectively before any loss of data occurs. In the real world, incidents occur quickly, without warning, and simultaneously with other problems.

Incident response activities need to be carried out with discretion. The suspected intruder need not know he or she is being observed. Regardless of who the attacker is or the origin of the incident (internal or external), sometimes it's best to allow the incident to continue for a while, if no serious damage is occurring. This gives you time to monitor and record the intruder's activities, and this information can be used to track down and capture him or her. The information you gather might also be needed for prosecution, if your organization elects to file charges. To gather this information, you might need to connect a surveillance computer to the network, making sure the intruder can't detect it and learn he or she is being monitored; sometimes it means analyzing a computer system's contents without altering anything (such as using the bit-stream backup technique discussed earlier), but it always means doing things quietly, efficiently, and promptly.

Always remember the goal of your actions, whether it's to gather evidence for prosecution or simply to discover the security flaw that allowed access so that it can be corrected. If prosecution is the goal, don't attempt to gather digital evidence unless you're competent in computer forensics techniques. Destroying potential evidence won't earn you a promotion. More likely, it will get you a one-way trip out of the building.

8

When you're working under pressure, the temptation is to proceed as quickly as possible and seal off any vulnerable computers or services so that nothing is lost. However, you also need to remember that the data you collect as a result of a real intrusion might need to be presented as evidence in a court of law. How you handle data collection can have a huge impact on how admissible it is. If the information could have been tampered with between the time it was detected and the time of the court date, it could become invalid.

Filling out a response checklist, such as the one in Table 8-3, is a good idea. Evidence intended for litigation must be traceable. A checklist such as the one in Table 8-3 keeps a record of intrusions and responses, aside from log files. If your log files are corrupted or lost, you have another record. Also, you can determine what action caused a problem if, for example, a change to the rule base causes unexpected or undesirable results. It can't be said enough: Document everything! Even things that seem insignificant at the time can prove important later. A sample pair of checklist entries is shown as an example.

Table 8-3 Intrusion response checklist

Date/Time	Occurrence	Response
10/20/04 07:58 a.m.	Received alert from IDS stating that an echo reply request had been received from IP address 62.126.0.34	Blocked request; changed firewall rules to block echo reply requests from 62.126.0.34
10/20/04 10:14 a.m.	Received alert from IDS stating that a series of echo requests had been sent from internal computer 192.168.20.38 with 200.46.101.1 as destination	Disconnected 192.108.20.4 from network. Ran anti-Trojan software. Blocked communications with 200.46.101.1

Gathering Data for Prosecution

You have to be as careful as possible when you're collecting evidence. Although the following list is by no means a complete report of computer forensics techniques, keep these rules of evidentiary handling in mind:

- *Make sure two people handle the data at all times*—Having one look "over the shoulder" of the other is essential; that way, no one can argue that one person alone might have fabricated or altered the data.

- *Write everything down*—Document every event that occurs and everything you do, no matter how trivial it might seem at the time. One of your team members should be designated for the task of note-taking to record exactly what was done and who did it.

- *Lock it up!*—After data is collected on hard disks, removable drives, CDs, or other media, it needs to be locked away and protected so that there's no danger of tampering with it. Also, duplicate the media and store the duplicate in a safe location. Do your analysis on the duplicate of the file and leave the original alone.

Early in the process of handling a legitimate security incident, SIRT members need to decide who will handle the evidence so that the **chain of custody** (the record of who handled an object to be used as evidence in court) is recorded. Each SIRT member needs to write down, step by step, his or her part in a response. Because some key personnel might not be present the next time you have an incident, checklists should include team members' phone numbers and e-mail addresses and any URLs used to research, report, or obtain repair assistance or tools for that response. Checklists should be inspected and updated regularly.

Before an incident occurs, you should determine whether you plan to prosecute offenders and include this decision in your security policy. If you intend to prosecute offenders who break into your network successfully, you need to respond with extra care and follow specific evidence-handling principles.

CAUTION

Don't attempt to perform computer forensics tasks (particularly if the evidence is important or related to a serious crime) if you don't know precisely what you're doing. A little knowledge can be dangerous; a little more knowledge can lead to disaster. Computer forensics is a highly specialized field, and becoming proficient at it takes intensive training and practice.

8

Handling Evidence

When investigating an incident within a legal framework, reliable and accurate electronic findings are critical to the success of an investigation. Computer forensics is a relatively new field, but the requirements for evidence handling and criteria for admissible evidence are well established. You must consider your position and the level of investigation required for the situation. If the issue is inappropriate use of the Internet and company resources, a full forensics investigation isn't warranted. If company computers might contain evidence of a criminal act, evidence gathering and handling must be considerably more detailed and careful. In this circumstance, you might recommend that your company hire a professional computer forensics technician or call local law enforcement for guidance.

How you handle each situation depends on the circumstances, but the general steps for handling and examining hard disks and other computer data are described in the following list:

1. *Secure the area*—Ask all unnecessary staff to leave the area; make sure no one disturbs you while you work.

2. *Prepare the system*—Before you begin working on the system, photograph it so that you have a record of how it was arranged when you started your investigation. Be sure to photograph all wires and connections, front and back, so that the configuration can be duplicated if necessary.

3. *Examine the system*—You might want to examine the system while the attack is actually taking place, if possible. You might be able to identify services the attacker is exploiting and detect suspicious connections to other computers on your network.

4. *Shut down the system*—Disconnect the computer from the network. Note, however, that some malicious programs are configured to erase themselves when the computer is shut down. There are some steps you can take to prevent this, depending on the system, but computer forensics are beyond the scope of this book. If the situation warrants, calling in a forensics expert might be advisable. Otherwise, do some research to find methods of shutting down a computer safely without loss of data.

5. *Secure the system*—After you disconnect the computer, if you plan to work on it in a lab, place it in an antistatic bag for transport. Insert blank disks in any disk drives so that the drives aren't damaged in transit.

6. *Prepare the system for acquisition*—Start the computer from a boot disk, a floppy disk that has been configured so that it doesn't communicate with the hard drive when the computer starts. Using a boot disk preserves the hard drive in its original state so that it can be examined.

7. *Examine the system*—Check the current system date and time to see whether it's accurate.

8. *Connect target media*—Place a clean disk drive in the system and make a forensic copy (a bit-stream copy or other forensic method) of the affected disk drive.

9. *Secure evidence*—Turn off the computer, disconnect the target media, seal the machine, and connect the target media to a lab computer so that you can begin analyzing the data. Be sure to keep the original media in a secure location with an evidence log recording the chain of custody. Never examine the original media! Use a forensic copy for all investigation and analysis.

During all these steps, take extensive notes recording everything that's done to the scene and anything that might contain evidence. Your notes should keep track of when each step was performed and who performed it to maintain the chain of custody.

Advanced computer forensics techniques are well beyond the scope of this book. What's important to remember is that you must have considerable training and experience to become proficient enough to collect, analyze, and preserve evidence. If you don't have this training, the smartest move is to call in someone who does. In reality, you probably wouldn't conduct computer forensics beyond securing the scene, which simply involves keeping the location and immediate surroundings (anywhere evidence might be located) from being disturbed until a properly trained computer forensics technician arrives to investigate. The Federal Rules of Evidence apply to digital data, and failure to maintain the strictest controls can result in data being lost or deemed inadmissible as evidence.

TIP

You can find out more about the Federal Rules of Evidence and guidelines for computer investigations by visiting the federal guide "Searching and Seizing Computers and Obtaining Electronic Evidence in Criminal Investigations" at *www.cybercrime.gov/s&smanual2002.htm*. You can also view the Federal Rules of Evidence online at Cornell University's Legal Information Institute (*www.law.cornell.edu/rules/fre/overview.html*). Also, Course Technology offers an excellent book on computer forensics, *Guide to Computer Forensics and Investigations, Second Edition* (2005, ISBN 0619217065).

CHAPTER SUMMARY

□ IDS devices can have their own set of filter rules, as packet-filtering routers and firewalls do. You can configure a set of rules to send alert messages if suspicious packets pass through packet filters on the network perimeter and reach the IDS. Rules can also be configured to log events or a range of subsequent packets. Rule options can assist in interpreting log files and determining how to react to attack attempts.

□ Security incident response team (SIRT) members should be drawn from all major departments in the organization and should have representatives from management, human resources, and legal counsel. Keeping the membership wide ranging gives the SIRT authority to take drastic measures to prevent attacks from spreading.

□ The speed and thoroughness with which the response occurs depends on the range of employees involved and how many other duties they're required to perform in the organization. Ideally, you can hire a team of people whose sole job is to respond to incidents full-time. Otherwise, you can assign people who have other jobs in the company to perform incident response on an as-needed basis. You can also outsource your incident response and security monitoring needs to contractors.

□ Specific issues and approaches are involved in responding to intrusions and security breaches that affect your network. First, you should establish a SIRT. The team's primary functions can be divided into six steps: preparation, notification, response, countermeasures, recovery, and follow-up.

□ The process of responding to security incidents should be defined clearly in a brief document to which all SIRT members can refer. The response should be based on principles spelled out in the company's security policy.

□ When notification of a security event does occur, the SIRT member on call should assess whether the incident is legitimate or a false positive. After the initial response and assessment, countermeasures should be taken. The two general types of countermeasures are containment and eradication. Containment involves preventing the malicious file or intruder from further accessing resources on the network. Eradication seeks to eliminate any malicious files, Registry keys, viruses, or other files that have been introduced.

□ After eradication is complete, the affected media, programs, or computers need to be recovered so that they can function on the network again. Finally, in follow-up, the incident should be described fully in a database or other file where future SIRT members can access it if similar events happen.

❑ False alarms are almost inevitable with any IDS. If they are reported, you can reduce their occurrence in the future by adjusting the rules your firewall, packet filter, or IDS use. You can also exclude an IP address from attempting to access your network or disable a signature if needed.

❑ Legitimate attacks require a calm, systematic, and thorough response. Legitimate attacks can be differentiated from events such as system crashes or new user accounts or files that suddenly appear on network computers. If a legitimate attack has been detected, you need to determine how many computers have been damaged. No matter how serious the event is, you should follow an action plan.

❑ External attacks by attackers you can identify might call for prosecution in court. To pursue a legal case, you need to use computer forensics techniques—the practice of collecting, handling, and analyzing evidence to track attacks, identify offenders, and develop a legal case. You need to document all steps and maintain a record of the chain of custody.

Key Terms

attack visualization — The process of replaying the attack so that the analyst can see what the attacker viewed.

chain of custody — The record of who handled an object to be used as evidence in court.

containment — The process of preventing a malicious file, intruder, or compromised media from spreading to other resources on the network.

countermeasures — Strategies and approaches that address threats to network security.

eradication — The process of removing any files or programs that result from an intrusion, including malicious code, Registry keys, unnecessary executable files, viruses, worms, or files created by worms.

follow-up — The process of documenting what happened when an intrusion was detected and a response occurred.

incident response — The actions taken after a computer security incident to determine what happened and what countermeasures need to be taken to ensure the network's continued security.

loose source and record routing (lsrr) — This option specifies a set of hops that the packet must traverse, but not necessarily every hop in the path.

notification — The process by which SIRT members receive news about security incidents.

out-of-band notification — Notification of a security incident that occurs not on a computer network, but on another communications device, such as a pager.

recovery — The process of putting media, programs, or computers that have been compromised by intrusions back in service so that they can function on the network again.

strict source and record routing (ssrr) — This option specifies every hop that the packet must traverse.

virtual team — A team that has other jobs to perform during regular business hours and exists only during meetings or when an incident becomes serious.

REVIEW QUESTIONS

1. What is the advantage of configuring IDS filter rules if you already have packet-filtering rules in place? (Choose all that apply.)

   a. You can attach messages to the alerts.

   b. The filters can be configured to match TCP flag combinations.

   c. The filters can be configured to match specific ports.

   d. You gain another layer of security.

2. How do the initial rules in an IDS filter differ from the initial rules in a packet filter, which usually begin by blocking all TCP traffic?

   a. They allow all TCP traffic.

   b. They log all TCP traffic.

   c. They send an alert for any TCP traffic.

   d. They log and alert all TCP traffic.

3. Which rule would cause Snort to log traffic from any computer to a computer at 192.168.10.1, port 23?

   a. log udp all all -> 192.168.10.1 23

   b. logging tcp any -> 192.168.10.1 23

   c. log tcp any any -> 192.168.10.1 23

   d. log snmp any any -> 192.168.10.1/23

4. The Snort msg option tells the logging and alerting engine to do which of the following?

   a. Match the ACK flag in a packet.

   b. Log files to a specified file name instead of the default log files.

   c. Print a message along with a packet dump or an alert.

   d. Record all TCP flags to a message in the log files.

5. Why does it make sense to look in-house for SIRT members? (Choose all that apply.)

   a. You can assemble the team more quickly than by hiring outsiders.

   b. Current employees are familiar with the organization.

   c. Current employees have the appropriate security clearance (if applicable).

   d. Current employees are more trustworthy than contractors brought in from outside.

6. Which Snort rule sends an alert if the word "Password" is detected in the packet's data payload?

   a. alert tcp any any -> any any (content: "Password" in data payload; msg: "password transmitted?";)

   b. alert tcp any any -> any any (content: "Password"; msg: "password transmitted?";)

   c. alert tcp any any -> any any (content Password; msg: password transmitted;)

   d. alert tcp all-> all (content "Password"; msg "password transmitted?";)

7. The process of determining the level of damage caused by an intrusion falls into which of the following intrusion response steps?

   a. response

   b. detection

   c. follow-up

   d. recovery

8. What is a virtual team?

   a. members who perform incident response full-time

   b. members who work in different geographical locations and only communicate electronically

   c. members who perform incident response on an as-needed basis

   d. members who assemble only when an incident actually occurs

9. Which of the following applies to "fire drills" that test intrusion response procedures?

   a. They should be unscheduled.

   b. They should be scheduled.

   c. They should involve an actual "test" attack.

   d. They should follow a scenario.

10. A group that exists to help organizations with incident response is called a(n) _____ .

    a. public resource team

    b. incident response group

    c. incident coordination center

    d. distributed intrusion detection system

11. Why would you consider outsourcing your incident response needs?

    a. better security

    b. lower cost

    c. faster response

    d. less strain on in-house staff

12. Which of the following is a way of reducing false alarms? (Choose all that apply.)

    a. adjusting rules

    b. decreasing network gateways

    c. excluding signatures or IP addresses

    d. restricting access control lists

13. When a system or media is to be transported for analysis, you should do which of the following? (Choose all that apply.)

    a. Place the evidence in plastic bags.

    b. Place the evidence in antistatic bags.

    c. Insert boot disks in all disk drives.

    d. Photograph the area before anything is disturbed.

8

14. A(n) _____ is a record of who handled a compromised device and how it was handled, and it can be used as evidence in court.

    a. incident-tracking form

    b. follow-up

    c. chain of custody

    d. audit

15. Who is likely to review the detailed information you record during follow-up after an incident? (Choose all that apply.)

    a. supervisors who are planning to leave the organization

    b. public resource team members aiding in the investigation of a security breach

    c. IT staff trying to determine whether new hardware or software is needed to enhance network performance

    d. future SIRT members who weren't involved in the original incident

16. During the recovery process, what resources should be checked on a computer that has been compromised? (Choose all that apply.)

    a. user accounts

    b. the BIOS boot sequence

    c. the Windows Registry

    d. the password file

17. Why is the complete elimination of false positives an unrealistic goal?

    a. Firewalls and IDSs might have code flaws that cause false alarms.

    b. As new users join the organization, they might set off false alarms.

    c. Creating too many rules can slow down network performance.

    d. all of the above

18. Why would you want to disable a signature on an IDS? (Choose all that apply.)

    a. You're upgrading your network.

    b. The signature is generating too many alerts.

    c. The signature is duplicated on another network segment.

    d. none of the above

19. What's the first thing you should do when handling evidence for prosecution?

    a. Call all senior staff members.

    b. Log the current user off the system and log on as administrator.

    c. Turn off the system and unplug it.

    d. Secure the area.

20. Why would you want to keep records of intrusions for internal use only? (Choose all that apply.)

    a. to prevent bad public relations

    b. to prevent disgruntled employees from attempting similar attacks

    c. to keep attackers from knowing they made the administrator angry

    d. to keep stock values from rising

HANDS-ON PROJECTS

HANDS-ON PROJECTS

Hands-On Project 8-1: Revising a Signature in Response to Incidents

Time Required: 15 minutes

Objective: Revise the Snort rule base in response to security incidents.

Description: In this project, you revise the default rule base Snort uses in response to two different security incidents—a scan of your own network by your network administrator to test for vulnerabilities and an ICMP request packet. You create a text-based rule file (with the .rules extension) that Snort can recognize and use IDS Policy Manager, the application you installed in Activity 8-1, to add the .rules file to the Snort rule base.

1. Click **Start**, point to **All Programs**, point to **Accessories**, and click **Notepad**.

2. When Notepad opens, type the following, which tells Snort not to send an alarm when you scan the network from your management console at 10.0.20.5:

```
pass icmp 10.0.20.5 any -> any any
```

3. Press **Enter** to start a new line.

4. Next, type the following, which tells Snort to send an alert message when it encounters a type of ICMP packet called a timestamp request, which is denoted by type 13 code 0:

```
alert icmp any any -> any any (itype:13; icode:0;)
```

5. Click **File**, **Save** from the menu. In the Save As dialog box, double-click the directory where Snort is installed (for example, C:\Snort or C:\Program Files\Snort). In the File name text box, type **"icmp-new.rules"** and then click **Save**. (Be sure to include the quotation marks so that Notepad saves the file with the .rules extension.)

6. Navigate to the C:\Program Files\Activeworx\IDSPolMan folder, and double-click **IDSPolicyMan.exe** to start IDS Policy Manager.

7. If a message box notifies you that a new build of the program has been found, click **No**.

8. When the Policy Manager window opens, click the **Policy Manager** tab.

9. Right-click **Official** under the Policy Name column, and click **Open in Policy Editor**. If the Check for new rules? dialog box opens, click **No**. If the Check for new Bleeding Snort rules? dialog box opens, click **No**.

10. The Policy Editor opens and displays Snort's default set of rules. Click **Options**, **Add .Rules file to Policy** from the menu.

11. Click the **Look in** list arrow in the Browse for File dialog box, click the **icmp-new.rules** file you saved earlier, and click **Open**. Note that the rules category icmp-new has been added.

12. Click **File**, **Exit**, and then click **Yes** to save your changes and close IDS Policy Manager.

CASE PROJECTS

Case Project 8-1: Locating a Virus on the Network

When you arrive at the office Monday morning, you discover antivirus system alerts telling you that a virus has been detected. You read about the virus on the Symantec Security Response Web site (*http://securityresponse.symantec.com*). An article about the virus states that it works by replicating itself throughout networked systems, attempting to connect to a file called Cmd.exe. Given that it has had all weekend to spread through the network, how would you track the virus down?

Case Project 8-2: Tracking Down a Trojan

You receive a call at home from the SIRT member on duty, informing you that someone on your internal network has logged in to the firewall with an administrator (root) password. You tell the caller to disconnect the firewall from the Internet immediately because it's a sign someone has intercepted the password and is attempting to gain access to the firewall to learn about the company's network. You don't know how long the intruder has been on the firewall or whether the firewall logs are reliable because the intruder might have been able to alter them. What could you do in response?

Case Project 8-3: Tracking Down Internal Misuse

Your IDS sends an alert notifying you that a confidential company file has been accessed on one of your organization's file servers. You check the server's logs and discover that the file was accessed by a computer on your internal network. You track the logs for that computer and find that some e-mails with sizeable attachments were sent around the same time to an address in Europe. The e-mail messages had the subject line "Family Photos." You suspect that confidential company files were being sent, not personal photos. How could you verify this?

Case Project 8-4: Designing an Incident Response Strategy

Now that LedGrafix has a comprehensive security policy and a well-designed and documented network configuration, including an intrusion detection system, it's time to develop the incident response strategy for this chapter's running case project.

First, you need to assemble a security incident response team (SIRT). This team will be responsible for determining whether intrusions are legitimate or false positives, determining how to escalate responses as needed, and deciding whether prosecution is viable or necessary. The team should be drawn primarily from current LedGrafix staff. Include IT staff members, an upper management representative, a financial representative, and a human resources representative. Also, designate a person to handle public relations. Include contact information for the company's legal counsel, and identify a local law enforcement officer to contact if the police need to be notified. Follow these steps to help plan LedGrafix's SIRT:

1. List who should be included in the SIRT, and explain briefly why you selected each member. It doesn't need to be a specific list of names, but a general guide for selection (including information such as skill sets needed, responsibilities the member is especially suited for, and so forth). For example, you might list the human resources director because she's familiar with all employees and can handle staff notification, if needed. You might also have the HR director handle public relations. This list is intended for the company's upper management, which will coordinate organizing the team with your guidance.

2. Plan the general agenda for the team's first meeting. The team must select a team leader, discuss how responsibilities should be divided, and design a plan for developing, testing, and maintaining incident response procedures. (As a consultant, you can't design these procedures. It's an ongoing task the SIRT must do. Your job is to offer guidance.) Prepare a short list of "talking points" the team must address.

3. Instruct the SIRT leader to develop an Initial Response Checklist that includes responsible parties, contact information, and notification and escalation procedures. This checklist should be posted for employees but not available for the general public (to protect team members' privacy). Develop a sample document the SIRT leader could use to organize this information.

Now that you have guided LedGrafix in developing an incident response strategy, you need to begin integrating it into the security policy. At this stage of development for a company such as LedGrafix, you should also begin planning who will handle ongoing maintenance of policies and begin preparing that person or group to take over the job. Because LedGrafix is a small company, it can't hire staff to take care of this task full-time. Someone within the company needs to take care of it.

Assume that the IT director, Jon Smith, will be handling the task of security policy and procedures maintenance. Develop a checklist of tasks he needs to do and a tentative schedule. Write a brief agenda for a meeting with him covering the key points of security policy maintenance, including the risk analysis cycle, security awareness training, and resources for monitoring current threats that might affect the company or its policies. Also, plan to review the policies and procedures manual with him and answer his questions, explaining how you developed each part of the manual.

After you have developed your list for upper management, the SIRT meeting agenda and talking points, the sample Incident Response Checklist, and your draft plan for turning over ongoing maintenance to Mr. Smith, proofread all documents carefully and submit them to your instructor.

You should begin thinking about finalizing your policies and procedures manual for your final draft soon. Be sure to review all previous chapters' running case projects and incorporate any feedback you have received. Don't wait until the last minute to do this because it's easy to overlook errors or omissions. Make sure you have included a references page listing all resources you've used for your project.

In addition to your network diagrams, you might want to include flowcharts, sample documents, or other supporting material appropriate to your design. For example, if you have designed a network that uses command-line tools heavily for testing or scripts for configuration, include tables or reference charts showing commonly used commands or scripts. However you have decided to proceed to this point, begin the process of preparing the final deliverable: a complete professional security policies and procedures manual.

CHAPTER 9

CHOOSING AND DESIGNING FIREWALLS

> **After reading this chapter and completing the exercises, you will be able to:**
>
> ◆ Explain what firewalls can and cannot do
> ◆ Describe common approaches to packet filtering
> ◆ Establish a set of rules and restrictions for a firewall
> ◆ Design common firewall configurations
> ◆ Compare hardware and software firewalls

When you travel by air, you have to pass through a variety of security checkpoints. First, your bags are checked, then you go through a security checkpoint, and when you board the plane, your tickets and identity are verified. The purpose of all this "filtering" is to keep people who shouldn't be on the plane from boarding.

In the same way, security devices placed at the perimeter of a computer network filter out packets of digital information. The arrangement of security devices is collectively called a firewall or firewall perimeter; in addition, at least one device in the arrangement is a program or hardware device called a firewall. When you begin designing network defenses, one of the first decisions to make is what components are needed to achieve your security goals and how to best arrange those components.

This chapter discusses the concept of firewalls—what they are and what they aren't. Then you learn about packet filtering and how to develop a rule base that implements your security policy. Finally, you learn the different ways firewalls can be arranged with routers or other firewalls and the various types of firewall hardware and software.

AN OVERVIEW OF FIREWALLS

As you learned in Chapter 1, a **firewall** is hardware or software that can be configured to block unauthorized access to a network. "Firewall" is often viewed as a catchall term representing any device that can block attackers or viruses. Managers commonly ask their network administrators to "get a firewall and put it on the network so that we have better security." This request implies that a firewall is one device that can single-handedly keep attackers away from a network, which is an incorrect assumption. Firewalls can't protect against malicious insiders who send proprietary information out of the organization through a network connection or by copying data onto a disk. A strong security policy and access controls on sensitive information must be used to protect against this type of incident. A firewall also can't protect connections that don't go through it, such as remote dial-up connections. These connections require a virtual private network (VPN) for protection. The following sections explain what firewalls are and are not so that you have a clearer idea of what they do.

What Firewalls Are

First, the term "firewall" doesn't necessarily refer to a single router, computer, VPN gateway, or software program. Any network firewall is actually a combination of multiple software and hardware components. The term "firewall" can refer to all the devices positioned on the perimeter of a network, so the term "firewall perimeter" might be more descriptive.

The earliest firewalls were packet filters; a single packet-filtering router was placed at the network perimeter to function as a firewall, although a rather weak one. Today's firewalls are more than just a hardware appliance, and many are strictly software based. Some firewall programs are designed for general consumer use, such as Norton Personal Firewall, ZoneAlarm, or Sygate Personal Firewall. They have fairly simple interfaces that give nontechnical users a minimal number of decisions to make for configuration, as shown in Figure 9-1.

Much of the work in establishing rules and blocking traffic is done on a case-by-case basis: When a firewall confronts a type of traffic it doesn't recognize, it prompts you to decide whether the traffic should be blocked or allowed. This process can seem quite bothersome until the firewall "learns" what is and isn't acceptable traffic, but it's well worth the effort.

In Figure 9-2, Norton Personal Firewall is reporting that an ICMP echo request packet is being received from an unknown host (IP address 64.91.96.108) on the Internet. The program offers simple decisions: Allow the traffic, block the traffic, or **customize access** (that is, identify criteria under which this request is allowed). In addition, as shown in Figure 9-2, you're asked to decide whether the firewall should consider converting the decision into a rule to be applied automatically to similar traffic in the future.

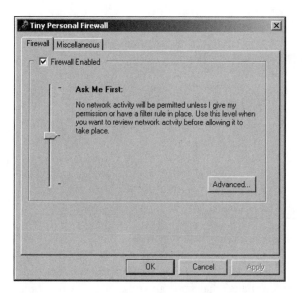

Figure 9-1   Tiny Personal Firewall's simple interface

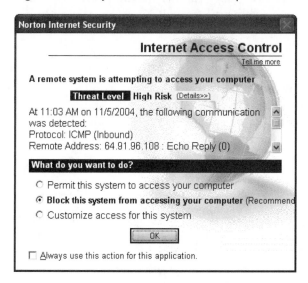

Figure 9-2   Personal firewalls establish rules on a case-by-case basis

Other firewall programs, such as Check Point Next Generation (NG), are designed to protect and monitor large-scale networks. They come with a variety of GUI tools for configuring and monitoring network traffic. The range of options in these programs can be quite complex, as shown in Figure 9-3.

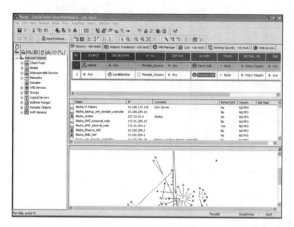

Figure 9-3   Check Point NG's more complex user interface

Still other firewalls, such as the Cisco PIX line of **firewall appliances**, are self-contained hardware devices with firewall functionality that you can add to a network. For a list of links to firewall appliances, you can check *http://directory.google.com/Top/Computers/Security/ Firewalls/Products*. For more information on the Cisco PIX line of devices, visit *www.cisco.com* and run a search for PIX.

Whether they are hardware or software based, firewalls are effective only if they are configured correctly to block undesirable traffic, such as a TCP SYN flood or an IP spoofing attack. The most sophisticated firewalls are useless if they have poorly configured rules that allow traffic from untrusted sources. In addition, because new threats and modes of attack are being devised all the time, firewalls can be configured correctly and still fail to block some harmful traffic from entering the system because the firewall doesn't yet recognize the traffic as something that should be blocked.

What Firewalls Are Not

Firewalls aren't a standalone solution, so they shouldn't be regarded as the only tool you need to protect a network. No firewall can protect a network from internal threats, such as disgruntled employees or those who try to find ways around security measures. In both cases, a strong security policy and employee education are essential. Your organization's security policy should include strict procedures for keeping patches updated and checking for any new vulnerabilities. Many cases have been reported of worms and viruses getting past expensive firewalls that weren't patched in a timely manner.

Ideally, a firewall should be combined with antivirus software and intrusion detection systems (IDSs) to create a more comprehensive solution. Strong network security architecture encompasses many components, including IDSs, firewalls, antivirus software, access control, and auditing. The defense in depth (DiD) approach discussed in Chapter 1 is the most effective method of securing resources, so keep layered defense strategies in mind.

Check Point NG integrates with products that provide antivirus protection, intrusion detection, and other solutions through the use of its own protocol, called **Open Platform for Security (OPSEC)**. Developers use OPSEC to create solutions that integrate well with Check Point NG to create a strong network security architecture. Examples of products you might integrate with a firewall include the following:

- eSafe Protect, a product by Aladdin Systems (*www.esafe.com*) that scans e-mail, Web pages, and FTP traffic for viruses.

- StoneBeat, an event-logging program by Stonesoft Corp. (*www.stonesoft.com*). You can use third-party applications such as this one to send log data to the central firewall log database, where it can be consolidated with other logs.

- WebTrends (*www.webtrends.com*), a program well known for its capability to create graphical reports from log database information.

The expense of purchasing and installing multiple software programs can be considerable, easily running into many thousands of dollars. The most important consideration is the need for an integrated security system in which a firewall plays an important—but by no means solitary—role.

9

APPROACHES TO PACKET FILTERING

Chapter 2 introduced packet filtering, and Chapter 3 discussed the importance of a security policy in creating a network defense program. In this chapter, you see how to put this information together to develop a packet-filtering rule base. First, you learn about stateless and stateful packet filtering, and then see how a packet filter's activities depend on the other security components it's intended to work with and its position in your perimeter security configuration.

Stateless Packet Filtering

As you have learned, packet filters work by screening traffic that arrives on the perimeter of a network. **Stateless packet filters** decide whether to allow or block packets based on information in the protocol headers. Most often, filtering is done on common IP protocol header features, such as the following:

- *IP address*—Each packet-filtering rule specifies a source IP address and a destination IP address.

- *Ports and sockets*—Ports give you more control over what's allowed and what's blocked when creating filtering rules. A socket is a software connection that enables an application to send and receive data using a network protocol.

- *ACK bits*—Acknowledgement bits are parts of TCP headers, discussed in more detail in "Filtering by ACK Bit" later in this chapter.

Table 9-1 shows the simple set of rules for a firewall located at 192.168.120.1 on network 192.168.120.0.

Table 9-1   Stateless packet-filtering rules

Rule	Source IP	Source Port	Destination IP	Destination Port	Action
1	Any	Any	192.168.120.0	Above 1023	Allow
2	192.168.120.1	Any	Any	Any	Deny
3	Any	Any	192.168.120.1	Any	Deny
4	192.168.120.0	Any	Any	Any	Any
5	Any	Any	192.168.120.2	25	Allow
6	Any	Any	192.168.120.3	80	Allow
7	Any	Any	Any	Any	Deny

The following list describes the rules in Table 9-1 in more detail:

- *Rule 1*—Many external hosts that are contacted by a host on the internal network respond by connecting to TCP ports above 1023; this rule enables such connections.

- *Rule 2*—This rule prevents the firewall from connecting to any other hosts, either external or internal. The firewall is supposed to monitor traffic, not make connections. An attacker who manages to get control of the firewall might try to use it to make a connection, and this rule would block it.

- *Rule 3*—This rule provides extra security for the firewall, in addition to Rule 2, by keeping external users from establishing a direct connection to the firewall.

- *Rule 4*—This rule enables internal hosts to make connections to computers outside the network.

- *Rule 5*—This rule enables external users to send e-mail into the network.

- *Rule 6*—This rule allows external users to access the network's Web server.

- *Rule 7*—This cleanup rule denies any other traffic that hasn't been allowed explicitly by previous rules.

However, intruders can still get around these defenses. For instance, in Rule 1 (hosts responding to connections are allowed access to ports above 1023), the problem is that this rule also allows connections that have been faked to seem as though they are responding to connections to gain access.

Stateless packet filters do have their advantages. One advantage is cost; they tend to be inexpensive, and many are free. Some are included with routers or open-source OSs. On the other hand, stateless filters can be cumbersome to maintain in a complex network. They are vulnerable to IP spoofing attacks, and they offer no form of authentication.

Stateful Packet Filtering

Stateless packet filters aren't enough for most organizations because they can't filter intrusions that occur when someone connects to a computer without the computer already having initiated a connection. Without a connection in place, an attacker can spoof the computer into creating one, and DoS and other attacks can result. Another potential vulnerability is that a stateless filter handles every packet individually and has no recollection of what packets have already passed through the filter. Previously forwarded packets belonging to a connection have no bearing on the filter's decision to forward or drop a packet.

Stateful packet filters, on the other hand, keep a record of connections a host computer has made with other computers. To do this, they maintain a file called a **state table** containing a record of all current connections. The packet filter allows incoming packets to pass through it only from external hosts already connected that have a record in the state table.

Here's a more concrete example: Suppose a firewall has Rule 1 of Table 9-1, allowing external connections on ports above 1023, in its rule base. One host on the internal network has specific connections underway, as shown in an excerpt from a state table in Table 9-2.

9

Table 9-2   State table example

Source IP	Source Port	Destination IP	Destination Port	Connection State
192.168.120.101	1037	209.233.19.22	80	Established
192.168.120.104	1022	165.66.28.22	80	Established
192.168.120.107	1010	65.66.122.101	25	Established
192.168.120.102	1035	213.136.87.88	79	Established
223.56.78.11	1899	192.168.120.101	80	Established
206.121.55.8	3558	192.168.120.101	80	Established
224.209.122.1	1079	192.168.120.105	80	Established

NOTE Ports 1023 and lower are reserved for specific protocols or other purposes. Therefore, when a Web page you request using your own port 80 is sent back to you, the Web server returns it using a TCP port higher than 1023. That's why it's important for a firewall to allow these connections.

In the state table, internal hosts on the network that have the address range 192.168.120.0 to 192.168.120.255 have established connections with hosts on the external network. Some are using HTTP port 80 to connect via the Web, and one has established a connection to an e-mail server on port 25. Near the bottom of the table, several external hosts have established connections to hosts on the internal network on port 80.

Suppose an attacker tries to connect to the network on port 10995 from IP address 201.202.100.1 by sending a packet with the ACK TCP header set. The ACK header is normally sent at the end of a "handshake" between two networked computers and means that a connection is established. When a stateful firewall receives this packet, it checks the state table to see whether a connection between any host on the internal network and the computer at 201.202.100.1 exists. If a connection is not found in the state table, the packet is dropped.

One of the most user-friendly packet filters is built into Windows XP. Windows Firewall is an improved version of XP's original packet filter, Internet Connection Firewall, and offers more control. You access it through Control Panel's Security Center, and then click the Windows Firewall link to open the configuration dialog box shown in Figure 9-4.

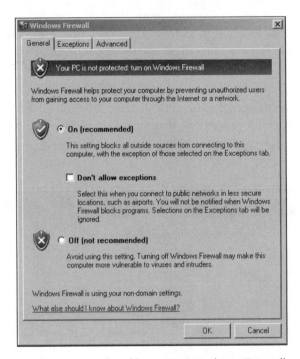

Figure 9-4   Packet filtering in Windows Firewall

Windows Firewall offers an improved level of protection over Internet Connection Firewall. You can limit the amount of traffic with more precision and specify exceptions, such as ports or programs (see Figure 9-5).

In the Advanced tab, you can access settings for a particular interface, such as logging and ICMP message handling. You can also control traffic for network services, such as DHCP, DNS, and FTP, as shown in Figure 9-6. You can use this dialog box to add, edit, or delete services and to configure more specific control over ICMP responses.

You can also reset the program to its default configuration in the Advanced tab. This setting can come in handy if a change you have made is causing problems, but you're unsure which change is the culprit.

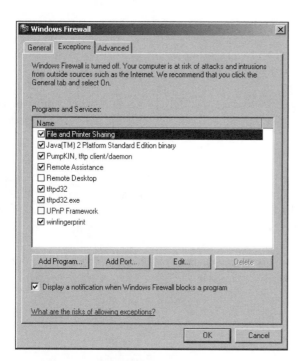

Figure 9-5 Specifying exceptions

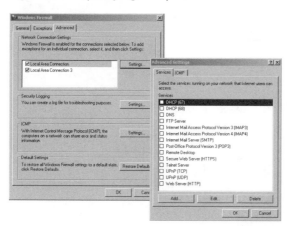

Figure 9-6 Configuring advanced settings in Windows Firewall

Stateful packet filtering doesn't necessarily address all problems with stateless filtering. Authentication, for instance, might not be addressed.

CAUTION

Packet Filtering Depends on Position

The type of filtering that a firewall, router, or other device performs depends on its position in the firewall perimeter configuration and on the other hardware or software with which its activities need to be coordinated. For instance, a packet filter positioned between the Internet and a host or network that provides the only protection for that host or network needs to be configured carefully; all inbound and outbound traffic needs to be accounted for in the packet filter's rule base.

In contrast, a packet filter placed between a proxy server and the Internet needs to help in shielding all internal users from external hosts. A company concerned about protecting the privacy of its employees and its data warehouses might install a proxy server on the network perimeter. A proxy server handles traffic on behalf of computers on the network it protects, rebuilding both outbound and inbound requests from scratch to hide internal IP address information. A packet filter between the proxy server and the Internet needs to direct traffic to and from the proxy server. A primary goal is to prevent direct connections between the internal network and the Internet (see Figure 9-7).

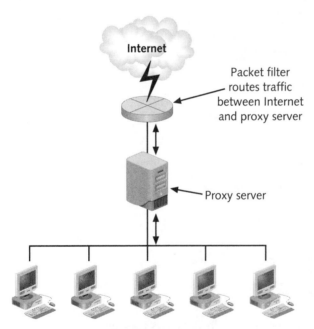

Figure 9-7   A packet filter connects a proxy server with the Internet

Proxy servers can perform stateful packet filtering on their own. They operate at the application layer of the OSI model, so they can make intelligent decisions about what traffic is allowed to pass. The tradeoff is the drop in performance that can result from the demand that proxy servers place on the host computer, which is much higher than for a traditional firewall.

Another type of configuration combines packet filtering with a DMZ. One common setup is placing packet-filtering devices (routers or firewalls) at either end of the DMZ. The packet filter on the DMZ's external interface needs to allow Internet users to gain access to servers on the DMZ but needs to block access to the internal LAN. The packet filter on the internal interface performs a similar function but for internal users; it enables them to access servers on the DMZ but not connect directly to the Internet. Instead, they connect to the Internet through a proxy server on the DMZ (see Figure 9-8).

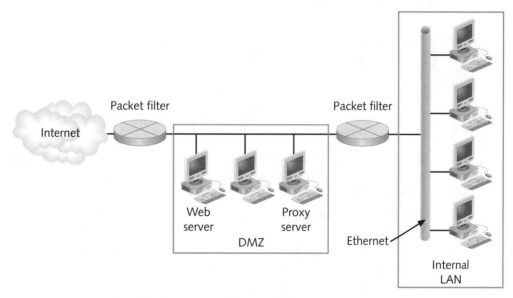

Figure 9-8   A packet filter routing traffic to and from a DMZ

The question of how many packet filters to use and where to place them depends on your needs. A simple home network might gain adequate protection from a single well-configured stateful packet filter. A small network that needs to protect proprietary information can use a proxy server–packet filter combination to prevent any external users from "seeing" IP or port information associated with hosts on the internal network. If no IP addresses or ports are visible through port scans or other means, no attacks can be launched. For large companies that run public Web servers and have proprietary information to protect, placing packet filters on either side of a DMZ can provide effective multilayered protection for public servers and employees.

Activity 9-1: Installing a Freeware Firewall Program

Time Required: 30 minutes

Objective: Install the freeware desktop firewall program ZoneAlarm.

Description: Freeware firewall programs aren't as full featured as commercial firewalls, but they're good for testing and learning how the programs work. In this activity, you need a Windows XP computer to download and use the freeware version of a popular personal firewall, ZoneAlarm by Zone Labs.

> You need to turn off Windows Firewall or any other firewall software before performing the activities in this chapter.
>
> **NOTE**

1. Start your Web browser. Enter the URL **www.download.com/** and press **Enter** to go to CNET's Download.com home page.

2. In the Search box, type **ZoneAlarm** and click **GO**. (You can also type the direct URL: **http://www.download.com/3000-2092-10039884.html?part= zonealarm&subj=dlpage&tag=button**.)

3. Click the first **Download Now** link, if necessary, and then click **Run** to begin downloading to a temporary location.

4. If a Security Warning dialog box opens, click **Run**, and then click **Next** in the ZoneAlarm Installation Wizard. Fill out the User Information dialog box, and then click **Next**. Accept the license agreement, and then click **Install**.

5. When the User survey dialog box opens, select the appropriate options in the drop-down lists, and then click **Finish**.

6. When the ZoneAlarm Setup dialog box asks if you want to start ZoneAlarm now, click **Yes**.

7. In the License Wizard dialog box, click **Select ZoneAlarm**. Click **Next** and then click **Finish**.

8. Click **Finish** and then click **Done**. You'll configure ZoneAlarm manually. Click **OK** to restart your computer and complete the installation.

9. If a License Wizard window appears, click **No, Thank you**. Click **Finish** in the ZoneAlarm - Getting Started window. The main ZoneAlarm Control Center window is displayed.

10. Click **Program Control** at the left. Leave the defaults selected in the main window, and click the **Programs** tab.

11. In the Program Control window shown in Figure 9-9, click the **Add** button.

12. In the Add Program dialog box, locate and open the Internet Explorer folder. Click the **iexplore.exe** file, and then click **Open**. The program is added to the list of programs in the ZoneAlarm Wizard.

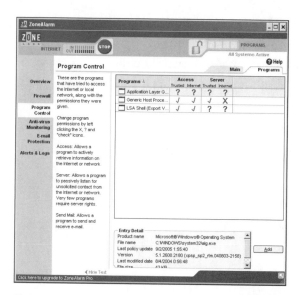

Figure 9-9   The ZoneAlarm Program Control window

13. Repeat Steps 11 and 12 for any other programs you want to access the Internet, such as your e-mail application, FTP programs, and so on. (For example, if you use Outlook Express for e-mail, the program name is Msimn.exe; for Netscape Navigator, the program name is Netscape.exe.) When you're done, close the ZoneAlarm Control Center.

14. In the ZoneAlarm tips window, click the **Don't show this message again** check box, and Click **OK**. ZoneAlarm now appears as an icon on the taskbar. To open the Control Center in the future, double-click this icon.

15. Leave ZoneAlarm open and your system running for the next activity.

CREATING RULES AND ESTABLISHING RESTRICTIONS

After you have determined where packet-filtering devices should be positioned and what their functions will be on the network, you need to establish the rule base that enables them to function. Firewalls can be expensive and elaborate and come in many varieties, but most network security professionals agree that even the most full-featured firewall depends on a good **rule base**. This set of rules tells the firewall what action to take when a certain kind of traffic attempts to pass through. A simple firewall with well-constructed rules is more effective than a complex product with rules that don't block the intrusion attempts they need to stop.

What makes an effective firewall rule base? The following sections describe some points to consider:

- It should be based on the organization's security policy.

- It should include a firewall policy that provides rules for how applications can access the Internet.

- It should be as simple and short as possible.

- It should restrict access to ports and subnets on the internal network from the Internet.

- It should control Internet services.

 A set of packet-filtering rules is frequently called an access control list (ACL) instead of a rule base.

NOTE

Base the Rule Base on Your Security Policy

When you're configuring the firewall rule base, you have the opportunity to put your organization's security policy rules and procedures into practice. Certain elements of filtering packets are especially important to configure rules and, therefore, implement the organization's security policy:

- *Logging and auditing*—Most security policies require methods for detecting intrusions and other security problems, such as viruses.

- *Tracking*—The rule base should include a procedure for initiating notification so that you can follow response procedures in case of intrusion.

- *Filtering*—One of the primary objectives of a rule base is to filter communications based on complex rules so that only traffic using approved protocols, ports, and source and destination IP addresses is allowed.

- *Network Address Translation (NAT)*—The rule base should provide for concealing internal names and addresses on the company LAN from those outside the network.

- *Quality of Service (QoS)*—QoS rules can be set up to enable the firewall to maintain a baseline level of functionality, which can be specified in your organization's security policy.

- *Desktop security policy*—This policy enables you to specify the level of access remote users have when they log on to the network.

A rule base is a practical implementation of the policies adopted by the organization. Consider the following common policies that need to be reflected in the rule base:

- Employees can have access to the Internet with certain restrictions, such as content filtering or controls on downloads.

- The public can access the company's Web server and e-mail server.

- Only authenticated traffic can access the internal LAN.

- Employees are not allowed to use instant-messaging software outside the internal LAN.

- Traffic from the company's ISP should be allowed.

- External traffic that attempts to connect to a port used by instant-messaging software should be blocked.

- Only the network administrator should be able to access the internal network directly from the Internet for management purposes.

Create a Firewall Policy That Covers Application Traffic

A **firewall policy** is an addition to your security policy that describes how your firewalls should handle application traffic, such as Web or e-mail applications. The risk analysis (covered in Chapter 2) should provide a list of those applications and associated threats and vulnerabilities, describe the impact if confidential data is compromised, and outline countermeasures for mitigating the risks. Before developing a firewall policy, you must understand these factors, because your risk analysis results dictate how firewall systems handle your network's application traffic (whether it blocks or allows traffic).

The firewall policy should explain how the firewall is set up, managed, and updated. Although each organization's needs are different, you follow the same general steps to create a firewall policy. First, you identify which network applications are needed and the vulnerabilities associated with each application. Next, you need to conduct a cost-benefit analysis to determine the most cost-effective and efficient method for securing application traffic. Remember that some traffic is more sensitive than others, and you must balance security and cost. Also, keep in mind that many networks have multiple firewalls at several locations, so you need to develop a traffic matrix like the one shown in Table 9-3 for each location.

Table 9-3 Application traffic matrix

Application or Service	Internal Host Type	Location	Host Security Policy	Firewall Internal Security Policy	Firewall External Security Policy
FTP	Windows	Any	Client only; antivirus	Permit	Deny

Table 9-3 Application traffic matrix (continued)

Application or Service	Internal Host Type	Location	Host Security Policy	Firewall Internal Security Policy	Firewall External Security Policy
FTP	UNIX	Any	Secure Shell (SSH); user ID/password; no anonymous traffic	Permit	Application proxy with user authentication
Telnet	Windows	Any	Client only	Permit	Application proxy with user authentication
Telnet	UNIX	Any	Secure Shell	Permit	Application proxy with user authentication
NetBIOS over TCP/IP	Windows 95/98/NT	Any	Limit access to shares	Permit local domain only; deny all others	Deny

When your traffic matrix is finished, you can develop the firewall rule base. Firewalls enable you to control access to your computer or network by controlling access to particular applications. Some Trojan programs work by gaining control of other applications (for instance, Outlook Express), which then access the Internet. Sometimes, attackers try to access applications on your computer or the ports they use. If a computer on your network has an instant-messaging application installed, such as MSN Messenger or ICQ, these applications probably launch on startup. The computer listens for incoming connections on the ports those applications use, and attackers can scan for these open ports.

Firewall software gives you a way to block applications from accessing the Internet so that these ports aren't left open—or, if the application needs to be used, the application can be flagged so that the user must be prompted if it's to access the Internet. Typically, you're given three options:

- *Allow*—The application can access the Internet at any time. (You'll probably want to establish this rule for Web browsers, e-mail applications, and other software you normally use.)
- *Block*—The application is blocked from accessing the Internet.
- *Ask or prompt*—The user is prompted when the application attempts to access the Internet.

Keep the Rule Base Simple

Keep the list of rules in your rule base as short as possible. The more complex the rule base is, the higher the chance of misconfiguring it. Some professionals suggest that a rule base contain no more than 30 rules and certainly no more than 50. The shorter the rule base, the faster your firewall can process requests because it has fewer rules to review.

Typically, a firewall processes rules in a particular order. The rules are usually numbered 1, 2, 3, and so on, and a list of firewall rules is usually displayed in the form of a grid. The first cell in the grid is the rule number. The subsequent cells describe the attributes the firewall should test for: an IP address, a protocol, and an action to be taken. Check Point NG's rule grid is shown in Figure 9-10.

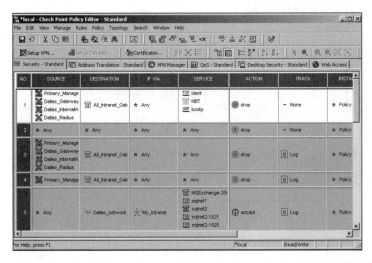

Figure 9-10 A firewall processes rules in order from top to bottom

The fact that rules are processed in order means that the most important ones—the ones that need to be processed first—should be put at the top of the list. (All firewalls have a way to reorder rules in the rule base.) It's a good idea to make the last rule in the rule base a **cleanup rule**, which is a rule that covers any other packets that haven't been covered in preceding rules. On a Cisco router, this cleanup rule is the explicit "deny all" at the end of the access list.

When a packet hits a firewall, rules are tested one after another. As soon as a match is found, the action corresponding to the rule is followed. Most often, there are two possible actions. The first is Allow (permit the packet to proceed through the firewall to its destination on the Internet or in the internal network). The second is Deny (drop the packet altogether). Usually, no notification is sent to the sender for a Deny action because it might give attackers clues about the network's characteristics; the packet is simply dropped. A third option, Reject, typically isn't used because it notifies the sender and could give clues about the network. The process by which the firewall reviews packets and decides whether to allow or deny them is shown in Figure 9-11.

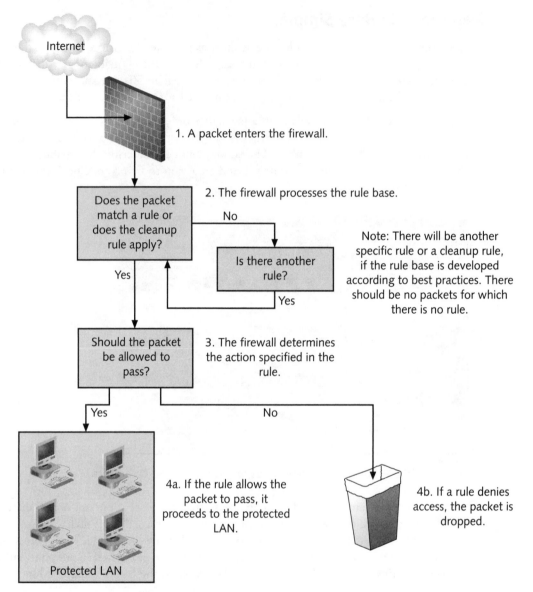

Figure 9-11   Firewalls process rules in order until a match is found

Restrict Subnets, Ports, and Protocols

Packet filters can usually give you more control over what traffic can be blocked or allowed. The more flexibility you have, the greater your ability to control specific types of traffic. The following sections give some examples of rules you might create to control traffic while still allowing needed connectivity.

NOTE Much of this information was introduced in Chapter 8, when you learned about creating a rule base for the IDS program Snort. The same principles apply here. In reality, a rule base is a rule base; it doesn't matter whether it's an IDS, firewall, router, or another piece of equipment applying the rules.

Filtering by IP Addresses

One way you can identify traffic is by IP address range. Some traffic is legitimate; it comes from a network you trust, such as your own network or your ISP's servers, and shouldn't be blocked by the firewall. However, most firewalls start from the sensible premise that all traffic should be blocked by default, and you need to identify "trusted" networks whose communications should be allowed.

For instance, if your network subnet contains IP addresses in the range of 10.10.56.0 to 10.10.56.255, you would specify that the firewall regard them as "trusted," as shown in one of ZoneAlarm's configuration dialog boxes (see Figure 9-12). Remember that 10.10.56.0 is the subnet address and 10.10.56.255 is the broadcast address for this range, and they can't be used as valid IP addresses for hosts.

9

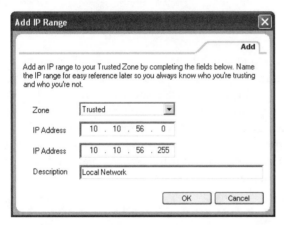

Figure 9-12   Identify trusted subnets or IP addresses

Activity 9-2: Adding Computers to a Trusted Zone

Time Required: 10 minutes

Objective: Specify trusted IP address ranges in ZoneAlarm.

Description: If you work on a network, you need to allow other computers to communicate with yours. By default, ZoneAlarm blocks all connections until you identify the computers you want to be able to access your machine freely. The following steps add a computer to your trusted zone.

NOTE

If you don't already have the information, you need to determine the IP addresses of other computers in your lab network. To do so, open a command prompt window, type ipconfig, and press Enter.

1. Open the ZoneAlarm window, if it's not open already.

2. Click **Firewall** in the list of program features.

3. Click the **Zones** tab. A list of computers in your "trusted zone" appears. If only one machine is listed, you probably need to add others to your zone.

4. Click the **Add** button, and then click **IP Range** from the popup menu.

5. In the Add IP Range dialog box, enter the starting address for the first IP address in your lab network or other local network in the first IP Address text box. Enter the ending address in the second IP Address text box. Then enter a name for the network, and then click **OK**.

6. Click **Apply**.

7. Close all ZoneAlarm windows, and leave your system running for the next activity.

Control Internet Services

The goal in coming up with packet-filtering rules is to account for all possible ports that a type of communication might use or for all variations of a protocol (for instance, passive and active FTP or standard and secure HTTP). Most businesses use the Internet heavily in daily business operations, and the challenge for security professionals is to balance the need for Internet connectivity with the need to secure LAN resources from the risks inherent in Internet access. The following sections discuss how to control access to commonly used Web resources, such as surfing the Internet, sending and receiving e-mail, and using FTP as a secure means of centralized data storage.

Web Services

A common first priority of employees in a protected network is (not surprisingly) to be able to surf the Web and exchange e-mail messages. The rules for accessing the Web need to cover standard HTTP traffic on TCP port 80, as well as Secure HTTP (S-HTTP) traffic on TCP port 443. These rules, shown in Table 9-4, assume that the local network being protected has an IP address range of 207.177.178.0/24.

Table 9-4   Outbound Web access

Rule	Protocol	Transport Protocol	Source IP	Source Port	Destination IP	Destination Port	Action
1	HTTP outbound	TCP	207.177.178.0/24	Any	Any	80	Allow
2	S-HTTP outbound	TCP	208.177.178.0/24	Any	Any	443	Allow

DNS

To connect to Web sites, employees need to be able to resolve the fully qualified domain names (FQDNs) they enter, such as *course.com*, to their corresponding IP addresses by using DNS. Internal users connect to external hosts via a DNS server in the DMZ of the security perimeter. DNS uses UDP port 53 for name resolution attempts and TCP port 53 for zone transfers. In addition, you need to set up rules that enable external clients to access computers in your own network using the same TCP and UDP ports, as shown in Table 9-5. (The rules in Table 9-5 assume that your organization's DNS server is located at IP address 208.177.178.31.)

Table 9-5   DNS resolution rules

Rule	Protocol	Transport Protocol	Source IP	Source Port	Destination IP	Destination Port	Action
3	DNS outbound	TCP	208.177.178.31	Any	Any	53	Allow
4	DNS outbound	UDP	208.177.178.31	Any	Any	53	Allow
5	DNS inbound	TCP	Any	Any	208.177.178.31	53	Allow
6	DNS inbound	UDP	Any	Any	208.177.178.31	53	Allow

E-Mail

To set up configuration rules, you need to assess whether your organization needs to accept incoming e-mail messages, whether internal users can access mail services outside your organization (such as Hotmail), and what e-mail clients your organization supports to ensure the highest level of security without blocking e-mail access.

Setting up firewall rules that permit filtering e-mail messages is not simple, however. One reason is the variety of e-mail protocols that can be used:

- POP3 and IMAP4 for inbound mail transport
- SMTP for outbound mail transport
- Lightweight Directory Access Protocol (LDAP) for looking up e-mail addresses
- HTTP for Web-based mail service

To keep things simple, consider a configuration that uses only POP3 and SMTP for inbound and outbound e-mail, respectively. However, SSL encryption (a form of encryption between Web server and client) should be used for additional security. Table 9-6 outlines rules for e-mail access, which assume that your SMTP mail server is located at 208.177.178.29. Note that the S following a protocol, such as POP3/S, indicates SSL encryption.

Table 9-6 E-mail rules

Rule	Protocol	Transport Protocol	Source IP	Source Port	Destination IP	Destination Port	Action
7	POP3 outbound	TCP	208.177.178.0/24	Any	Any	110	Allow
8	POP3/S outbound	TCP	208.177.178.0/24	Any	Any	995	Allow
9	POP inbound	TCP	Any	Any	208.177.178.0/24	110	Allow
10	POP3/S inbound	TCP	Any	Any	208.177.178.0/24	995	Allow
11	SMTP outbound	TCP	208.177.178.29	Any	Any	25	Allow
12	SMTP/S outbound	TCP	208.177.178.29	Any	Any	465	Allow
13	SMTP inbound	TCP	Any	Any	208.177.178.29	25	Allow
14	SMTP/S inbound	TCP	Any	Any	208.177.178.29	465	Allow

FTP

Two kinds of FTP transactions can take place on networks: active FTP or passive FTP. The rules you set up for FTP need to support two separate connections: TCP port 21, the FTP control port, and TCP 20, the FTP data port. If some clients in your network support active FTP, you can't specify a particular port because the client can establish a connection with the FTP server at any port above 1023. Instead, you specify the IP address of your FTP server (in this example, 208.177.178.25), as shown in Table 9-7.

Table 9-7 FTP rules

Rule	Protocol	Transport Protocol	Source IP	Source Port	Destination IP	Destination Port	Action
15	FTP control inbound	TCP	Any	Any	208.177.178.0/25	21	Allow
16	FTP data inbound	TCP	208.177.178.0/25	20	Any	Any	Allow
17	FTP PASV	TCP	Any	Any	208.177.178.0/25	Any	Allow

Table 9-7 FTP rules (continued)

Rule	Protocol	Transport Protocol	Source IP	Source Port	Destination IP	Destination Port	Action
18	FTP control outbound	TCP	208.177.178.0/25	Any	Any	21	Allow
19	FTP data outbound	TCP	Any	20	208.177.178.25	Any	Allow

Filtering by Ports

You already know that TCP/IP and UDP both provide for the transmission of information by breaking it into segments of uniform length called packets (or datagrams). Packets can vary in length from, say, 54 bits of information to 1,054 bits; however, what's important to remember is that a system that uses TCP or UDP sends packets in a particular transmission that are the same length so that they are more easily sent and received. An individual file might be broken into multiple packets, but those packets are all the same length.

Filtering by TCP or UDP port numbers is commonly called port filtering or protocol filtering. Using TCP or UDP port numbers can help you filter a wide variety of information, including SMTP and POP e-mail messages, NetBIOS sessions, DNS requests, and Network News Transfer Protocol (NNTP) newsgroup sessions. You can filter out everything but TCP port 80 for Web, TCP port 25 for e-mail, or TCP port 21 for FTP. The port-filtering process is shown in Figure 9-13.

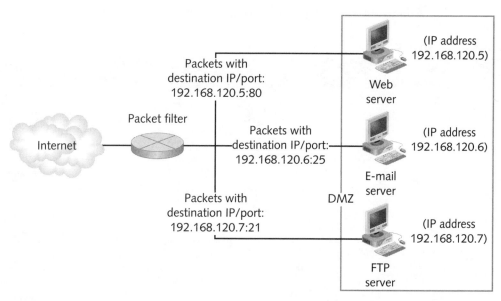

Figure 9-13 Port numbers direct packets to the client or server that needs them

Figure 9-13 indicates that ports are filtered by a router and directed to the correct combination of computer and software by their IP address and port number. The port numbers in Figure 9-13 are technically correct; port 80 is reserved for HTTP Web pages, port 25 for SMTP e-mail, and so on. However, in practice, when two computers exchange information, they use two different port numbers: the port from which data is sent (the source port) and the port at which the response data is received (the destination port). It's quite normal for network communications between two computers to use different source and destination ports. (In fact, it's rare for source and destination ports to be the same.) However, the fact that ports are different and the destination port is determined dynamically (determined on a per-connection basis and, therefore, impossible to predict) makes filtering by port number complicated.

NOTE   There isn't a magic solution to filtering services based on port number, especially when the ports are above 1023 in the registered or dynamic port number ranges as assigned by IANA. You have to know what services you're running on your network and what ports are used by those services; you block the ports you don't need and allow the ones you do. Refer to *www.iana.org/assignments/port-numbers* for current port number assignments.

For instance, if you're on a Windows-based network, your computers probably use NetBIOS name service to find one another on NetBIOS ports 137, 138, and 139. NetBIOS traffic should originate inside your internal network and stay inside the firewall; any traffic coming from the Internet that attempts to use these ports should be dropped. You should also block inbound traffic that attempts to use ports assigned to other Windows networking services. Table 9-8 lists some examples of filtering common Windows services and ports.

Table 9-8   Filtering Windows services and ports

Rule	EXT	Protocol	Source IP	Source Port	Destination IP	Destination Port	Action	Service
1	X	TCP	Any	Any	Any	135	Deny	NetBIOS RPC
2	X	UDP	Any	Any	Any	135	Deny	NetBIOS RPC
3	X	TCP	Any	Any	Any	137	Deny	NetBIOS Name Service
4	X	UDP	Any	Any	Any	137	Deny	NetBIOS Name Service
5	X	TCP	Any	Any	Any	445	Deny	SMB/File Sharing
6	X	UDP	Any	Any	Any	445	Deny	SMB/File Sharing
7	X	TCP	Any	Any	Any	1720	Deny	Net Meeting
8	X	UDP	Any	Any	Any	1720	Deny	Net Meeting
9	X	TCP	Any	Any	Any	1755	Deny	Windows Media
10	X	UDP	Any	Any	Any	1755	Deny	Windows Media

Table 9-8   Filtering Windows services and ports (continued)

Rule	EXT	Protocol	Source IP	Source Port	Destination IP	Destination Port	Action	Service
11	X	TCP	Any	Any	Any	3389	Deny	Remote Desktop Protocol
12	X	UDP	Any	Any	Any	3389	Deny	Remote Desktop Protocol

UNIX also has its own set of services that should be blocked when they are inbound from the Internet. Some examples are shown in Table 9-9.

Table 9-9   Filtering UNIX services and ports

Rule	Protocol	Source IP	Source Port	Destination IP	Destination Port	Action	Service
1	TCP	Any	Any	Any	17	Deny	QOTD
2	UDP	Any	Any	Any	17	Deny	QOTD
3	TCP	Any	Any	Any	111	Deny	Portmapper
4	UDP	Any	Any	Any	111	Deny	Portmapper
5	TCP	Any	Any	Any	513	Deny	Remote Login
6	TCP	Any	Any	Any	514	Deny	Syslog
7	UDP	Any	Any	Any	514	Deny	Syslog
8	TCP	Any	Any	Any	635	Deny	mountd (NFS Service)

CAUTION The problem with specifying a port number for filtering is that some applications don't use a fixed port number when they reply to a client. AOL Instant Messenger and ICQ are known for this; they assign themselves dynamic port numbers, which are used only for the length of a particular communication. You have to filter these communications by IP address instead.

Activity 9-3: Tracking Connection Attempts

ACTIVITY

Time Required: 15 minutes

Objective: Analyze a problem scenario to determine a solution for preventing intrusions on a specific port.

Description: After installing a firewall program on your computer, you receive a number of alerts about connection attempts on UDP port 1027. You go to *www.iana.org/assignments/port-numbers*, where you learn that the instant-messaging program ICQ uses this port. You know that attackers commonly exploit ICQ, and your organization doesn't use the program. You suspect the connection attempts are actually attempted intrusions. The firewall has blocked the attempts successfully, but you're concerned that future attempts could be successful. What can you do to prevent attackers from getting through on ICQ port 1027?

_____

_____

_____

_____

ICMP Message Type

Internet Control Message Protocol (ICMP) functions as a sort of housekeeping protocol for TCP/IP, helping networks cope with communication problems. From a security standpoint, ICMP packets have a downside: Attackers can use them to crash computers on your network. Because ICMP packets have no authentication method to verify the packet recipient, attackers can attempt man-in-the-middle attacks, in which they impersonate the intended recipient; they can also send packets of the ICMP redirect message type to direct traffic to a computer they control outside the protected network. A firewall/packet filter must be able to determine whether an ICMP packet, based on its message type, should be allowed to pass. Some rules you can use to block common ICMP message types are shown in Table 9-10.

Table 9-10 Filtering ICMP message types

Rule	INT	EXT	Protocol	ICMP Type	Source IP	Source Port	Destination IP	Destination Port	Action
1			ICMP	Source Quench	Any	Any	Any	Any	Deny
2	X		ICMP	Echo Request	Any	Any	Any	Any	Deny
3		X	ICMP	Echo Reply	Any	Any	Any	Any	Deny
4	X		ICMP	Destination Unreachable	Any	Any	Any	Any	Deny
5		X	ICMP	Redirect	Any	Any	Any	Any	Deny
6		X	ICMP	Destination Unreachable	Any	Any	Any	Any	Deny
7			ICMP		Any	Any	Any	Any	Deny

The INT and EXT (internal and external) columns are left empty for Rules 1 and 7 because that enables them to apply to both inbound and outbound traffic. Rule 7 in Table 9-10 is a cleanup rule that drops all ICMP packets that haven't been filtered by previous rules.

Filtering by Service

With some firewalls, you can filter by naming the service you want to use. You don't have to specify a port number. Check Point NG does this in its rule base; the rules shown in the Service column in Figure 9-14, for instance, specify Telnet, SMTP, and HTTP by name.

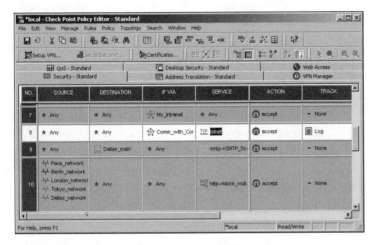

Figure 9-14   Some rule bases let you filter by service

Remember from Chapter 8 that packets can also be filtered based on the IP protocol ID field in the header. This works in much the same way for firewalls as it does for IDSs. Firewalls can also filter by the six TCP control flags you learned about in Chapter 8:

- URG (urgent)
- ACK (acknowledgment)
- PSH (push function)
- RST (reset the connection)
- SYN (synchronize sequence numbers)
- FIN (no more data from sender)

You have also learned about IP options, the set of flags that can optionally appear in an IP header. Options add information to a packet, as in these examples:

- *Security*—This option enables hosts to send security parameters, handling restrictions, and other information.
- *Loose source and record routing*—This option enables the source computer sending the packet to specify the routers that should be used in forwarding the packet to its destination.

- *Strict source and record routing*—Same as loose source and record routing, except that the host computer must send the packet directly to the next address in the source route.

- *Internet timestamp*—Provides a timestamp indicating when the packet was sent.

Packet-filtering rules can and should be tailored to meet a network's special needs. However, every rule base should follow a few general practices:

- A firewall or packet filter that follows a "Deny All" security policy should start from a clean slate; in other words, it should begin by allowing services selectively as needed and end by blocking all other traffic of any sort.

- The rule base should keep everyone except network administrators from connecting to the firewall. (Anyone who accesses the firewall can learn all the IP addresses on the internal network and open up access to the internal network.)

- The rule base should block direct access from the Internet to any computers behind the firewall or packet filter. All inbound traffic, in other words, should be filtered first.

- The rule base should permit access to public servers in the DMZ and enable users in the organization to access the Internet.

A rule base, then, is a mixture of rules that selectively allow or deny access. Table 9-11 lists a typical set of rules that assume the firewall is at 192.168.120.1, the e-mail server at 192.168.120.2, the Web server at 192.168.120.3, and the DNS server at 192.168.120.4. The internal network is represented by 192.168.120.0.

Table 9-11   A typical packet-filtering rule base

Rule	Source IP	Source Port	Destination IP	Destination	Action	What It Does
1	192.168.120.1	Any	Any	Any	Deny	Prevents the firewall itself from making any connections
2	Any	Any	192.168.120.1	Any	Deny	Prevents anyone from connecting to the firewall
3	192.168.120.0	Any	Any	Any	Allow	Allows internal users to access external computers
4	192.168.120.0	Any	192.168120.4	53	Allow	Enables internal users to connect to the DNS server

Table 9-11   A typical packet-filtering rule base (continued)

Rule	Source IP	Source Port	Destination IP	Destination	Action	What It Does
5	Any	Any	192.168.120.2	25	Allow	Allows external and internal users to access the e-mail server via SMTP port 25
6	192.168.120.0	Any	192.168.120.2	110	Allow	Enables internal users to connect to the e-mail server using POP3 port 110
7	Any	Any	192.168.120.3	80	Allow	Enables both external and internal users to connect to the Web server
8	Any	Any	Any	Any	Deny	Blocks all traffic not covered by previous rules

ACTIVITY

Activity 9-4: Tracing a Blocked IP Address

Time Required: 15 minutes

Objective: Determine the source of packets logged by ZoneAlarm.

Description: ZoneAlarm blocks all traffic from outside computers unless you specifically tell it that a particular type of traffic is to be allowed. When you first start using the program, you're likely to get a flood of alert messages and corresponding log file entries for each type of connection attempt that's blocked. Some connections might be legitimate communications from your own ISP. However, many others are from attackers. You can use the Tracert program, included with Windows 2000 and XP (as well as Linux and other versions of Windows), to determine whether the server from which the packet is originating is coming from your own ISP or school or from a server you don't recognize.

1. To use Tracert to determine the origin of a packet, open a command prompt window, type **tracert *IPaddress*** (substituting the IP address you want to investigate for *IPaddress*), and press **Enter**.

2. Using the information you gathered in Step 1, determine what IP addresses aren't suspicious. To do this, contact your school's network administrator or the office that manages Internet services, and ask what range of IP addresses are commonly used to give access to on-campus computers. If you use an ISP to connect to the Internet, contact the ISP and ask what IP address ranges it uses for its customers.

3. Double-click the **ZoneAlarm** icon in the Windows taskbar to start the program.

9

4. To make sure alerts are on, click **Alerts & Logs** at the left of the ZoneAlarm window (see Figure 9-15), and click the **Log Viewer** tab, if necessary.

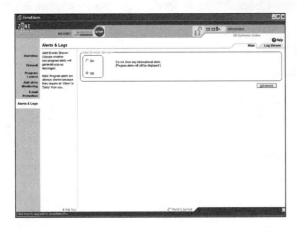

Figure 9-15 The ZoneAlarm Alerts & Logs window

5. Keep track of the kinds of alert messages you get. Do you receive any NetBIOS connection attempts from IP addresses that aren't on your network? What could be the source of a NetBIOS scan? Write down the information on the following lines.

_____

_____

6. Do you get any attempts to connect on ports such as 1243 or 53001? Write down the port numbers displayed in the Destination IP column after the IP addresses shown, and see whether any match the list of ports that well-known Trojan programs attempt to use. (Do an Internet search for "common Trojan ports" or similar keywords to locate this information.)

_____

_____

7. Do you get any attempts to connect on port 137? This port is commonly used by WINS registration. What could be the cause of this common connection attempt that's related to Windows networking services?

_____

8. When you're finished evaluating alert messages, click **Alerts & Logs** at the left in the ZoneAlarm window, click the **Main** tab, and click the **Off** option button under Alert Events Shown to stop the program from showing you alert messages.

9. Close all ZoneAlarm windows, and leave your system running for the next activity.

DESIGNING FIREWALL CONFIGURATIONS

Firewalls can be deployed in different ways on a network: as part of a screening router, a dual-homed host, a screened host, a screened subnet DMZ, multiple DMZs, multiple firewalls, or a reverse firewall setup.

Screening Router

A single router on the network perimeter that has been configured to filter packets is the simplest kind of firewall you can have. This **screening router** determines whether to allow or deny packets based on their source and destination IP addresses or other information in their headers (see Figure 9-16).

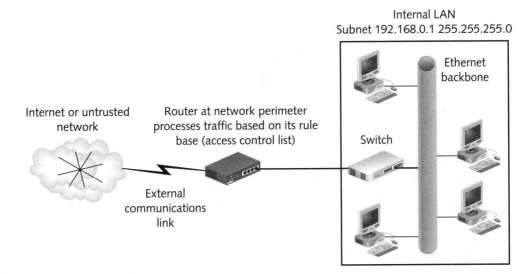

Figure 9-16 A screening router

However, this device alone doesn't stop many attacks, especially those that use spoofed or manipulated IP address information. A router should be combined with a firewall or proxy server for added protection.

Dual-Homed Host

A common arrangement is to install firewall or other security-related software (such as a proxy server) on a **dual-homed host**, a computer that has been configured with more than one network interface. The capability to forward packets is disabled on the computer, so only the firewall software on the computer can forward traffic from one interface to another (see Figure 9-17). This type of setup is also used by millions of PC users connected to the

Internet. Rules are established so that the firewall moves traffic between the Internet and the home computer or network.

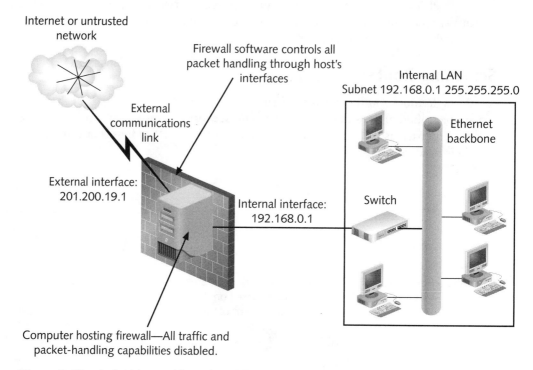

Figure 9-17   A dual-homed host firewall configuration

Originally, the term "dual-homed host" was used for a computer equipped with two separate network interface cards (NICs), with one NIC for each interface. Now this term is used to describe the setup in Figure 9-17, where a firewall is placed between the LAN and the Internet.

A dual-homed host is limited in the security it can provide, because the firewall depends on the same computer system used for day-to-day communication. Any problem with the host machine weakens the firewall. The big disadvantage is that the host serves as a single point of entry to the organization. Having a simple checkpoint means that an attacker has only one layer of protection to break through to infiltrate the local network. Therefore, a multilayered DiD arrangement proves even more important with a dual-homed host.

NOTE

The machine that hosts the firewall software might have more than two network interfaces. It might be connected to the DMZ, to the Internet, and to the internal LAN, for example. In that case, it's called a "multihomed host."

Screened Host

A **screened host** setup is similar to a dual-homed host, but the big difference is that a router is often added between the host and the Internet to carry out IP packet filtering. It's essentially a combination of the dual-homed host and screening router configurations, blending the two to provide an added layer of functionality, security, and performance (see Figure 9-18).

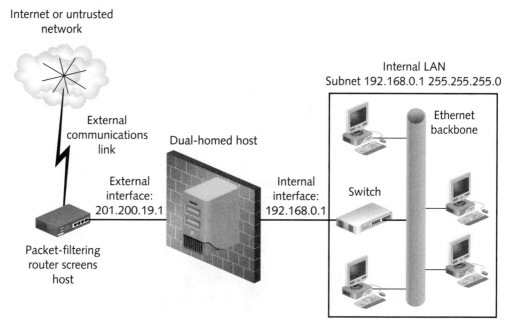

Figure 9-18   A screened host

You might choose this setup for perimeter security on a corporate network, for instance. A common enhancement is to have the screened host function as an application gateway or proxy server. The only network services allowed to pass through the proxy server are those for which proxy applications are already available.

Screened Subnet DMZ

As you learned in Chapter 1, a DMZ is a subnet of publicly accessible servers placed outside the internal LAN. Because this subnet contains a substantial amount of information important to the company, a packet filter or other security software should screen the DMZ. A common solution is to make the servers a subnet of the firewall (see Figure 9-19).

Because the firewall that protects the DMZ is also connected to the Internet and can be connected to the internal LAN, the firewall is often called a **three-pronged firewall**. You might choose this setup when you need to provide services to the public, such as an FTP

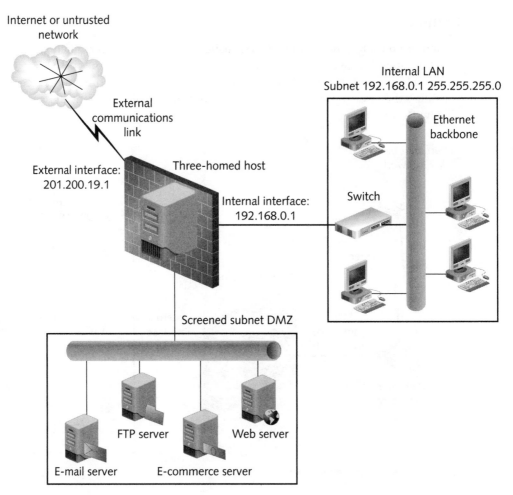

Figure 9-19   A screened subnet DMZ

server, a Web server, or an e-mail server, but want to make sure attackers don't gain access to your Web site or FTP resources.

The subnet attached to the firewall and contained in the DMZ is sometimes called a "service network" or "perimeter network" by those who dislike the military connotations of the term DMZ. The services provided in the DMZ vary, depending on the organization, but typically include a Web server, an FTP server, and outgoing and incoming e-mail servers.

Multiple DMZ/Firewall Configurations

One DMZ isn't enough security for many large-scale corporations that are connected to the Internet or do business online. To handle a large demand from the Internet while keeping the response time of Web servers and other public servers as fast as possible, you should set up multiple DMZs. Each DMZ is a **server farm**, a group of servers connected in their own subnet that work together to receive requests with the help of **load-balancing software**. This software prioritizes and schedules requests and distributes them to servers based on each server's current load and processing power.

NOTE Remember that some people prefer to call DMZs service or perimeter networks because they dislike the military connotation of the term DMZ. The terms are used interchangeably in this book.

Installing clusters of servers in DMZs outside the internal network helps protect the internal network from becoming overloaded. Placing the company's Web server in the outer subnet makes the server better equipped to handle heavy traffic because there's less filtering of packets. If a Web server behind the firewall gets as many as 20,000 hits a minute, that amount of traffic could crash or at least seriously slow the firewall's performance, as well as other traffic that needs to pass through. If the Web server is outside the protected network but in the DMZ, the firewall's performance isn't compromised. To protect the local network, inbound connectivity from the Web server to the internal network should be blocked, and access attempts should be logged carefully.

Each server farm/DMZ can and should be protected by its own firewall or packet-filtering router. A possible configuration is shown in Figure 9-20. The service networks don't necessarily need to be protected from one another directly; instead, they all feed into a single router, which sends traffic into the internal network. The service subnets aren't connected directly to the Internet; a packet-filtering router screens each one.

A service network has also been established to allow resource sharing with a business partner. This network configuration should be handled with care, as some of the information being exchanged could be moderately sensitive; in this situation, placing a firewall between the packet-filtering router and the partner access subnet might be wise. As you learned in Chapters 5 and 6, a VPN can be a secure remote access solution. A screened DMZ is also sufficient, as long as the screening router is configured carefully, strict authentication methods are used, and access controls are placed on information at the file and folder level. Encryption of sensitive data can add another layer of protection.

Finally, an additional firewall is placed inside the internal network to protect network management systems. The advantage of locating management software out of band—outside the internal network on a protected subnet of its own—is that the management servers gain an extra level of protection from intruders. If intruders gain control of the firewall or network management software, they could potentially gain access to all hosts on the network.

9

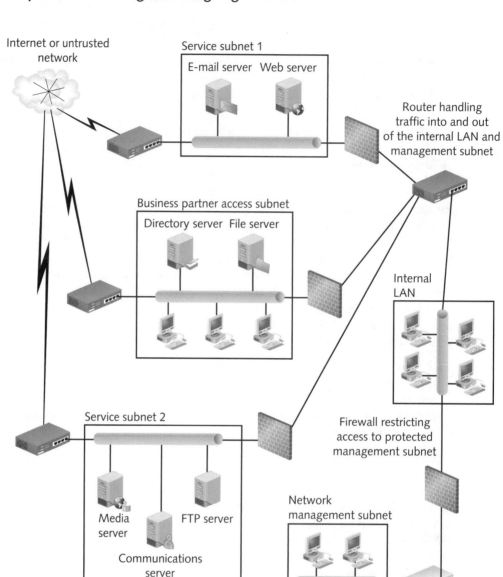

Figure 9-20 Multiple DMZs protected by multiple firewalls

A protected subnet within an already protected internal LAN could be used as an extra layer of protection for other types of confidential information, such as customer or personnel data. The extra protection might protect the servers from disgruntled employees in the organization, as well as attackers from the Internet.

Multiple Firewall Configurations

As you learned in Chapter 1, defense in depth (DiD) is a term used often in network security; it simply means multiple security devices configured to work together to provide protection. DiD makes use of many different layers of network security. To achieve this level of protection, many organizations find that they need more than one firewall, either throughout the network or on a particular subnet.

The following sections describe how two or more firewalls can be used to protect not only an internal network, but also one DMZ, two DMZs, and branch offices that need to connect to the main office's internal network. In addition, multiple firewalls can help you achieve load distribution that keeps heavy traffic flowing through the gateway smoothly.

Protecting a DMZ with Two or More Firewalls

When multiple firewalls are deployed around the perimeter of a network, they can work together to balance the traffic load into and out of the network. When two firewalls are used in tandem, they must be configured identically and use the same firewall software. That way, traffic coming from the Internet can be balanced between them by using routers or switches on either side, as shown in Figure 9-21.

In Figure 9-21, the two firewalls have an external interface on the Internet. You can also have a configuration in which one firewall has an interface on the Internet and the second has an interface on the internal LAN; the DMZ being protected is positioned between them. In any case, using two firewalls helps in the following ways:

- One firewall can control traffic between the DMZ and the Internet, and the other can control traffic between the protected LAN and the DMZ.

- The second firewall can serve as a **failover firewall**, which is a backup that can be configured to switch on if the first one fails, thus ensuring uninterrupted service for the organization.

One of the biggest advantages of setting up a DMZ with two firewalls is that you can control where traffic goes in the three networks you're dealing with: the external network outside the DMZ, the external network within the DMZ, and the internal network behind the DMZ. You can identify certain protocols, such as outbound HTTP port 80, that should go to the external network within the DMZ and allow other protocols to pass through to the internal network.

CAUTION

Using multiple interior routers to connect your DMZ subnet to parts of your internal subnets can cause problems. For example, using Routing Information Protocol (RIP) on an internal system could determine that the most direct route to another internal system is through the DMZ. As a result, confidential internal traffic flows across your DMZ, where it can be intercepted if an attacker manages to break into a host computer. Having multiple interior routers also makes overall network configuration more difficult.

9

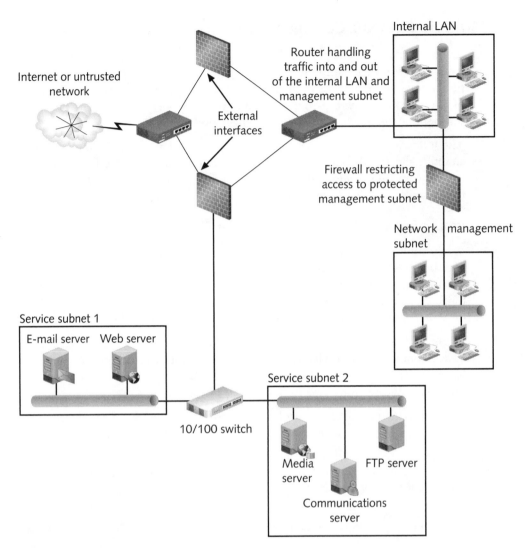

Figure 9-21 Two firewalls used for load balancing

Activity 9-5: Designing a Failover Firewall

Time Required: 15 minutes

Objective: Analyze a set of requirements and design a configuration to meet those requirements.

Description: Your organization's security policy calls for your Web site to be online 95% to 100% of the time, even during a firewall failure caused by a DoS attack or other problem. You know that one way to ensure the availability of the Web server and other publicly accessible computers in your DMZ is to protect them with two firewalls. What are the requirements for this setup? How might you configure the two firewalls?

_____

_____

_____

_____

_____

_____

Protecting Branch Offices with Multiple Firewalls

A multinational corporation that needs to share information among branch offices in outlying locations can communicate securely by using a single security policy implemented by multiple firewalls. The central office has its own centralized firewall, which directs traffic for branch offices and their firewalls. The central office develops the security policy and deploys it through the centralized firewall with its associated rules on a dedicated computer called a **security workstation** (see Figure 9-22). Each office has its own firewall, but the central office can develop and control the security policy. The policy is then copied to other firewalls in the corporation.

One notable aspect of Figure 9-22 is that the two firewalls have a path for communicating with one another and a router to direct traffic to each firewall. However, traffic from the Internet or the corporate LAN doesn't travel between the two firewalls; only traffic from the security workstation travels on the connection between the DMZs, carrying configuration information to the firewalls and receiving log file data from them.

Reverse Firewall

Some forward-thinking companies have taken to installing a **reverse firewall**, a device that monitors connections headed out of a network, instead of trying to block what's coming in. Sometimes the biggest threats facing an internal network come from its own users. Consider a university that makes certain applications available to researchers but restricts access to those applications to scientists who need them. Some clever computer science students might try to break into the server that stores these applications so that they can download and use them free. A reverse firewall would help by monitoring connection attempts out of a network that originate from internal users and then filtering out unauthorized attempts.

Reverse firewalls have other purposes. A company concerned about how its employees use the Web and other Internet services can set up a reverse firewall to log connections to Web sites. It can then block sites that are accessed repeatedly and considered unsuitable for employees to visit during work hours.

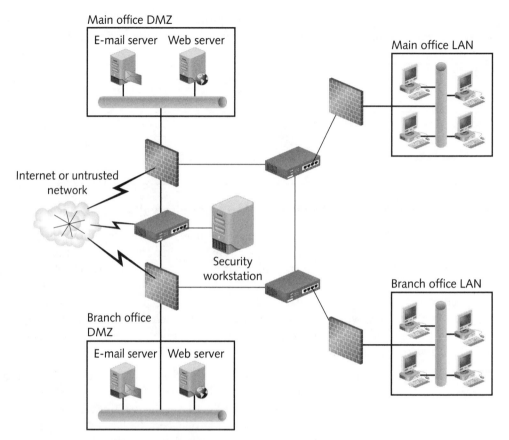

Figure 9-22   Multiple firewalls protecting branch offices

In a DoS attack, information floods out of the network from infected computers, thus overloading the network. A reverse firewall, such as the hardware device Reverse Firewall sold by Cs3 (*www.cs3-inc.com/rfw.html*), inspects outgoing packets and tracks where they're originating within the network. If many unexpected packets are noticed leaving the network, the firewall sends a notification to the network administrator. This feature, however, could be part of any firewall and programmed into a hardware or software firewall to avoid the need to purchase a specialized reverse firewall.

Much of this chapter assumes that you're building a firewall to protect your internal network from the Internet. However, you might also want to protect segments of your internal network from other segments, such as isolating lab or test networks. Some networks might need to be more secure than the rest of your site—for instance, where projects are being developed or where financial data or grades are stored. In these situations, internal firewalls can be positioned between two parts of the same organization or two separate organizations that share a network instead of between a single organization and the Internet. In this case, you need to set up packet-filtering rules that isolate the internal network being protected from the Internet and from your own bastion host. This way, if the bastion host is compromised, it won't lead to a compromise of the internal firewall. (Bastion hosts are covered in Chapter 10.)

Proxy servers also monitor traffic moving in the outbound direction—that is, from the internal LAN to the Internet. However, proxy servers have the advantage of shielding information about internal computers by hiding internal IP addresses.

Activity 9-6: Monitoring Outbound Network Traffic

Time Required: 20 minutes

Objective: Analyze a problem scenario to determine a solution.

Description: Your company is concerned about the amount of employee time spent surfing entertainment and shopping sites on the Web during office hours. You're asked to come up with a way to monitor and track (and possibly block) connections from hosts on the internal network trying to make outbound connections to the Internet. How could you do this with a firewall?

_____

_____

_____

_____

_____

_____

Which firewall configuration is the best one for your needs? Each has its advantages and disadvantages. It's important to remember that firewall setups aren't an either-or decision. You can combine a screened host with a multiple firewall setup, for instance; you can also have a reverse firewall in addition to a conventional firewall. The advantages and disadvantages of each setup are summarized in Table 9-12.

Table 9-12   Firewall configuration advantages and disadvantages

Configuration	Advantages	Disadvantages
Screening router	Simplicity, cost; good for home applications if a stateful packet filter is used	Provides only minimal protection; viruses, Trojan horses, and some malformed packets might get through
Dual-homed host	Simple, economical; can provide effective protection if configured correctly	Provides a single point of entry (and fault); firewall depends entirely on the host computer
Screened host	Provides two layers of protection for home and small business networks	Provides a single point of entry (and fault); firewall depends on the host computer and on the router that protects it
Screened subnet DMZ	Protects public servers by isolating them from the internal LAN	Servers in the DMZ are highly vulnerable and need to be hardened
Multiple DMZ/ firewalls	Provides layers of protection for a business network	Expensive
Single DMZ/two firewalls	Balances traffic load in heavy load situations	Expensive
Branch offices/ multiple firewalls	Provides protection for all offices in a corporate network as well as central administration	Firewalls must be purchased, installed, and configured at each office location
Reverse firewall	Monitors attack from inside the network; enables organizations to monitor user activity	Can slow down user access to external networks or other parts of the internal LAN

COMPARING SOFTWARE AND HARDWARE FIREWALLS

As a network administrator whose responsibilities include security for your organization, you'll be called on to evaluate firewall software and hardware packages and recommend the best choice for your company's needs. Firewalls come in many varieties, but they all handle the core functions: filtering, proxying, and logging. Some packages add "bells and whistles," such as caching and address translation. However, don't let price rule your decision. With some freeware products, you can perform some of the same functions as a more expensive commercial enterprise package.

The following sections show how the basic strategies and concepts governing firewalls are implemented in a range of software and hardware combinations you're likely to encounter in the workplace. This overview should help you choose your own package when the time comes. The discussion is divided into software and hardware.

Software-Based Firewalls

The kinds of firewalls most people are familiar with consist solely of firewall software. They can be combined with hardware devices to create an extra-secure checkpoint. The downside of software-based firewalls is that they require a lot of administration to configure the software and secure the OS through patches or removal of vulnerable services. On the other hand, they also tend to be less expensive than hardware firewalls and, therefore, are easier to deploy in multiple locations. Security professionals often debate the question of whether software firewalls are more secure than hardware firewalls. Many believe the level of security depends more on the skill in configuring the firewall and the regularity of maintenance and updates than the specific program or device.

Free Firewall Programs

Free firewall programs aren't perfect. Their logging capabilities aren't as robust as some commercial products, and configuration can be difficult. In addition, they might not include a way to monitor traffic passing through the firewall in real time or to manage firewall settings for a network of computers from a centralized location. Nonetheless, they have a place in small-business and home networks because of their convenience, simplicity, and unbeatable price (free!). Some popular free firewall programs include the following:

- *Netfilter*—This firewall software, which comes with the Linux 2.4 kernel, is a powerful solution for stateless and stateful packet filtering, NAT, and packet processing. Netfilter is good at logging copious information about traffic in a well-organized, easy-to-review manner. For more information, visit *www.netfilter.org*.

- *ZoneAlarm*—The free version of this firewall program (which you installed in Activity 9-1) is so effective that you might lose your Internet connectivity when you first set it up. Correct configuration to allow just the software and IP addresses you want is critical to maintaining Internet connectivity.

- *Sygate Personal Firewall*—An excellent program for general home use, it includes extensive logs containing header information about packets. You can also configure packet-filtering rules. You can find Sygate products at *www.sygate.com*.

Some of these programs are stripped-down versions of more elaborate products from the same companies. You can try an evaluation version of these programs (ZoneAlarm Pro and Sygate Personal Firewall Pro) and then decide whether to purchase them.

Commercial Firewall Software: Personal Firewalls

Personal firewall products are located between the Ethernet adapter driver of the machine on which they're installed and the TCP/IP stack, where they inspect traffic going between the driver and the stack. They include programs such as the following:

- *Norton Personal Firewall*—This excellent, easy-to-use program for home users comes as a standalone product or as part of the Norton Internet Security package with antivirus software. You can download Norton Personal Firewall at *www.symantec.com/sabu/nis/npf/*.

- *ZoneAlarm Pro*—Along with firewall software, you get antivirus protection and the capability to block pop-up ads and cookies. ZoneAlarm and ZoneAlarm Pro can be downloaded from *www.zonelabs.com*.

- *BlackICE PC Protection*—This program combines intrusion detection with firewall functionality. Information and downloads can be found at *www.digitalriver.com/dr/v2/ec_dynamic.main?SP=1&PN=10&sid=26412.*

- *Sygate Personal Firewall Pro*—Along with firewall and intrusion detection, this program can do content filtering; it matches attack patterns to block possible intrusions. You can find more information on it at *http://smb.sygate.com/products/pspf/pspf_ov.htm.*

Despite the features in the preceding list, these well-known personal firewall products are considered "lightweight" in terms of firewall protection. Some work with multiple protocols, but most guard only against IP threats. Some programs don't handle outbound connection blocking, and others do. Some are inconvenient to configure because they don't work on a "configure as you compute" basis. Instead, you set a general security level (such as Cautious, Nervous, or Paranoid), and the software adjusts its security settings accordingly.

Commercial Firewall Software: Enterprise Firewalls

Enterprise firewalls are programs that come with a centralized management option and sometimes the capability to install multiple instances of the software from a centralized location. Following are some examples:

- PGP Desktop 9.0 is a combined firewall and encryption package that makes use of Pretty Good Privacy (PGP) encryption; it's available from PGP Corporation (*www.pgp.com*). One disadvantage is pricing: A one-year license costs $79, and a "perpetual license" costs $199 for a single user at the time of this writing.

- Check Point NG (*www.checkpoint.com*) is a suite of management and configuration tools for real-time monitoring, remote administration, and log file analysis.

- The Proventia security products (*www.iss.net/products_services/products.php*) by Internet Security Systems, Inc., offer a variety of security tools and packages with an emphasis on centralized management for enterprise applications.

- Novell's BorderManager (*www.novell.com/products/bordermanager*) uses a proxy server to protect employees and give employers a way to monitor employees' online activities.

Firewalls that used to consist primarily of packet-filtering tools have added user authentication, NAT, encryption, and centralized management to their list of features to stay ahead in an increasingly competitive market.

Hardware Firewalls

One advantage of hardware firewalls is that they don't depend on a conventional OS, such as Windows, Solaris, or Linux, which can provide openings through bugs or other flaws. On the other hand, hardware firewalls *do* run on an operating system—some of Cisco's hardware firewalls run on Cisco's own Internetwork Operating System (IOS), for instance—and they can be subject to the same sorts of flaws as computer OSs. Hardware firewall devices are generally more scalable than software firewalls, and they can handle more data with faster throughput. On the downside, hardware firewalls tend to be more expensive than software products.

Hybrid Firewalls

A **hybrid firewall** combines aspects of hardware and software firewalls in one package. As a hardware appliance, it can offer high performance. However, it can also perform functions normally available only in software firewalls, such as protection against DoS attacks or even integrated antivirus scanning. A hybrid solution is a good choice in a large-scale organization, where the appliance needs to protect hundreds or even thousands of users and provide good throughput and virus protection.

Which firewall product is best for your needs? That depends on the number of users you plan to protect, the amount of network traffic that needs to pass through the firewall, your budget, and your overall level of concern about security. Budget shouldn't always be the primary consideration. An inexpensive software program can quickly become inadequate as a network grows. It pays to buy the strongest program you can afford at the outset. Table 9-13 lists some advantages and disadvantages you should consider when determining whether to choose a hardware or software product.

Table 9-13   Firewall advantages and disadvantages

Type of Firewall	Advantages	Disadvantages
Software—freeware	Unbeatable price; small file size; ease of installation	Only a minimal set of features is offered; lack of technical support
Software—commercial personal firewalls	Simple to install; economical price; auto-configuration features help novice users	Not as full-featured as enterprise products; not as robust as appliances; tend to be installed on single-computer systems, which reduces security
Software—commercial enterprise firewalls	Usually installed on dedicated host for maximum security; centralized administration available for large networks; real-time monitoring and other administrative features	Can be difficult to install and configure
Hardware appliances	More scalable than software firewalls, and can handle faster throughput	Can be very expensive, and difficult to patch if bugs or security alerts require it
Hybrid firewall	Provides throughput and security of an appliance with features of a software firewall	Just as expensive or more expensive than other appliances

CHAPTER SUMMARY

❑ A firewall is hardware or software that can be configured to block unauthorized access to a network. A firewall is actually a combination of multiple software and hardware components, and the term "firewall" can refer to all the devices positioned on the perimeter of a network, whether they are hardware or software based.

❑ Firewalls aren't a standalone solution, so they shouldn't be regarded as the only tool you need to protect a network. Strong network security architecture encompasses many components, including IDSs, firewalls, antivirus software, access control, and auditing.

❑ Firewalls are effective only if they are configured correctly to block undesirable traffic and allow necessary traffic to pass. An effective firewall rule base should be based on the organization's security policy, provide rules for how applications can access the Internet, and be as simple and short as possible. The rule base should also restrict access to ports and subnets on the internal network from the Internet and control Internet services.

❑ You can use several different firewall configurations to protect a network. You can set up a simple packet-filtering router that screens your network, but this setup offers only minimal security. A dual-homed host that runs a firewall is more secure, but the combination of a packet-filtering router and a dual-homed host provides layers of security and is more effective. Multiple firewalls can be used for load balancing or for protecting different branch networks within an organization. In addition, a reverse firewall can be used to monitor communications from the internal network to the Internet.

❑ Software firewalls come in many varieties: freeware, shareware, and enterprise. Hardware firewall "appliances" are more expensive, but they can handle more traffic. Hybrid firewalls combine the scalability of hardware devices with content filtering that's normally provided only by software firewalls.

KEY TERMS

cleanup rule — A packet-filtering rule that comes last in a rule base; it covers any other packets that haven't been covered in preceding rules.

customize access — Identify criteria for a firewall to allow a connection request, instead of allowing the firewall to deny or allow all requests automatically.

dual-homed host — A computer that has been configured with more than one network interface.

failover firewall — A backup firewall that can be configured to switch on if the first one fails, thus ensuring uninterrupted service for the organization.

firewall — Hardware or software that can be configured to block unauthorized access to a network.

firewall appliances — Hardware devices that have firewall functionality.

firewall policy — An addition to a security policy that describes how firewalls should handle application traffic, such as Web or e-mail applications.

hybrid firewall — A product that combines aspects of both firewall appliances and software firewalls in one package.

load-balancing software — Software that prioritizes and schedules requests and distributes them to a group of servers based on each machine's current load and processing power.

Open Platform for Security (OPSEC) — A protocol developed by Check Point Technologies that enables its firewall products to integrate with software that provides antivirus protection, intrusion detection, and other solutions.

reverse firewall — A device that monitors information going out of a network rather than trying to block what's coming in.

rule base — A set of rules for telling a firewall what action to take when a certain kind of traffic attempts to pass through.

screened host — Similar to a dual-homed host, but the main difference is that a router is often added between the host and the Internet to carry out IP packet filtering.

screening router — A router placed between the Internet and the protected LAN that determines whether to allow or deny packets based on their source and destination IP addresses or other information in their headers.

security workstation — A dedicated computer that deploys a security policy through a centralized firewall to other firewalls that protect branch offices or other networks in the organization.

server farm — A group of servers connected in their own subnet that work together to receive a large number of requests; the load is distributed among all the servers.

stateful packet filters — Similar to stateless packet filters, except stateful packet filters also determine whether to allow or block packets based on information maintained about current connections.

stateless packet filters — A simple filter that decides whether to allow or block packets based on information in the protocol headers.

state table — A file maintained by stateful packet filters that contains a record of all current connections.

three-pronged firewall — A firewall that has three separate interfaces—for example, one to a DMZ, one to the Internet, and one to the internal LAN.

9

REVIEW QUESTIONS

1. A firewall can do which of the following? (Choose all that apply.)

   a. Screen traffic for viruses.

   b. Prevent theft of proprietary information.

   c. Filter traffic based on rules.

   d. Provide a layer of protection for the network.

2. What is the primary difference between a screened host and a dual-homed host setup?

   a. A dual-homed host has two network interface cards.

   b. IP forwarding is disabled.

   c. A packet filter shields the screened host.

   d. The host is screened by a firewall.

3. A firewall is an effective standalone security solution. True or False?

4. What is the main problem with a screening router setup?

   a. The router can be configured incorrectly.

   b. The router might not provide an adequate screen.

   c. The router can't be used with a firewall.

   d. The router alone can't stop many types of attacks.

5. Name three functions that most firewalls can't handle that need to be performed by additional software products.

6. What enables servers in a server farm to work together to handle requests?

   a. a router

   b. a switch

   c. a network hub

   d. load-balancing software

7. Why would a company consider the expense and extra work of purchasing and installing clusters of servers and creating multiple DMZs?

   a. The network can handle high traffic better.

   b. The company can put more information online.

   c. The company improves security.

   d. The company gains another layer of defense.

8. Why create a protected subnet within an already protected internal network? (Choose all that apply.)

   a. to protect Web servers

   b. to protect customer information

   c. to protect management servers

   d. to protect the company's reputation

9. Stateless packet filters allow or block packets based on which of the following?

   a. status of the connection

   b. information in protocol headers

   c. state table

   d. packets that have been handled previously

10. A corporation with several branch offices has decided to maintain multiple firewalls, one to protect each branch office's network. What's the most efficient way to maintain these firewalls?

   a. Use a centralized security workstation.

   b. Send security policy information to each network administrator.

   c. Set up remote desktop management software, such as pcAnywhere.

   d. Broadcast configuration instructions periodically by e-mail.

11. Software or hardware configured to monitor traffic from the internal network to the Internet is called which of the following? (Choose all that apply.)

   a. stateful packet filter

   b. proxy server

   c. reverse firewall

   d. Network Address Translation (NAT)

12. Which of the following is an advantage of using a software firewall rather than a hardware firewall?

   a. throughput

   b. reliability

   c. cost

   d. availability

13. Which of the following is an advantage of using a hardware firewall rather than a software firewall? (Choose all that apply.)

   a. scalability

   b. cost

   c. ease of maintenance

   d. increased throughput

14. Almost every type of firewall depends on what configurable feature for its effectiveness?

   a. network connection

   b. state table

   c. rule base

   d. management console

9

15. Given that many kinds of network traffic can pass through a network gateway, what's the problem with creating a long complex rule base designed to handle every possible situation? (Choose all that apply.)

    a. disk space

    b. slower performance

    c. danger of misconfiguration

    d. danger of missing attack attempts

16. Where should the most important rules in a rule base go?

    a. in the connection log file

    b. at the bottom of the rule base

    c. in the state table

    d. at the top of the rule base

17. Which of the following is a guideline for developing a firewall rule base?

    a. The rule base should restrict all Internet access.

    b. The rule base should restrict access to ports and subnets on the internal network from the Internet.

    c. The rule base should be as detailed as possible.

    d. The rule base should not interfere with application traffic.

18. A firewall policy does which of the following? (Choose all that apply.)

    a. Describes how employees can use the firewall.

    b. Identifies and mitigates the risks an organization faces.

    c. Explains how the firewall is set up, managed, and updated.

    d. Details how the firewall should handle application traffic.

19. A rule base should end with a(n) _____ rule.

    a. reject

    b. allow

    c. cleanup

    d. block

20. The rule base should allow internal clients unrestricted and unfiltered Internet access. True or False?

HANDS-ON PROJECTS

Hands-On Project 9-1: Creating a Firewall Configuration Diagram

Time Required: 30 minutes

Objective: Diagram firewall configuration designs.

Description: When you're called on to create and install a firewall configuration for a network, you need to be able to create a diagram showing how the system will be set up. A diagram can be useful at the planning phase or when you're proposing a security setup for the network.

1. Draw a diagram of a screening router configuration. Use a simple circle or rectangle to represent the LAN being protected.

2. Draw a dual-homed host configuration. Be sure to label the external and internal interfaces of the dual-homed host.

3. Draw a screened host configuration. Again, be sure to label the external and internal interfaces of the screened host.

CASE PROJECTS

Case Project 9-1: Setting up Layers of Defense for High-Traffic Networks

You install a firewall at the perimeter of your company network and create a DMZ that contains a Web server and FTP server, so that visitors can access your Web site and download trial and commercial versions of your company's software. Over time, your company's products gain in popularity to the point that your Web server is receiving several thousand hits per hour. Diagram a setup that would enable your Web server to handle a steadily increasing amount of traffic yet still provide security for the internal LAN.

Case Project 9-2: Designing a Perimeter Network for LedGrafix

LedGrafix management is pleased with the work you have done so far, and the network design is almost finished. In your last progress meeting, the vice president said the company is interested in making its products available via Internet download with an e-commerce server-processing payments. He expressed concern about the security aspects of this goal and wants you to incorporate a security framework to support this goal. Your job is to create a "placeholder" in the network for the servers when they're ready. The VP also asked if you could make sure the company would be able to add an FTP server, an e-mail server, and other functions to the network without compromising security.

Before you begin, you need your most recent network design and risk analysis.

1. First, you need a firewall policy to guide you in developing and deploying a solution. Remember that a firewall policy tells you how the firewall is set up, managed, and updated; the policy also tells you how application traffic should be handled, which certainly includes Web traffic. Draft an initial firewall policy.

2. Create an application traffic matrix. Refer back to Table 9-3 for help, if needed. Which applications are needed? Which direction does traffic from each application need to travel and how should that traffic be controlled in each direction? (*Hint*: Your risk-analysis documentation should contain most of this information.)

3. Based on your firewall policy, the traffic matrix, and the stated requirements for security of Web and e-commerce servers (allowing for scalability), draft a basic rule base for inbound and outbound traffic.

4. Now examine your current design. How can you incorporate a Web server and an e-commerce server yet allow for future growth and controlled access from internal and external sources?

5. What software do you need? What equipment do you need to purchase? (Remember to include items such as additional IDS sensors.)

6. Modify your network design to reflect your solution. (Remember to update previous installations, such as IDS sensors and remote access, to account for the revision.)

TIP
Use your network diagram and plenty of scratch paper to chart the current logical and physical flow of traffic. This helps you visualize where controls must be placed and how rules should work. Don't try to visualize the entire network at once; start with a single piece, such as a logical segment or physical office. Follow the flow of traffic through the internal network, being careful to account for mobile devices or unauthorized connections. Next, follow the flow of traffic outbound from all internal locations, noting all interfaces leading out of the trusted network. Then follow the flow of traffic inbound. Remember that you don't need to secure everything through hardware. File and folder level permissions, group and role access controls, and authentication play an important role, too.

Make sure you review your design for accuracy and update your policies and procedures. Be prepared to justify your choices and include any references used. When you have finished proofreading your documents, submit them as directed by your instructor. For this project, you should submit the following:

- Firewall policy draft
- Application traffic matrix

- Draft rule base

- Hardware and software inventory listing everything needed to deploy this solution

- Updated network design

As the end of this book (and your course) draws near, you should continue to refine all documentation completed for submission in final draft form at the end of the course. If you haven't already started this process, don't wait until the last minute! You might also want to review your school's policies on formatting technical papers and academic honesty and review any other presentation requirements your instructor might have.

9

10

FIREWALL TOPOLOGY

After reading this chapter and completing the exercises, you will be able to:

♦ Explain the goal of securing the network perimeter

♦ Describe factors in choosing a bastion host

♦ Explain how to supplement a firewall with a proxy server

♦ Set up Network Address Translation (NAT)

♦ Decide when to use user, session, or client authentication

After you have determined the best firewall configuration for your network defense needs, you can get down to the details of configuring the perimeter network to carry out tasks to protect your entire network. First, you learn how to work with proxy servers to make network defense more effective, and then you review factors in choosing a bastion host for your network.

Depending on the type of firewall you've installed, you can also set up Network Address Translation (NAT) and authentication. In fact, firewalls are now handling more security activities than in the past.

SECURING NETWORK PERIMETERS

You've learned about traffic signatures, VPNs, intrusion detection systems (IDSs), and firewalls. In this chapter, you see how all these components are combined in the network perimeter to protect the internal LAN and to provide and protect services in the DMZ. Businesses need a variety of services within their LANs and on the Internet. They also need a network area where resource access is more flexible, allowing internal hosts and external systems to gain access. The problem is providing adequate access without jeopardizing confidential or mission-critical areas. To accomplish this goal, perimeter networks host Web, e-commerce, FTP, remote access services, databases, DNS servers, and more. Securing these systems requires firewalls, but firewalls can't do the job alone.

To design a secure perimeter network, you must understand how firewalls, IDSs, and other security measures are combined with bastion hosts, Network Address Translation (NAT), proxy servers, and authentication methods to provide the versatility needed for secure productivity. A bastion host can provide Web, FTP, e-mail, or other services running on a specially secured server. Proxy servers can enhance performance; more importantly, they enhance security by hiding internal clients from the outside world. NAT performs a function similar to proxies and allows the use of private IP addresses in the LAN, conserving scarce public IP addresses. Authentication and encryption also play a prominent role in security, giving remote users a way to access resources from locations outside the network.

In the following sections, you learn how to select, harden, and use bastion hosts in a perimeter network to provide the services businesses rely on. Then, you see how proxy servers can enhance your perimeter network security and improve performance for internal hosts. Next, you learn the function of NAT and how to use NAT modes. Finally, you explore authentication methods in more depth and learn other methods of setting up remote access.

CHOOSING A BASTION HOST

Security software doesn't operate on its own. You install it on a computer that runs on an OS platform; this computer needs to be as secure as possible because of the important security software on it and its position on the network perimeter. Often, the computer also functions as a server providing Web pages, e-mail, or other services to users inside and outside the network being protected. This practice is discouraged because of vulnerabilities introduced with the complexity of configuring this type of system; however, small companies might not have the resources to host these services separately. In this situation, the company should consider hiring a security specialist.

To protect security software as well as the network, the computer needs to be turned into a **bastion host**, a computer that sits on the network perimeter and has been specially protected through OS patches, authentication, and encryption. A computer hosting a firewall that's riddled with OS vulnerabilities gives attackers a way to compromise the entire network. They might even be able to disable firewall software if they can gain administrative privileges or crack passwords on the server.

The following sections describe how to choose and configure a bastion host that can safely host firewall or other security software: how to choose the machine, how to limit its functionality so that it discourages attackers, and how to handle backups and auditing.

General Requirements

In general, a bastion host should be a computer running an OS that is already secure or has been in release long enough that patches for potential security vulnerabilities are available. When the OS is made as secure as possible, the computer is said to be **hardened**, or more secure than any others on the network, by eliminating all unnecessary software and services, closing potential openings, and protecting the information on it with encryption and authentication.

In general, these are the steps in creating a bastion host (covered in more detail in the following sections):

1. Select a machine with sufficient memory and processor speed.

2. Choose and install the OS and any patches or updates.

3. Determine where the bastion host will fit in the network configuration, and make sure it's in a safe and controlled physical environment.

4. Install the services you want to provide or modify existing services.

5. Remove services and accounts that aren't needed.

6. Back up the system and all data on it, including log files.

7. Run a security audit.

8. Connect the machine to the network.

Selecting the Bastion Host Machine

You don't need to select the latest hardware and software combination to configure a bastion host. Instead, you should choose a combination of machine type and software that you're familiar with and can work with easily. You don't want to be repairing or rebuilding a machine under pressure and learning to operate it at the same time.

In an ideal situation, you can designate one host for each service you want to provide to the public: one FTP server/bastion host, one Web server/bastion host, one SMTP server/ bastion host, and so on. However, buying and installing so much hardware can be prohibitively expensive. Budget constraints might force you to combine two or more services on one bastion host. In this case, a comprehensive risk analysis of the services and hardware you need to protect the most can be helpful. (See Chapter 2 for a review of risk analysis.) The following sections discuss essential components of a secure bastion host: the operating system, memory and processor speed, and location on the network.

Operating System

The most important requirements for a bastion host are your own level of comfort with the operating system and its inherent security and reliability. Management probably isn't concerned about what OS you install; from a management perspective, the priority is that the machine protects the internal network and you can get it running and maintain it easily.

Running a close second is the security level of the OS. Whatever OS you decide on, be sure to pick a version that's stable and secure. To ensure its security, check the operating system's development Web site (as shown in the following list) for a list of patches, and update any that are available:

- Windows Server 2003 (*www.microsoft.com/windowsserver2003/default.mspx*)
- Red Hat Linux (*www.redhat.com*)
- Linux (*www.linux.org*)
- FreeBSD Project (*www.freebsd.org*)
- SANS Institute's list of the Top Twenty Most Critical Internet Security Vulnerabilities, which includes subsections on UNIX and Windows vulnerabilities (*www.sans.org/top20.htm*)
- U.S. Department of Energy's Computer Incident Advisory Capability (CIAC) site (*www.ciac.org/ciac*), which lists newly discovered security advisories on its home page

Memory and Processor Speed

Bastion hosts don't need to have the most recent or expensive memory-processor combinations. Memory is always important when operating a server, but because the bastion host might be providing only a single service, you aren't likely to need several gigabytes worth of RAM. You might, however, need to match processing power to the server load, which could mean simply upgrading the processor or perhaps adding processors.

Location on the Network

Bastion hosts are typically located outside the internal network and are frequently combined with packet-filtering devices on either side, as shown in Figure 10-1. Combining a bastion host with packet-filtering devices (such as routers and firewall appliances) further protects the bastion host from attack; these devices can filter tampered-with packets from reaching the bastion host in the first place. In addition, a packet-filtering server (proxy server) can filter out any suspicious packets coming from *inside* the network as a result of Trojan programs or viruses that have circumvented existing network defenses.

More often, multiple bastion hosts are set up in the DMZ, where each machine provides a single service to the public (see Figure 10-2). This configuration is more secure because you can allow general access to the Web server yet limit access to the mail server to only employees.

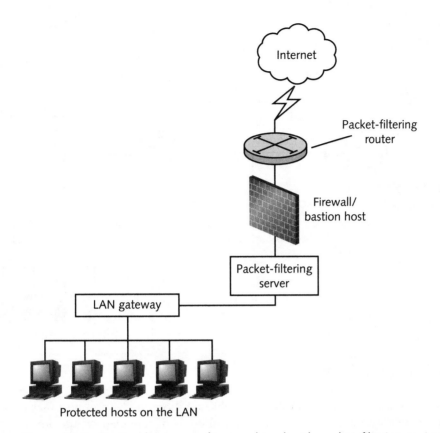

Figure 10-1   Bastion hosts are often combined with packet-filtering routers

Hardening the Bastion Host

A bastion host can be any server that hosts a Web server, an e-mail server, an FTP server, or other network service. However, the more services offered on the bastion host, the higher the chance of a security vulnerability in a service installed on the system.

Therefore, one way to harden a bastion host is by removing all unnecessary software, services, and user accounts. The simpler your bastion host is, the easier it is to secure. In addition, any service the bastion host offers could have software bugs or configuration errors, which could lead to security problems. Only the minimum number of services and open ports should be available on the network to give intruders fewer opportunities to exploit these ports.

Selecting Services to Provide

A bare-bones configuration reduces the chance of attacks and has the extra benefit of boosting efficiency. By closing unnecessary ports and disabling user accounts and services you don't plan to use, you give attackers far fewer ways to gain access to the system. Perhaps

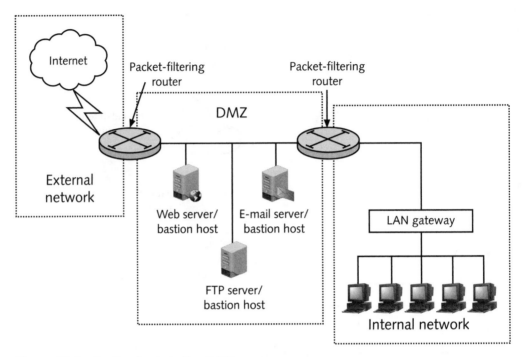

Figure 10-2   Bastion hosts in the DMZ

the most important services you should disable are those the bastion host uses to perform routing or IP forwarding—unless, of course, the host is intended to function as a router. Disabling IP forwarding makes it more difficult for attackers to communicate with internal computers on your LAN.

When you're stopping or removing services, you should not disable any **dependency services**—services the system needs to function correctly. For example, the Telnet service should be disabled in most cases; normally, it's not required by other services. The RPC service, however, shouldn't be disabled because almost everything else depends on it to function correctly. In addition, stopping services one at a time to see what effect it might have on the system is advisable. You should also get in the habit of documenting every change you make and recording how the system reacts, so that you have a record in case you're called on to troubleshoot that system later. This documentation process, called **change management**, could be added as a requirement of your security policy.

Activity 10-1: Limiting Unnecessary Services

Time Required: 15 minutes

Objective: Stop unnecessary services to reduce security vulnerabilities.

Description: When setting up a bastion host, one important task is to stop any unnecessary services running on that machine. Often, an OS has a number of services running by default that you don't really need; for example, a Windows XP system with a typical setup might have as many as 80 services running at one time. The following steps show you how to inventory and stop running services on a Windows XP computer.

1. Open Control Panel, and in Category view, click **Performance and Maintenance**.

2. Click **Administrative Tools**, and then double-click **Services**. If necessary, click the **Standard** tab at the bottom of the Services dialog box.

3. Scroll down the list of services and see whether there are any you don't need. (You might want to check Microsoft's Web site for full product documentation of Windows XP to find out whether you can safely disable a service.) For instance, check Routing and Remote Access. If this service is listed as Started in the Status column, double-click it.

4. In the Routing and Remote Access Properties dialog box, click the **Stop** button to stop the service.

5. Click **Disabled** in the Startup type drop-down list to stop the service from restarting automatically in the future.

6. Click **OK** to close the Routing and Remote Access Properties dialog box and return to the Services dialog box.

7. Repeat Steps 3 through 6 for other services you want to stop.

8. When you're done, close all open windows to return to the Windows desktop. Leave your system running for the next activity.

Using Honeypots

A **honeypot** is a computer placed on the network perimeter to attract attackers so that they stay away from critical servers on the network (see Figure 10-3); it may or may not be a bastion host. This computer is equipped with software and, possibly, data files that look like they're used by the company but are not, in reality, used at all. A honeypot might also be configured with some security holes so that it seems vulnerable to known attacks. A honeypot can be located between the bastion host and the internal network; if an attacker manages to get past the external packet filter to the DMZ and is scanning for open ports, the honeypot could act as a place for the attacker to get "stuck" (in other words, diverted from your real files by being misdirected to files that are of no value).

Network security experts are divided over honeypots. Some think they have value; some think they are outdated and not worth using; some think they are unnecessary and even potentially dangerous if they contain actual information about your company and its bastion hosts. Laws on the use of honeypots are confusing at best; consult your legal department before setting one up to avoid possible legal violations. Honeypots are worth mentioning not only because you're likely to be asked about them in certification tests, but also because they are still discussed as options in a perimeter security configuration.

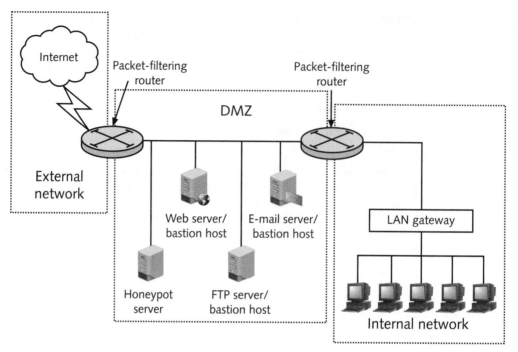

Figure 10-3   A honeypot in the DMZ

Another goal of a honeypot is logging. Because you expect that intruders who can't tell the difference between the honeypot and a legitimate target will attack it, you can configure the honeypot to log every access attempt to identify who's trying to attack your network. Because your employees aren't accessing resources in the honeypot, any access attempt is probably from an attacker. A honeypot can also give you some indication of how someone might try to attack your real network computers. By reviewing what OS flaws, open ports, or other vulnerabilities are exploited on the honeypot, you can take steps to address these vulnerabilities on other machines.

Disabling User Accounts

Default accounts are sometimes created during installation of OSs and application software, and some of these accounts have blank or default passwords. Accordingly, you should delete or disable all user accounts from the bastion host. They aren't needed because users shouldn't be able to connect to the bastion host from their computers. Each user account on the bastion host increases the chances of a security breach.

You should also rename the Administrator account as another way to thwart intruders. Many attackers can gain access to computers through Administrator accounts that use the default account name "Administrator" and are never assigned a password. Renaming these accounts and using passwords of at least six or eight alphanumeric characters can prevent these types of attacks.

It's a good idea to assume that the bastion host will be compromised in some way and then take proactive steps to secure it. The bastion host is the machine most likely to be attacked because of its availability to external Internet users.

NOTE

Activity 10-2: Eliminating Unnecessary Accounts

ACTIVITY

Time Required: 10 minutes

Objective: Delete or disable unnecessary user accounts.

Description: Another important aspect of creating a bastion host is eliminating user accounts you don't need that give attackers potential vulnerabilities they can exploit. Often, the Guest account on Windows systems gives attackers a way to get in. In addition, you should have only one Administrator account. The following steps show you how to eliminate or disable unnecessary accounts on a Windows XP computer.

1. Open Control Panel in Category view, and click **User Accounts**.

2. If you see the text "Guest account is on" at the bottom of the User Accounts window, click **Guest**. The User Accounts window for the Guest account opens. Click the **Turn off the guest account** link. The account is disabled, and you're returned to the previous User Accounts window.

3. If you see more than one account labeled Computer administrator, decide which administrator account you want to keep. Click the others in succession. In the next User Accounts window, click **Delete the account** or **Change the account type** to reduce access privileges.

4. Close Control Panel and return to the Windows desktop. Leave your system running for the next activity.

Handling Backups and Auditing

Setting up a bastion host requires being more systematic and thorough than you might be used to; backups, detailed recordkeeping, and auditing are essential steps in hardening a computer.

Bastion hosts can generate a lot of log files and other data (such as alert messages). You need to copy this information to other computers in your network regularly. When you do this recordkeeping, keep in mind that the information goes through some layers of network defense you have set up already. Because of its high security configuration, your bastion host will probably be in a vulnerable location on the DMZ and outside the internal LAN. Log files and system data, which need to be backed up regularly, should go through the firewall protecting the internal LAN to screen them for viruses and other vulnerabilities, such as manipulated packets. (Recall that attackers might insert falsified information into those packets to enable them to access computers on the internal LAN.)

10

Auditing should be configured for all failed and successful attempts to log on to the bastion host and any attempts to access or change files. Administrators rarely have enough time to review log files, but you should make time every day to review logs for any devices in the DMZ, as well as your routers and packet-filtering servers. These logs can give you advance warning of intrusion attempts.

To avoid using network resources, be sure that machines used as bastion hosts have CD-RW drives, removable disk drives, or tape drives so that you can make backups.

NOTE

WORKING WITH PROXY SERVERS

Your organization's security policy might call for installing a proxy server—software that forwards packets to and from the network being protected and caches Web pages to speed up network performance. For many organizations, a proxy server is the only type of firewall installed, except for the company's router. The following sections describe the goals of setting up a proxy server and explain how proxy servers work, how to choose a proxy server, and how proxy servers can filter content for your network.

Proxy servers provide effective protection because they work at the application layer of the OSI model. They can interpret what application is being used to make a request and forward the request on behalf of that application. In contrast, firewalls primarily interpret IP and TCP header information at the lower OSI levels.

NOTE

Goals of Proxy Servers

Originally, speeding up network communications was the primary goal of proxy servers. The process, shown in Figure 10-4, works like this: As Web pages are requested from a company's Web server, the proxy server receives the Web pages and forwards them to the computer making the request. At the same time, it caches the page's text and image files—in other words, stores those files on disk for later retrieval if needed. Computers requesting the same Web page more than once have their requests received by the proxy server rather than the Web server. The proxy server checks its cache for the Web page being requested and compares the page's contents against the contents of the page currently published on the Web server. If no changes are found, the files are retrieved from the cache rather than from the original Web server. Storing documents in disk cache reduces the load on the Web server and speeds up network traffic.

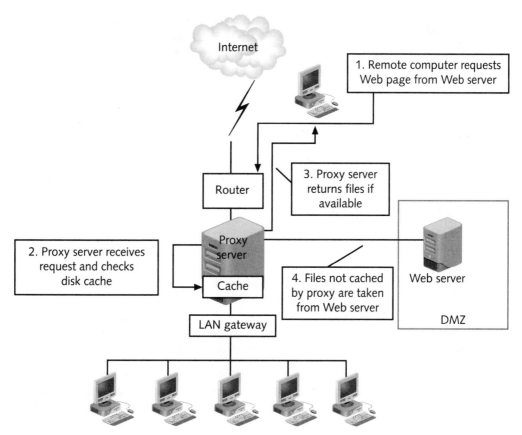

Figure 10-4   Proxy servers cache Web pages and other files

TIP   Microsoft Internet Security and Acceleration (ISA) Server also caches documents to speed up network performance and is discussed in Chapter 11.

The primary goal of proxy servers these days is to provide security at the application layer and shield hosts on the internal network. A secondary goal is controlling the Web sites users are allowed to access. Proxy servers can use IP addresses or domain names to block access to specific Web sites or to entire top-level domains. For example, an administrator could allow access to only the .gov top-level domain so that employees can view government forms online.

CAUTION

Many proxy servers come with default configurations that enable users to access the Internet using multiple services. However, these default configurations can open security holes. They might be set up to enable Telnet access, for example, or enable Web access around the clock, which most users don't need. For better security, you might want to disable services that most users don't need.

How Proxy Servers Work

Network-layer packet filters look only at the header part of a TCP/IP packet. Their goal is to block unauthorized packets and allow only authorized packets to reach their destination. If packets are authorized, the packet filter enables host and client computers to communicate with one another directly.

In contrast, the goal of proxy servers is to prevent a direct connection between an external computer and an internal computer. One way proxy servers do this is by working at the application layer. When a request is received from an internal computer, the proxy server opens the packet and examines the data. If, for example, the request is for a Web page and uses the standard GET method, the proxy server reconstructs the packet and forwards it to the requested Web server, acting as a proxy Web browser. By acting at the application layer, the proxy server can interpret which application was originally used to make a request and which application is needed to forward that request.

What does it mean to "reconstruct" a packet? When a proxy server receives a request, it opens the packet, examines the contents, and replaces the original header with a new header containing the proxy's own IP address instead of the original client's. An example is shown in Figure 10-5.

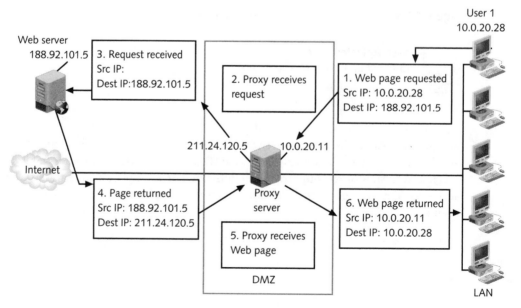

Figure 10-5   Proxy servers replace source IP addresses with their own addresses

As you can see in Figure 10-5, the proxy server is in the DMZ. The following procedure occurs:

1. User 1 requests the Web page at IP address 188.92.101.5.

2. The proxy server receives a request from User 1's Web browser in the internal LAN, examines the request, and strips off the packet header. The proxy server replaces the header with its own public-source IP address before sending the packet on its way.

3. The Web server receiving the request interprets it as coming from the proxy server's IP address instead of from User 1's computer. In fact, the Web server (or an attacker who intercepts the request) has no way of knowing that User 1's computer exists.

4. The Web server then sends its response with the Web page to the proxy server.

5. The response goes through the proxy server for processing, and the IP header sent by the Web server is replaced.

6. The proxy server sends the requested Web page to User 1's computer, where the browser displays it.

The proxy server is configured to receive traffic before it goes to the Internet; client programs, such as Web browsers and e-mail applications, are configured to connect to the proxy rather than the Internet. A typical browser configuration is shown in Figure 10-6.

10

Figure 10-6   Configuring client programs to connect to the proxy server rather than the Internet

In Figure 10-6, the proxy server's IP address of 192.168.0.1 has been entered in the Proxy address to use text box. Port 8080, normally used for proxy services, is also specified. This configuration results in the proxy server forwarding requests to external hosts over port 8080 while using a source IP address of 192.168.0.1. Proxy servers require all users on a network to configure client programs accordingly. Depending on the number of users in your network, configuration can be time consuming. If you don't have time to make all these configurations, you can prepare a set of instructions that users follow to configure their own software so that you have to deal with problems only as they come up.

Many older proxy server programs come with an auto-configuration script that enables client programs to be set with the proxy server's address and port number automatically. Newer proxy servers, such as Microsoft ISA Server, no longer need a separate client program loaded on users' computers. Table 10-1 summarizes some advantages and disadvantages of using proxy servers.

Table 10-1   Proxy server advantages and disadvantages

Advantages	Disadvantages
Examines contents of packets and filters based on contents	Can be weak
Shields internal host IP address	Can slow down network access
Caches Web pages for faster access	Might require configuration of client programs to use proxy server
Provides a single point of logging	Provides a single point of failure

Choosing a Proxy Server

Different proxy servers perform different functions to strengthen your existing firewall configuration. The type of proxy server you install depends on your network's needs. You can install a simple freeware proxy server if you're satisfied with the level of protection your existing firewall provides and simply want to add functions the firewall can't perform (such as filtering out pop-up ads, executable code, or other types of content).

On the other hand, if you want to strengthen existing firewall protection, a commercial proxy server can perform many functions that improve your overall network security, including a single point of logging and hiding internal IP addresses. If you need to save installation time and want to have only one program to manage, an enterprise-level firewall with proxy server, packet filtering, and other functions is a good choice. The basic types of proxy servers you can choose—freeware proxy servers, commercial proxy servers, or a firewall that includes proxy server functions—are described in the following sections.

Freeware Proxy Servers

Freeware proxy servers tend to offer a specific function rather than the full range of proxy server functions, so they're often described by names such as "content filter." An Internet search for freeware proxy-servers returns dozens of links, but be aware that most of these products don't have the features needed for business applications. One freeware proxy that's worth mentioning is Squid Proxy for Linux (*www.squid-cache.org*). It's an open-source product, so plenty of documentation and support are available.

Commercial Proxy Servers

The many benefits of commercial proxy servers become evident when you install a program such as Microsoft ISA Server. This commercial program combines the capabilities to cache Web pages and translate source and destination IP addresses with content filtering and traditional firewall functions, such as packet filtering and NAT. To compete with other security programs, most proxy servers aren't advertised as having these features. Instead, they are described as part of a more comprehensive firewall package. A commercial proxy server is a good choice for a business network if you plan to upgrade the software as new versions become available. Any commercial program should offer technical support to help with installation and configuration problems.

Proxy Servers That Can Include Firewall Functions

Some proxy servers, such as Microsoft ISA Server, can be set up to act as firewalls (in addition to performing other duties). Having an all-in-one program simplifies installation, product updating, and day-to-day management. On the other hand, all your network security needs are being handled by a single program. If something goes wrong with your proxy server, your firewall also goes down. If feasible, using several software and hardware programs in a coordinated network defense layer is preferable. For example, you could use ISA Server for your proxy server needs and Cisco PIX as your firewall.

Filtering Content

A useful feature of proxy servers is their capability to open TCP/IP packets, inspect the data portion, and take action based on the contents. This capability enables proxy servers to filter out content that would otherwise appear in a user's Web browser. In a business environment, proxy servers can be configured to block Web sites containing content employees shouldn't be allowed to view. They can also drop any executable programs, such as Java applets or ActiveX controls, embedded in Web pages that can potentially damage files or replicate files when they run on a user's computer.

NOTE Most Web pages don't have embedded executable code. However, attackers have attempted to distribute malicious code by adding executable code to Web pages. An example is the well-known W32/Nimda worm that, according to a security alert issued by the CERT Coordination Center (*www.cert.org/ advisories/CA-2001-26.html*), can propagate itself when Web browsers open Web pages or when e-mail programs receive certain attachments.

Using Network Address Translation (NAT)

If a port number is similar to specifying an apartment number for a postal address, NAT functions much like a mailroom worker receiving mail and routing it to the correct location without the sender knowing the correct address. With mail addressed to "Santa Claus, North Pole," for example, mailroom workers route the letters to people who have taken on the responsibility of replying to them, but their exact locations and identities are kept secret from the general public.

NAT works in much the same way: Computers outside the internal network don't see the IP addresses of host computers on the protected internal network. The device that performs NAT (such as a firewall or router) acts as a go-between, receiving requests at its own IP address and forwarding them to the correct IP addresses in the organization. Using NAT means you don't have to assign public IP addresses to each computer in your organization for it to send and receive information on the Internet. A NAT-enabled firewall or router is the only device that needs to have a public, routable IP address for use on the Internet. Internal hosts can be assigned private IP addresses set aside for use on LANs.

NAT is one of the essential functions that many firewalls or routers perform. The reason for enabling NAT, from a security standpoint, doesn't have to do with conserving IP addresses, however. By shielding the IP addresses of internal host computers, the NAT-enabled device makes it more difficult for attackers to find computers to exploit. Many attacks begin with an intruder locating a computer with a static, public IP address; the intruder can then scan the machine for open ports to exploit. If the intruder can't find the computer's IP address, attacks might never start. NAT can be carried out in two different ways—hide-mode mapping and static mapping—which are described in the following sections.

Hide-Mode Mapping

You might already be using a form of NAT called **hide-mode mapping**—the process of hiding multiple private IP addresses behind one public IP address—in your home or classroom network. Consider a computer that functions as a server for a network, has a gateway to the Internet, and uses Dynamic Host Configuration Protocol (DHCP), a protocol that enables IP addresses to be assigned dynamically among hosts on a network. The server might have a public IP address, such as 213.141.56.8, but the addresses on the internal network might be private ones, such as 192.168.120.5, 192.168.120.6, 192.168. 120.7, and so on. This address configuration enables computers on your network to share a single Internet connection at 213.141.56.8.

Hide-mode NAT enables multiple computers to communicate with the Internet while having their IP addresses hidden from other computers on the Internet, as shown in Figure 10-7. The computers on the Internet see only the NAT device's IP address; the packets that actually originate from internal hosts all seem to be coming from the NAT device. There are disadvantages to this mode. First, you can hide only so many clients behind a single IP address. For most networks, this isn't a big problem; but for a large network, performance can begin to degrade as the number of connections increases. In addition, hide-mode NAT doesn't work with some types of VPNs because the two endpoints must have unique addressing. Finally, hide-mode NAT uses only a single public IP address, so you can't provide other services, such as a Web server, unless you obtain another IP address for them.

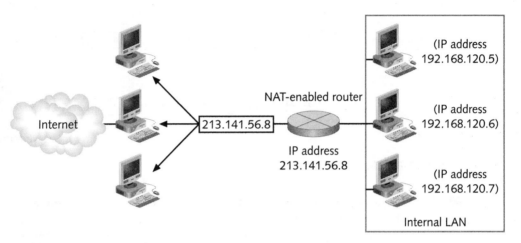

Figure 10-7   NAT in hide mode

NOTE   A single NAT device essentially sets up a firewall for an internal network. In fact, any security scheme that shields computers from external attack is called a firewall in a generic sense. That applies regardless of whether the hardware or software device actually contains the label "firewall."

Static Mapping

Static mapping is a form of NAT in which internal IP addresses are mapped to external, routable IP addresses on a one-to-one basis. The internal IP addresses are still hidden, but the computers appear to have public, routable IP addresses. Neither the public nor private IP addresses change dynamically; instead, they are static. A NAT device's static translation from private to public IP addresses is shown in Figure 10-8.

As you can see in Figure 10-8, each internal IP address has a corresponding public IP address that's visible to external hosts. External hosts think they're making a direct connection to an internal computer; but in reality, they are still connecting directly to the NAT device, which forwards the request to the internal computer. Static NAT can be used when you have internal clients that need more bandwidth instead of sharing available bandwidth with all other clients.

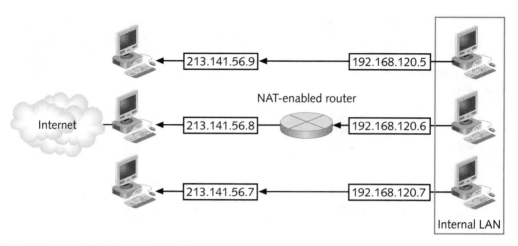

Figure 10-8   Static NAT translations

NOTE

Because NAT devices function as a sort of digital go-between for internal and external computers, they can be confused with proxy servers. Proxy servers, too, shield internal hosts by forwarding requests from the Internet to computers, and vice versa. However, proxy servers completely rebuild packets from scratch before sending them on, and NAT simply forwards packets.

ACTIVITY

Activity 10-3: Designing a Rule Base

Time Required: 30 minutes

Objective: Create basic rule sets for packet filtering.

Description: In this activity, you configure your own set of basic rules for packet filtering for a network with the following characteristics: The internal network is represented by 192.168.120.0; the firewall is hosted at 192.168.120.1; the e-mail server is at 192.168.120.2; the Web server is at 192.168.120.3; and the DNS server is at 192.168.120.4.

TIP

You might find it helpful to use a table similar to Table 9-11 for writing your rules, although you can use the lines supplied in the following steps.

1. Create a rule that allows internal hosts to access the external network.

   _____

   _____

2. Create a rule that prevents any access to the firewall.

   _____

   _____

3. Create a rule that allows internal and external access to the e-mail server and Web server.

_____

_____

4. Create a rule that allows internal access to the DNS server.

_____

_____

5. For extra credit, what additional rule could you write that involves the firewall?

_____

_____

AUTHENTICATING USERS

10

Authentication is the process of identifying users who are authorized to access the network. This important element in a network defense program is one that many full-featured firewalls and IDSs perform. Authentication plays an important role in firewall or other security configurations. In general, authentication depends on the exchange of information that tells one entity that the other entity is recognized as an authorized user. That information can be a password; a long encrypted block of code called a key; a checksum (a formula for verifying digital information); a physical object, such as a smart card; or biometric information from fingerprints, retina scans, or voiceprints.

The following sections describe different authentication schemes you can use when configuring a firewall. First, you examine what should be authenticated: users, clients, or sessions. Next, you see how authentication is actually carried out, such as by exchanging passwords or keys. Then you review authentication methods that combine a variety of approaches for dial-up users (such as RADIUS) and users on the internal network (such as Internet Protocol Security combined with Internet Key Exchange).

Step 1: Deciding What to Authenticate

You're probably already familiar with the type of authentication you use to get your e-mail, access a file server, or dial up your ISP. Authentication by a firewall adds another level of security to these logins. When a connection is made to the firewall, you can have the firewall authorize the connection by requesting a user name and password or by exchanging information "behind the scenes" so that users don't have to log in at every session. Of course, not all firewalls perform authentication, and the ones that do might handle only simple user authentication. The Check Point NG firewall handles three different types of authentication—user, client, and session authentication—and is used as an example in the following sections.

User Authentication

User authentication is the process of identifying a person who has been authorized to access network resources. A user who submits the correct credentials can log on to the network from any location or any computer, which offers a measure of flexibility. You don't need to require users to log on every time they access the firewall; instead, you can configure the authentication to be automatic and based on the exchange of keys.

First, you have to define users. In Check Point NG, you assign a user to a user group; you can then set up access rules for that group. You can also specify source and destination addresses, which allows you to restrict resources to which the user group has access. If a user group can have unrestricted access, you specify Any in the Source and Destination text boxes in the Location tab of the User Properties dialog box (see Figure 10-9).

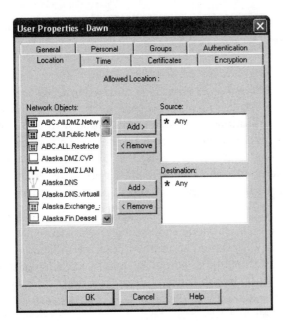

Figure 10-9 Restricting user access

In addition, you can specify time-based restrictions that control when a user is allowed to access the network, such as only on weekdays during daytime hours (see Figure 10-10). Setting time-based restrictions adds another level of security for your network if you don't have IT staff available around the clock to handle intrusion attempts. By blocking authorized access during overnight hours, you make it more difficult for attackers to launch exploits in the middle of the night.

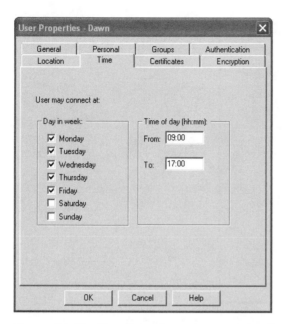

Figure 10-10   Time-based user access restrictions

If you prevent users from accessing the network on evenings or weekends, you might run into complaints from employees who need to work after hours. Make sure employees don't need to work during off hours before you set time-based restrictions.

Client Authentication

Client authentication is the process of granting access to network resources based on a source IP address, computer MAC address, or computer name rather than user information. With client authentication, as with user authentication, the identification process can be automatic or manual. If you require computers to authenticate themselves manually, users have to enter a user name or password. Manual authentication requires extra effort for users to access the resources they want, but it increases security because you restrict access based on the source computer *and* user name/password in one process.

If the IP addresses on your network are assigned dynamically and change often, enterprise-level firewalls, such as Check Point NG, account for this by using computer names (such as Email Server) rather than IP addresses to perform client authentication. You can also configure the client authentication process to be automatic. In Check Point NG, you do this by choosing an option in the Sign On Method section of the Client Authentication Action Properties dialog box (see Figure 10-11).

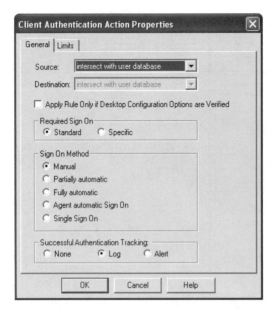

Figure 10-11   Client authentication can be manual or automatic

Even if an intruder steals a user's user name and password, having that user log on with client authentication means that the computer could be accessed only with the required IP address—or by spoofing the IP address, which the intruder would also have to obtain.

Session Authentication

Session authentication is the process of authorizing a user or computer on a per-connection basis by using special authentication software installed on the client computer that exchanges information with the firewall. Session authentication gives the user even more flexibility than user or client authentication; it enables any user and any computer (configured with the client software) to access network resources of any sort. The connection between the client computer and firewall is authorized instead of the person or a machine name or address.

For session authentication to work with Check Point NG, you need to install the Session Authentication Agent on any client computer where authentication needs to be carried out. The client computer and firewall authenticate in the background; however, the user making the connection does need to enter a password. You can configure session authentication so that a user is asked to enter a password every time a file or other resource is requested, once per session, or after a specified number of minutes of inactivity. The third option prevents unauthorized users from working at a machine connected to a protected resource that the original user has abandoned.

How do you decide which type of authentication is right for your needs? Table 10-2 compares the advantages and disadvantages of these three authentication approaches.

Table 10-2   User, client, and session authentication

Method	Advantages	Disadvantages
User authentication	Gives the user flexibility in being able to access the network from any location	If user name/password information is stolen, an unauthorized user can gain access
Client authentication	Provides better security than user authentication; can be configured to work with all applications and services	User must work at a computer configured for a client authentication
Session authentication	Gives the user the highest amount of flexibility; provides both password and session authentication	Session Authentication Agent must be installed on each client computer

The type of authentication you want your firewall to perform is only one aspect of authentication you have to determine. Another is the type of information to be exchanged for the authentication to work reliably, as described in the next section.

Step 2: Deciding How to Authenticate

Determining the type of authentication to use depends, in part, on that method's level of security, which largely depends on the type of information exchanged to verify the user or computer's identity. When you make a purchase at a retail store, often you're asked to show an identification card and sign a receipt to verify your identity. Over a network, computers or users present other types of digital information to declare who they are. This section examines types of information firewalls can exchange with clients to authenticate themselves or their users.

Password Security

Password-based authentication, in which a user name and password is compared against a database of approved users, is probably the simplest and most straightforward authentication a firewall can perform. However, because passwords can easily be lost, cracked, or misappropriated by unauthorized users, some variations on the usual password system have been developed for increased security. Firewalls can use a number of password systems, including:

- *OS password*—The firewall refers to the user's password stored on the host computer's operating system for authentication.

- *Firewall password*—Some firewalls include their own system of user passwords, such as the "enable" password on Cisco routers and PIX firewalls.

10

- *S/Key password*—S/Key uses a special application to generate a one-time password that's encrypted. The user is given the password and enters it once to authenticate. The password is not used again.

- *SecureID*—This form of two-factor authentication from RSA Security (*www.rsasecurity.com*) consists of a password (something the user knows) combined with something the user possesses (a small electronic device called a token that generates a random number every 60 seconds). Combining a random number with a password produces a one-time combination with secure authentication.

The OS password system is simple but won't work if the firewall is hosted on a standalone computer, because users probably won't have an account on a computer that's designated only for the firewall system. The S/Key one-time password system is far more secure and highly configurable; Check Point NG's configuration options for S/Key are shown in Figure 10-12.

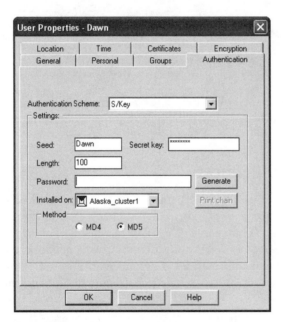

Figure 10-12   S/Key configuration options

As you can see in Figure 10-12, to use S/Key authentication, a seed is used to generate a one-time password. You enter the user's password in the Secret key text box; this secret password is used with the seed to create a one-time password. You can use the Length text box to specify the number of one-time passwords generated by the seed and the secret password.

The S/Key one-time password system enables you to generate a list of passwords used in succession. These password lists are one type of one-time passwords. The other type of one-time password is the challenge-response system, such as MS-CHAP in Windows. In this system, the client computer receives an identifier and then submits a challenge value. The server or firewall performing the authentication response returns a response value that the user submits to complete the authentication.

Smart Cards and Tokens

As mentioned, objects that a user possesses can be combined with passwords to create secure two-factor authentication. The most common objects used in authentication are smart cards and tokens. You're probably familiar with smart cards because credit cards and ATM cards fall into this category; they're small plastic cards with a magnetic stripe that stores information about the cardholder. For smart cards to work, the user's computer needs to have a card reader installed.

Any object that enables users to authenticate themselves with a network can also be called a **token**. A smart card is a form of a token; other types are handheld or key fob electronic devices that generate random numbers. The numbers are changed periodically (perhaps every five minutes). The user authenticates by entering the current number from the token, as well as a PIN or password. Although smart cards and other tokens can easily be lost or stolen, requiring a PIN or password makes it difficult for a thief to use them.

You can find out more about security tokens by visiting the RSA Security Web site (*www.rsasecurity.com*). RSA Security sells a variety of tokens for its SecureID authentication system.

Exchanging Public and Private Keys

A password is a "code" you use when you want to authenticate yourself on a network. Computers can also authenticate themselves to one another (or to programs that use encryption, such as enterprise-level firewalls) by exchanging codes. As you might expect, because of the power of computers to carry out calculations and store information, the codes computers exchange can be long and complicated. The longer the code and the more complex the formula used to create it, the more secure the level of authentication.

The codes that computers exchange to be authenticated to servers, firewalls, or other computers are called keys. Keys are blocks of encrypted code generated by mathematical formulas called algorithms; they are very long (1024, 2048, or 4096 bits or even longer) and, therefore, difficult (and often nearly impossible) to crack. Keys can be issued to people as well as to computers. One of the most popular and secure forms of authentication on the Internet, **public key cryptography**, authenticates through the exchange of public and private keys.

How Public Key Cryptography Works

Data encrypted with your public key can be decrypted only with your private key. Figure 10-13 shows a simplified view of the way public key cryptography works.

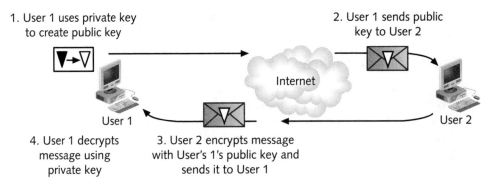

1. User 1 uses private key
   to create public key

2. User 1 sends public
   key to User 2

Internet

User 1

User 2

4. User 1 decrypts
   message using
   private key

3. User 2 encrypts message
   with User's 1's public key and
   sends it to User 1

Figure 10-13   Public key cryptography involves exchanging a public key created with a
private key

The encryption scheme shown in Figure 10-13 enables you to distribute a public key freely. Only you can read data encrypted with this key. In general, to send encrypted data to someone, you encrypt the data with the recipient's public key, and the recipient decrypts the encrypted data by means of the corresponding private key. Compared with symmetric key encryption (in which the same key is used rather than a pair of public and private keys), public key cryptography requires more computation, so it's not always appropriate for large amounts of data.

The reverse of the encryption scheme shown in Figure 10-13 also works: Data encrypted with your private key can be decrypted only with your public key. This scheme isn't the best way to encrypt confidential data, however, because anyone with your public key, which is, by definition, published, could decrypt the data. Nevertheless, private key encryption is useful because you can use your private key to sign data with your digital signature—an important requirement for e-commerce and other commercial applications of cryptography. Web browsers can then use your public key to confirm that the message was signed with your private key and hasn't been tampered with since being signed.

Digital Signatures

Encryption and decryption address the problem of eavesdropping but don't address two other security issues: tampering and impersonation. A **digital signature** is an attachment to an e-mail or other message that enables the recipient to authenticate the sender's identity. It provides tamper detection and authentication through a mathematical function called a **one-way hash**. A one-way hash is also known as a **message digest** (a code of fixed length that results from processing a message or other input through a mathematical function, usually resulting in a shortened version of the original input). A one-way hash has the following characteristics:

- The value of the hash is unique for the hashed data. Any change in the data, even deleting or altering a single character, results in a different value.

- The content of the hashed data can't, for all practical purposes, be deduced from the hash, which is why it's called "one-way."

Instead of encrypting the data, the signing software creates a one-way hash of the data and then uses your private key to encrypt the hash. The encrypted hash along with other information, such as the hashing algorithm, creates a digital signature.

To validate data integrity, the receiving software uses the signer's public key to decrypt the hash and then uses the same hashing algorithm that generated the original hash to generate a new one-way hash of the same data. (Information about the hashing algorithm is sent with the digital signature.) Finally, the receiving software compares the new hash against the original hash. If the two hashes match, the recipient can be certain that the public key used to decrypt the digital signature corresponds to the private key used to create the digital signature. If they don't match, the data might have been tampered with since it was signed, or the signature might have been created with a private key that doesn't correspond to the signer's public key.

Some firewalls can generate digital signatures so that users on the network can identify themselves to one another. Make sure your firewall supports the MD5 **hash functions**—common mathematical functions that create digest versions of messages.

10

Step 3: Putting It All Together

Passwords, tokens, keys, digital signatures, and certificates are often used on the Internet to secure communications and authenticate users, which has an impact on firewalls because they provide a gateway for communication between external computers on the Internet and internal computers on the LAN. If any users on the internal network use encryption to authenticate themselves, that communication goes through the firewall.

Firewalls, therefore, need to be able to recognize and process a variety of authentication methods to enable users to make purchases from Web sites, send and receive encrypted e-mail, or log on to databases. The following sections explain some of the common authentication methods firewalls use.

S-HTTP

Secure Hypertext Transfer Protocol (S-HTTP) refers to using a common security protocol, such as Secure Sockets Layer (SSL) or Transport Layer Security (TLS), to encrypt communication between a Web server and a Web browser. SSL, which is used more often than TLS, involves exchanging public and private keys and uses a digital certificate to verify the server's identity.

From the standpoint of a firewall, SSL doesn't present an inherent problem. In an SSL packet, the data portion is encrypted, but the IP and TCP/UDP headers are not, so the firewall can filter and route the packet as needed. The firewall can't, however, scan or filter the data portion because of the encryption. Although SSL does provide a way to encrypt credit card numbers and other confidential information when it's submitted to a Web site, it doesn't provide user authentication.

You can learn more about S-HTTP by reading the original proposal for it at *www.ietf.org/rfc/rfc2660.txt.*

TIP

IPSec/IKE

Internet Protocol Security (IPSec) works by encrypting communication at the network layer (layer 3) of the OSI model. IPSec can automatically protect e-mail, Web traffic, and file transfers using FTP. As you learned in Chapter 5, IPSec is widely used because of its strong encryption algorithms and effective authentication methods. Firewalls that support IPSec can give users a way to secure their network communication effectively.

NAT can interfere with some forms of IPSec and other encryption methods. If the firewall is used to configure rules for IPSec encryption, there should be no problem with NAT or filtering by the firewall. However, if IPSec is implemented by software inside the firewall (such as an OS or a VPN appliance) and IPSec communications are intended to pass through the firewall, some IPSec-protected packets won't be read by the firewall. Specifically, because Authentication Header (AH) encrypts the IP header portion of packets, firewalls that perform NAT can't read the encrypted headers and, therefore, can't translate them into other IP addresses. In addition, because Encapsulating Security Payload (ESP) doesn't encrypt the IP header but does encrypt the TCP or UDP header port number, firewalls can't perform NAT on these packets because NAT changes port information as well as IP addresses.

Refer to Chapter 5 for a review of AH, ESP, and IKE.

NOTE

In addition to its encryption schemes, IPSec includes a variety of software components, including Internet Key Exchange (IKE), which provides for the exchange of public and private keys to authenticate users. Another IPSec protocol, Internet Security Association Key Management Protocol (ISAKMP), enables two computers to reach agreed-on security settings and securely exchange security keys so that they can encrypt communications.

IPSec incompatibilities with NAT have largely been addressed by NAT Traversal (NAT-T), which has been standardized by the IETF's IP Security Protocol Working Group and is defined in RFCs 3947 and 3948.

NOTE

Dial-in Authentication: RADIUS and TACACS+

Laptops, handheld devices, and tablet PCs mean that employees can stay connected to the office while working at home or during business trips. Each time an employee dials in to the corporate network remotely, however, a potential security breach is possible. An intruder or unauthorized user who gains access to the remote user's system could also access files on the corporate network. To address this problem, firewalls can use special authentication systems designed for use with dial-in users. These are the two best-known systems:

- **Terminal Access Controller Access Control System (TACACS+)**, commonly called "Tac-plus," is a set of authentication protocols developed by Cisco Systems. TACACS+ uses the MD5 algorithm to produce an encrypted digest version of transmitted data.

- **Remote Authentication Dial-In User Service (RADIUS)** is generally considered to provide less security than TACACS+, even though it's more widely supported. RADIUS transmits authentication packets unencrypted across the network, which means they are vulnerable to attacks from packet sniffers.

These systems are becoming less critical because more remote employees and business partners have direct connections to the Internet and can establish connections through VPNs. However, they still play a role in many corporate networks' security schemes.

NOTE TACACS+ is not backward compatible with Standard TACACS or Extended TACACS (XTACACS). For more information on TACACS, TACACS+, or XTA-CACS, perform a search at *www.cisco.com*.

In TACACS+ or RADIUS, authentication is carried out by a server set up to perform authentication. A TACACS+ server or a RADIUS server is set up with the usual dial-up access server the network uses to receive connection requests from remote users. The dial-up server can usually be set to configure requests to the TACACS+ or RADIUS server for authentication. The TACACS+ or RADIUS authentication server needs to have its own IP address and uses special ports for communications, which means the network administrator must configure authentication for filtering, proxying, and NAT, as discussed in the following list:

- *Filtering characteristics*—TACACS+ uses TCP port 49; RADIUS uses UDP port 1812 for authentication and UDP port 1813 for accounting. (For more information on RADIUS client/server accounting, see RFC 2866.) You need to set up packet-filtering rules that enable clients to exchange authorization packets with the TACACS+ or RADIUS server.

- *Proxy characteristics*—A RADIUS server can function as a proxy server, but it doesn't work with generic proxy systems you might have set up for Web access or other services. TACACS+, however, does work with generic proxy systems.

- *NAT characteristics*—RADIUS simply isn't compatible with NAT, but TACACS+ does work with NAT systems. However, static NAT works best because some TACACS+ systems use the source IP address to create the encryption key.

NOTE Wireless users connecting to the corporate network need to connect to a wireless LAN access point. These users can be authenticated in a manner that conforms to the IEEE 802.11 standard. VPNs should be used for wireless access because of the high vulnerability of wireless transmissions; network traffic or Internet access can be intercepted by unauthorized wireless users who manage to get close enough to a wireless access point. The highly secure nature of VPN tunneling and encryption offers protection for wireless clients. You can learn more about securing wireless access at *www.sans.org/rr/whitepapers/wireless/158.php*.

CHAPTER SUMMARY

❏ Modern networks require a variety of services, including Web, e-mail, databases, VPNs and other remote access configurations, e-commerce, and other resources to enhance productivity. The need for access must be balanced with the need for security, however, and that can require using many hardware and software products in various configurations on the network perimeter and inside the protected LAN.

❏ Firewalls can't secure a network alone. Perimeter security involves a layered approach to provide services and protect internal hosts. Bastion hosts, honeypots, proxy servers, NAT, and authentication can be combined to address your organization's security needs.

❏ A bastion host is a computer on the network perimeter that has been specially protected through OS patches, authentication, and encryption. Bastion hosts can be combined with firewalls and packet-filtering devices for security and can provide Web, FTP, e-mail, and other network services. A honeypot is a vulnerable computer deliberately placed on the network perimeter to draw attackers' attention away from critical systems. Honeypots act as "decoys."

❏ A proxy server forwards packets to and from the network being protected and caches Web pages to speed up network performance. It also acts on behalf of internal hosts, preventing direct connections between internal hosts and the Internet. Proxy servers work at the application layer of the OSI model to interpret which application is making a request.

❏ Network Address Translation (NAT) conceals the IP addresses of computers on the internal network from external locations. NAT also enables networks to use private IP addressing for internal clients, thus conserving public IP addresses. Hide-mode NAT conceals multiple IP addresses behind a single IP address; static NAT maps each internal IP address to a public IP address.

❏ Many firewalls perform user, client, or session authentication. They can authorize by accepting one-time or multiple-use passwords, by using two-factor authentication systems such as SecureID, by exchanging public and private keys, and by issuing digital signatures.

❏ Many enterprise-level firewalls can operate with encryption schemes, such as Secure Sockets Layer (SSL) and Internet Protocol Security (IPSec). In addition, firewalls can work with a server configured so that remote employees can dial up the network and access resources they need.

Key Terms

bastion host — A computer that sits on the network perimeter and has been specially protected through operating system patches, authentication, and encryption.

change management — The process of documenting changes made to hardware or software. This documentation helps administrators roll back a configuration correctly if changes have an adverse affect.

client authentication — The process of granting access to network resources based on a source IP address, computer MAC address, or computer name rather than user information.

dependency services — Services a computer system needs to function correctly. Usually, key system processes depend on other processes to function.

digital signature — An attachment to an e-mail or other message that enables the recipient of the message to authenticate the sender's identity.

hardened — The process of making a computer more secure by eliminating unnecessary software and services, closing potential openings, and protecting the information on it with encryption and authentication.

hash function — A mathematical function (such as MD5) that creates a digest version of a message.

hide-mode mapping — The process of hiding multiple private IP addresses behind one public IP address.

honeypot — A computer placed on the perimeter of a network to attract attackers. A honeypot acts as a diversion, drawing attackers' attention away from other hosts.

message digest — A code of fixed legnth that results from processing a message or other input through a mathematical function, usually resulting in a shortened version of the original input.

one-way hash — *See* message digest.

public key cryptography — A form of network authentication that identifies participants through the exchange of public and private keys.

Remote Authentication Dial-In User Service (RADIUS) — An authentication method that identifies and verifies the authorization of users who dial up a central server to gain access to networked resources.

session authentication — The process of authorizing a user or computer on a per-connection basis using special authentication software installed on the client computer that exchanges information with the firewall.

static mapping — A form of NAT in which internal IP addresses are mapped to external, routable IP addresses on a one-to-one basis.

Terminal Access Controller Access Control System (TACACS+) — A set of authentication protocols developed by Cisco Systems that uses the MD5 algorithm to produce an encrypted digest version of transmitted data. TACACS+ is usually used to authenticate dial-up remote users.

token — A small electronic device that generates a random number or password used in authentication.

user authentication — The process of identifying a person who has been authorized to access network resources.

10

REVIEW QUESTIONS

1. When you request a Web page, the Web server storing the page sends it back to you using which port?

   a. 80

   b. 443

   c. one higher than 1023

   d. one lower than 1023

2. Which of the following functions can a bastion host perform? (Choose all that apply.)

   a. FTP server

   b. e-mail server

   c. security management server

   d. domain controller

3. It doesn't matter what operating system runs on a bastion host. True or False?

4. A packet filter located between a proxy server and the Internet needs to route traffic to and from which of the following? (Choose all that apply.)

   a. Internet

   b. internal network

   c. DMZ

   d. proxy server

5. Which of the following can hide internal IP addresses from the Internet? (Choose all that apply.)

   a. packet filters

   b. NAT

   c. proxy servers

   d. state tables

6. Hardening a bastion host involves which of the following? (Choose all that apply.)

   a. disabling unnecessary services

   b. removing unnecessary accounts

   c. installing current patches

   d. all of the above

7. Disabling _____ makes it more difficult for attackers to communicate with internal hosts.

   a. IP filtering

   b. IP forwarding

c. IP routing

d. IP lookup

8. Which accounts should you delete on the bastion host?

a. all system accounts

b. all accounts

c. all user accounts

d. default administrator accounts

9. Goals of proxy servers include which of the following? (Choose all that apply.)

a. enhancing network communication performance

b. caching user account data and passwords

c. hiding internal hosts

d. facilitating direct communications between internal hosts and the Internet

10. What are the advantages of NAT? (Choose all that apply.)

a. rebuilding packets from scratch

b. storing files in a cache for improved performance

c. shielding internal IP addresses from attackers

d. using private IP addressing internally instead of public IP addresses

11. Why would you use static NAT mapping rather than hide-mode mapping? (Choose all that apply.)

a. Static NAT mapping translates internal addresses to one IP address.

b. Hide-mode mapping doesn't work with some VPNs.

c. Static NAT mapping assigns IP addresses dynamically.

d. With hide-mode mapping, performance on large networks could degrade as the number of connections increases.

12. What do proxy servers do that NAT does not do?

a. perform encryption

b. rebuild packets from scratch

c. packet filtering

d. work with static IP addresses

13. In which situation should you choose user authentication rather than the more secure client authentication?

a. Users move around a lot and need to log on from different locations.

b. Client IP addresses are assigned dynamically.

c. Client IP addresses are private.

d. Users work at the same location and don't move around frequently.

10

14. What kinds of restrictions can you impose on user authentication? (Choose all that apply.)

   a. IP address

   b. network resources being requested

   c. time

   d. user's physical location

15. What would an attacker have to do to gain access to an account protected with client authentication? (Choose all that apply.)

   a. be physically located inside the company's building

   b. discover the correct user name/password

   c. log on at the correct time

   d. discover the correct IP address

16. For session authentication to work with Check Point NG, you need to do which of the following? (Choose all that apply.)

   a. Identify the computer name.

   b. Install a Session Authentication Agent on clients.

   c. Determine how often the user is prompted for a password.

   d. Determine the user name to be used during the session.

17. Which of the following characteristics describes TACACS+? (Choose all that apply.)

   a. works with NAT systems

   b. is backward compatible with Standard TACACS

   c. uses TCP port 49

   d. doesn't work with generic proxy systems

18. Which elements are used together to create two-factor authentication? (Choose all that apply.)

   a. something the user requests

   b. something the user lacks

   c. something the user possesses

   d. something the user knows

19. Name three methods that some firewalls use to incorporate encryption and protect users.

20. When you're stopping or removing services, you should be careful not to disable any _____ services.

   a. system

   b. remote access

   c. dependency

   d. encryption

HANDS-ON PROJECTS

Hands-On Project 10-1: Filtering UDP Traffic

Time Required: 10 minutes

Objective: Use advanced TCP/IP properties to configure UDP filtering.

Description: When you install and configure the freeware firewall program ZoneAlarm (as described in Chapter 9) to send you alert messages, you'll probably notice many alerts from computers attempting to connect to yours on a UDP port. Because UDP is used less often than TCP and is considered less secure than TCP, you might be inclined to block it altogether. However, UDP is commonly used by computers on your network as well as your DNS server and your ISP's servers, all trying to connect to yours. One way to block UDP communications selectively is to use Windows 2000 or XP's built-in TCP/IP filtering function.

In this project, you need to specify what services are allowed to use specific UDP ports instead of blocking UDP specifically. To enter these ports, you need to know what services to run. You can scan a list of ports at *www.iana.org/assignments/port-numbers*. For this project, you enable the common UDP ports for DNS (port 53) and NetBIOS (port 137).

1. Open Control Panel, and in Category view, click **Network and Internet Connections**.

2. Click **Network Connections**, right-click the icon representing your computer's connection to the Internet, and then click **Properties**.

3. In the General tab of the Properties dialog box, click **Internet Protocol (TCP/IP)**, and then click the **Properties** button.

4. Click the **Advanced** button, and then click the **Options** tab.

5. Click **TCP/IP filtering**, and then click the **Properties** button.

6. In the TCP/IP Filtering dialog box, click to select the **Enable TCP/IP Filtering (All adapters)** check box.

7. In the UDP Ports column, click the **Permit Only** option button.

8. Click **Add**. In the Add Filter dialog box, type **53**, and then click **OK**. The number 53 is listed under UDP Ports.

9. Click **Add**. In the Add Filter dialog box, type **137**, and then click **OK**. The number 137 is added to the list of UDP ports.

10. Click **OK** to close all dialog boxes.

11. Close any remaining open windows to return to the Windows desktop. If a message box prompts you to restart your computer, click **No**. Leave your system running for the next activity.

10

Hands-On Project 10-2: Troubleshooting a Rule Base

Time Required: 15 minutes

Objective: Examine a rule base for any security concerns.

Description: As a security professional, you might be asked to edit packet-filtering rule bases or improve rules that leave security holes open. Analyze the rule base in Table 10-3, and then answer the following questions:

Table 10-3   Rule base

Rule	Source IP	Source Port	Destination IP	Destination Port	Action
1	Any	Any	192.168.120.0	>1023	Allow
2	192.168.120.1	Any	Any	Any	Deny
3	Any	Any	192.168.120.1	Any	Deny
4	192.168.120.0	Any	Any	Any	Any
5	Any	Any	192.168.120.2	25	Allow
6	Any	Any	192.168.120.3	80	Allow
7	Any	Any	Any	Any	Allow

1. Examine Rule 1 and explain what security risk it poses in its current configuration. Describe how this rule could be improved.

_____

_____

_____

_____

_____

_____

2. Describe a problem with the cleanup rule in the rule base.

_____

_____

Case Projects

Case Project 10-1: Designing a Test Methodology for the LedGrafix Network

Your planning and design work for LedGrafix is almost finished. You have designed the network, conducted risk assessments, written a security policy, and investigated tools for log file analysis. You have also planned a remote access solution, designed an IDS, and designed the configuration of the perimeter network. You've documented your design and conducted a second round of risk analysis. Based on your findings, you've handled revisions to the security policy throughout the process.

You have followed industry best practices and learned that technical expertise must be combined with a solid understanding of a business's needs and goals. Now you have another important task to address. As you should know from previous security and networking training, testing a configuration before putting it online in a production environment is wise so that you can discover and correct any issues before they cause a major problem in the real environment. For this running case project, you develop a testing methodology for the LedGrafix network:

1. First, you need to determine what to test. A typical system contains applications, operating systems, network equipment and configurations, security measures, data storage and organization facilities, backup procedures, and so forth. Using the Application Testing Checklist your instructor supplies, you can get a good idea of what you need to test in your design. You also need to refer back to your hardware and software inventory lists. The checklist is a sample testing form for a Windows keyboarding application, but you can modify it for hardware, network, security, and other systems you have integrated into your network design for LedGrafix.

2. Next, you must document your configurations using the Test Configuration Documentation example your instructor supplies. Modify this example as needed to document your configurations.

3. It's highly unlikely that you won't encounter problems when testing at this stage. You need to document any error messages or dysfunctional systems along with possible causes and solutions using the Testing Error Documentation form your instructor supplies. Again, modify the form as needed to fit your design.

4. Many stress-testing and load-testing simulation applications are available. Locate and research other tools to use for stress testing your network. A great place to start is *www.snapfiles.com*. You can also find security-testing tools, such as vulnerability scanners, port scanners, and protocol analyzers.

Because each design will be different, you might have other functions that require testing. Be sure to plan for them, too. After you have finished your testing methodology design, proofread your work and submit it to your instructor. Be sure to place all documentation in an appendix to your final draft of the policies and procedures manual for your LedGrafix network design.

Make sure you don't wait until the last minute to develop your final draft, which will be submitted at the end of this book as the culmination of all the material you've studied.

10

CHAPTER

11

STRENGTHENING AND MANAGING FIREWALLS

After reading this chapter and completing the exercises, you will be able to:

♦ Manage firewalls to improve security

♦ Describe the most important issues in managing firewalls

♦ Know how to install and configure Check Point NG

♦ Know how to install and configure Microsoft ISA Server 2000

♦ Know how to manage and configure Iptables for Linux

Firewalls can go a long way toward blocking traffic that's attempting to access your network from external networks, such as the Internet. However, when you actually set up a firewall at your network perimeter, a number of issues come up. The basic purpose of a firewall is to filter inbound traffic. Monitoring outbound traffic can also be important because focusing solely on inbound traffic could leave your network vulnerable to malicious programs, which often work by installing themselves on an internal host and then attempting to connect to an external location. Your best defense is to manage the firewall so that it runs efficiently and allows you to track possible intrusions and respond to them quickly.

This chapter examines ways in which you can strengthen and manage firewall configurations. The next step is to put these principles into practice by examining three popular firewall applications: Check Point NG, Microsoft ISA Server 2000, and Iptables.

MANAGING FIREWALLS TO IMPROVE SECURITY

A firewall's effectiveness depends on ongoing attention from a network administrator. All too often, firewalls are installed and left to do their job without any adjustments to address new types of attacks. If intrusion attempts aren't detected in log files, attackers could succeed in gaining access to your network's computers.

Firewall maintenance can be a difficult task in light of other duties that might seem more urgent. However, because of its importance as a gateway for the network, managing the firewall to improve security is essential. Poor management affects the network in the following ways:

- *Security*—A firewall that isn't protecting the network the way it should leaves everyone in the organization in danger of having their privacy violated and their files damaged. Worse, a poorly configured firewall could give everyone a false sense of security, thus dangerously eroding vigilance. Managing the firewall enables the organization to cope with new threats and continue to block attacks effectively.

- *Throughput*—The term "throughput" refers to a device or connection's capacity to move data in a specific period of time. A firewall configured with too many filtering rules reduces network traffic throughput because it must process packets against each rule, one by one. Adjusting the firewall so that it performs better speeds up your entire network's throughput.

- *Disaster recovery*—If you haven't been diligent about making backups of the firewall configuration and storing them in a secure location, you won't be able to restore the firewall quickly after a disaster.

The following sections examine some administrative tasks that should be carried out regularly to keep your firewall performing effectively:

- Editing the rule base to conform to your organization's security policy
- Managing firewall log files
- Improving firewall performance
- Configuring advanced firewall functions that can keep the entire network running more smoothly

Editing the Rule Base

Editing rules in a firewall's rule base is one of the best ways to improve security and performance. Making the rule base more effective also has the benefit of enabling the firewall to carry out your organization's security policies more effectively. Keep the following guidelines in mind to improve your firewall's rule base:

- Make sure the most important rules are near the top of the rule base.
- Make sure you don't make the firewall do more logging than it has to.

- Reduce the number of domain objects in the rule base (see the following Note).
- Keep rules that cover domain objects near the bottom of the rule base.

NOTE

Domain objects are named or identified resources in an organization's domain—remember that a domain in this context is simply a security boundary. The problem with using domain objects in the rule base is that it could lead to a security breach. When the firewall encounters a rule that includes a computer or other domain object as the source or the destination, it attempts to look up the object's domain name from its IP address. Through a type of attack called DNS spoofing or DNS poisoning, this object could make it possible for an attacker who has gained control of the network's DNS server to identify a computer on the internal network that can be targeted for attack. In addition, an intruder might attempt a zone transfer of the DNS database to acquire information about your internal network. A zone transfer is a special query that secondary DNS servers use to update their DNS records.

Reducing Rules

One of the simplest and most effective ways to improve a firewall's rule base is to see whether it contains any unnecessary rules. You want to keep the number of rules to a minimum. There's no hard-and-fast rule for the exact number you should have; what's important is checking for duplicates or unnecessary listings.

Don't forget that the security policy plays a primary role in determining what rules are necessary. For example, say you have a network with IP addresses in the range 210.100.101.0 to 210.100.101.255. The firewall is at 210.100.101.1, and the Web server is at 210.100. 101.2. Your organization's security policy calls for users on the internal LAN to be able to use HTTP to access Web sites and S-HTTP on the Internet, but not on the Web server in the organization's own DMZ. You could write the rules as shown in Table 11-1.

Table 11-1   Too many firewall rules

Rule	Source IP	Destination IP	Protocol	Action	Track	Comments
1	Any	210.100.101.1	Any	Deny	Alert	Block access to firewall
2	210.100.101.0 to 210.100.101.255	210.100.101.2	S-HTTP	Deny	None	Block LAN access to Web server using S-HTTP
3	210.100.101.0 to 210.100.101.255	Any	HTTP, S-HTTP	Allow	None	Allow LAN access to all Web sites

11

Table 11-1 Too many firewall rules (continued)

Rule	Source IP	Destination IP	Protocol	Action	Track	Comments
4	Any	210.100.101.2	HTTP	Allow	None	Allow all computers to access the Web server using HTTP
5	Any	Any	Any	Deny	Log	Cleanup rule

This rule base has three rules to allow internal and external users to connect to the Web server with HTTP but not S-HTTP. A more efficient method is to consolidate two of the rules (2 and 3 in Table 11-1) into one rule (3 in Table 11-2).

Table 11-2 More efficient firewall rules

Rule	Source IP	Destination IP	Protocol	Action	Track	Comments
1	Any	210.100.101.1	Any	Deny	Alert	Block access to firewall
2	Any	210.100.101.2	HTTP	Allow	None	Allow full access to Web server using HTTP
3	210.100.101.0 to 210.100.101.255	All except 210.100.101.2	HTTP, S-HTTP	Allow	None	Enable LAN access to Web using HTTP and S-HTTP but not to DMZ Web server
4	Any	Any	Any	Deny	Log	Cleanup rule

NOTE Tables 11-1 and 11-2 include a rule base column called Track. Some firewall programs use this column to determine whether the firewall should record the action it performs when a match to a rule is found. Typical options in the Track column are Alert (which causes the firewall to send an alert message), Log (which tells the firewall to log the event), and None (which tells the firewall not to track the event).

Reordering and Editing Rules

Another way to improve your firewall rule base is to make sure the most frequently matched rules are near the top rather than the bottom. This ordering is beneficial because a firewall checks rules in top-to-bottom order until a match is found. If a firewall has to proceed from rule 1 through rule 11 before finding the first match at rule 12, it spends unnecessary time processing rules 1 to 11. Moving rule 12 closer to the top makes it easier for the firewall to find the match quickly and allows traffic through with less delay.

To reorder your rules, scan log files to find commonly used services (those with the highest number of log file entries), and then move rules for those services closer to the top of the rule base. For example, one of the most common services is SMTP for outgoing e-mail. (This service is followed closely by POP3 for incoming e-mail and HTTP for the Web.) A rule base that allows internal users to connect to the SMTP server in the DMZ, for example, should not be number 20 in the rule base; it should be in the top five. Similarly, rules for traffic going to or from your network's DNS server should be near the top of the rule base, after the rule that prevents access to your firewall.

Your goal should be to reduce the number of rules with Log as the action to the bare minimum. In doing so, you improve firewall rule base efficiency even further. You should log only events that occur as a result of attempts to access resources you have restricted (such as the firewall itself) or that occur on resources whose activities you need to track (such as your external Web server's level of activity).

Activity 11-1: Improving a Rule Base

Time Required: 15 minutes

11

Objective: Review a sample rule base and make improvements.

Description: Reviewing and rewriting your firewall's packet-filtering rule base can speed up your firewall's performance and improve security. The sample rule base in Table 11-3 has some rules that could be edited and rearranged. The LAN has IP addresses from 210.100.101.0 to 210.100.101.255. The firewall is at 210.100.101.1, the Web server is at 210.100.101.2, the DNS server is at 210.100.101.3, the SMTP server is at 210.100.101.4, and the POP3 server is at 210.100.101.5. The firewall using this rule base works correctly, but some simple changes could improve its performance dramatically.

Table 11-3 Sample firewall rule base

Rule	Source IP	Destination IP	Protocol	Action	Track	Comments
1	Any	210.100.101.1	Any	Deny	Alert	Block access to firewall
2	210.100.101.0 to 210.100.101.255	210.100.101.2	S-HTTP	Deny	None	Block LAN access to Web server using S-HTTP
3	210.100.101.0 to 210.100.101.255	Any	HTTP, S-HTTP	Allow	None	Allow LAN access to all Web sites
4	Any	210.100.101.2	HTTP	Allow	Log	Allow all computers to access the Web server using HTTP

Table 11-3 Sample firewall rule base (continued)

Rule	Source IP	Destination IP	Protocol	Action	Track	Comments
5	210.100.101.0 to 210.100.101.255	210.100.101.3	UDP	Allow	Log	Enable LAN to make queries to DNS server
6	210.100.101.3	Any except 210.100.101.0 to 210.100.101.255	TCP	Allow	Log	Enable DNS server to make look-ups on the Web but not in LAN
7	210.100.101.0 to 210.100.101.255	210.100.101.5	TCP	Allow	None	Allow LAN access to POP3 server
8	Any	210.100.101.4	TCP	Allow	None	Allow any computer to access the SMTP server
9	Any	Any	Any	Deny	Log	Cleanup rule

1. Which rules cover the same sort of communication?

   _____

   _____

2. Which rule is too far down the list and should be moved up?

   _____

3. Which rules give the firewall more work to do than is necessary? (*Hint:* Look in the Track column.)

   _____

   _____

   _____

4. On a separate piece of paper, create a rule base table like the following sample or ask your instructor for a blank form. Using as few rows as possible, write a new rule base that addresses the questions in the preceding steps.

Sample rule base table

Rule	Source IP	Destination IP	Protocol	Action	Track	Comments

Sample rule base table (continued)

Rule	Source IP	Destination IP	Protocol	Action	Track	Comments

Managing Log Files

Log files generated by firewalls and other security devices provide critical information about network traffic and attempts to attack hosts on your internal network. You can control exactly what the firewall records in the log files and how those files are stored to improve the firewall's performance yet maintain network security. The following sections explain how to configure a firewall to generate log files more efficiently. You can control what the firewall logs, modify the log file format, prepare log file summaries, and generate reports that help you make changes to the firewall for more effective operation.

CAUTION

Assembling a team of network administrators to manage tasks helps distribute the workload, but be aware that having too many administrators making changes can result in confusion and misconfiguration of the firewall. Make sure team members keep a record of every change they make, including the time the change was made and the reason for the adjustment.

Deciding What to Log

Every firewall includes default settings for events it logs. By default, some firewalls, such as Microsoft ISA Server 2000, log only packets subject to a rule with a Deny action. This makes sense because it enables administrators to keep track of unsuccessful attempts to access the network. However, you can also choose to log all packets, including those that have been allowed, but this option slows the operation of the firewall, proxy server, or IDS dramatically.

Many firewalls offer different kinds of log files, such as the following:

- *Security log*—Records any specific security events the firewall has detected, such as DoS attempts or port scans.

- *System log*—Records when the firewall was started and stopped so that you can keep track of who attempts to use or configure it.

- *Traffic log*—Captures each packet that enters or leaves the firewall. You can use it for preparing reports that describe when traffic is heaviest, lightest, and so on.

- *Active log (Check Point NG)*—Displays currently active connections and is used for real-time traffic monitoring.

- *Audit log (Check Point NG)*—Enables you to keep track of who accesses the firewall and what actions were performed.

Sometimes firewalls come with so many types of logging data that including them all would make log files unwieldy. On the other hand, some options that can give you useful

11

information are easily overlooked, simply because they make log file entries difficult to view without scrolling across a computer screen or they won't fit on a standard sheet of paper. Table 11-4 lists some log file data you might find useful. The first seven types are "must haves"; the remaining types are useful but not essential.

Table 11-4   Types of log file data

Log File Data	What It Records
Date	The date when the event occurred
Time	The time when the event occurred, usually in Greenwich Mean Time (GMT)
Source IP	The IP address of the computer that made the request
Destination IP	The IP address of the computer that is being asked to provide a service to the requesting computer
Protocol	The name of the application protocol used to make the connection
Source port	The port number being used to provide the requested service to the requesting computer
Destination port	The port number being used to provide the requested service to the requesting computer
Authentication status	Whether the client making the request has been authenticated
Interface	The firewall interface on which the request was received (such as INT for internal interface or EXT for external interface)
Service	The name of the service (such as DNS, HTTP, or FTP) that was used to make the request or connection
Rule	The number of the rule that was used to process the request
Processing time	The time, in milliseconds, that was required to process the request
Bytes sent	The number of bytes sent from the internal host to the external computer as a result of the connection
Cache info	Indicates whether the requested object was cached

Some firewalls include a GUI interface that enables you to alter the log file display by customizing which fields are included in the log. For example, Check Point NG has a wide range of data fields to choose from in the SmartView Tracker Log tab (see Figure 11-1). In the Query Properties pane, you can include a field by simply selecting the corresponding check box. To exclude the field, click the check box again to clear it. To display the Query Properties pane, choose View, Query Properties from the menu.

Configuring the Log File Format

Many firewalls and IDSs generate log files formatted in plain text that you can view with a text editor, such as Notepad. Most text editors, however, require scrolling sideways to view lines, and often there's no word wrapping, which makes viewing log files tedious. Additionally, plain text log files can have a problem with field separators occurring within a field. A separator might be a comma or a tab. For example, in the "Date" field, a tab might appear

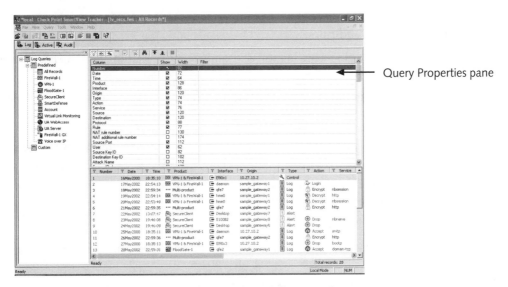

Query Properties pane

Figure 11-1   Check Point NG's SmartView Tracker interface

between the day and month, which can make a log entry difficult to read. Some sophisticated firewalls, such as Microsoft ISA Server 2000, give you the option to save log files in different formats, such as:

- *Native format*—You view log files within the firewall's interface.

- *Open Database Connectivity (ODBC) format*—Log files saved in this format can be viewed with Microsoft SQL Server or another ODBC-compliant database program, which makes it easy to run reports on the data or pull out certain fields for further analysis.

- *W3C Extended format*—This customizable, ASCII text-based format, developed by the World Wide Web Consortium (W3C), is viewed with a text editor, not in a Web browser. You can choose which fields to include, and tools using this format can usually generate summaries. W3C also supports logging needs of proxy caches and captures a wider range of information. For more on this format, visit *www.w3.org/TR/WD-logfile.html*.

You can edit and reconfigure log file formats as a first step toward improving firewall efficiency. Fine-tuning log file formats to log the information you actually need makes it easier to review the files, helps with optimizing the firewall rule base, and can aid in improving performance and security by eliminating useless or duplicate entries. For example, you wouldn't want to log all connections to your Web server, as that would yield a log file larger than the server could hold. Similarly, you wouldn't want to log internal DHCP broadcasts from hosts seeking IP configuration from the nearest available DHCP server.

Log files should also be reviewed regularly for any problems, signs of attacks, duplicate entries, or unnecessary logging (such as the DHCP broadcasts mentioned previously), and firewall rules should be edited to improve security. Here's the general process to follow for reviewing log files and rules:

1. Start your log-viewing software and review the summary of recent log file events.

2. Display the raw data in the form of a report. You might create a report that sorts access attempts by source IP address so that you can see who's been attempting to connect to your network or by destination address to see where users are going on the Internet. (This information could be useful to track down the source of a downloaded Trojan or complaint of someone viewing objectionable content.)

3. Review the data and identify traffic patterns that point to problems with the firewall rules. For instance, log files with duplicate entries are evidence that rules should be reconfigured to eliminate repetition.

4. Adjust the rules accordingly.

5. Review subsequent log file data to make sure changes to the rules reduced the number of unnecessary log file entries.

Log files can also indicate signatures of attack attempts, such as port scans. A signature might be a sequence of log file entries in which one computer makes connection attempts to consecutive ports on a single computer (such as 192.168.0.1:234, 192.168.0.1:235, and so on); this signature could indicate that the computer attempting connections is scanning for open ports. You should respond by blocking all connection attempts from the source computer and making sure no unnecessary ports are open on the targeted computer or others on the internal network.

Preparing Log File Summaries and Generating Reports

A log file summary shows the major events that generated log file entries over a particular period, such as a day, week, or month. These summaries aren't reports, but they list totals of how many events occurred and what type and can be used to prepare reports.

Some firewall programs include log file analysis tools that prepare summaries of raw data over a certain period and then give you options for organizing the information into report forms. Other programs require using an add-on log analyzer. The freeware firewall Zone Alarm by Zone Labs is popular enough that another company, MCS (*http://zonelog.co.uk*), has created a log file analysis tool for it, called ZoneLog Analyser. Viewing raw data can be tedious and prone to errors. As you can see in Figure 11-2, the raw data in ZoneLog Analyser is difficult to read and interpret. Some columns serve no purpose for a general log review and make the file harder to read.

Generating a report that displays data in an easy-to-read format is preferable, and sorting features are particularly useful. Figure 11-3 shows a log file report that ZoneLog Analyser generated from the same data you viewed in raw format in Figure 11-2. You can customize the report further to display only the information you want by removing columns, as shown in Figure 11-3.

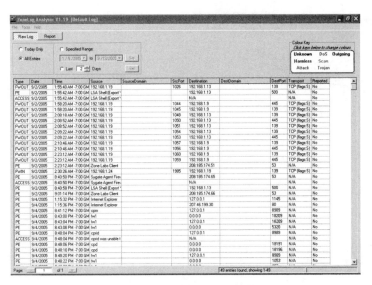

Figure 11-2   Raw data in ZoneLog Analyser

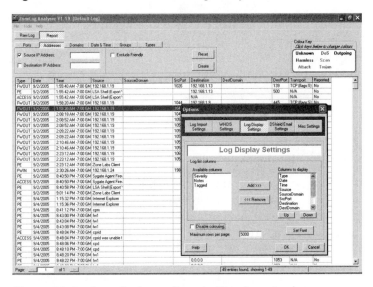

Figure 11-3   Log display options in ZoneLog Analyser

In Figure 11-3, the Type, SourceDomain, and DestDomain columns are shown. To generate the report in Figure 11-4, these columns were removed to make the data easier to read. (The column widths in Figure 11-4 were also adjusted manually to improve readability.)

ZoneLog Analyser is a helpful log file analysis tool capable of displaying basic information about traffic ZoneAlarm has logged, but with many comprehensive firewall programs, you can produce reports with statistics, such as the number of visitors to your Web site, the types of browsers visitors used, and the pages that were accessed most often. These reports are

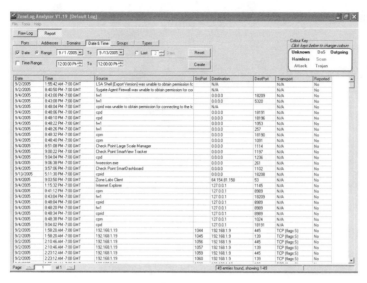

Figure 11-4   ZoneLog Analyser report sorted by date

similar to the reports a Web server generates, but firewall programs also report on security-related events, such as attack attempts. A Web server doesn't have a way to determine what constitutes a suspicious packet or an intrusion attempt; it simply serves Web page files and receives data submitted by clients.

Activity 11-2: Analyzing a Log File

Time Required: 10 minutes

Objective: Analyze a log file for duplicate entries.

Description: In this activity, you analyze the set of log file entries in Table 11-5 so that you can identify duplicate entries that need to be eliminated, thus improving firewall efficiency and security. You also examine the log file for possible attacks and any missing information. The LAN has IP addresses from 210.100.101.0 to 210.100.101.255. The firewall is at 210.100.101.1, the Web server is at 210.100.101.2, the DNS server is at 210.100.101.3, the SMTP server is at 210.100.101.4, and the POP3 server is at 210.100.101.5.

Table 11-5   Sample log file entries

Entry	Date	Source	Destination	Destination Port	Action	Type	Protocol
1	21Mar2004	67.23.89.9	210.100.101.23	137	Deny	Log	UDP
2	21Mar2004	67.23.89.9	210.100.101.23	137	Deny	Log	UDP
3	21Mar2004	189.101.10.88	210.100.101.151	114	Deny	Log	TCP
4	21Mar2004	189.101.10.88	210.100.101.151	115	Deny	Log	TCP
5	21Mar2004	210.100.101.3	155.201.8.83	37	Allow	Log	TCP

Table 11-5 Sample log file entries (continued)

Entry	Date	Source	Destination	Destination Port	Action	Type	Protocol
6	21Mar2004	67.23.89.9	210.100.101.23	137	Deny	Log	UDP
7	21Mar2004	210.100.101.35	210.100.101.3	137	Allow	Log	TCP
8	21Mar2004	189.101.10.88	210.100.101.151	116	Deny	Log	TCP
9	21Mar2004	189.101.10.88	210.100.101.151	117	Deny	Log	TCP
10	21Mar2004	210.100.101.126	210.100.101.2	80	Allow	Log	TCP
11	21Mar2004	225.23.202.5	210.100.101.2	80	Allow	Log	TCP
12	21Mar2004	189.101.10.88	210.100.101.151	118	Deny	Log	TCP

1. Are there any duplicate log file entries? What do they indicate, and how could you cut back on the duplication?

   _____

   _____

2. Are there any events that don't need to be logged?

   _____

   _____

3. Identify any attack attempts.

   _____

   _____

4. Is any type of information missing from the log files that needs to be there?

   _____

   _____

Improving Firewall Performance

After you install your firewall, you might notice it takes longer to connect to the Internet or receive files from external hosts. The problem could be that the firewall's default settings are causing it to perform unnecessary lookups and other operations. Here are some examples:

- *Host lookups*—Make sure the firewall uses the list of host names in the host computer to look up computers instead of having to resolve a domain name to an IP address every time a request is received. Remember that a computer hosting a firewall can maintain a list of internal hosts the firewall can use for internal communications. For external communications, a DNS server is required to resolve names to IP addresses. If the internal network is large, an internal DNS server is more efficient. Different firewalls have different methods for specifying the location of the Hosts file or DNS servers.

- *Decryption*—Check Point FireWall-1 (part of the Check Point NG security suite described later in this chapter) decrypts packets that arrive at the firewall, regardless of whether they are encrypted. You can modify this behavior in the Global Properties dialog box, as shown in Figure 11-5 later in this chapter.

- *Logging*—Many firewalls are set up by default to log events multiple times or to log events that aren't critical, such as internal hosts using native Windows networking communications (WINS or NetBIOS). By changing the default settings, you can save the firewall some work and reduce the disk space that log files take up.

The host computer's processor speed has the most impact on firewall performance. Choose a machine with the fastest CPU available. A dual-processor configuration can maintain a better performance level when the network traffic level increases.

Calculating Memory Requirements of Firewalls

For the firewall to operate smoothly, it must have at least the minimum required RAM, if not more. System requirements for the firewall are listed on the manual that comes with the software and on the manufacturer's Web site. For instance, a proxy server such as ISA Server 2000 needs a minimum of 256 MB RAM (refer to *www.microsoft.com/isaserver/evaluation/ sysreqs/2000.mspx*). In most cases, however, 512 MB to 1 GB of available RAM is preferred. The system also requires storage space to **cache** Web pages and other files. A standard formula for determining cache memory is [100 MB + (0.5 MB x number of users)]. If the program is intended to serve 500 users, for example, you need a minimum of 100 MB + (0.5 x 500), or 350 MB of cache space.

Testing the Firewall

After you have configured the firewall, testing it before and after it goes online helps ensure that users won't run into access problems. Ideally, you should test the firewall before you install it on the network so that you can shut down the software and make changes, if needed, without interrupting network traffic. An ideal environment for testing is a lab with two client computers: one connected to the external interface (to simulate a machine on the Internet) and another on the internal interface (to simulate a computer on the internal LAN). It's an especially good idea to equip one client computer with a network vulnerability scanner, such as WebSAINT (mentioned in Chapter 8), to scan it for open ports and services that might give attackers a way to circumvent the firewall.

If you don't have two computers, you can use one test machine and connect it to the internal interface and then connect to the firewall's external interface through a dial-up connection.

TIP

Configuring Advanced Firewall Functions

After you have the firewall's basic functions set up, you can add advanced features if they are supported, such as the following:

- *Data caching*—Storing Web pages in cache has already been discussed in connection with proxy servers in Chapter 10, but firewalls can also cache Web pages.

- *Remote management*—You can install remote management software, if available with your firewall, on remote computers to make monitoring and configuration easier, especially if you have several firewalls to manage or your firewalls aren't easy to access physically.

- *Application filtering*—You can configure many firewalls to perform inspection at the application protocol level so that filtering is based on application-level protocols, such as HTTP, SMTP, POP3, and IMAP.

- *Voice protocol support*—Voice protocols, such as H.323v2 or Session Initiation Protocol (SIP), are used for Voice over IP (VoIP) services, in which the IP network also provides telephone service.

- *Authentication*—High-end firewalls include authentication methods as an additional security feature.

- *Time-based access scheduling*—You can configure policies (access lists or rules) based on day of the week and time of day, for example.

In addition, you might also want to set up a form of load balancing, such as **load sharing**—the practice of configuring two or more firewalls to share the total traffic load. Each firewall in a load-sharing setup is active at the same time and uses a specialized protocol to communicate with the other firewalls. In Check Point NG, you configure load sharing in the Global Properties dialog box (see Figure 11-5).

11

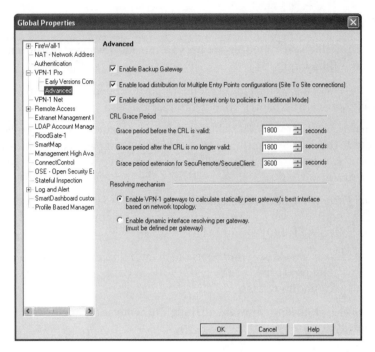

Figure 11-5   Advanced settings in Check Point NG

INSTALLING AND CONFIGURING CHECK POINT NG

In this section, you examine the decisions you need to make to install and configure Check Point NG, an enterprise-level firewall. This overview of the installation and configuration procedure shows how Check Point's components work together to protect a network. With Check Point NG, as with the other firewall applications, you start by reviewing your organization's security policy for the firewall's goals, which indicate what rules should be configured. As you learned in Chapters 9 and 10, the placement of the firewall is also important: A firewall that's the sole gateway for a network should be configured differently from one that shares a DMZ with a second firewall or is just one of several firewalls on a network.

To plan for installation, you need to answer questions such as the following:

- Is the firewall on the outside of the DMZ, or does it protect one part of the internal network from another part?

- How important is it to monitor employees' activities on the network?

After you've determined what security functions the firewall is to perform and its position on the network, you can begin installing and configuring it, as explained in the following sections.

Installing Check Point Modules

You can install Check Point NG on a computer running Windows 2000 Professional or Server or later, Windows NT with Service Pack 4 or later installed, Sun Solaris 7 and later, or Red Hat Linux 6.2 or later. You can also install it on a dedicated hardware appliance, such as the Nokia IP series.

A component is part of an application that performs a specific range of functions. Check Point NG contains a variety of components that work together to create an overall security architecture for a network. The Check Point NG CD has an option to select the components you need early in the installation process. They include the following:

- *Check Point Management Server*—This module maintains the Check Point databases, including network objects and definitions, policies, and logs.

- *Policy Editor*—You'll probably use this module most often; it enables you to create filter rules and identify network objects to protect.

- *VPN/FireWall*—This module includes the Inspection module for examining traffic and the VPN-1/FireWall-1 Security Servers, which provide authentication and content security features at the application level.

- *Log Viewer*—You use this module to configure and organize log files the firewall generates.

- *Inspection*—You use this module for traffic monitoring. It ensures that packets comply with the security policy. It also provides an auditing mechanism and a centralized location for logs and alerts at the network administrator's computer.

TIP

For more information on the modules in Check Point NG or other Check Point products, visit *www.checkpoint.com/support/technical/documents/docs_ng. html*. The Check Point NG Getting Started Guide is a good place to start. You might find it helpful to download a copy of this document for reference throughout this section.

Check Point NG integrates with products that provide antivirus protection and other functions through the use of its own protocol, Open Platform for Security (OPSEC). Developers use OPSEC to create solutions that integrate with Check Point NG to create a strong network security architecture. Examples of products you might integrate with the firewall include eSafe Protect (*www.esafe.com*), a program that scans e-mail, Web pages, and FTP traffic for viruses, and WebTrends (*www.webtrends.com*), a program well known for its capability to create graphical reports from log database information.

Step 1: Preparing to Install Check Point NG

Before you install Check Point NG, you need to determine where the program will be installed and prepare the host computer. Pick a directory on a standalone server, if possible. The default location for Check Point is the C:\WINNT directory. If you select another location, you must include a FWDIR variable pointing to the directory where the product is installed. (Refer to Check Point documentation for instructions on how to do this.) Eliminate all unnecessary services, as described in Chapter 10, and install all service packs and patches.

You also need to enable IP forwarding on the host computer (see Hands-on Project 11-1 later in this chapter). Check Point controls IP forwarding on the host computer by default to enable the gateway to forward packets to other IP addresses, and IP forwarding is enabled only when Check Point is running.

After you have the host computer prepared, go to the Check Point User Center (*https:// usercenter.checkpoint.com/usercenter/index.jsp*) to obtain a license key to use the software. To add the license, click Add in the Licenses tab of the Check Point Configuration Tool dialog box (see Figure 11-6).

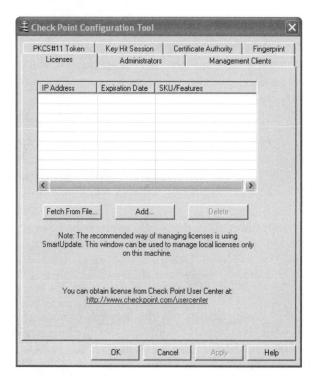

Figure 11-6   Adding a license key in Check Point NG

Remember that the type of license key you obtain determines how long you can use the software and the IP address on which the software has been installed. Be sure to get a license key that covers the length of time you plan to use Check Point NG before you renew or update the license.

Step 2: Select Check Point Modules to Install

When the installation program starts, you need to specify which components to install from the Product Menu. You can choose between Server/Gateway Components or Mobile/Desktop Components. Next, you're asked which product to install: Enterprise Primary Management, Enterprise Secondary Management, Enforcement Module & Primary Management, or Enforcement Module. Each one installs a slightly different set of modules, as follows:

- *Enterprise Primary Management or Enterprise Secondary Management*—Installs the Management Server

- *Enforcement Module & Primary Management*—Installs the VPN/FireWall module and Management Server

- *Enforcement Module*—Installs the VPN/FireWall module

Next, you need to decide whether to install NG with backward compatibility with previous versions and where to install the product.

Selecting which Management Clients you want to install is the next step, and you can choose from Log Viewer, Traffic Monitoring, System Status, and more. Management Clients can be added or removed later. Next, the Check Point Configuration program asks a series of questions to configure the product. After all configurations have been finished, a Setup Complete window is displayed, and you must restart the host to activate the software. You can make additional settings when the host restarts by running the Check Point Configuration program from the Start menu or by typing cpconfig at the command prompt.

Step 3: Configuring Network Objects

After you have installed the software, you can begin to define the objects on the network that the firewall needs to protect. Object definition and policy configurations for objects, along with most other Check Point configurations and management, are performed through "smart" management interfaces, such as SmartDashboard or the SmartView Tracker. In Check Point's management interfaces, you define the gateway and computers that the firewall needs to protect, which the program interface calls "network objects." After a network object is defined, you can specify policies for an object or group of objects. As you can see in Figure 11-7, the SmartDashboard window has a substantial amount of information and configuration options.

The SmartDashboard window is divided into these panes:

- *Object tree*—This pane displays a hierarchical list of objects in your network. A network object can be a gateway, computer, node, domain, service, or other device.

- *Rules*—This pane lists rules in the rule base derived from your network security policy.

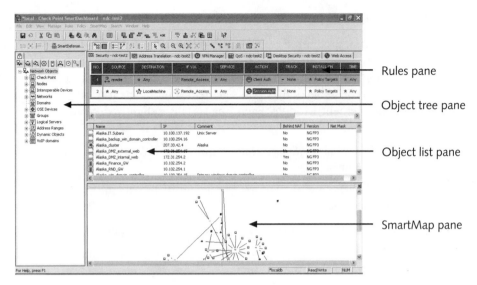

Figure 11-7   Check Point's SmartDashboard interface

- *Object list*—This pane, displayed under the Rules pane by default, is an alternative to the tree view. Network objects in this list can be sorted by name, IP address, or comments you add about each object.

- *SmartMap*—This pane shows a visual and interactive topology map of all objects being protected on your network. (You can configure the SmartMap in the Global Properties dialog box.)

The easiest way to define objects is to use Network Objects Manager, a GUI tool included in SmartDashboard. To open Network Objects Manager, choose Manage, Network Objects from the menu. You can add, delete, or edit the objects listed, as shown in Figure 11-8.

The objects you'll most likely use are Check Point Gateway (a gateway managed by the Management Server) and Check Point Node (a host computer on the network). A **node** can be a single computer, VPN appliance, gateway, host, or any combination of these devices.

Step 4: Creating Filter Rules

After you have defined the essential objects in your network, you can begin developing a set of packet-filtering rules. Check Point calls this rule base a "Policy Package." You can create separate sets of rules for different parts of your network, such as a VPN.

To create a new Policy Package, click File, New from the menu. A dialog box opens, prompting you to save your work. Click OK, and the New Policy Package dialog box opens. Assign a name to the Policy Package, select the policy types to be installed, as shown in Figure 11-9, and then click OK. After the Policy Package is installed, you can tailor the rule base to fit your needs.

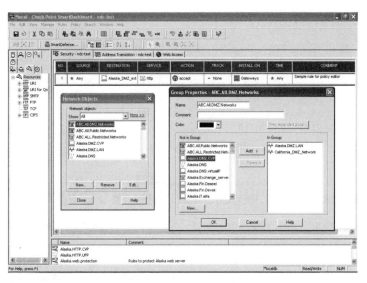

Figure 11-8   Managing network objects in SmartDashboard

11

Figure 11-9   Adding a new policy

What's New in Check Point NGX

Check Point NGX includes improved security and management capabilities, such as centralized management for an organization's perimeter, internal, and Web security needs. VPN security has also been enhanced by enforcing VPN rules by direction (inbound or outbound), and support for backup links and on-demand links is enabled by multiple VPN links between gateways. Backward compatibility for older authentication schemes, such as Firewall-1 password, OS password, RADIUS, LDAP, and TACACS, are supported for L2TP clients. For a complete list of NGX's features, visit *www.checkpoint.com/ngx/upgrade/index.html*.

INSTALLING AND CONFIGURING MICROSOFT ISA SERVER 2000

Microsoft ISA Server 2000 is a firewall designed to protect business networks and performs a variety of proxy server functions in addition to packet filtering, NAT, and other traditional firewall functions. The proxy server features include screening communication at the application level and caching Web pages to reduce network server load and improve the speed of accessing Web server pages.

The first step in installation is selecting the version of ISA Server 2000 you want: Standard Edition or Enterprise Edition. Table 11-6 summarizes the main differences between the two editions.

NOTE   The SCNP exam focuses on ISA Server 2000; however, the basic concepts and strategies for deploying a proxy/firewall server are the same. If you're interested in learning more about ISA Server 2004, visit *www.microsoft.com/isaserver/default.mspx*. At the time of this writing, a 120-day evaluation version was available. Another site with interesting ISA toys and information is *www.isaserver.org*.

Table 11-6   ISA Server 2000: Standard versus Enterprise

Feature	Standard	Enterprise
Server	Standalone	Multiple
Processors	One	Up to four
Policy	Simple	Multilevel

NOTE   ISA Server 2000 doesn't run on Windows XP or 2000 Professional. ISA Server is usually run on a hardened version of Windows 2000 Server or Windows Server 2003 and is often purchased as a preconfigured package (ISA Server, OS, and hardware) from a third-party vendor.

Licensing ISA Server 2000

You need to obtain a license to use ISA Server 2000 on a permanent basis. It's licensed on a per-processor basis, meaning you need to purchase one license for each processor on the host where ISA Server 2000 is installed. You can then use as many clients as you need to connect to the server. Although trial software for ISA Server 2000 is no longer available, as of this writing you can download a 120-day trial version of ISA Server 2004 from the Microsoft Web site (*www.microsoft.com/isaserver*). Microsoft also has trial versions of Windows Server 2003 available if you need the operating system.

Installing ISA Server 2000

Installation of ISA Server 2000 is simplified by a wizard that guides you through the installation steps. However, after you begin to install the program, Windows 2000 Server's built-in Web server, Internet Information Services (IIS), is stopped. After ISA Server 2000 is installed, you have to uninstall IIS or reconfigure it to work with ISA Server 2000.

NOTE   If you install the Enterprise Edition, you need to run the ISA Server Enterprise Initialization Tool, which modifies Windows 2000 Active Directory so that ISA Server 2000 can use it.

11

The following sections describe the basic steps for installing ISA Server 2000: choosing a server mode, configuring cache locations, and setting IP addresses of the internal address space.

TIP   Make sure you have the latest updates installed before you install ISA Server 2000. You can find the current Windows service pack and check for other relevant updates at the Microsoft Windows Update Web site.

Step 1: Choosing a Server Mode

One of the first decisions to make during installation is the mode in which the server operates, which determines the features the firewall offers. Figure 11-10 shows the options for each server mode:

- *Firewall*—In this mode, ISA Server 2000 can perform stateful packet filtering at multiple layers of the OSI model.

- *Cache*—In this mode, ISA Server 2000 stores Web pages in cache.

- *Integrated*—This mode enables you to use functions in both Firewall and Cache modes.

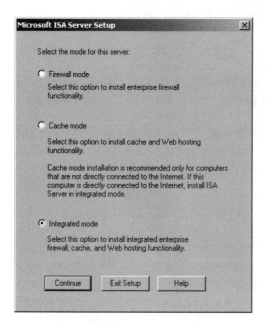

Figure 11-10   ISA Server modes

Integrated mode seems an obvious choice because it gives you the most flexibility. However, you might choose Firewall mode if you already have a proxy server on the network that stores Web pages in cache or if you don't want to cache Web pages. You might choose Cache mode if you already have a stateful packet filter in place. You can't change the server mode after installation, so you must be certain of the tasks you want ISA to perform and install accordingly.

Step 2: Configuring Cache Locations and Setting Addresses

If you specified Cache or Integrated mode, the installation wizard prompts you to select the location where you want to store cached files (see Figure 11-11). Cached Web pages need to be stored on an NTFS-formatted drive. You also specify the amount of disk storage space set aside for cache; the amount depends on the number of users (see "Calculating Memory Requirements of Firewalls" earlier in this chapter).

After configuring the disk cache space, you create a **local address table (LAT)** that defines your network's internal addressing scheme (see Figure 11-12), which is the range of IP addresses that span your network's address space. You also identify the network adapter of the host computer. After you have completed the LAT, the installation finishes, and the Getting Started Wizard opens automatically so that you can begin configuring ISA Server.

Make sure there are no addresses in the LAT other than your internal network addresses.

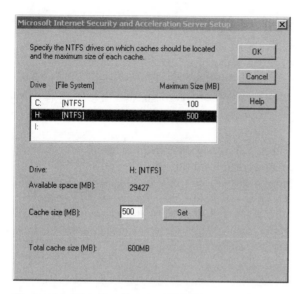

Figure 11-11   Configuring ISA Server caching

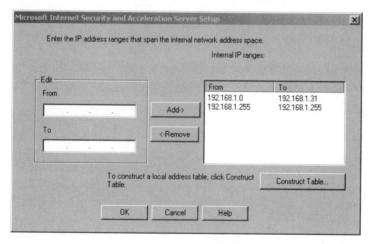

Figure 11-12   Creating the local address table

Configuring ISA Server 2000

If you have done your homework and planned your installation carefully, configuring ISA Server shouldn't be too complicated. Part of your planning should have included a risk assessment and review of your security policy. These critical facets of securing your network provide most of the information you need to configure the rule base, logging, and alerts and to fine-tune ISA's services. If you installed ISA as a Web proxy only, much of the work is already done when the installation is finished. If you selected Integrated or Firewall modes, you have a bit more work to do.

Step 1: Creating a Rule Base from Your Security Policy

ISA Server 2000's Getting Started Wizard leads you through the steps in creating the rule base derived from your security policy. This wizard makes ISA Server 2000 especially easy to configure because it helps you create the filtering rules that govern Internet access for your organization. The Getting Started Wizard runs in the ISA Management Console (shown in Figure 11-13), which you can use to change settings after the program is running.

NOTE ISA Server 2000 comes with a pair of built-in application filters designed to defeat two of the most common types of attacks. The first type is the DNS host name overflow, in which long host names are sent to the DNS server, which can cause the server to stop running and, therefore, open it to an attacker's control. The second type is the POP buffer overflow, in which the attacker sends more data than a POP server's buffer can handle. This overflow makes it possible for an attacker to gain access to the server's root level.

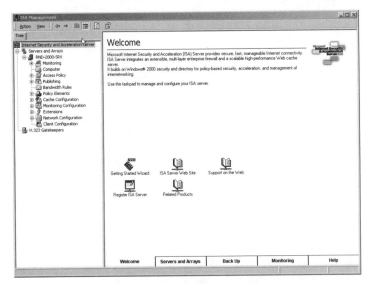

Figure 11-13 The ISA Management Console

The following sections describe the basic concepts in configuring ISA Server, including policy elements, monitoring the server, and the ISA Management Console. Along with most features of ISA Server, policy elements are created and managed in the ISA Management Console. If you take a closer look at Figure 11-13, you can see a Policy Elements folder in the tree view at the left.

ISA Server is designed to integrate with Microsoft Active Directory, and the ISA Management Console is usually added to the Microsoft Management Console (MMC) for Active Directory during the ISA installation as an **MMC snap-in**. As you can see in Figure 11-13,

ISA Server also has a Getting Started Wizard that walks you through the process of configuring the server.

Step 4: Selecting Policy Elements

One of the first steps in configuring ISA Server 2000 (or any firewall) is identifying the policy elements you want the program to filter and protect. ISA Server 2000 can work with several types of policy elements, as shown in Figure 11-14.

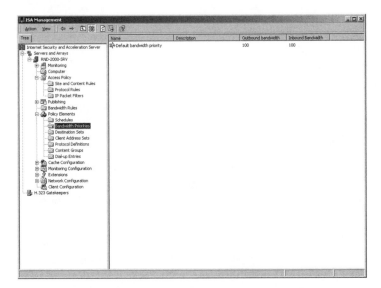

Figure 11-14   Policy elements in ISA Server 2000

- *Schedules*—Specifies when a rule is in effect. ISA Server has two preconfigured schedules: Work Hours, which is Monday through Friday, 9 a.m. through 5 p.m., and Weekends, which is all day Saturday and Sunday.

- *Bandwidth Priorities*—Defines the priority level applied to connections passing through ISA Server. Connections with an assigned priority have a higher priority than those without, by default. Bandwidth priorities are directional, meaning they can be controlled for outbound and inbound requests. Bandwidth priorities have an assigned number from 1 to 200; the higher the number, the higher the priority.

- *Destination Sets*—A destination is a computer name, IP address, or IP address range and can include a path. A **destination set** includes one or more computers or folders on specific computers. There are internal destination sets (groups of computers in the local intranet) and external destination sets (computers outside the intranet).

- *Client Address Sets*—Client computers that are grouped and managed by IP address. You can specify rules to apply to or exclude specific **client address sets** instead of configuring rules for each client computer.

- *Protocol Definitions*—Specifies the port number for the initial connection, the low-level protocol (TCP or UDP), the direction (Send only, Receive only, Send receive, or Receive send for UDP or Inbound or Outbound for TCP), and secondary connections (optional, specifying the range of port numbers, protocol, and direction used for additional packets following the initial connection). Protocol rules refer to the protocol definitions to determine handling of requests. For example, if a client requests access to a resource using a specific protocol, ISA checks the protocol rules. If the rules deny use of that protocol, the request is denied.

- *Content Groups*—Specifies MIME types and file extensions for HTTP and FTP traffic passing through ISA's Web Proxy service.

- *Dial-up Entries*—Specifies how ISA Server connects to the Internet. A dial-up entry includes the name of the network connection, the user name, and the password for a user who has permission to access the dial-up connection.

Monitoring the Server

After you have created a set of filtering rules, you restart your computer and log on as Administrator so that you can manage the program. You reopen the ISA Management Console so that you can refine security settings and configure additional options for server management.

You can also use the ISA Server Performance Monitor for real-time monitoring of the server, including viewing alerts as soon as they are issued. To configure monitoring and alerts, you need to set up **counters**—utilities that keep track of the number of active TCP, UDP, or other connections currently forwarding data on the network. To access ISA Server Performance Monitor (see Figure 11-15), click Start, point to Programs or All Programs, point to Microsoft ISA Server, and click ISA Server Performance Monitor.

Activity 11-3: Analyzing How Proxy Servers Handle Packets

Time Required: 20 minutes

Objective: Learn how proxy servers shield internal computers.

Description: Proxy servers shield internal computers by rebuilding packets and changing IP addresses. In this activity, you improve your understanding of how proxy servers process IP addresses by analyzing the process step by step. Figure 11-16 shows LAN clients with Web browsers, a proxy server, and a Web server and how they interact. Use this diagram to guide you through this activity.

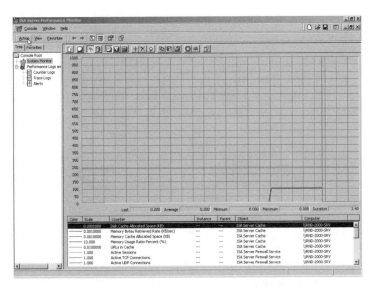

Figure 11-15   ISA Server Performance Monitor

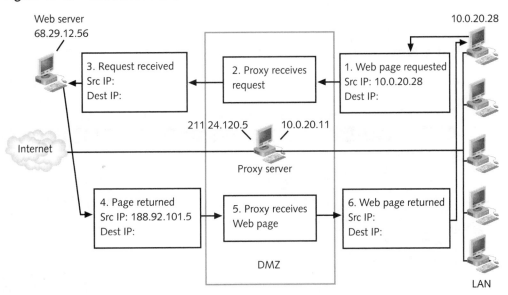

Figure 11-16   Interaction of elements in a packet transaction

List the source and destination IP addresses for each step in the process to show how IP addresses change as they go through the proxy server:

1. A computer on the internal network with the source IP address 10.0.20.28 makes a request to view a Web page from the server shown in the upper-left corner of Figure 11-16. Fill in the destination IP address for box 1 that appears in the packet the proxy server receives.

   _____

2. In box 3, what source and destination IP addresses appear in the packet sent by the proxy server to the external Web server?

   _____

3. In box 4, what destination IP address does the proxy server receive in the response sent to it by the external Web server?

   _____

4. In box 6, what are the source and destination IP addresses in the packet sent by the proxy server to the original host after processing the response from the Web server?

   _____

What's New in ISA Server 2004

ISA Server 2004 also comes in Standard and Enterprise editions, compared in Table 11-7.

Table 11-7   ISA Server 2004: Standard versus Enterprise

Feature	Standard Edition	Enterprise Edition
Server	Single server	Up to 32 nodes through Network Load Balancing (NLB)
Processors	Up to four	Unlimited (depends on OS)
Policies	Local	Array and enterprise policies use Active Directory Application Mode (ADAM)
Windows Network Load Balancing (NLB)	Not supported	Included
Caching	Single server store	Unlimited using Cache Array Routing Protocol (CARP)

ISA Server 2004's HTTP policy allows application layer filtering on a per-rule basis to enable custom constraints for HTTP inbound and outbound access. The HTTP policy can also be configured to block any connection attempts to the OS executable content. A key feature is the capability to block content regardless of file extension. ISA Server 2004 has extensive support for complex protocols to give you control over streaming media and voice/video applications. Protocol support also includes IP-level protocols, meaning IPSec traffic can be enabled. The configuration wizard is one of the easiest Microsoft has created, and ISA Server 2000 users should be up to speed in no time.

Managing and Configuring Iptables

Iptables, which is included in version 2.4.x and later of the Linux kernel, is used to configure packet filter rules for the Linux firewall Netfilter. It replaces Ipchains (which was developed from a Linux firewall called Ipfwadm). Unlike Ipchains, Iptables enables Netfilter to perform stateful rather than stateless packet filtering. You can also filter packets based on a full set of TCP option flags instead of just the SYN flag, which was the only filtering flag available in Ipchains. Unlike Check Point NG and Microsoft ISA Server 2000, Iptables is a command-line tool. It can be used to set up logging, NAT, and forwarding packets from one port to another.

Like other packet-filtering programs, Iptables works with sets of rules. Unlike other programs, however, the rules are grouped in the form of **chains**. Because you're already familiar with the idea of a rule base—a set of packet-filtering rules used by a firewall or router—you might think of a chain as being similar to a rule base. The differences are that Linux makes use of multiple rule bases/chains, and a rule in one chain can activate a specific rule in another chain.

Built-in Chains

When Iptables receives a packet, the chains are reviewed. Iptables comes with three built-in chains:

- *Output*—This chain of rules is reviewed when packets are received that originate from inside a LAN with a destination address on an external network.

- *Input*—This chain of rules is for packets that originate from an external network destined for a location on the internal network.

- *Forward*—This chain is used when a packet needs to be routed to another location.

The packet then moves through all the rules in a chain until a match is found. If a match is found, one of four decisions is made on how to handle it:

- *Accept*—The packet is accepted.

- *Drop*—The packet is dropped without any error message, which provides effective security because it doesn't let outside users know anything about the system that received and processed the request.

- *Queue*—The packet is queued for processing by a specific application.

- *Return*—Tells Iptables to stop checking rules in the chain and return to the original chain.

The chains of rules work together, as shown in Figure 11-17.

11

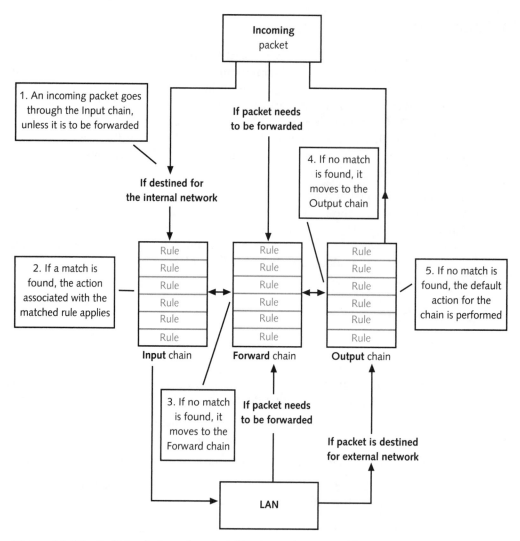

Figure 11-17   Built-in chains of packet-filtering rules in Iptables

NOTE   An incoming packet goes through the Input chain, unless it's forwarded.

The following process takes place in Figure 11-17:

1. Incoming packets that aren't forwarded go through the Input chain.

2. If a match is found, the action associated with the matched rule applies.

3. If no match is found, it moves to the Forward chain.

4. If no match is found, it moves to the Output chain.

5. If no match is found, the default action for the chain is performed.

In the iptables command, you can configure the default action for a chain with the use of the -P option, which sets the default policy for a built-in chain. Then comes the chain name, OUTPUT, and the new policy, ACCEPT. The following command sets the default action Accept for any packets originating from the internal network destined for the Internet:

```
iptables -P OUTPUT ACCEPT
```

The following command blocks all incoming connection attempts by default:

```
iptables -P INPUT DROP
```

After you set the default action, you can configure more specific actions on a case-by-case basis. The two preceding commands are optional starting points for more restrictive rules that follow.

Another default command rejects all forwarded packets by default. For example, the following command blocks, by default, any packets the firewall forwards to a destination computer:

```
iptables -P FORWARD DROP
```

Blocking packets from being forwarded by default prevents external users from accessing internal computers in case a user activates a service on a port by accident, which could allow an attacker to exploit the opening.

To see other options that can be used with the iptables command, type iptables –h at the command prompt to access the Help file, as shown in Figure 11-18.

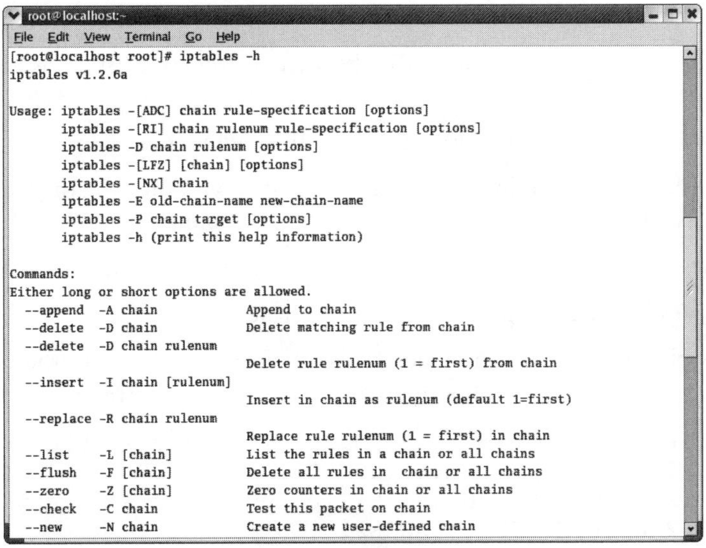

Figure 11-18 A list of Iptables options for chains

After you set the default rules, you can create specific rules by using the commands described in the following section.

 One advantage of using Iptables rather than an add-on firewall is that because it's part of the Linux kernel, it runs through its packet-filtering rule base and makes decisions quickly.

NOTE

User-Defined Chains

In addition to built-in chains, user-defined chains can be established. You create them by using the commands for configuring individual rules. Some of the available commands are described in the following list (with *chain* representing the name of the chain to which the rule belongs):

- -A *chain rule*—Adds a new rule to the chain.
- -I *chain rule-number rule*—Enables you to place a new rule in a specific location in the chain, as indicated by *rule-number*.
- -R *chain rule-number rule*—Enables you to replace a rule with a new one in the location specified by *rule-number*.
- -D *chain rule-number*—Deletes the rule at the position specified by [rule-number].
- -D *chain rule*—Deletes a rule.

Commands used to create rules include the following:

- -s *source*—Identifies the source IP address.
- -d *destination*—Identifies the destination IP address.
- -p *protocol*—Identifies the protocol to be used in the rule (such as TCP, UDP, ICMP).
- -i *interface*—Identifies the network interface the rule uses.
- -j *target*—Identifies the action (or **target**) associated with the rule; the target can be an action (such as Allow or Drop), a network, or a subnet.
- !—Negates whatever follows it, such as an IP address you want to exclude.
- -l—Activates logging if a packet matches the rule.

Some examples should make these commands clearer. For example, refer to the set of rules in Table 11-2 earlier in this chapter. The following commands create the same rules:

```
iptables -A OUTPUT -s any -d 210.100.101.1 -p any -j DROP
iptables -A OUTPUT -s any -d 210.100.101.2 -p HTTP -j ACCEPT
iptables -A OUTPUT -s 210.100.101.0-210.100.101.255 -d any !
   210.100.101.2 HTTP,HTTPS -j ACCEPT
iptables -A OUTPUT -s any -d any -p any -j DROP -l
```

In addition, you can identify a service rather than a protocol: www for the World Wide Web, smtp for outgoing e-mail, and pop3 for incoming e-mail. The following rule enables all users on the 10.0.20.0/24 network to access the company Web server at 10.0.20.2 using the World Wide Web service:

```
iptables -A OUTPUT -s 10.0.20.0/24 -d 10.0.20.2 www -j ACCEPT
```

Configuring Iptables is complex; this overview is intended only to give you a starting point. For more information, see the main pages for Iptables in the Red Hat Linux Help files. An excellent resource for Netfilter and Iptables is *www.netfilter.org*.

ACTIVITY

Activity 11-4: Configuring Iptables

Time Required: 20 minutes

Objective: Use a Linux system to configure Iptables rules.

Description: Iptables is a packet-filtering tool that allows the Netfilter application to perform stateful packet filtering, NAT, logging, and other security functions for the Linux kernel. In this activity, you activate Iptables and begin configuring it. You need a computer equipped with Red Hat Linux 8.0 or later to perform this activity. Assume the following about the network you're configuring: The network is at 10.0.20.0/24, the firewall is at 10.0.20.1, the e-mail server is at 10.0.20.2, and the Web server is at 10.0.20.3.

1. Click the **Red Hat** icon or equivalent for your OS, point to **System Tools**, and click **Terminal**.

2. To configure Iptables to run whenever you start your computer, enter **chkconfig --level 345 iptables on** at the command prompt, and then press **Enter**.

3. If necessary, turn off any other security programs you have running by entering the following:

```
service ipchains off
service ip6tables off
```

4. Type **iptables –L**, and then press **Enter** to view the default chains and their policies. What do you notice about the default actions?

_____

_____

_____

_____

5. Type the following commands to set default policies for the built-in chains. After each line, press **Enter**:

```
iptables -P OUTPUT ACCEPT
iptables -P INPUT DROP
iptables -P FORWARD DROP
```

11

6. Type **iptables –L** and press **Enter** to verify the policy changes. (*Hint:* You can press the up arrow key to cycle through previous commands.)

7. Create a rule for the following security policy statement: Anyone on the internal network can access the Web server on the DMZ, as well as external Web sites.

_____

_____

_____

_____

_____

8. Create a rule that prevents hosts on the Internet from accessing internal hosts directly using the World Wide Web service.

_____

_____

_____

_____

_____

9. Create two rules that enable anyone on the internal network to connect to the company e-mail server but not to any external e-mail servers using SMTP.

_____

_____

_____

_____

_____

10. To save your changes, type **service iptables save**, and then press **Enter**.

TIP

At this writing, the domain requirements for the Security Certified Professional Network Defense and Countermeasures (NDC) exam cover the installation of Ipchains. However, Iptables is covered in this book because it has replaced Ipchains and because the two programs have similar configurations. For more information on Ipchains, visit *www.tldp.org/HOWTO/IPCHAINS-HOWTO.html*.

These three products, Check Point NG, ISA Server 2000, and Iptables, clearly have many capabilities not discussed in this chapter. In fact, it would take an entire book to cover even one of these products! You should do extensive research using many different resources, especially reviewing full product documentation, before attempting this (or any) exam.

CHAPTER SUMMARY

- Improving a firewall configuration often involves optimizing existing resources, such as the rule base and log files. Optimizing the rule base can enhance efficiency and improve security by eliminating redundant or unnecessary rules or reordering rules so that the most important and common ones are near the top of the rule base.

- Log files provide critical information about network traffic and attempts to attack computers on your internal network. You can control what the firewall logs and how those files are stored to improve the firewall's performance. Some firewalls come with so many types of log data that including them all would make the files unwieldy. Log only the traffic representing the most serious security concerns and manage the size of log files so that they don't consume too many resources.

- Many firewalls and IDSs generate log files formatted in plain text that you can view with a text editor, such as Notepad, but text-based log files can be difficult to read. Other firewalls give you the option of saving log files in different formats, such as ODBC or W3C Extended format. Another option for viewing log files is to use the firewall's built-in interface.

- Fine-tuning log file formats to log only the information you actually need makes it easier to review files, helps with optimizing the firewall rule base, and can aid in improving performance and security by eliminating useless or duplicate entries.

- Some firewall programs include log file analysis tools that prepare summaries of raw data over a certain period and then give you options for organizing the information into report forms. Other programs require using an add-on log analyzer.

- After you install your firewall, you need to configure basic functions, such as host lookup, encryption/decryption settings, and logging. The host computer's processor speed has the most impact on firewall performance. After you have the firewall's basic functions set up, you can add advanced features, such as data caching, remote management, application filtering, voice and multimedia application support, load balancing, and failover redundancy.

- For the machine hosting the firewall, choose a machine with the fastest processor available and at least the minimum required RAM, if not more. A standard formula for determining requirements for cache memory is [100 MB + (0.5 MB x number of users)].

- After you have configured the firewall, testing it before and after it goes online helps ensure that users won't run into access problems. Ideally, you should test the firewall before you install it on the network so that you can shut down the software and make changes, if needed, without interrupting network traffic.

- Check Point NG is a suite of firewall modules used to implement a security policy through stateful packet filtering, Network Address Translation, and authentication. Log file analysis, real-time monitoring, and remote management are also available.

- Microsoft ISA Server 2000 improves network security through traditional firewall filtering and NAT and improves network performance through caching Web pages.

- Iptables is a Linux command-line tool for creating packet filter rules. It includes three built-in chains of filter rules that monitor inbound and outbound packets, as well as packets the firewall needs to forward to specific destinations.

KEY TERMS

cache — Store data on disk for later retrieval; also a hard disk area where files are stored.

chains — Sets of packet-filtering rules used by the Linux tool Iptables.

client address sets — Client computers that are grouped and managed by IP address.

counters — Utilities that keep track of the number of active TCP, UDP, or other connections currently forwarding data on the network.

destination set — Includes one or more computers or folders on specific computers. There are internal destination sets (groups of computers in the local intranet) and external destination sets (computers outside the intranet).

Iptables — A packet-filtering command-line tool that comes with version 2.4.x or later of the Linux kernel.

load sharing — The practice of configuring two or more firewalls to share the total traffic load.

local address table (LAT) — A set of IP addresses that defines a network's internal addressing scheme for a firewall or proxy server.

MMC snap-in — A management utility added to the Microsoft Management Console (MMC) in Microsoft server operating systems. Snap-ins for a variety of administrative functions are available.

node — A single computer, VPN appliance, gateway, host, or any combination of these devices.

target — In the Linux tool Iptables, the target determines what action is taken on packets matching a specific criteria.

REVIEW QUESTIONS

1. Which of the following guidelines should you keep in mind when editing your rule base? (Choose all that apply.)

   a. Place rules governing domain objects near the bottom of the rule base.

   b. Make your rule base as detailed as possible.

   c. Place the most frequently matched rules near the top of the rule base.

   d. Adjust default logging so that the firewall logs all traffic.

2. One of the simplest and most effective ways to improve a rule base is to do which of the following?

   a. Reduce the number of rules.

   b. Remove duplicate or unnecessary listings.

   c. Make sure the rule base contains the recommended number of rules.

   d. Reverse the order of rule processing.

3. You shouldn't log events resulting from attempts to access restricted resources. True or False?

4. The firewall host computer's _____ has the most impact on firewall performance.

   a. RAM cache

   b. network card speed

   c. available hard drive space

   d. processor speed

5. How can effective firewall administration play a role in disaster recovery?

   a. by keeping the rule base simple

   b. by keeping backups of the current configuration

   c. by keeping copies of the most recent log files

   d. by testing the firewall on a regular basis

6. What is the advantage of saving firewall logs in Open Database Connectivity (ODBC) format?

   a. reading logs using the firewall itself

   b. presenting logs in a graphical format

   c. opening logs in a Web browser

   d. opening logs with a database application

7. Having several administrators available to configure a firewall can _____ . (Choose all that apply.)

   a. make developing content filters easier

   b. create multiple packet-filtering rules

   c. speed up periodic firewall maintenance

   d. cause confusion

8. Why do so many firewalls, by default, log packets that are denied?

   a. to keep log file size to a minimum

   b. to track unsuccessful access attempts

   c. to have a record on file in case users complain

   d. to be able to correct rules to allow access to the same packets

11

9. If a firewall doesn't look up host names on the host computer, what happens? (Choose all that apply.)

   a. Performance slows.

   b. The firewall has to resolve domain names.

   c. The firewall drops all packets.

   d. The firewall could potentially crash.

10. Voice protocols, such as _____ , are used for Voice over IP (VoIP) services, in which the IP network also provides telephone service. (Choose all that apply.)

    a. H.323v2

    b. ODBC

    c. Session Initiation Protocol (SIP)

    d. L2F

11. Which program decrypts incoming packets by default?

    a. Microsoft ISA Server 2000

    b. Iptables

    c. Ipchains

    d. Check Point NG

12. Which of the following is a common formula for determining cache memory needs?

    a. 1 GB + (0.5 MB x [1.5 x number of users])

    b. 100 MB + (0.5 MB x number of users)

    c. 0.5 MB x number of users

    d. 350 MB + (0.5 MB x number of users)

13. Check Point NG integrates with products that provide antivirus protection and other functions through the use of _____ .

    a. Compatibility Server

    b. Management Server

    c. OPSEC

    d. System Status

14. ISA Server 2000 can be installed on which operating systems? (Choose all that apply.)

    a. Windows 2000 Professional

    b. Windows 2000 Server

    c. Windows XP Professional

    d. Windows Server 2003

15. Iptables built-in chains include _____ . (Choose all that apply.)
    a. Inbound
    b. Output
    c. Reverse
    d. Forward

16. The default location for Check Point is in the C:\WINNT directory. If you select another location, you must include which of the following to point to the location where the product is installed?
    a. MKDIR variable
    b. RMDIR variable
    c. PTR record
    d. FWDIR variable

17. What do Iptables chains consist of?
    a. IP addresses
    b. packet-filtering rules
    c. log file listings
    d. encrypted packets

18. The SmartMap in Check Point NG's SmartDashboard is which of the following?
    a. a hierarchical list of all objects in the network
    b. a GUI tool in SmartDashboard for defining objects
    c. a list of rules derived from your network security policy
    d. an interactive display of all objects in your network

19. To configure Iptables to run whenever you start your computer, which of the following commands do you use?
    a. chk --level 375 chains run
    b. config --level 345 iptables run
    c. chkconfig --level 345 iptables on
    d. chkconfig --level iptables on

20. Which of the following defines your network's internal addressing scheme?
    a. routing table
    b. network address table
    c. local address table
    d. intranet routing table

11

HANDS-ON PROJECTS

Hands-On Project 11-1: Enabling IP Forwarding

Time Required: 10 minutes

Objective: Enable IP forwarding in Windows XP.

Description: In this activity, you enable IP forwarding in Windows XP. IP forwarding, as discussed in the chapter, must be enabled for Check Point to manage traffic effectively.

 Warning! You will be modifying the Windows Registry directly in this activity. If Registry Editor isn't used correctly, you can cause serious problems, some of which can be corrected only by reinstalling the operating system. Be sure you have a backup of the current system state in case anything goes wrong, and follow these instructions carefully.

1. To create a backup for Windows XP, you need to create a restore point as a backup. Click **Start**, **Help and Support**. The Windows Help and Support Center opens.

2. Under Pick a task, click **Undo changes to your computer with System Restore** to open the System Restore window. In the pane on the right, click the **Create a restore point** option button, then click **Next**.

3. Enter a restore point description, such as "Before enabling IP forwarding." Click **Create**, and the restore point is created. Now you have a backup in case something goes wrong.

4. Click **Close** to close the System Restore window and the Help and Support Center window.

5. To open Registry Editor, click **Start**, **Run**, type **regedit.exe** in the Open text box, and click **OK**.

6. In the Registry Editor window, click to expand the listings until you're at the Registry key HKEY_LOCAL_MACHINE\SYSTEM\CurrentControlSet\Services\Tcpip\Parameters. (You have to scroll through the list of services to locate Tcpip.)

7. Make sure Parameters is highlighted, as shown in Figure 11-19. (Note that your Registry items might differ from what's shown in the figure.)

8. In the pane on the right, locate and right-click the **IPEnableRouter** value, and then click **Modify** to open the Edit DWORD Value dialog box.

9. In the Value text box, change the 0 to a **1**. A value of 1 enables TCP/IP forwarding for all network connections. Click **OK**.

10. Close Registry Editor.

11. Close all open windows, and shut down your computer, unless your instructor tells you otherwise.

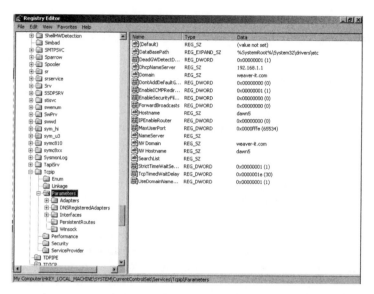

Figure 11-19   Configuring TCP/IP parameters in Registry Editor

NOTE

After you have completed Hands-On Project 11-1, you should disable IP forwarding unless you have Check Point NG running and intend to practice using it. To reverse the changes made in the project, return to the System Restore window as instructed in Steps 1 and 2, except click **Restore my computer to an earlier time** rather than **Create a Restore point**. Select the restore point you created in Step 3, and follow the instructions to undo your changes.

CASE PROJECTS

CASE PROJECTS

Case Project 11-1: Peer Reviews and Final Project Revisions

As you near the end of this running case project, it's important to realize that your peers are a valuable resource. In a professional setting, you'll likely spend most of your time working in a team environment, so learning how to work well with others is essential. Often, this means giving and taking constructive criticism, evaluating differing opinions and ideas, and choosing the solution that achieves the organization's goals, regardless of whose idea it is. Most successful projects are a culmination of the work of many people.

This running case project has been an individual effort so far, although you might have exchanged papers for a brief peer review in previous chapters. For this chapter, you exchange papers with other students for a full peer review of your project.

First, review your paper to make sure it contains all the required information. Refer to previous chapters to make sure you haven't missed anything, and double-check for accuracy. (For example, if you added firewalls, make sure you updated your network diagram to reflect the new configuration.) When you're satisfied that your paper is ready, exchange it with a classmate as directed by your instructor. Be sure to keep a clean backup copy in digital form.

After everyone has exchanged papers, your instructor will hand out a Peer Review Form. Fill it out and answer the questions, including any comments you might have about the project you're reviewing. You can also enter comments, correction, or questions on the project itself (digital or hard-copy format). Be professional and remain objective, and remember to be respectful of the author. When you have finished your review, submit the completed Peer Review Form and the marked project to your instructor or return it to the author (as directed by your instructor).

After your paper is returned with a completed Peer Review Form, read your classmate's comments. Evaluate his or her ideas and opinions carefully. Remember, this feedback is not a personal attack; it's intended to help you produce the best possible project. Revise your project as needed, correcting spelling, grammar, and punctuation errors, clarifying any areas, if necessary, and including missing information the reviewer might have pointed out. When you're finished, remember to proofread again, and check accuracy, completeness, content, and references.

CHAPTER 12

STRENGTHENING DEFENSE THROUGH ONGOING MANAGEMENT

After reading this chapter and completing the exercises, you will be able to:

♦ Strengthen network control by managing security events

♦ Improve analysis by auditing network security procedures

♦ Strengthen detection by managing an intrusion detection system

♦ Improve network defense by changing a defense in depth configuration

♦ Strengthen network performance by keeping pace with changing needs

♦ Increase your knowledge base by keeping on top of industry trends

In previous chapters, you've learned about designing and configuring an intrusion detection system (IDS). This chapter discusses how to manage the information from an IDS and other security systems in your network defense. Through efficient management, you can maximize the performance level of your IDS and other areas of your network's overall security configuration.

Many organizations create positions, such as computer security manager (CSM), to cover the ongoing management of network security systems. The responsibilities of a CSM should be spelled out clearly in the organization's security policy. In this chapter, you learn about these managerial responsibilities, including security event management, security auditing, managing an IDS, improving a defense in depth configuration, keeping pace with network needs, and maintaining your knowledge base to keep up with fast-changing events in network security.

STRENGTHENING CONTROL: SECURITY EVENT MANAGEMENT

If you're hired by a large multinational corporation to "manage security," your initial tasks are likely to include cataloguing the various security devices you need to manage. You might discover that the organization already has a range of devices, such as:

- Packet-filtering routers
- VPN appliances
- An IDS at each branch office
- One or more firewalls at each office
- Event logs or syslogs (system logs) for selected systems in each office

The flow of information from these devices is shown in Figure 12-1.

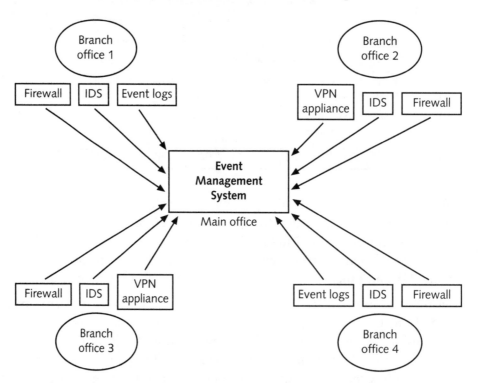

Figure 12-1   Flow of information from multiple sources

You could easily have 10, 20, or more devices sending log file data that you need to manage. How do you keep track of all the information and respond to legitimate security concerns without becoming overwhelmed? You need to create and manage a security incident response team (SIRT), as described in Chapter 8. You also need to establish a **security event management program** for gathering and consolidating events from multiple sources so that you can analyze the information to improve network security. The following sections discuss different aspects of this program to improve procedures and strengthen security while maintaining productivity:

- Monitoring events
- Managing data from multiple sensors
- Managing IDS signatures
- Managing change

Monitoring Events

Network protection needs to be conducted on an ongoing basis to keep up with new vulnerabilities. You need to establish a process for securing, monitoring, testing, and continually strengthening your network's level of protection. One way to improve network defenses is through ongoing **event monitoring**—reviewing alert and event logs your security devices and operating systems produce and testing the network periodically to identify any weak points. The goal is to strengthen defenses by gathering information, changing procedures, and improving the network. You need to monitor the following events:

- Logins
- Creation of user accounts and groups
- Correct handling of e-mail attachments
- Backups and other ways to maintain and protect sensitive information
- Antivirus scanning and control
- Procedures for granting mobile users secure remote access

For example, suppose your network's database server contacts a remote host via the Internet. The IDS sends an alarm because you have configured notifications for these types of events; the database server is supposed to receive only incoming connections, not initiate its own outgoing connections. The port the database server uses to connect to the remote host, 40449, indicates that the connection is a suspicious one because this port is normally closed.

To verify this connection, you run the Netstat utility by opening a command prompt window and entering the netstat -a command on the database server to review current connections. Netstat reports that the server is listening for connections on the expected ports, such as port 1028 for NetBIOS connections. It also reports that the server is listening for connections on port 40449, which indicates that a Trojan program might have been installed on the database server and is initiating a connection to the remote host over this port. This, in turn, indicates that an attacker might have been able to log in to the database server with a legitimate password that he "cracked" or obtained through other fraudulent means. Your response needs to incorporate several steps:

- Block the connection
- Locate and eradicate the Trojan program
- Determine how the intrusion occurred
- Change network passwords
- Possibly change the way users safeguard their passwords

To be effective, your responses need to occur as quickly as possible. Your ability to detect intrusions into your systems and determine the identity of the intruder might be limited. Carrying out an information attack doesn't take long, and damage can occur in an instant. You need to develop a team approach to network security and make use of automated responses, such as alarm systems built into an IDS. You also need to coordinate data from multiple sources and keep aware of new network security threats.

Managing Data from Multiple Sensors

Consider a multinational organization with offices in several different countries or a national organization with branch offices in separate states. Each office network has its own firewall and IDS. Each IDS has sensors that gather data passing through the gateway. Some of that data contains alert messages that need to be reviewed in a timely fashion. How do you process all the events occurring at these offices? Obviously, you need to install database software that sorts through the events and enables you to view them systematically. As a security manager, you need to address the following questions, discussed in more detail in the following sections:

- Should all the data be consolidated and flow through a central security location?
- Should the data from sensors go to security managers at each office?

Centralized Data Collection

Centralized data collection results in an organization's event and security data being "funneled" to a centralized management console in the main office. Depending on the number of branch networks and security devices, the amount of data traversing network gateways and passing through the firewall at the main office can be considerable.

When you set up a firewall or IDS, typically you're required to identify the location of a host computer running a management console application. Data from security devices in your organization's network and its remote networks can be transmitted to that console by using its IP address. Figure 12-2 shows this arrangement, in which event data from separate offices is sent to a management console in the organization's main office.

Centralized data collection offers the following benefits:

- Reduced cost because you have fewer systems to maintain
- Less administrative time required
- Improved efficiency

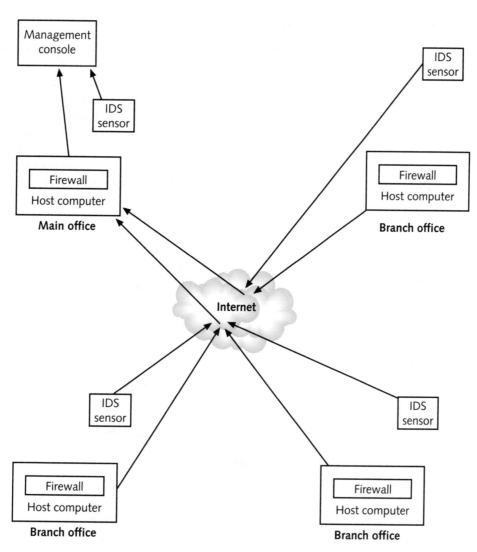

Figure 12-2   Centralized data collection

On the downside, you need to find a way to transmit data from each collection point to the centralized management console. In addition, the traffic needs to be protected by encryption and encapsulation; this is an ideal situation for a VPN connection of the sort described in Chapter 5. However, most security devices can communicate with one another by using their own encrypted "handshake" mechanism, and many companies rely on this feature instead of setting up a VPN. Unfortunately, most security devices, such as IDSs, use standard ports by default that attackers can exploit.

Distributed Data Collection

The second option, distributed data collection, reduces the amount of network traffic (see Figure 12-3). In a **distributed data collection** arrangement, the data from security devices, such as firewalls and IDSs, goes to a management console on its own local network. Security managers in each network review the data separately and analyze and respond to events as needed. A distributed data collection setup requires the organization to maintain separate security managers in each branch office, as well as separate management console software. This arrangement saves bandwidth, but it still requires offices to communicate with one another about security incidents. If an event occurs at one office that could affect other offices, the security manager dealing with that event should notify other branch managers so that they can take steps to prevent these events from occurring in their offices.

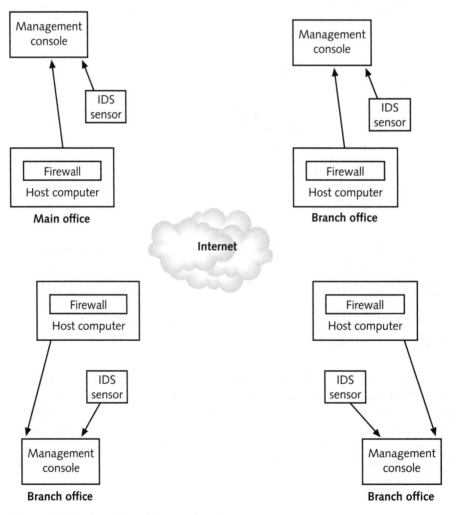

Figure 12-3 Distributed data collection

Evaluating IDS Signatures

The reason for monitoring and evaluating network traffic is not to have a large quantity of data to analyze. Instead, you want to gather evidence that indicates whether your IDS signatures are working well enough or need to be updated. A variety of IDS vendors are available, each with its own set of signatures for suspicious events. How do you evaluate signatures for each one? One vendor, Neohapsis, has proposed a standard for reviewing signatures called the **Open Security Evaluation Criteria (OSEC)**. OSEC includes a core set of tests that any network security product has to follow. In version 1.0 of OSEC, the tests include the following:

- Device integrity checking
- Signature baseline
- State test
- Discard test
- Engine flex
- Evasion list
- In-line/tap test

TIP

You can learn more about OSEC and the test criteria at *http://osec.neohapsis. com/criteria/nids-v1/testsummary.html*.

The process of updating IDS signatures varies, depending on the vendor. Check the vendor's Web site for complete instructions and visit it often to download new signatures. Your organization might also want to hire a security management firm on a contract basis to handle these routine tasks. For instance, the Swiss firm Celeris (*www.celeris.ch/en*) performs routine signature analysis on an ongoing basis. In addition, its service agreements call for the company to notify you of security incidents within 30 minutes of detection and to make major configuration changes in a 48- to 96-hour period, depending on the level of service you pay for.

ACTIVITY

Activity 12-1: Developing Test Criteria

Time Required: 15 minutes

Objective: Create test criteria for your network.

Description: In this activity, you develop a set of test criteria for your own network, using the OSEC criteria from Neohapsis, Inc. as a starting point. You need a computer with an Internet connection and a Web browser installed to complete this activity.

1. Start your browser, enter the URL **http://osec.neohapsis.com/criteria**, and then press **Enter**.

2. Click **Test descriptions** at the bottom of the page. Scroll down the Test Details page to view the descriptions of tests included in the current version of OSEC.

3. In Section D, Discard Tests, what type of attack targets ports you should test for?

   _____

   _____

4. Scroll down to Section F, Evasion Tests. What two types of attacks described in this section should you test for yourself?

   _____

   _____

5. Scroll down the list and look for an attack involving 100,000 separate connection attempts (sessions) followed by an attack attempt. Write down the name of this type of attack.

   _____

   _____

6. Read the Baseline Attacks section. Write down three types of HTTP obfuscation tests involving mangled or malformed URLs or URIs that you should perform on your own servers.

   _____

   _____

   _____

   _____

7. Close any open windows, and leave your system running for the next activity.

Managing Change

The process of making a change in a procedure, a network defense component, or another administrative matter doesn't have to be a long, complex chain of events. However, you can run into serious problems if you make a change abruptly that has an impact on the way employees work. The impact, in fact, can be more harmful than the original problem. Suppose you determine, as a result of an alert received from an IDS, that access to a database server needs to be severely restricted to select administrative staff because an intruder nearly gained access to that server. If you make the change without assessing its impact or without notifying all employees affected by it, you're likely to be flooded with a stream of protests because employees won't be able to access files.

In an administrative sense, it's best to make sure significant changes are carried out systematically so that they occur smoothly. Change management involves modifying equipment, systems, software, or procedures in a sequential, planned way. The process should include an assessment of the change's impact and a decision about whether the change should be made based on that impact. You might consider using change management for the following types of changes:

- Significant changes to firewall or IDS rules that affect users
- New VPN gateways
- Changes to access control lists
- New password systems or procedures

The full process of evaluating and making a change is shown in Figure 12-4.

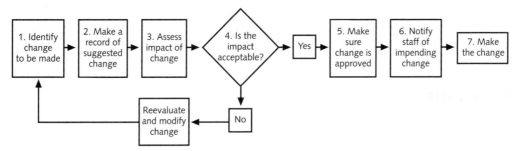

Figure 12-4   Significant changes should be evaluated and communicated systematically

The process shown in Figure 12-4 might seem involved, but being systematic and thorough helps an organization run smoothly. You ensure that everyone is informed, you get the approval of managers, and you make sure the change should take place. The following list describes the process in Figure 12-4 in more detail:

1. Identify the change to be made. You might decide to make a change after reviewing log files, after an intrusion, or after an alert message.

2. Make a record of the suggested change. Write down the situation that prompted you to consider the change and describe the change so that you can communicate it to management and staff later.

3. Assess the impact of the change. Will the change inconvenience employees by making it more difficult to access resources they need? Will the change slow down network traffic by creating another layer of security? Think through all possible implications of the change.

4. Decide whether the impact of the change is acceptable. Discuss this question with the head of your department or your colleagues. You might also want to consult financial staff if the change has cost implications. If the impact isn't acceptable, reevaluate it and determine whether a modification will reduce the impact. If the impact is acceptable, proceed to the next step.

12

5. Make sure the appropriate administrators approve the change. The approval process can add a considerable amount of time to the change. If you circulate a memo describing the change and a meeting needs to be held to discuss the change, you might not be able to carry it out for a week or more. If the change seems urgent and not making it could result in a security risk, try to talk to managers yourself and get approval immediately.

6. Notify staff of the impending change. After approval is given, tell all employees affected by the change when it will take effect. Give people several days or even a week to prepare for it. However, if there's an urgent need for the change, simply make the change after receiving approval, and tell people after the fact.

7. After notifying the involved employees and answering any questions they have, make the change.

You don't necessarily have to follow all these steps for every change. For a slight modification in a firewall or an IDS rule, you don't need to tell the entire staff. You should follow this decision procedure only for significant changes that affect the way others in the organization do their daily business.

STRENGTHENING ANALYSIS: SECURITY AUDITING

Security auditing is the process of testing the effectiveness of a network defense system. You can attempt break-ins to test network defenses, for example. Recording and analyzing events such as logons, logouts, and file accesses can also supply useful information. In addition, you should examine the security procedures in your organization, such as the way confidential information is handled.

In the past, groups known as **tiger teams** were assembled to actively test a network. Tiger team members usually had expertise in one or more areas of security, and each contributed to the overall effectiveness of the team. These teams can still be used on a contract basis, but you can also do testing yourself. You might have to put together data from several sources, such as the following:

- Packet filters
- Application logs
- Router logs
- Firewall logs
- Event monitors
- Host-based IDS (HIDS) logs
- Network-based IDS (NIDS) logs

One way to consolidate the data these devices generate is to transfer (or "push") the information to a central database. Most IDSs have a feature for transferring data; even the freeware IDS program Snort can be used to transmit data to a database directly. At the very least, you should store the time of the incident, the data collected about the incident, the application affected, the OS in use, the user ID, the process ID, and log entry ID.

With multiple security devices, you accumulate so much data from log files that you need to manage it before it takes up your available storage space. Choose a time period for retaining detailed information from IDS logs. Ninety days is a common target. When the data is older than 90 days, you can archive it to long-term storage, such as tape, DVD, or CD. Also, consider paring data down to only the most essential information, as discussed in the previous section.

Operational Auditing

In an **operational audit**, a company's IT staff examines system logs to see whether they're auditing the information that's needed and not getting bogged down with unnecessary information. They should look for the following:

- Accounts that have weak passwords or no passwords
- Accounts assigned to employees who have left the company or user group
- New accounts that need to be checked against a list of authorized users

Financial institutions have to undergo security audits regularly because of government regulations. These audits might involve attempts at **social engineering**—attempting to trick employees into giving out passwords or other information. Auditors who work onsite in financial institutions even look in trashcans to see whether computer printouts containing confidential information have been discarded without being shredded. Another auditing strategy is a **Tinkerbell program**, in which network connections are scanned and alerts are generated when connection attempts are made from sites identified as suspicious or when logons using suspicious IDs are attempted.

NOTE Tinkerbell is a monitoring program used to scan incoming network calls and generate alerts when calls are received from particular sites or when logins are attempted with certain IDs. It was named after Project Tinkerbell, an experimental phone-tapping program that British Telecom developed in the early 1980s.

CAUTION Because of its highly sensitive nature, information gathered as a result of a security audit should be protected rigorously. (This information might include passwords, for instance.) If an unauthorized employee or intruder gained access to the files, network resources could be compromised. Your organization should have a clearly defined plan for handling and protecting audit data and follow it accordingly.

12

Independent Auditing

In an **independent audit**, you hire an outside firm to come in and inspect your audit logs to make sure you're getting the information you want and not gathering unnecessary information that consumes system and network resources. The outside firm attempts to detect any flaws or vulnerabilities in your system—not just in your IDS, but in other locations, such as files or applications. The audit firm might examine where your security equipment is located, how well it's protected from unauthorized users or environmental disasters, and how thoroughly data is erased when you dispose of it. Because you need to give this outside firm access to sensitive data, be sure to have the auditors sign a nondisclosure agreement (NDA), in which they state that they won't release your information to anyone outside the audit firm.

Auditing might uncover information about your organization's employees that they consider confidential. Ask your Legal Department to review the audit information and determine whether simply searching through the information constitutes an invasion of privacy. If you work for a government agency, the concern over privacy increases: The Privacy Act of 1974 requires government agencies to notify citizens when the government gathers information about them.

STRENGTHENING DETECTION: MANAGING AN IDS

As your network grows, the amount of traffic and information on your IDS and other security devices increases, too. To keep the IDS running smoothly, you might need to make adjustments to the IDS rule base and the amount of storage space available to the IDS. This section briefly examines how to strengthen an IDS by maintaining the current system, changing or adding software, or changing or adding hardware.

Maintaining Your Current System

You don't always need to add new systems or components to make an IDS stronger. You can boost efficiency and strengthen detection by maintaining the resources you currently have more efficiently. The following sections discuss how to do this through backups, managing accounts, managing IDS rules, and user management.

Backups

You need to back up your firewall and IDSs in case of disaster. With a backup stored in a secure location, you can restore the systems if they become corrupted or intruders gain access to them. You should also keep backups of other security components, including:

- Routers
- Bastion hosts

- Servers

- Special-purpose devices

Automated backup software, such as the EMC Dantz Retrospect series of products by Dantz Development Corp. (*www.dantz.com*), is advisable, especially for a large-scale network, because built-in backup software often isn't full-featured enough.

Managing Accounts

Account management is another aspect of ongoing security maintenance. This task, which is often neglected, involves adding new accounts, recovering old ones, and changing passwords. Make sure user accounts are reviewed every few months. You want to make sure no accounts have been added by attackers and no accounts belonging to terminated employees are still active.

TIP Your security policy should include procedures for the Human Resources Department to notify you whenever someone leaves the organization (whether that person quits or is terminated) so that you can disable or delete the account immediately.

Managing IDS Rules

Scale back on the number of IDS rules by eliminating unnecessary rules, as discussed in Chapter 8. If you reduce the amount of unnecessary processing the IDS must perform, the IDS can keep up with information that passes through fast networks, such as ones that use gigabit-speed interfaces.

TIP Be sure you keep your IDS audit logs in a secure location so that intruders can't tamper with them or erase evidence of their intrusions.

User Management

Remember from Chapter 2 that a security user awareness program consists of training procedures to make sure employees, contractors, and business partners understand the company's security policy and how it should affect their behavior. Simply developing and following this program can improve security by teaching employees how to use the system more securely.

You can raise employee awareness in a variety of ways. You can give a lecture on security in the organization and include a demonstration of how easy it is to crack weak passwords. You should also prepare booklets for employees to read and sign. Signing the booklets ensures that they have read the security policy and its procedures and regulations.

Changing or Adding Software

Once or twice a year, IDS software vendors usually release updated software. When a vendor releases an updated version of your command console software, be sure to get details on what sort of upgrade path is needed. Be sure to ask whether the new version requires working with new data formats that you don't already use and require installing new supporting software.

Changing or Adding Hardware

Adding hardware, such as new network sensors to an IDS, can be expensive, but the cost is usually outweighed by the cost to the organization of lost data, erosion of customer trust, or network downtime, which can occur as a result of an intrusion. You might be able to address your company's needs with just the addition of a second network card to monitor the network, or you might need to consider more expensive options. In addition, you could consider adding consoles to reduce the **target-to-console ratio**—the number of target computers on your network managed by a single command console. You might also want to reevaluate the placement of sensors in your network. If you aren't catching all the traffic on a network segment, you might want to move a sensor to a new location or add a sensor. You could also convert your host-based system into a hybrid configuration by adding a network sensor.

Strengthening Defense: Improving Defense in Depth

The principle of defense in depth (DiD) should guide you in carrying out ongoing maintenance of your perimeter security configuration. This approach, as you've learned in previous chapters, calls for security through a variety of defensive techniques that work together to block attacks. On the simplest level, DiD can be achieved with a personal firewall and antivirus software to protect a single computer. When applied to network services, DiD calls for maintenance of the following areas:

- *Availability*—Information is made available to authorized users when it's needed.

- *Integrity*—The information exchanged by network users is accurate.

- *Authentication*—Users prove their identity to other users or computers so that they can exchange information.

- *Confidentiality*—Information can't be read by anyone but intended recipients.

- *Nonrepudiation*—Both the recipient and sender of information across the network can't deny their participation in a business transaction.

The last item in this list—nonrepudiation—requires more explanation. Repudiation sometimes occurs in business transactions, particularly those in which one business makes a purchase from or delivers supplies to another business. Often, because of the ease with which records can be accessed online, transactions are initiated electronically. For instance, company

A orders 10,000 widgets from company B via an e-mail message. The order is placed, the goods are shipped, and the payment is made electronically. However, if company A receives the bill and then denies it placed the order, it's said to have repudiated the transaction. Similarly, if company B denies it received the electronic payment, it's also said to have repudiated the transaction. Nonrepudiation is the use of authentication as a way to guarantee that the sender of a message can't deny sending a message and the recipient can't deny receiving a message. Through public key infrastructure, the sender and receiver are authenticated through the exchange of digital certificates. Both have electronic records that the transaction actually took place, in addition to records of the date and time it occurred.

Active Defense in Depth

Active defense in depth is a particularly strong implementation of the DiD concept. Instead of passively waiting for attacks to occur and then reacting, security personnel expect that attacks will occur and try to anticipate them. Active defense in depth calls for multiple levels of protection, as well as security approaches that overlap one another. It also calls for defending against major and serious network threats first. The additional layers of protection address other, less serious threats.

Active defense in depth requires respondents to think creatively and counter every possible threat, whether familiar or unfamiliar. In an active approach, the defense method changes based on the threat. Security personnel have the ability to "flex" and change based on where the threat occurs or what it is.

One "layer" of security is training. Security personnel should be training and learning constantly to keep up with attacks and countermeasures. Efforts to improve their knowledge enable the organization to remain flexible when it comes to network defense. The following steps can be used to create a training cycle for strengthening defenses:

1. *Training*—Security staff are trained in the network defense configuration.

2. *Perimeter defense*—After training, security staff can establish a perimeter defense configuration for the network.

3. *Intrusion detection*—After defenses are arranged and put online, IDSs alert security staff to potential vulnerabilities by sending alerts.

4. *Intrusion response*—Security staff evaluate alerts and respond to block attacks.

5. *New security approaches*—Countermeasures are taken to reduce the number of false positives as well as true positives (actual attacks) the IDS encounters, which strengthens perimeter defense and helps security staff learn more about network vulnerabilities and defenses.

By seeing training as an ongoing process instead of something that occurs only before hiring, an organization improves its overall security stance while its personnel improve their ability to prevent attacks.

12

Adding Security Layers

An active defense in depth posture takes into account the fact that a single network can't be protected fully unless all interconnecting networks are protected. Your goal is to establish trust—to provide nonrepudiation for your network and ensure the integrity and confidentiality of information passing into and out of it. To improve security, you might need to add new layers of security measures. For example, you might need to add an IDS to supplement your firewall and VPN. If you already have an NIDS, you might want to add an HIDS or a hybrid IDS to strengthen detection and response.

To see how this strategy works, take a look at how it was carried out by the U.S. Navy. In a 1998 article, "Defense in Depth: Security for Network-Centric Warfare," Capt. Dan Galik described the layers or "zones" of defense created to protect one of the U.S. Navy's intranets (*www.chips.navy.mil/archives/98_apr/Galik.htm*). These layers included the following:

- A firewall
- Encryption
- Virus protection to filter out potentially harmful e-mail attachments
- Authentication
- Intrusion detection
- Access control
- Information integrity through SSL and IPSec
- Auditing

In addition, four defensive "zones" were created to protect users and communication between zones. The following zones allowed protection to extend from the network perimeter to users' desktops:

- Zone 1 includes users' desktops, which are protected through passwords, access control lists, VPN encryption, and virus protection.
- Zone 2 is described as a single "community of interest" or group of computers joined in a network. Routers, firewalls, virus protection, and VPN encryption protect this zone.
- Zone 3 encompasses multiple communities of interest so that communication can be carried out securely between them. Protection methods include network intrusion detection, firewalls, VPN encryption, and virus protection.
- Zone 4 is the outermost zone, which is the boundary between a U.S. Navy information system and a public network, such as the Internet. Defensive mechanisms at this level include authentication for routers and DNS servers, VPN encryption, and firewalls.

By dividing its communication needs into separate systems and relying on multiple security methods, the U.S. Navy achieved effective external security. However, this system doesn't always provide strong defense from vulnerabilities, such as accidental misuse of resources or malicious attacks from insiders. Defense in depth can often be improved by placing more emphasis on access control, user education and awareness, and increased levels of auditing.

STRENGTHENING PERFORMANCE: KEEPING PACE WITH NETWORK NEEDS

IDS performance refers to its capability to capture packets and process them according to the rule base. Ideally, an IDS captures all the packets that reach it, sends alarms on all suspicious packets, and allows legitimate packets to pass through to the internal network. This level of performance, however, can be hampered by a number of factors, discussed in the following sections.

Managing Memory

IDS performance depends largely on the number of signatures it has to review when receiving a packet. For signatures of events that consist of only a single packet, memory requirements are almost nonexistent. However, for signatures requiring a sequence of packets to reach the IDS, the IDS needs to maintain the connection state in memory. Memory is also needed to store information in cache and for any databases containing IDS configuration settings. The primary consideration is that the IDS should have more than the minimum amount of RAM to maintain state information and, therefore, thwart attacks that take place over extended periods.

Managing Bandwidth

Firewalls, packet sniffers, and IDSs need to be able to process data as fast as it moves through the network. If your network has a gigabit Ethernet gateway, but your IDS runs on a host with only a 100-MB Ethernet connection, data passes through more slowly than it should. An IDS, for example, should be capable of handling 50% of bandwidth utilization without losing the capacity to detect. Intrusion detection often begins to break down if your bandwidth use exceeds 80% of network capacity.

TIP Run Performance Monitor on Windows or the Top utility on UNIX/Linux to gauge how much overhead your IDS is consuming. Make sure host computers that provide network sensors and IDS management consoles run as fast as possible. If performance lags, upgrade immediately to a faster computer or network card.

Managing Storage

Some intrusions take place over long periods, and storage of a sizeable amount of historical data from IDS log files can be essential to tracking long-term attacks. One aspect of managing an IDS is ensuring enough storage space (typically, a gigabyte or more) for current IDS data and making sure data is archived or deleted securely when it's no longer needed.

Clearing out media when it's full and the information on it is no longer needed is an important—and often overlooked—network security consideration. To make sure intruders, criminals, or malicious employees can't recover this data, you need to shred documents and files completely.

For systems storing highly sensitive information, you might want to physically remove and degauss the physical drives. **Degaussing** is the process of magnetically erasing an electronic device, such as a monitor or a disk, to remove any stray data or magnetic fields. Simply deleting or erasing files doesn't completely remove all information from the disk. When you use a delete or erase command, you simply remove pointers that tell the computer what clusters are storing the information. That way, the computer can reuse those sectors if needed. However, until the sectors are overwritten, the information in them can be recovered. Programs that overwrite disk media completely include Mutilate File Wiper (shown in Figure 12-5), Shredder, Secure Clean, BC Wipe, and Norton Utilities Wipeinfo.

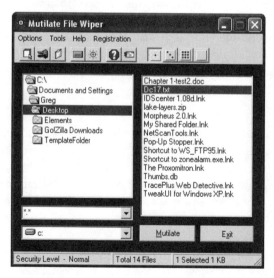

Figure 12-5   File shredder software removes all traces of files permanently

CAUTION   Don't allow employees to maintain company information on their own laptop or home computers. You have no way of knowing what kind of security mechanisms are on employees' personal computers. They are, for the most part, highly vulnerable and easy to attack.

ACTIVITY

Activity 12-2: "Deleting" a File and Recovering It

Time Required: 30 minutes

Objective: Use PC Inspector to recover a deleted text document.

Description: One aspect of ongoing security management is managing files on your network's computer systems. At times, you might need to delete files containing sensitive information. However, deleting a file by moving it into your operating system's trash can or Recycle Bin doesn't mean it's gone forever. Intruders or criminals can still manage to recover it, as you'll discover in this activity. You need a Windows XP computer with WinZip or another file-archiving utility installed and a blank, formatted floppy disk.

1. Start Notepad.

2. In a new document, type the following text: **"Sensitive--Top Secret--Plans for Upcoming Product Line"**.

3. Click **File**, **Save** from the menu. In the Save in drop-down list, click **3 1/2" Floppy (A:)**.

4. Type the name **SensitiveFile.txt** in the File name text box, and then click the **Save** button.

5. Click **File**, **Exit** from the menu to close Notepad.

6. In Windows Explorer, navigate to and expand the A: drive, right-click the **SensitiveFile.txt** file, and then click **Delete**.

7. When prompted to verify deleting the file, click **Yes**.

8. Right-click the **Recycle Bin** icon, and then click **Empty Recycle Bin**.

9. When prompted to verify emptying the Recycle Bin, click **Yes**. Click **View**, **Refresh** from the Windows Explorer menu to confirm that the file isn't on the floppy disk.

10. Start your browser, enter the URL **http://www.snapfiles.com/download/dlpcinspector.html**, and press **Enter**.

NOTE

Windows XP SP2 users might see an information bar stating that the download has been blocked by Internet Explorer. Click the bar and follow the prompts to allow the download.

11. When the File Download dialog box opens, click **Save**. Select a location for saving the file, and then click **Save**.

12. When the download is finished, close your Web browser, and double-click the **pci_filerecovery.exe** file. If necessary, click **Run** in the Open File – Security Warning dialog box to proceed.

12

13. In the Choose Setup Language dialog box, verify that English is selected, and click **OK**.

14. When the InstallShield Wizard starts, click **Next**. Follow the instructions in subsequent windows to install PC Inspector File Recovery on your computer.

15. When the installation is finished, click **Start**, point to **All Programs**, point to **PC Inspector File Recovery**, and click **PC Inspector File Recovery.**

16. In the Choose Language dialog box, verify that English is selected, and click the **check mark** icon.

17. In the Welcome to PC Inspector File Recovery dialog box, click the **Recover deleted files** tab at the upper left.

18. In the Select drive dialog box, click the **Logical drive** tab, if necessary, click **Windows drive A:**, and click the **check mark** icon.

19. A list of folders appears under the Deleted heading. (If it doesn't, click the plus sign next to Deleted to view the folders.)

20. Right-click the **SensitiveFile.txt** file, and then click **View as text**.

21. When the Select FAT dialog box opens, click **noFAT (consecutive)** in the drop-down list, and click the **check mark** icon. A text box opens, and your file is displayed.

_____

_____

22. Exit PC Inspector File Recovery, and leave your system running for the end-of-chapter projects.

Maintaining Your Own Knowledge Base

You can't carry out ongoing security maintenance in isolation. To remain effective, you need to maintain your knowledge base and industry contacts, just as you maintain software and hardware configurations. Visiting security-related Web sites and holding online discussions with other professionals in the field are good uses of your work time. Make sure management understands that you need to stay informed by visiting Web sites, participating in mailing lists and newsgroups, subscribing to trade publications, and taking certification tests to keep up with the fast-changing field of network security.

Web Sites

You'll find no shortage of Web sites with news on virus outbreaks and security breaches that affect prominent corporations. The challenge is to choose one or two sites you scan daily or every few days, looking for security issues that might affect your own network. You might visit sites such as the following:

- Center for Internet Security (*www.cisecurity.org*)

- SANS Institute (*www.sans.org*)

- CERT Coordination Center (*www.cert.org*)

TIP

Create a set of bookmarks for Web sites you visit regularly (see Hands-on Project 12-1 for suggestions on setting up this list).

Mailing Lists and Newsgroups

Mailing lists often provide more up-to-date information about security issues and vulnerabilities than Web sites or periodicals. You get first-hand information from security professionals about problems they're facing and opinions on security-related issues. Often, you can also read about suggested solutions to those problems. Investigate these mailing lists as a starting point:

- NTBugtraq (*www.networksecurityarchive.org*)

- Firewalls Mailing List (*www.isc.org/index.pl?/ops/lists/firewalls/*)

- SecurityFocus HOME Mailing Lists (*http://online.securityfocus.com/archive*)

CAUTION

Be careful about posting messages on newsgroups or mailing lists that describe specifics of security breaches you have experienced. You don't want attackers who might be monitoring communications in those groups to know that your network has been vulnerable. Don't give out specifics about your network configuration or give out the name of your company. Consider using another e-mail address besides your company e-mail for posting to newsgroups and mailing lists.

Trade Publications

Newsletters and trade publications on information security, such as the following, often contain useful reviews of hardware and software products:

- Compsec Online (*www.compseconline.com*)

- Cisco Systems (*www.cisco.com/public/support/tac/tools.shtml#alerts*)

- SANS newsletters (*www.sans.org/newsletters/*)

12

CAUTION Subscribing to publications you receive by e-mail or conventional mail can be useful, but be aware of privacy issues and the possibility of receiving unwanted mail. When you subscribe, give as little personal information as possible. For online subscriptions, clear any check boxes selected by default that give the publisher permission to send you other publications or sell your e-mail address to other mailing lists.

Certifications

Many certifications need to be renewed periodically by retesting. Make sure management understands that studying and certification benefit the company, too. Visiting the following certification Web sites can help you keep up with tests you've taken or hope to take in the future:

- Security Certified Program (*www.securitycertified.net*)
- International Information Systems Security Certification Consortium (*www.isc2.org*)
- CompTIA (*www.comptia.org*)
- GoCertify (*www.gocertify.com*)

Be aware of when your current certifications need to be renewed. Discuss with your supervisor whether the company will help defray the cost of study materials and testing or at least give you time off so that you can study and travel as needed.

CHAPTER SUMMARY

- ▢ Security event management involves accumulating data from a wide range of security devices by means of a coordinated program. This program includes monitoring of alert and event logs produced by security devices and OSs and collecting data from multiple sensors through a centralized or a distributed system. It also requires reviewing IDS attack signatures to make sure they are up to date.

- ▢ Another aspect of event management (one that's often overlooked) is the need to make a change in a procedure in a systematic way. Change management describes the modification of systems or procedures in a way that includes management approval and notifies staff of the impending change before it occurs.

- ▢ Security auditing is used to test the effectiveness of network defenses after they have been established. In an operational audit, a company's IT staff examine system logs and look for vulnerabilities, such as weak passwords or unnecessary user accounts. An independent audit is performed by an outside auditing firm.

- ▢ Another aspect of ongoing security maintenance is managing an IDS to keep it running smoothly through measures such as making backups, managing user accounts, reducing unnecessary rules, and adding hardware or software as needed. Also, institute an awareness program to make sure employees, contractors, and business partners understand and observe the security policy.

❏ By strengthening a network's defense in depth configuration, you improve overall network defense, ensure the availability and integrity of information, and provide for nonrepudiation. Active defense in depth calls for trying to anticipate and thwart attack attempts before they occur. This can be done through training or adding layers of security.

❏ Keep pace with your network's needs by ensuring there's enough memory for an IDS to process long-term attacks, enough network speed to capture and process all packets, and enough storage space for log and alert files.

❏ Make sure files are deleted completely by "shredding" them electronically—in other words, overwriting them so that all traces are removed from the media where they're stored.

❏ Maintain your knowledge base to stay up to date on security breaches and virus outbreaks. Visiting security-related Web sites, joining mailing lists, subscribing to newsletters, and posting on newsgroups are ways to keep informed. In addition, keep your security certifications up to date to maintain your level of expertise.

Key Terms

active defense in depth — A particularly strong implementation of the defense in depth concept, in which security personnel expect that attacks will occur and try to anticipate them instead of passively waiting for attacks and then reacting.

centralized data collection — A system in which an organization's event and security data is "funneled" to a centralized management console in the main office.

degaussing — The process of magnetically erasing an electronic device, such as a monitor or a disk, to remove any stray data or magnetic fields.

distributed data collection — A system in which data from security devices goes to a management console on its own local network.

event monitoring — Reviewing alert and event logs produced by security devices and operating systems and testing the network periodically to identify any weak points.

independent audit — An audit in which you hire an outside firm to inspect your audit logs to make sure you're getting the information you need and not gathering unnecessary information that consumes system and network resources.

Open Security Evaluation Criteria (OSEC) — A framework for evaluating security products, developed by Neohapsis Labs.

operational audit — An audit in which an organization's own staff examines system and security logs to analyze information about intrusions and other unauthorized accesses.

security auditing — The process of checking the effectiveness of a network defense system by testing the system, analyzing event logs, or observing procedures.

security event management program — A program that gathers and consolidates events from multiple sources so that the information can be analyzed to improve network security.

social engineering — A technique of tricking employees into giving out passwords or other information.

target-to-console ratio — The number of target computers on your network managed by a single command console.

12

tiger teams — Special teams assembled to actively test a network.

Tinkerbell program — A program in which network connections are scanned and alerts are generated when logons are attempted or when connection attempts are made from sites identified as suspicious.

REVIEW QUESTIONS

1. Which of the following is a type of security audit? (Choose all that apply.)
   a. automated
   b. independent
   c. centralized
   d. operational

2. Why is it important to protect the confidentiality of information you gather through auditing? (Choose all that apply.)
   a. Employees' privacy could be compromised.
   b. It might become corrupted when you store it.
   c. Intruders could discover passwords.
   d. Viruses could infect it.

3. When should you follow the elaborate procedure for carrying out change shown in Figure 12-3?
   a. when many employees will be affected by the change
   b. when the change needs to be made urgently
   c. whenever a change needs to be made to security configurations
   d. when the change will have a substantial impact

4. If the impact of a security or procedural change in your organization seems too substantial, what should you do?
   a. Forget about making the change.
   b. Document the fact that you considered the change and move on.
   c. Reevaluate and modify the change.
   d. Discuss the situation with your supervisors.

5. How much time should you give employees to prepare for a major change in your organization's security processes? (Choose all that apply.)
   a. several weeks
   b. several days to a week
   c. no time at all, if the change needs to be made immediately
   d. several hours

6. What is the name for an auditing program in which current connections are scanned and alerts are generated when logons are attempted?

   a. social engineering

   b. port scan

   c. event monitoring

   d. Tinkerbell program

7. An employee whose primary responsibilities include maintaining and strengthening network defenses is called which of the following?

   a. security incident response team leader

   b. computer security manager

   c. chief information officer

   d. security auditor

8. What is a realistic goal of ongoing security management? (Choose all that apply.)

   a. blocking all suspicious packets

   b. tracing all attacks

   c. tracing as many intrusion attempts as possible

   d. continually strengthening and modifying defenses

12

9. Which of the following describes a goal of a security event management program? (Choose all that apply.)

   a. consolidating events from multiple sources

   b. responding to events as quickly as possible

   c. conducting forensics to trace and prosecute offenders

   d. managing IDS signatures

10. How can you gather information on a variety of security events and respond to it quickly?

    a. Assemble a large response team.

    b. Use distributed data collection.

    c. Automate data collection and analysis.

    d. Outsource security management.

11. Which of the following is an advantage of centralized data collection? (Choose all that apply.)

    a. reduced traffic through network gateways

    b. reduced administrative costs

    c. reduced software and hardware costs

    d. only one person needed to review data

12. Why would you choose distributed rather than centralized data collection?

    a. to reduce traffic through gateways

    b. to reduce the load on security managers

    c. to reduce cost

    d. to reduce hardware and software costs

13. What is a potential security risk with a centralized data collection system?

    a. More time is required to respond to alerts.

    b. There are more gateways for attackers to exploit.

    c. There is a dependence on remote network hosts that might fail.

    d. Data might not be encrypted as it passes through the Internet.

14. Before installing new signatures for an IDS, what do you need to do?

    a. Back up the IDS.

    b. Stop the IDS.

    c. Change passwords.

    d. Double-check to verify whether new signatures are necessary.

15. What can happen if you make a change in security configurations too abruptly and without proper authorization? (Choose all that apply.)

    a. Employees might ignore the change.

    b. The change might surprise other security managers.

    c. You might be flooded with protests from employees.

    d. You could face disciplinary action.

16. The change management process might apply when which of the following occurs? (Choose all that apply.)

    a. New password logon procedures are needed.

    b. You need to block access to DMZ servers.

    c. A new VPN gateway is installed.

    d. You need to change a fragmentation rule in a packet filter.

17. If your assessment is that the impact of a change is too substantial to justify the change, what should you do?

    a. Don't make the change.

    b. Modify the change and reassess the impact.

    c. Modify the impact but make the change.

    d. Seek approval from management.

18. Security auditing involves which of the following? (Choose all that apply.)

   a. reviewing log files

   b. reviewing hardware and software costs

   c. testing defenses

   d. rotating firewall logs

19. Why should you review your user accounts regularly? (Choose all that apply.)

   a. to make sure passwords have not expired

   b. to eliminate accounts attackers have created

   c. to reduce disk space

   d. to delete accounts of former employees

20. What is nonrepudiation?

   a. the capability of a system to authenticate users

   b. the capability to rely on information gained through a security audit

   c. legal defense used by employees whose privacy has allegedly been violated

   d. the capability to validate transactions through electronic documentation

12

HANDS-ON PROJECTS

HANDS-ON PROJECTS

Hands-On Project 12-1: Assembling Security-Related Bookmarks

Time Required: 20 minutes

Objective: Create a list of Web sites to use as resources for keeping updated on the latest developments in security.

Description: As part of your ongoing security management program, you need to visit Web sites and other resources on network defense issues. One way to ensure that you visit these resources regularly (for example, once a week) is to assemble a list of bookmarks that you can access quickly. You can then set up an e-mail reminder notifying you that you need to check for updated software and other security-related news. For this activity, you need a computer with an Internet connection and Internet Explorer installed.

1. Start your browser, enter the URL **http://online.securityfocus.com**, and then press **Enter**.

2. Click **Favorites**, **Organize Favorites** from the menu.

3. Click the **Create Folder** button. Replace "New Folder" with the name **Security**, and then press **Enter**.

4. Click **Create Folder**. Replace "New Folder" with the name **News**, and then press **Enter**.

5. Click the **Move to Folder** button. In the Browse for Folder dialog box, click the **Security** folder, and then click **OK**.

6. Repeat Steps 4 and 5 for two more new folders named **Discussions** and **Other Resources**.

7. Click **Close**.

8. Add the SecurityFocus Online home page to the News folder by clicking **Favorites**, **Add to Favorites** from the menu. In the Add Favorite dialog box, click the **Create in** button. Click the **Security** folder, click the **News** folder, and then click **OK**.

9. On the SecurityFocus Online home page, look for a security-related resource that isn't a news source or a discussion group. Click the link for the resource, click **Favorites**, **Add to Favorites** from the menu, and add the page to the **Other Resources** folder. What resources did you find?

    _____

    _____

10. Click the **Mailing Lists** link.

11. Scan the list of mailing lists and choose three that seem relevant to the subjects covered in this book. Add them to the Discussions folder. Record the mailing lists you added:

    _____

    _____

12. As an optional final step, add the URLs listed in the section "Maintaining Your Own Knowledge Base" to the appropriate folders in your Security favorites folder.

CASE PROJECTS

CASE PROJECTS

Case Project 12-1: Completing the LedGrafix Project

Now that you have reviewed other students' papers and received feedback on your own, you can complete your work. Evaluate the feedback you received for incorporation into your project. Make your final revisions, proofread carefully, and check to make sure all components are present and all your references are correct.

Your school or instructor might have specific formatting guidelines, so make sure you have followed them. When you're satisfied that your paper is complete and ready to be graded, submit it to your instructor. Congratulations! You're officially done with the design project for LedGrafix.

A

SC0-402 OBJECTIVES

Table A-1 maps the Network Defense and Countermeasures objectives in the Security Certified Professional's (SCP's) SC0-402 course to the corresponding chapter and section title where the objectives are covered in this book. Because the SCP exams undergo periodic updating and revising, you should check the SCP Web site for the latest developments at *www.securitycertified.net*.

Table A-1 Objectives-to-chapter mapping

Domain Objective	Chapter and Section(s)
Domain 1.0 Network Security Fundamentals	
Examine Network Defense Fundamentals	Chapter 1
Identify Network Defense Technologies	Chapter 1: Using Network Defense Technologies in Layers
Examine Access Control Methods	Chapter 1: Routing and Access Control Methods
Define the Principles of Network Auditing	Chapter 1: Network Auditing and Log Files Chapter 12: Strengthening Analysis: Security Auditing
Identify the Impact of Defense	Chapter 1: The Impact of Defense
Domain 2.0 Security Policy Design and Implementation	
Examine the Concepts of Risk Analysis	Chapter 2: Fundamental Concepts of Risk Analysis
Define the Methods of Risk Analysis	Chapter 2: Approaches to Risk Analysis, Deciding How to Minimize Risk
Describe the Process of Risk Analysis	Chapter 2: Approaches to Risk Analysis, Risk Analysis: An Ongoing Process Chapter 3: Conducting Ongoing Risk Analysis
Examine Techniques to Minimize Risk	Chapter 2: Deciding How to Minimize Risk
Examine the Concepts of Security Policies	Chapter 3: What Makes a Good Security Policy? Chapter 12: Strengthening Control: Security Event Management, Strengthening Defense: Improving Defense in Depth
Identify Security Policy Categories	Chapter 3: Formulating a Security Policy
Define Incident-Handling Procedures	Chapter 2: Handling Security Incidents Chapter 3: Responding to Security Incidents Chapter 8: Developing a Security Incident Response Team (SIRT), How to Respond: The Incident Response Process, Dealing with False Alarms, Dealing with Legitimate Security Alerts, Gathering Data for Prosecution
Domain 3.0 Network Traffic Signatures	
Describe the Concepts of Signature Analysis	Chapter 4: Understanding Signature Analysis, Detecting Traffic Signatures Chapter 12: Strengthening Control: Security Event Management
Examine the Common Vulnerabilities and Exposures	Chapter 4: Using the Common Vulnerabilities and Exposures (CVE) Standard
Examine Normal Network Traffic Signatures	Chapter 4: Capturing Packets, Detecting Traffic Signatures

Table A-1   Objectives-to-chapter mapping (continued)

Domain Objective	Chapter and Section(s)
Domain 3.0 Network Traffic Signatures	
Examine Abnormal Network Traffic Signatures	Chapter 4: Capturing Packets, Detecting Traffic Signatures, Identifying Suspicious Events, Advanced Attacks, Remote Procedure Calls
Domain 4.0 VPN Concepts and Implementation	
Identify Concepts of VPNs	Chapter 5: Understanding VPN Concepts, VPN Core Activity 1: Encapsulation, VPN Core Activity 2: Encryption, VPN Core Activity 3: Authentication, Advantages, and Disadvantages of VPNs Chapter 6: Auditing VPNs and VPN Policies
Describe IP Security Protocol (IPSec)	Chapter 5: IPSec/IKE
Examine VPN Design and Architecture	Chapter 6: Designing a VPN, Configuring VPNs, VPN Topology Configurations
Describe the Process of VPN Configuration	Chapter 6: Adjusting Packet-Filtering Rules for VPNs, Using VPNs with Firewalls, Auditing VPNs and VPN Policies
Domain 5.0 IDS Concepts and Implementation	
Identify the Goals of an IDS	Chapter 7: Examining Intrusion Detection System Components, Examining Intrusion Detection Step by Step
Examine Host-Based Intrusion Detection	Chapter 7: Host-Based Intrusion Detection Systems, Hybrid IDS Implementations, Evaluating Intrusion Detection Systems
Examine Network-Based Intrusion Detection	Chapter 7: Network-Based Intrusion Detection Systems, Hybrid IDS Implementations, Evaluating Intrusion Detection Systems
Describe IDS Log Analysis	Chapter 12: Strengthening Detection: Managing an IDS, Strengthening Control: Security Event Management
Describe Methods of Using an IDS	Chapter 7: Examining Intrusion Detection System Components, Examining Intrusion Detection Step by Step, Options for Implementing Intrusion Detection Systems Chapter 8: Developing IDS Filter Rules
Configure an Intrusion Detection System	Chapter 7 Chapter 8: Developing IDS Filter Rules
Domain 6.0 Firewall Concepts and Implementation	
Recognize Firewall Components	Chapter 9: Designing Firewall Configurations, Comparing Software and Hardware Firewalls
Create a Firewall Policy	Chapter 9: Establishing Rules and Restrictions, Creating a Firewall Policy

Table A-1 Objectives-to-chapter mapping (continued)

Domain Objective	Chapter and Section(s)
Domain 6.0 Firewall Concepts and Implementation	
Define Firewall Rule Sets and Packet Filters	Chapter 9: Creating Rules and Establishing Restrictions Chapter 11: Managing Firewalls to Improve Security
Perimeter Networks	Chapter 10: Using Network Address Translation (NAT), Putting It All Together
Examine the Proxy Server	Chapter 10: Working with Proxy Servers, Putting It All Together
Examine the Bastion Host	Chapter 10: Choosing a Bastion Host
Define a Honeypot	Chapter 10: Choosing a Bastion Host
Install and Configure Firewall-1	Chapter 11: Installing and Configuring Check Point NG
Install and Configure ISA Server	Chapter 11: Installing and Configuring Microsoft ISA Server 2000
Install and Configure Ipchains	Chapter 11: Managing and Configuring Iptables

NOTE

Although the objective mentions Ipchains, this book covers Iptables because it's the most recent version. Commands and options in both tools are similar.

B

SECURITY RESOURCES

Intrusion detection and network security are constantly changing fields. To keep up with the latest developments, you should visit the Web sites and other resources mentioned in this appendix. Many of the sites offer white papers, research papers, and other background information on topics such as firewalls, packet filtering, authentication, and encryption. You can find policy hints and resources, disaster-planning guides, and tools to help you do your job. In addition, you should visit these sites to learn about the latest threats. Bugs, security holes, and patches to plug them will be available online before you read about them in a book.

SECURITY RESOURCES

New threats surface daily, and you need ways to keep up with them. The Web sites in Table B-1 list links to helpful sites you can use to enhance your skills and knowledge.

Table B-1   Helpful sites for IT security professionals

Web Site	Description
Common Vulnerabilities and Exposures (CVE), *www.cve.mitre.org*	The CVE standard enables security devices to share information about attack signatures and other vulnerabilities so that they can work together.
Symantec Security Response, *http://securityresponse.symantec.com*	Symantec maintains an extensive database of viruses. The site includes information about security incidents, but the emphasis is on protecting against and eliminating viruses and other harmful code.
Internet Storm Center, *http://isc.sans.org/*	This site, which is affiliated with SANS, specializes in how to repond to intrusions, incidents, and security alerts. A world map shows security breaches reported by geographic region. The site also includes a list of current attack trends, such as frequently attacked ports and recently reported malicious software.
Dshield.org, *www.dshield.org*	This site is the home of the distributed intrusion detection system, in which network administrators from around the world share firewall and intrusion detection log information in an effort to track attack patterns.
The Center for Internet Security, *www.cisecurity.org*	This nonprofit organization is devoted to developing security standards it calls "benchmarks." Benchmarks are available for Linux, UNIX, and other operating systems.
System Administration, Networking and Security (SANS) Institute, *www.sans.org*	This research and education organization focuses on network security. SANS conducts seminars and workshops on security around the country.

Table B-1 Helpful sites for IT security professionals (continued)

Web Site	Description
The Cert Coordination Center, *www.cert.org*	This group, affiliated with the Carnegie-Mellon Institute, lists security alerts, incident notes, and vulnerabilities on its home page. CERT also offers tips and articles about aspects of network security and training courses.
Forum of Incident Response and Security Teams (FIRST), *www.first.org*	This group is a coalition of security incident response teams working in government, commercial, and academic organizations that seek to promote rapid reaction to security incidents by coordinating communication and sharing information.
The National Institute of Standards and Technology (NIST), *www.nist.gov* NIST Computer Security Division, Computer Security Resource Center (CSRC), *http://csrc.nist.gov*	NIST is a nonregulated U.S. federal agency with the mission to develop and promote measurement, standards, and technology to enhance productivity, facilitate trade, and improve the quality of life. The division that addresses information security is the Information Technology Security and Networking Division.
Internet Assigned Numbers Authority (IANA), *www.iana.org*	IANA assigns and maintains number assignments for the Internet, including port numbers and protocol numbers. Also coordinates DNS and IP addressing.
Internet Engineering Task Force (IETF), *www.ietf.org/home.html*	The IETF is an international body of network designers, vendors, operators, and researchers cooperatively working toward the Internet's evolution and smooth operation.
IEEE Computer Society, *www.ieee.org/portal/site*	This organization is a major international membership association for computer professionals. Membership isn't free, but the organization offers online courses, information, and professional networking opportunities for members.

B

Other Resources

You should also join newsgroups and mailing lists for IT professionals as a way to network with your peers and learn from their experiences. Sometimes, you run into a problem that you can't solve, despite poring through manuals and textbooks, searching the Internet, and running every test you can think of. Table B-2 lists two places to start when looking for other professionals who might have a solution to your problem.

Table B-2 Information security news sources

Web Site	Description
SecurityFocus Mailing Lists, *http://online.securityfocus.com/archive*	SecurityFocus runs security-related mailing lists on topics ranging from intrusion detection to firewalls to honeypots. One of the best features is being able to search archived messages by topic without having to subscribe. However, by joining a list, you can get news daily.
SANS Computer Security Newsletters and Digests, *www.sans.org/newsletters*	The set of newsletters published by the SANS Institute includes a weekly News Bites publication and a weekly Security Alert Consensus listing current security threats and countermeasures.

SECURITY CERTIFICATION SITES

The following sites offer certification through exams that can be invaluable for finding employment in network security.

Global Information Assurance Certification (GIAC)

The GIAC Web site (*www.giac.org*) provides information about the SANS Institute certification exams. Programs range from the entry-level Basic Information Security Officer to more specialized certifications, such as the GIAC Certified Firewall Analyst (GCFW).

The International Information Systems Security Certification Consortium (ISC²)

ISC² (*www.isc2.org*) is an international nonprofit organization dedicated to maintaining a common body of knowledge on security. ISC² prepares and administers two of the most common certifications in network security: Certified Information Systems Security Professional (CISSP) and Systems Security Certified Practitioner (SSCP).

B

CompTIA Certification

The Computing Technology Industry Association (*www.comptia.org/default.aspx*) is best known for the A+ series of certifications. The CompTIA Security+ Certification exam is also available to establish fundamental security competency in firewalls, encryption, and intrusion detection.

The Security Certified Program

The Security Certified Program (*www.securitycertified.net/index.htm*) is the vendor-neutral administrator of the Security Certified Network Professional (SCNP) and Security Certified Network Architect (SCNA) exams. The SCNP certification consists of two tests: Network Defense and Countermeasures (NDC) SC0-402 (which this books covers) and Hardening the Infrastructure (HTI) SC0-411. The lower-level certification, SCNP, is comparable in content and skill level to the ISC^2 certification Systems Security Certified Practitioner (SSCP).

Glossary

acceptable use policy — This policy section establishes what constitutes acceptable use of company resources and usually offers some specifics about what's considered unacceptable use.

accountability — The capability to track an attempted attack or intrusion back to the responsible party.

acknowledgement (ACK) flag — A TCP header field that contains the value of the next sequence number the sender is expecting to receive. After a connection is established (TCP three-way handshake), the ACK flag is significant and this value is always sent.

active defense in depth — A particularly strong implementation of the defense in depth concept, in which security personnel expect that attacks will occur and try to anticipate them instead of passively waiting for attacks and then reacting.

anomaly detection — A type of intrusion detection that causes an alarm to be sent when an IDS detects an event that deviates from behavior defined as "normal"; also called profile-based detection.

ASCII payload — The actual data part of the packet, given in ASCII format.

assets — The hardware, software, and informational resources you need to protect by developing and implementing a comprehensive security policy.

asymmetric cryptography — A type of encryption in which two different keys are used; also called public key cryptography. A private key is kept by the certificate holder and never shared; a public key is shared among users to encrypt and decrypt communications. *See also* symmetric cryptography.

attack visualization — The process of replaying the attack so that the analyst can see what the attacker viewed.

auditing — The process of reviewing records of activities of computers on the network; these records include who is connecting to a computer, what resources are being requested, and whether access is granted or blocked.

authentication — The process of determining the identity of an authorized user through matching a user name and password, a fingerprint or retinal scan, a smart card and PIN, and so on.

Authentication Header (AH) — An IPSec protocol that provides authentication of TCP/IP packets to ensure data integrity.

availability — Making sure those who are authorized to access resources can do so in a reliable and timely manner.

back doors — A way of gaining unauthorized access to a computer or other resource, usually through an opening in a program that's supposed to be known only to the program's author.

bastion host — A computer that sits on the network perimeter and has been specially protected through operating system patches, authentication, and encryption.

cache — Store data on disk for later retrieval; also a hard disk area where files are stored.

CAN — A prefix the CVE Web site uses to identify candidate vulnerabilities. As of October 2005, this prefix was replaced with "CVE," and a vulnerability's status is noted as Entry, Candidate, or Deprecated.

centralized data collection — A system in which an organization's event and security data is "funneled" to a centralized management console in the main office.

certification authority (CA) — A trusted organization that issues digital certificates that can be used to generate keys. *See also* digital certificate.

chain of custody — The record of who handled an object to be used as evidence in court.

chains — Sets of packet-filtering rules used by the Linux tool Iptables.

change management — The process of documenting changes made to hardware or software. This documentation helps administrators roll back a configuration correctly if changes have an adverse affect.

cleanup rule — A packet-filtering rule that comes last in a rule base; it covers any other packets that haven't been covered in preceding rules.

client address sets — Client computers that are grouped and managed by IP address.

client authentication — The process of granting access to network resources based on a source IP address, computer MAC address, or computer name rather than user information.

client-to-site VPN — A type of VPN connection that makes a network accessible to remote users requiring dial-in access; also called a remote access VPN.

command console — Software that provides a graphical front-end interface to an IDS.

Common Gateway Interface (CGI) scripts — Scripts used to process data submitted over the Internet.

Common Vulnerabilities and Exposures (CVE) — A standard that enables security devices to share information about attack signatures and other vulnerabilities so that they can work together to provide network protection.

confidentiality — The goal of preventing intentional or unintentional disclosure of communication between a sender and recipient.

connectionless — A feature of the UDP protocol, which does not depend on a connection actually being established between a host and client for a UDP packet to be sent from host to client.

containment — The process of preventing a malicious file, intruder, or compromised media from spreading to other resources on the network.

control connection — An initial FTP connection between client and server.

cost-benefit analysis — A technique for comparing the costs of an investment with the benefits it proposes to return.

countermeasures — Strategies and approaches that address threats to network security.

counters — Utilities that keep track of the number of active TCP, UDP, or other connections currently forwarding data on the network.

cracker — A person who attempts to gain access to unauthorized resources on a network, usually by finding a way to circumvent passwords, firewalls, or other protective measures.

customize access — Identify criteria for a firewall to allow a connection request, instead of allowing the firewall to deny or allow all requests automatically.

cyber risk insurance — Like business liability insurance, a cyber risk insurance policy protects businesses from losses resulting from attacks, viruses, worms, sabotage, and so on. Each policy has specific coverages and exclusions, as with any other insurance policy.

Cyclic Redundancy Check (CRC) — An error-checking algorithm sometimes added to the end of a TCP/IP packet.

data — The part of a packet that contains the actual data being sent from client to server.

Data Encryption Standard (DES) — An encryption scheme developed by IBM in the mid-1970s that was adopted as an encryption standard in 1977.

datagrams — Discrete chunks of packets, each of which contains source and destination addresses, control settings, and data.

dedicated computer — A computer used solely for running IDS software and logging traffic.

defense in depth (DiD) — A layering approach to security that protects a network at many different levels by using a variety of strategies and methods.

degaussing — The process of magnetically erasing an electronic device, such as a monitor or a disk, to remove any stray data or magnetic fields.

demilitarized zone (DMZ) — A subnetwork of publicly accessible Web, e-mail, and other servers that's outside the LAN but still protected by the firewall.

dependency services — Services a computer system needs to function correctly. Usually, key system processes depend on other processes to function.

destination sets — Includes one or more computers or folders on specific computers. There are internal destination sets (groups of computers in the local intranet) and external destination sets (computers outside the intranet).

digital certificate — An electronic document issued by a certification authority that contains information about the certificate holder and can be used to exchange public and private keys. *See also* certification authority (CA).

digital signature — An attachment to an e-mail or other message that enables the recipient of the message to authenticate the sender's identity.

distributed data collection — A system in which data from security devices goes to a management console on its own local network.

distributed IDS (DIDS) — A type of hybrid IDS that uses multiple IDS devices deployed on a network to monitor traffic and report suspicious events.

dual-homed host — A computer that has been configured with more than one network interface.

due process — A legal concept that ensures the government respects a person's rights or places limitations on legal proceedings to guarantee fundamental fairness, justice, and liberty.

electronic assets — The word processing, spreadsheet, Web page, and other documents on your network computers.

Encapsulating Security Payload (ESP) — An IPSec protocol that encrypts both the header and data parts of each TCP/IP packet.

encapsulation — The process of enclosing a packet within another one that has different IP source and destination information to ensure a high degree of protection.

encryption — The process of rendering information unreadable by all but the intended recipient.

eradication — The process of removing any files or programs that result from an intrusion, including malicious code, Registry keys, unnecessary executable files, viruses, worms, or files created by worms.

escalated — The process of increasing the response to an intrusion to a higher level.

escalation procedure — A set of roles, responsibilities, and measures taken in response to a security incident.

event horizon — The entire length of an attack, from the first packet the IDS receives to the last packet needed to complete the attack signature.

event monitoring — Reviewing alert and event logs produced by security devices and operating systems and testing the network periodically to identify any weak points.

exposure — Vulnerability to loss resulting from the occurrence of a threat, such as accidental or intentional disclosure or destruction or modification of information resources. Exposure increases with the presence of multiple threat factors.

failover firewall — A backup firewall that can be configured to switch on if the first one fails, thus ensuring uninterrupted service for the organization.

false negatives — Attacks that occur but aren't detected by the IDS.

false positives — Alarms generated by legitimate network traffic rather than actual attacks.

fault tolerance — The capability of an object or a system to continue operations despite a failure.

firewall — Hardware or software that can be configured to block unauthorized access to a network.

firewall appliances — Hardware devices that have firewall functionality.

firewall policy — An addition to a security policy that describes how firewalls should handle application traffic, such as Web or e-mail applications.

follow-up — The process of documenting what happened when an intrusion was detected and a response occurred.

footer — Another section added to a TCP/IP packet that tells a computer it's the end of the packet.

Fourth Amendment — The Fourth Amendment is contained in the Bill of Rights and provides constitutional protection from illegal search and seizure and guarantees the right to due process. It is from the Fourth Amendment that an expected right of privacy is implied, even though no such right is stated specifically.

fully qualified domain name (FQDN) — The complete DNS name of a computer, including the computer name, domain name, and domain name extension, such as *www.course.com*.

Generic Routing Encapsulation (GRE) — An encapsulation protocol (protocol ID 47) commonly used in VPNs.

hardened — The process of making a computer more secure by eliminating unnecessary software and services, closing potential openings, and protecting the information on it with encryption and authentication.

hash function — A mathematical function (such as MD5) that creates a digest version of a message.

header — The part of a packet that contains source and destination information and general information about the packet.

hexadecimal payload — The actual data the packet is communicating, expressed in hexadecimal format.

hide-mode mapping — The process of hiding multiple private IP addresses behind one public IP address.

honeypot — A computer placed on the perimeter of a network to attract attackers. A honeypot acts as a diversion, drawing attackers' attention away from other hosts.

host address — The part of an IP address that's unique to a computer in its subnet.

host-based IDS (HIDS) — An IDS deployed on each host in the LAN that's protected by the firewall.

hybrid configuration — A VPN configuration that combines characteristics of the mesh and star configurations.

hybrid firewall — A product that combines aspects of both firewall appliances and software firewalls in one package.

hybrid IDS — An IDS implementation that combines the features of HIDSs and NIDSs to gain flexibility and increase security.

Hypertext Transport Protocol (HTTP) — A protocol used by Web services that communicates via TCP/IP port 80.

ID number — For packets in general, it's an identifying number that can be used to reassemble a packet in case it's divided into fragments. For ICMP packets, it identifies the ICMP packet so that the originating computer can make sure the response came from its original request.

incident response — The actions taken after a computer security incident to determine what happened and what countermeasures need to be taken to ensure the network's continued security.

independent audit — An audit in which you hire an outside firm to inspect your audit logs to make sure you're getting the information you need and not gathering unnecessary information that consumes system and network resources.

integrity — The goal of ensuring the accuracy and consistency of information during all processing (storage, transmission, and so forth).

Internet Control Message Protocol (ICMP) — A protocol that reports network communication errors to support IP communications. The Ping command is a common troubleshooting utility based on ICMP.

Internet Key Exchange (IKE) — A form of key exchange used to encrypt and decrypt data as it passes through a VPN tunnel. IKE uses tunnel method encryption to encrypt and then encapsulate packets for extra security. *See also* tunnel method encryption.

Internet Protocol Security (IPSec) — A set of standard procedures that the Internet Engineering Task Force (IETF) developed for enabling secure communications on the Internet.

Internet Protocol version 4 (IPv4) — The IP addressing system currently in widespread use on the Internet, in which addresses are created with 32 bits (4 bytes) of data.

Internet Protocol version 6 (IPv6) — A new version of IP that's gaining support among software and hardware manufacturers and that will eventually replace IPv4; this version calls for 128-bit IP addresses.

Internet Security Association Key Management Protocol (ISAKMP) — An IPSec-related protocol that enables two computers to agree on security settings and establish a Security Association so that they can exchange keys using Internet Key Exchange. *See also* Internet Key Exchange (IKE) *and* Security Association (SA).

Internet use policy — A policy that defines how users can access and use the Internet and specifies what rules apply to e-mail and other communications. Internet use, e-mail use, and other forms of communication, such as instant messaging, can be included in a single section or addressed separately in an Internet use policy and a digital communications policy.

intrusion — An attempt to gain unauthorized access to network resources and to compromise the integrity and confidentiality of network data or users' privacy.

intrusion detection — The process of monitoring network traffic to detect attempts to gain unauthorized access to a system or resource and notifying the appropriate professionals so that countermeasures can be taken.

intrusion detection system (IDS) — A network security measure that can consist of multiple applications and hardware devices deployed on the network, hosts, or both to prevent, detect, and respond to traffic interpreted as an intrusion.

IP spoofing — The process of inserting a false address into the IP header to make the packet more difficult to trace back to its source.

IPSec driver — Software that handles the actual tasks of encrypting, authenticating, decrypting, and checking packets in an IPSec connection.

Iptables — A packet-filtering command-line tool that comes with version 2.4.x or later of the Linux kernel.

Kerberos — An IETF standard for secure authentication of requests for resource access. Kerberos is defined in RFC 1510.

key — An encoded block of data generated by an algorithm and used to encrypt and decrypt data.

Key Distribution Center (KDC) — A Kerberos component that holds secret keys for users, applications, services, or resources that use Kerberos; creates and distributes session keys by using symmetric cryptography.

LAN security policy — This type of policy defines and establishes responsibility for the protection of the LAN itself and for information that is processed, stored, and transmitted on the LAN.

load sharing — The practice of configuring two or more firewalls to share the total traffic load.

load-balancing software — Software that prioritizes and schedules requests and distributes them to a group of servers based on each machine's current load and processing power.

local address table (LAT) — A set of IP addresses that defines a network's internal addressing scheme for a firewall or proxy server.

loose source and record routing (lsrr) — This option specifies a set of hops that the packet must traverse, but not necessarily every hop in the path.

macro viruses — A type of malware that performs the same functions as a macro but tends to be harmful.

malware — Software, such as viruses, worms and Trojans, designed to purposely cause harm, allow theft, or otherwise compromise a computer system.

maximum transmission unit (MTU) — The maximum packet size that can be transmitted over a type of computer network, such as an Ethernet network.

mesh configuration — A VPN configuration in which all participants in the VPN are connected to one another. This configuration is commonly arranged as a full mesh or partial mesh setup.

message digest — A code that results from processing a message or other input through a mathematical function, usually resulting in a shortened version of the original input.

misuse detection — A type of intrusion detection in which an IDS is configured to send an alarm in response to sets of characteristics that match known examples of attacks.

MMC snap-in — A management utility added to the Microsoft Management Console (MMC) in Microsoft server operating systems. Snap-ins for a variety of administrative functions are available.

Monte Carlo simulation — An analytical method meant to simulate a real-life system by randomly generating values for variables.

multiple entry point configuration — A type of VPN configuration in which multiple gateways are used, each with a VPN tunnel connecting a different location.

multiple-packet attacks — Attacks that require a series of packets to be transmitted for the attack to be completed.

network address — The part of an IP address that a computer has in common with other computers in its subnet.

Network Address Translation (NAT) — NAT translates internal network address into external interface address, which hides the internal LAN addressing scheme and decreases the need for Internet-usable addresses.

network assets — The routers, cables, bastion hosts, servers, and firewall hardware and software that enable employees to communicate with one another and other computers on the Internet.

network-based IDS (NIDS) — A set of components that includes a command console and sensors positioned at locations where they can monitor network traffic.

network uptime — The amount of time a network is available for users to connect successfully and access resources.

node — A single computer, VPN appliance, gateway, host, or any combination of these devices.

nonrepudiation —Ensuring that the sender can't deny sending a message and the receiver can't deny receiving it.

notification — The process by which SIRT members receive news about security incidents.

null packets — TCP packets with no flags set.

one-way hash — *See* message digest.

Open Platform for Security (OPSEC) — A protocol developed by Check Point Technologies that enables its firewall products to integrate with software that provides antivirus protection, intrusion detection, and other solutions.

Open Security Evaluation Criteria (OSEC) — A framework for evaluating security products, developed by Neohapsis Labs.

operational audit — An audit in which an organization's own staff examines system and security logs to analyze information about intrusions and other unauthorized accesses.

out-of-band notification — Notification of a security incident that occurs not on a computer network, but on another communications device, such as a pager.

packet filters — Devices or software that block or allow the transmission of packets of information based on port, IP address, protocol, or other criteria.

packet monkey — An attacker who's primarily interested in blocking the activities of a Web site through a distributed denial-of-service attack.

packet sniffer — Software or hardware that monitors traffic going into or out of a network device and captures information about each TCP/IP packet it detects.

password security — Selecting good passwords, keeping them secure, and changing them as needed contributes to password security. Using multiple passwords, including screen-saver passwords and passwords for protecting critical applications, also helps guard against unauthorized access.

physical security — A term that refers to measures taken to physically protect a computer or other network device from theft, fire, or environmental disaster.

ping sweep — The act of sending a series of ICMP echo request packets in a range of IP addresses to see whether any computers respond.

Point-to-Point Tunneling Protocol (PPTP) — A tunneling protocol used for dial-up access to a remote server.

port scan — An attempt to connect to a computer's ports to see if any are active and listening.

privileged access policy — A policy detailing additional access, functions, and responsibilities of users with privileged (administrative or root) access to resources.

probability — The possibility that a threat will actually occur, influenced by geographic, physical, habitual, or other factors that increase or decrease the likelihood of occurrence.

profiles — Sets of characteristics that describe the services and resources a user normally accesses on the network.

promiscuous mode — A mode of operation in which an IDS or packet sniffer detects and analyzes each packet in its entirety.

proxy server — A program that provides Web browsing, e-mail, and other services for network users to conceal their identity from those outside the network.

public key cryptography — A form of network authentication that identifies participants through the exchange of public and private keys.

recovery — The process of putting media, programs, or computers that have been compromised by intrusions back in service so that they can function on the network again.

remote access policy — A policy that defines what security measures need to be in place on a remote desktop before the user or that desktop can connect to the organization's network.

Remote Authentication Dial-In User Service (RADIUS) — An authentication method that identifies and verifies the authorization of users who dial up a central server to gain access to networked resources.

Remote Procedure Calls (RPC) — A standard set of communication rules that allows one computer to request a service from another computer on a network.

residual risk — The risk remaining after countermeasures and defenses are implemented.

return on investment (ROI) — The total value gained after a solution has been deployed. A positive return on investment is desirable because it means the solution has solved more problems than it creates.

reverse firewall — A device that monitors information going out of a network rather than trying to block what's coming in.

risk — The possibility of incurring damage or loss.

risk analysis — A process of analyzing the threats an organization faces, determining precisely what resources are at risk, and deciding the priority to give each asset.

risk management — The process of identifying, choosing, and setting up countermeasures justified by the risks you identify.

role-based authentication — A method of authentication that grants users limited access based on the role they are assigned in the company and defines what resources that role is allowed to use.

rule base — A set of rules for telling a firewall what action to take when a certain kind of traffic attempts to pass through.

safeguards — Measures you can take to reduce threats, such as installing firewalls and intrusion detection systems, locking doors, and using passwords and encryption.

scalable — The capability to maintain a consistent level of operation as a network grows.

scanner — A device that scans a network for open ports or other potential vulnerabilities.

screened host — Similar to a dual-homed host, but the main difference is that a router is often added between the host and the Internet to carry out IP packet filtering.

screening router — A router placed between the Internet and the protected LAN that determines whether to allow or deny packets based on their source and destination IP addresses or other information in their headers.

script kiddies — Attackers (often young people) who spread viruses and other malicious scripts and use techniques to exploit weaknesses in computer systems.

search warrant — A legal document issued by the court allowing a search of a specified place for specific evidence. The warrant must detail what the search is seeking and where law enforcement is permitted to look for it.

Secure Shell (SSH) — A VPN authentication protocol that works with UNIX-based systems to create a secure transport layer connection between participating computers; SSH makes use of public key cryptography.

Secure Sockets Layer (SSL) — A protocol developed by Netscape Communications Corporation as a way of enabling Web servers and browsers to exchange encrypted information.

Security Association (SA) — A designation for users, computers, or gateways that can participate in a VPN and encrypt and decrypt data using keys.

security auditing — The process of checking the effectiveness of a network defense system by testing the system, analyzing event logs, or observing procedures.

security event management program — A program that gathers and consolidates events from multiple sources so that the information can be analyzed to improve network security.

security incident response team (SIRT) — A group of staff people designated to take countermeasures when an incident is reported.

security policy — A statement that spells out exactly what defenses will be configured to block unauthorized access, what constitutes acceptable use of network resources, how the organization will respond to attacks, and how employees should safely handle the organization's resources to discourage loss of data or damage to files.

security user awareness program — A training program designed to educate users about security topics, answer their questions about security, and prepare users to accept changes made for security purposes.

security workstation — A dedicated computer that deploys a security policy through a centralized firewall to other firewalls that protect branch offices or other networks in the organization.

selective acknowledgements — Acknowledgements that selected packets in a sequence have been received; this process is in contrast to having to acknowledge every packet.

sensor — A component of the IDS (hardware, software, or combination of the two) that monitors a host or network segment for misuse or attacks.

server farm — A group of servers connected in their own subnet that work together to receive a large number of requests; the load is distributed among all the servers.

session authentication — The process of authorizing a user or computer on a per-connection basis using special authentication software installed on the client computer that exchanges information with the firewall.

shim IDS — A type of hybrid IDS in which sensors are installed on selected hosts as well as network segments.

signature — A set of characteristics—such as IP numbers and options, TCP flags, and port numbers—used to define a type of network activity.

signature analysis — The practice of analyzing TCP/IP communications to determine whether traffic is legitimate or suspicious.

signatures — Combinations of flags, IP addresses, and other characteristics indicating an attack that are detected by a firewall or IDS.

single entry point configuration — A VPN configuration in which all traffic to and from the network passes through a single gateway, such as a router or firewall.

single-packet attack — An attack that can be completed by sending a single network packet from client to host.

site-to-site VPN — A VPN that uses hardware devices, such as routers, to connect two networks; also called a gateway-to-gateway VPN.

sniff — The process of receiving and analyzing packets as they pass into and out of the network; sniffing is carried out by packet-sniffing programs, network traffic analyzers, or IDSs.

social engineering — A technique of tricking employees into giving out passwords or other information.

socket — A network connection that uses a TCP/IP port number combined with a computer's IP address.

Socks — A communications protocol that provides proxy services for applications that don't normally support proxying and enables applications to set up a secure tunnel using encryption and authentication.

split tunneling — The term used to describe multiple paths. One path goes to the VPN server and is secured, but an unauthorized and unsecured path permits the user to connect to the Internet or some other network while still connected to the corporate VPN.

star configuration — A VPN configuration in which a single gateway is the "hub" and other networks that participate in the VPN are considered "rim" networks.

state information — Information about a network connection that is typically kept in a state table.

state table — A file maintained by stateful packet filters that contains a record of all current connections.

stateful packet filters — Similar to stateless packet filters, except stateful packet filters also determine whether to allow or block packets based on information maintained about current connections.

stateless packet filters — Simple filters that decide whether to allow or block packets based on information in the protocol headers.

static mapping — A form of NAT in which internal IP addresses are mapped to external, routable IP addresses on a one-to-one basis.

strict source and record routing (ssrr) — This option specifies every hop that the packet must traverse.

strobe scan — A type of port scan that probes ports that are commonly used by specific programs, in an attempt to see if such a program is presented and can be utilized.

subnet mask — A value that tells another computer which part of a computer's IP address is its network address and which part is the host address.

subpoena — A legal document requiring a person to appear, provide testimony, or cooperate with law enforcement. Testimony consists of written or oral declaration of fact under penalty of law.

survivability — The capability to continue functioning in the presence of attacks or disasters.

Survivable Network Analysis (SNA) — A security process that starts with the assumption that a computer system will be attacked and follows a set of steps to build a system that can survive such an attack.

symmetric cryptography — A type of encryption in which the sender and recipient exchange the same key. *See also* asymmetric cryptography.

target — In the Linux tool Iptables, the target determines what action is taken on packets matching a specific criteria.

target-to-console ratio — The number of target computers on your network managed by a single command console.

Terminal Access Controller Access Control System (TACACS+) — A set of authentication protocols developed by Cisco Systems that uses the MD5 algorithm to produce an encrypted digest version of transmitted data. TACACS+ is usually used to authenticate dial-up remote users.

Threat and Risk Assessment (TRA) — An approach to risk analysis that starts from the standpoint of threats and accounts for risks to an organization's assets and the consequences of those threats and risks if they occur.

threats — Events and conditions that haven't occurred but could potentially occur; the presence of these events or conditions increases risk.

three-pronged firewall — A firewall that has three separate interfaces—for example, one to a DMZ, one to the Internet, and one to the internal LAN.

ticket-granting server (TGS) — The part of the KDC that creates and distributes session keys clients use to access resources. *See also* Key Distribution Center (KDC).

ticket-granting ticket (TGT) — The TGT is essentially a digital token sent from the Authentication Server to the client. The client presents the TGT to the TGS to obtain a session key to access the resource. *See also* Key Distribution Center (KDC) *and* Ticket-Granting Server (TGS).

tiger teams — Special teams assembled to actively test a network.

time to live (TTL) — An instruction that tells a router how long a packet should remain on the network before it's discarded.

Tinkerbell program — A program in which network connections are scanned and alerts are generated when logons are attempted or when connection attempts are made from sites identified as suspicious.

token — A small electronic device that generates a random number or password used in authentication.

topology — The way in which participants in a network are connected physically to one another.

Transmission Control Protocol/Internet Protocol (TCP/IP) — This suite of protocols allows information to be transmitted from point to point on a network.

transport method encryption — A method of encryption in which only the data portion of a packet is encrypted, not the header. This method results in improved performance.

trigger — A set of circumstances that causes an IDS to send an alert message.

Triple Data Encryption Standard (3DES) — A stronger variation of DES that uses three separate 64-bit keys to process data, making the encryption much harder to break.

Trojan programs — A type of program that appears to be harmless but that actually introduces viruses or causes damage to a computer or system.

Trojan scan — A type of port scan that looks for active Trojan programs that have already circumvented security measures and are running on the scanned system. If attackers can find one already installed, they can use it instead of having to install a new one.

true negatives — Legitimate communications that don't cause an IDS to set off an alarm.

true positive — A genuine attack detected successfully by an IDS, in contrast to a true negative or a false positive.

tunnel — The connection between two endpoints in a VPN.

tunnel method encryption — A method of key exchange that encrypts both the header and data parts of a packet and encapsulates the packet within a new packet that has a different header.

tunneling protocols — Network protocols that encapsulate (surround or envelope) one protocol or session inside another.

two-factor authentication — Authentication requiring at least two forms of verification from a user to be granted access. Verification requires something the user possesses, knows, and/or is.

type of service (TOS) — The part of a packet header that can be used to express a packet's precedence—whether it should have low delay, whether it needs high reliability, and so on.

user authentication — The process of identifying a person who has been authorized to access network resources.

vanilla scan — A type of port scan in which all ports from 0 to 65,535 are probed, one after another.

virtual private network (VPN) — A set of technologies that provides a cost-effective way for two or more networks to make a secure private connection using public connections, usually the Internet. VPN endpoints establish connections (tunnels) to transmit and receive data, and then tear the connections down when they're no longer needed. Combinations of encryption, authentication, and encapsulation help ensure confidentiality, privacy, and integrity of transmitted information.

virtual team — A team that has other jobs to perform during regular business hours and exists only during meetings or when an incident becomes serious.

virus — Computer code that copies itself from one place to another surreptitiously and performs actions that range from benign to harmful.

VPN appliance — A hardware device designed to terminate VPNs and join multiple LANs.

VPN client — A router or an operating system that initiates a connection to a VPN server.

VPN domain — A group of one or more computers that the VPN hardware and software handle as a single entity. This group uses the VPN to communicate with another domain.

VPN protocols — Sets of standardized communication settings that software and hardware use to encrypt data that's sent through a VPN.

VPN server — A computer configured to accept VPN connections from clients.

vulnerabilities — Situations or conditions that increase threat, which in turn increases risk.

worm — A type of malware that creates files that copy themselves repeatedly and consume disk space. Worms don't require user intervention to be launched; they are self-propagating.

worst-case scenarios — Descriptions of the worst consequences that befall an organization if a threat occurs.

Index